The Complete History of the Indiana High School Football State Tournament

1973 to 2018
1st Edition

Copyright © 2018 by Almanac Sports, LLC

All rights reserved. No part of this publication may be reproduced, distributed, or transmitted in any form or by any means, including photocopying, recording, or other electronic or mechanical methods, without the prior written permission of the publisher, except in the case of brief quotations embodied in critical reviews and certain other noncommercial uses permitted by copyright law. For permission requests, write to the publisher, addressed "Attention: Permissions Coordinator," at the address below.

Published By: Engler Publishing

Almanac Sports, LLC
5625 Pearl Drive #102
Evansville, IN 47712

EnglerPublishing.com

Contact: dan@englerpublishing.com

Published in United States of America

Table of Contents

Evolution of the state tournament... Page 2
Tournament scores (1973 to 2018)... Page 3
Postseason champions by class.. Page 157
Most times qualifying for the playoffs... Page 183
IHSAA Football State Tournament records & championships by school........... Page 184
Most tournament games played.. Page 192
Most tournament wins.. Page 192
Best tournament win percentage... Page 192
Most sectional championships.. Page 193
Most regional championships... Page 195
Most semi-state championships.. Page 197
Most IHSAA state championships.. Page 198
Teams that have won IHSAA state championships in more than one class........ Page 199
Coaching records in the state tournament.. Page 200
About the Author.. Page 201

Evolution of the Indiana High School Athletic Association Football State Tournament

MYTHICAL STATE CHAMPIONSHIP (~1890s to 1972)
Before the IHSAA sanctioned a postseason playoff, there was no official state champion. Much like college football, they used human polls and computer rankings to settle the debate, but oftentimes there was no clear-cut winner.

- **BENEFITS:** lots of fun controversy
- **DRAWBACKS:** no way to determine true state champion; almost no chance for smaller schools to compete for title

POINTS SYSTEM (1973-82)
As early as the 1930s, a postseason playoff was discussed to determine a state champion that would have matched the best team in the north against the best team in the south, but talks didn't begin in earnest until the mid-1960s. Formats from every state with a playoff were studied, and, in 1971, the IHSAA announced they would implement a state tournament beginning in 1973.

For the first three years, only 12 teams qualified. The state was separated into three classes based on enrollment. In each class, the state was divided into four geographical areas (called districts), and the team from each district with the highest points qualified.

How they qualified
Teams earned points only by winning, with the amount earned based solely on the enrollment class of their opponent.

Class 3A	Class 2A	Class 1A
beats 3A = 3 points	beats 3A = 4 points	beats 3A = 5 points
beats 2A = 2 points	beats 2A = 3 points	beats 2A = 4 points
beats 1A = 1 point	beats 1A = 2 points	beats 1A = 3 points

The total points earned was divided by the number of games played to calculate a team's rating. Scratch games were also introduced, allowing a team to omit a specific game (this was usually done to maintain a rivalry against a smaller school).

Expansion
In 1976, this system was expanded to allow the top two teams in each disctrict to qualify for the tournament, bringing the total number of postseason participants from 12 to 24. In 1981, the playoff was again expanded to include the top four teams in each district, allowing 48 teams teams to qualify.

- **BENEFITS:** Teams could compete for a sanctioned state title
- **DRAWBACKS:** Several undefeated teams did not qualify and never had a chance to play for a state championship

CLUSTERS (1983-84)
In 1983, the method of qualifying was completely changed. The points system was scrapped and teams were now separated into four classes based on enrollment, each divided into 16 clusters, with each containing four to six teams. (Check out our book *What A Cluster!* for more information)

How they qualified
Each school played every other team in its cluster and the champion advanced to the postseason. Ties were broken by head-to-head results. If there was a three-way tie, a cluster-buster was played, where two of the three would meet in an overtime-type scenario, with the winning team immediately facing the third. The winner of that would earn the district's playoff berth.

- **BENEFITS:** Teams could now play their way into the playoffs; an undefeated season guaranteed a spot
- **DRAWBACKS:** A 9-1 team that finished second in its cluster did not qualify for the postseason; also, several traditional conferences and rivalries were almost destroyed because of the dramatic change in schedules

ALL-IN (1985-preseent)

In 1985, the IHSAA changed the format again, this time to allow every team into the state tournament, just as in every other IHSAA-sanctioned sport. Teams were separated into five classes based on enrollment. Each class was grouped into eight sectionals with six to eight teams. A random draw is performed about two weeks before the end of the regular season to determine the sectional pairings. Class 5A was subdivided in 2013 to add a sixth enrollment classification.

- **BENEFITS:** A poor start or early injury to a key player does not kill a team's state championship hopes; teams can schedule who they want
- **DRAWBACKS:** No reward for regular season performance; also, because of the blind draw, two undefeated teams could square off in the first round while two 0-9 teams face off in the other side of the bracket

IHSAA Football State Tournament Scores

1973

Class 3A
Semifinals
S.B. Washington 27, Hammond Gavit 14
Indpls. Cathedral 32, Bloomington South 27
State Championship
S.B. Washington 19, Indpls. Cathedral 13

Class 2A
Semifinals
Blackford 28, Wawasee 14
Greenfield-Central 28, Tell City 7
State Championship
Greenfield-Central 21, Blackford 12

Class 1A
Semifinals
Mishawaka Marian 42, Woodlan 0
Providence 40, Hamilton Heights 0
State Championship
Mishawaka Marian 21, Providence 14

1974

Class 3A
Semifinals
Mishawaka 28, Portage 21
Indpls. Washington 21, Richmond 14
State Championship
Indpls. Washington 19, Mishawaka 12

Class 2A
Semifinals
Boonville 21, Greenfield-Central 6
Blackford 21, NorthWood 13
State Championship
Blackford 28, Boonville 14

Class 1A
Semifinals
Garrett 7, Whiting 0
North Knox 21, Westfield 13
State Championship
Garrett 20, North Knox 6

1975

Class 3A
Sectional Championships
Valparaiso 31, Penn 19
Carmel 27, Richmond 18
State Championship
Valparaiso 14, Carmel 13

Class 2A
Sectional Championships
Mishawaka Marian 34, Blackford 0
Greenfield-Central 7, Castle 3
State Championship
Mishawaka Marian 34, Greenfield-Central 0

Class 1A
Sectional Championships
Wes-Del 27, Fountain Central 18
Lawrenceburg 26, Indian Creek 7
State Championship
Lawrenceburg 28, Wes-Del 14

1976

NOTE: 1976 saw the expansion of the playoffs from 12 to 24 teams. The method was not not changed, but the top two teams in each district qualified instead of one.

Class 3A
District 1 Sectional Championship
Merrillville 35, Valparaiso 14
District 2 Sectional Championship
S.B. St. Joseph 7, Fort Wayne Snider 3
District 3 Sectional Championship
Indpls. Cathedral 7, North Central (Indpls.) 6
District 4 Sectional Championship
Evansville Reitz 10, New Castle 7

Regional Championships
Merrillville 21, S.B. St. Joseph 0
Indpls. Cathedral 7, Evansville Reitz 0

State Championship
Merrillville 28, Indpls. Cathedral 24

Class 2A
District 5 Sectional Championship
Mishawaka Marian 34, Plymouth 0
District 6 Sectional Championship
McCutcheon 21, Bellmont 14
District 7 Sectional Championship
Roncalli 27, Noblesville 7
District 8 Sectional Championship
Jasper 7, Castle 6

Regional Championships
Mishawaka Marian 14, McCutcheon 7
Jasper 7, Roncalli 6

State Championship
Mishawaka Marian 34, Jasper 7

Class 1A
District 9 Sectional Championship
Lafayette C.C. 16, Fountain Central 8
District 10 Sectional Championship
Oak Hill 7, Jimtown 6
District 11 Sectional Championship
Sheridan 31, Eastern Hancock 28
District 12 Sectional Championship
Lawrenceburg 28, South Spencer 16

Regional Championships
Lafayette Central Catholic 14, Oak Hill 0
Lawrenceburg 22, Sheridan 16

State Championship
Lafayette Central Catholic 8, Lawrenceburg 6

1977
Class 3A
District 1 Sectional Championship
Portage 3, Merrillville 0
District 2 Sectional Championship
S.B. Washington 21, Mishawaka 14
District 3 Sectional Championship
Ben Davis 24, Carmel 7
District 4 Sectional Championship
Evansville Reitz 22, Martinsville 6

Regional Championships
Portage 14, S.B. Washington 7
Evansville Reitz 14, Ben Davis 13

State Championship
Portage 33, Evansville Reitz 14

Class 2A
District 5 Sectional Championship
Plymouth 21, Columbia City 7
District 6 Sectional Championship
Delphi 35, Delta 0
District 7 Sectional Championship
Mooresville 30, Crawfordsville 8
District 8 Sectional Championship
Jasper 55, Clarksville 14

Regional Championships
Plymouth 21, Delphi 20
Jasper 21, Mooresville 12

State Championship
Plymouth 21, Jasper 14, 2 OT

Class 1A
District 9 Sectional Championship
Seeger 6, North Judson 0
District 10 Sectional Championship
Tippecanoe Valley 21, Leo 15, OT
District 11 Sectional Championship
Indpls. Ritter 20, Eastern (Greentown) 0
District 12 Sectional Championship
Paoli 13, Brownstown Central 6

Regional Championships
Tippecanoe Valley 20, Seeger 0
Indpls. Ritter 48, Paoli 0

State Championship
Indpls. Ritter 15, Tippecanoe Valley 6

1978
Class 3A
District 1 Sectional Championship
Hammond 25, Highland 0
District 2 Sectional Championship
Fort Wayne Dwenger 22, Penn 18
District 3 Sectional Championship
Carmel 38, Indpls. Chatard 15
District 4 Sectional Championship
Columbus East 20, Richmond 18

Regional Championships
Fort Wayne Dwenger 21, Hammond 0
Carmel 49, Columbus East 14

State Championship
Carmel 35, Fort Wayne Dwenger 18

Class 2A
District 5 Sectional Championship
Goshen 19, Homestead 0
District 6 Sectional Championship
Delta 12, Peru 3
District 7 Sectional Championship
Brownsburg 13, Noblesville 12
District 8 Sectional Championship
Vincennes Lincoln 35, Brazil 0

Regional Championships
Goshen 27, Delta 0
Brownsburg 17, Vincennes Lincoln 7

State Championship
Goshen 9, Brownsburg 0

Class 1A
District 9 Sectional Championship
Fountain Central 35, North Newton 6
District 10 Sectional Championship
Tippecanoe Valley 36, West Noble 0
District 11 Sectional Championship
Hamilton Southeastern 20, Monrovia 14
District 12 Sectional Championship
Lawrenceburg 60, Paoli 0

Regional Championships
Fountain Central 27, Tippecanoe Valley 21
Lawrenceburg 22, Hamilton Southeastern 6

State Championship
Lawrenceburg 34, Fountain Central 6

1979
Class 3A
District 1 Sectional Championship
Hobart 35, Munster 20
District 2 Sectional Championship
Penn 7, Lafayette Jefferson 0
District 3 Sectional Championship
Indpls. Chatard 17, North Central (Ind.) 10
District 4 Sectional Championship
Columbus East 21, Bedford NL 0

Regional Championships
Hobart 27, Penn 20
Columbus East 20, Indpls. Chatard 13

State Championship
Columbus East 21, Hobart 14

Class 2A
District 5 Sectional Championship
Concord 10, Goshen 7
District 6 Sectional Championship
Blackford 28, Lewis Cass 0
District 7 Sectional Championship
Noblesville 27, Franklin Central 7
District 8 Sectional Championship
Tell City 26, Providence 0

Regional Championships
Blackford 17, Concord 14
Noblesville 12, Tell City 0

State Championship
Blackford 24, Noblesville 22

Class 1A
District 9 Sectional Championship
North Judson 6, Bremen 0
District 10 Sectional Championship
Tippecanoe Valley 67, Central Noble 0
District 11 Sectional Championship
Hamilton Southeastern 14, Oak Hill 10
District 12 Sectional Championship
Lawrenceburg 33, Paoli 0

Regional Championships
Tippecanoe Valley 63, North Judson 6
Hamilton SE 27, Lawrenceburg 0

State Championship
Tippecanoe Valley 44, Hamilton SE 14

1980
Class 3A
District 1 Sectional Championship
Hobart 23, Hammond 0
District 2 Sectional Championship
Mishawaka 28, Lafayette Jefferson 7
District 3 Sectional Championship
Carmel 21, Indpls. Marshall 9
District 4 Sectional Championship
Martinsville 38, Columbus East 7

Regional Championships
Hobart 33, Mishawaka 14
Carmel 21, Martinsville 14

State Championship
Carmel 13, Hobart 7

Class 2A
District 5 Sectional Championship
NorthWood 21, New Haven 15
District 6 Sectional Championship
Norwell 26, Blackford 14
District 7 Sectional Championship
Franklin Central 24, Brownsburg 7
District 8 Sectional Championship
East Central 8, Providence 6

Regional Championships
NorthWood 10, Norwell 7
Franklin Central 28, East Central 14

State Championship
Franklin Central 19, NorthWood 13

Class 1A
District 9 Sectional Championship
North Judson 34, Fountain Central 0
District 10 Sectional Championship
Southwood 33, Central Noble 12
District 11 Sectional Championship
Sheridan 35, North Putnam 7
District 12 Sectional Championship
Lawrenceburg 20, Tecumseh 12

Regional Championships

North Judson 19, Southwood 0
Sheridan 9, Lawrenceburg 0

State Championship
Sheridan 27, North Judson 0

1981
NOTE: 1981 saw the expansion of the playoffs from 24 to 48 teams and implemented a semi-state championship round. The method was not not changed, but the top four teams in each district qualified instead of two.

Class 3A
District 1 Sectional Championships
Hobart 22, Hammond Noll 7
Griffith 27, Hammond 18
District 1 Regional Championship
Hobart 21, Griffith 0

District 2 Sectional Championships
Lafayette Jefferson 36, FW Dwenger 35
FW Snider 16, S.B. St. Joseph 13, OT
District 2 Regional Championship
Fort Wayne Snider 18, Lafayette Jeff 17

District 3 Sectional Championships
Carmel 21, North Central (Indpls.) 7
Indpls. Marshall 12, Roncalli 7
District 3 Regional Championship
Carmel 7, Indpls. Marshall 3

District 4 Sectional Championships
Martinsville 22, Seymour 8
Castle 18, Richmond 17
District 4 Regional Championship
Castle 35, Martinsville 7

Semi-State Championships
Fort Wayne Snider 37, Hobart 0
Carmel 49, Castle 13

State Championship
Carmel 27, Fort Wayne Snider 0

Class 2A
District 5 Sectional Championships
Goshen 22, Peru 7
New Haven 24, Concord 13
District 5 Regional Championship
Goshen 14, New Haven 0

District 6 Sectional Championships
Delta 17, Alexandria 14
Harrison (W.L.) 19, West Lafayette 14
District 6 Regional Championship
Delta 16, Harrison (W.L.) 15, 2 OT

District 7 Sectional Championships
Franklin Central 42, Franklin 14
Brownsburg 23, Danville 14
District 7 Regional Championship
Franklin Central 2, Brownsburg 0

District 8 Sectional Championships
Jasper 35, Edgewood 0
Tell City 34, Providence 7
District 8 Regional Championship
Jasper 20, Tell City 14

Semi-State Championships
Goshen 16, Delta 7
Franklin Central 14, Jasper 13

State Championship
Franklin Central 34, Goshen 20

Class 1A
District 9 Sectional Championships
North Judson 22, Frontier 9
John Glenn 28, South Newton 21
District 9 Regional Championship
North Judson 21, John Glenn 0

District 10 Sectional Championships
Woodlan 14, Tippecanoe Valley 7
Adams Central 28, West Noble 16
District 10 Regional Championship
Woodlan 7, Adams Central 6

District 11 Sectional Championships
Hamilton Southeastern 42, Tri 27
Sheridan 63, Knightstown 33
District 11 Regional Championship
Hamilton Southeastern 35, Sheridan 28

District 12 Sectional Championships
Lawrenceburg 20, Southridge 7
North Posey 33, Brownstown Central 20
District 12 Regional Championship
North Posey 20, Lawrenceburg 14, OT

Semi-State Championships
Woodlan 14, North Judson 7
Hamilton Southeastern 48, North Posey 8

State Championship
Hamilton Southeastern 7, Woodlan 6

1982
Class 3A
District 1 Sectional Championships
Highland 14, Merrillville 13
Hobart 25, Gary Roosevelt 12
District 1 Regional Championship
Hobart 27, Highland 0

District 2 Sectional Championships

Lafayette Jefferson 20, Mishawaka 6
Fort Wayne Snider 20, Penn 7
District 2 Regional Championship
Fort Wayne Snider 27, Lafayette Jefferson 14

District 3 Sectional Championships
Indpls. Chatard 7, Indpls. Cathedral 0
Carmel 24, North Central (Indpls.) 14
District 3 Regional Championship
Carmel 21, Indpls. Chatard 13

District 4 Sectional Championships
Martinsville 35, Columbus East 0
Castle 23, Richmond 7
District 4 Regional Championship
Castle 24, Martinsville 21

Semi-State Championships
Hobart 15, Fort Wayne Snider 0
Castle 21, Carmel 8

State Championship
Castle 26, Hobart 23

Class 2A
District 5 Sectional Championships
Peru 20, New Haven 14
Norwell 12, Angola 0
District 5 Regional Championship
Peru 23, Norwell 6

District 6 Sectional Championships
McCutcheon 27, Western 3
Twin Lakes 13, Blackford 7
District 6 Regional Championship
McCutcheon 16, Twin Lakes 13

District 7 Sectional Championships
Franklin Central 9, Crawfordsville 6
Avon 14, Pike 0
District 7 Regional Championship
Franklin Central 30, Avon 15

District 8 Sectional Championships
Jasper 28, Tell City 10
Providence 9, Edgewood 6
District 8 Regional Championship
Jasper 24, Providence 7

Semi-State Championships
McCutcheon 27, Peru 0
Franklin Central 33, Jasper 6

State Championship
Franklin Central 40, McCutcheon 13

Class 1A
District 9 Sectional Championships
Carroll (Flora) 26, North Judson 8
LaVille 20, Attica 0
District 9 Regional Championship
LaVille 23, Carroll (Flora) 21

District 10 Sectional Championships
Oak Hill 13, Jimtown 7
Woodlan 13, Bluffton 6
District 10 Regional Championship
Oak Hill 12, Woodlan 6, OT

District 11 Sectional Championships
Hagerstown 27, Hamilton Southeastern 20
Frankton 14, Tri-West 7
District 11 Regional Championship
Hagerstown 28, Frankton 14

District 12 Sectional Championships
Southridge 40, Linton-Stockton 0
North Decatur 24, North Posey 22
District 12 Regional Championship
Southridge 40, North Decatur 8

Semi-State Championships
Oak Hill 28, LaVille 6
Southridge 24, Hagerstown 13

State Championship
Oak Hill 14, Southridge 7

1983

NOTE: 1983 saw the expansion of the playoffs from three classes to four. Sixteen teams still qualified in each class, but the extra class expanded the number of qualifying teams from 48 to 64. This was done using a new system, commonly known as the cluster system.

Class 4A
Sectional Championships
Hobart 21, Munster 6
Portage 36, Michigan City Elston 3
Penn 34, Fort Wayne Northrop 7
Anderson Highland 34, Carmel 14
North Central (Indpls.) 34, Anderson 8
Indpls. Washington 32, Lawrence North 9
Bloomington South 12, Columbus East 9
Castle 28, Jeffersonville 0

Regional Championships
Hobart 23, Portage 8
Penn 35, Anderson Highland 8
Indpls. Washington 30, North Central (Indpls.) 3
Bloomington South 25, Castle 21

Semi-State Championships
Penn 17, Hobart 0
Indpls. Washington 22, Bloomington South 0

State Championship
Penn 25, Indpls. Washington 14

Class 3A
Sectional Championships
Hammond 20, Griffith 6
S.B. St. Joseph 14, Concord 7
Fort Wayne Dwenger 41, New Haven 0
Mississinewa 21, Twin Lakes 20
McCutcheon 28, Muncie North 14
Roncalli 35, Plainfield 7
Rushville 14, Seymour 0
Jasper 27, Vincennes Lincoln 20, OT

Regional Championships
S.B. St. Joseph 14, Hammond 8
Fort Wayne Dwenger 55, Mississinewa 6
Roncalli 19, McCutcheon 6
Jasper 31, Rushville 6

Semi-State Championships
Fort Wayne Dwenger 14, S.B. St. Joseph 0
Roncalli 17, Jasper 6

State Championship
Fort Wayne Dwenger 22, Roncalli 21

Class 2A
Sectional Championships
Tippecanoe Valley 35, Rensselaer 0
Fort Wayne Luers 21, Lakeland 0
Oak Hill 20, Western 3
Crawfordsville 21, Edgewood 14
Indpls. Chatard 42, Speedway 0
Yorktown 14, New Palestine 7
Mitchell 19, Batesville 8
Evansville Mater Dei 7, Providence 6

Regional Championships
F.W. Luers 27, Tippecanoe Valley 24, OT
Crawfordsville 16, Oak Hill 14
Indpls. Chatard 31, Yorktown 0
Evansville Mater Dei 42, Mitchell 14

Semi-State Championships
Fort Wayne Luers 19, Crawfordsville 7
Indpls. Chatard 40, Evansville Mater Dei 6

State Championship
Indpls. Chatard 20, Fort Wayne Luers 16

Class 1A
Sectional Championships
Bremen 13, Winamac 12, 2 OT
Jimtown 39, Fremont 13
Churubusco 16, Northfield 3
Frontier 26, Attica 13
Sheridan 42, Lapel 6
Eastern Hancock 12, Tri 10
Fountain Central 24, Tri-West 13
North Daviess 32, Springs Valley 0

Regional Championships
Jimtown 20, Bremen 17, OT
Churubusco 22, Frontier 6
Sheridan 18, Eastern Hancock 0
Fountain Central 24, North Daviess 0

Semi-State Championships
Churubusco 6, Jimtown 0
Fountain Central 19, Sheridan 14

State Championship
Fountain Central 12, Churubusco 3

1984
Class 4A
Sectional Championships
Hobart 20, Crown Point 7
Michigan City Elston 32, Portage 0
Fort Wayne North 34, Penn 20
Carmel 27, New Castle 6
North Central (Indpls.) 17, Lafayette Jefferson 6
Warren Central 20, Indpls. Washington 18
Martinsville 7, Shelbyville 3
New Albany 12, Castle 10

Regional Championships
Hobart 21, Michigan City Elston 13
Fort Wayne North 28, Carmel 21, OT
Warren Central 19, North Central (Indpls.) 9
Martinsville 16, New Albany 14

Semi-State Championships
Hobart 27, Fort Wayne North 7
Warren Central 38, Martinsville 6

State Championship
Warren Central 28, Hobart 8

Class 3A
Sectional Championships
Griffith 9, Hammond Noll 7
Concord 14, S.B. St. Joseph 7
Fort Wayne Dwenger 28, DeKalb 14
Kankakee Valley 16, Blackford 14
Brownsburg 16, Delta 0
Roncalli 35, Plainfield 0
Franklin 13, Seymour 8
Boonville 14, Tell City 13

Regional Championships
Concord 10, Griffith 0
Fort Wayne Dwenger 26, Kankakee Valley 13
Brownsburg 14, Roncalli 6
Boonville 56, Franklin 0

Semi-State Championships

Concord 21, Fort Wayne Dwenger 12
Brownsburg 17, Boonville 14

State Championship
Brownsburg 17, Concord 12

Class 2A
Sectional Championships
NorthWood 10, North Newton 6
Fort Wayne Luers 27, Lakeland 14
Western 11, Oak Hill 7
West Lafayette 28, Edgewood 21
Indpls. Chatard 7, Hamilton Southeastern 0
Hagerstown 11, New Palestine 6
Lawrenceburg 33, Charlestown 6
Evansville Mater Dei 10, Providence 7

Regional Championships
NorthWood 21, Fort Wayne Luers 17
West Lafayette 17, Western 14
Indpls. Chatard 28, Hagerstown 3
Lawrenceburg 21, Evansville Mater Dei 14

Semi-State Championships
West Lafayette 14, NorthWood 13
Indpls. Chatard 26, Lawrenceburg 14

State Championship
Indpls. Chatard 35, West Lafayette 7

Class 1A
Sectional Championships
North Judson 15, Bremen 12
Mishawaka Marian 35, Prairie Heights 14
Adams Central 20, Eastern (Greentown) 10
Carroll (Flora) 23, Attica 9
Sheridan 70, Wes-Del 14
Eastern Hancock 33, Milan 15
Tri-West 21, Rockville 0
Linton-Stockton 9, Tecumseh 6

Regional Championships
North Judson 13, Mishawaka Marian 9
Adams Central 21, Carroll (Flora) 0
Sheridan 20, Eastern Hancock 0
Tri-West 44, Linton-Stockton 12

Semi-State Championships
North Judson 14, Adams Central 13
Sheridan 6, Tri-West 0

State Championship
Sheridan 19, North Judson 10

1985
NOTE: 1985 saw the expansion of the state tournament from four classes to five, and implemented the all-in format, where every team qualifies regardless of regular season performanace. This is in line with how the IHSAA administers all other team sports.

Class 5A
Sectional 1 First Round
Merrillville 36, Gary Roosevelt 14
Portage 27, Highland 21
Crown Point 14, Lake Central 0
Gary Wallace 36, Gary West 20
Sectional 1 Second Round
Merrillville 21, Portage 0
Crown Point 18, Gary Wallace 12, OT
Sectional 1 Championship
Merrillville 14, Crown Point 7

Sectional 2 First Round
Valparaiso 56, South Bend LaSalle 7
Mishawaka 27, Michigan City Rogers 0
Michigan City Elston 26, Chesterton 14
LaPorte 27, South Bend Riley 13
Sectional 2 Second Round
Valparaiso 27, Mishawaka 0
LaPorte 7, Michigan City Elston 0
Sectional 2 Championship
Valparaiso 34, LaPorte 0

Sectional 3 First Round
Fort Wayne North 42, Huntington North 14
Elkhart Memorial 23, Fort Wayne Northrop 21
Penn 47, Warsaw 0
Fort Wayne Snider 49, Elkhart Central 7
Sectional 3 Second Round
Elkhart Memorial 12, Fort Wayne North 7
Fort Wayne Snider 13, Penn 12
Sectional 3 Championship
Fort Wayne Snider 21, Elkhart Memorial 6

Sectional 4 First Round
Jay County 32, Anderson Highland 14
Anderson 28, Marion 13
Kokomo 40, Muncie Central 0
And. Madison-Heights 10, Lafayette Jefferson 7
Sectional 4 Second Round
Jay County 40, Anderson 14
Kokomo 39, Anderson Madison-Heights 0
Sectional 4 Championship
Kokomo 34, Jay County 7

Sectional 5 First Round
Carmel 46, Lawrence North 12
Lawrence Central 55, Indpls. Marshall 0
North Central (Indpls.) 35, Indpls. Northwest 3
Indpls. Arlington 13, Indpls. Broad Ripple 0
Sectional 5 Second Round
Carmel 21, Lawrence Central 7
North Central (Indpls.) 37, Indpls. Arlington 0
Sectional 5 Championship
Carmel 40, North Central (Indpls.) 20

Sectional 6 First Round
New Castle 31, Connersville 7
Richmond 32, Indpls. Tech 0
Warren Central 52, Ben Davis 20
Indpls. Howe 10, Indpls. Manual 6
Sectional 6 Second Round
Richmond 14, New Castle 0
Warren Central 45, Indpls. Howe 0
Sectional 6 Championship
Warren Central 37, Richmond 0

Sectional 7 First Round
Columbus North 50, Jennings County 12
Southport 32, Center Grove 6
Jeffersonville 33, New Albany 6
Perry Meridian 14, Columbus East 7
Sectional 7 Second Round
Southport 14, Columbus North 7
Perry Meridian 21, Jeffersonville 16
Sectional 7 Championship
Southport 7, Perry Meridian 0

Sectional 8 First Round
Bloomington North 17, Bedford N.L. 12
Castle 23, Terre Haute South 20
Terre Haute North 28, Martinsville 8
Bloomington South 42, Evansville Central 6
Sectional 8 Second Round
Bloomington North 14, Castle 6
Bloomington South 22, Terre Haute North 16
Sectional 8 Championship
Bloomington South 17, Bloomington North 7

Regional Championships
Valparaiso 14, Merrillville 2
Fort Wayne Snider 7, Kokomo 0
Warren Central 17, Carmel 15
Bloomington South 9, Southport 0

Semi-State Championships
Valparaiso 20, Fort Wayne Snider 7
Warren Central 31, Bloomington South 0

State Championship
Warren Central 41, Valparaiso 7

Class 4A
Sectional 9 First Round
Hammond Morton 28, Lowell 6
Hammond Noll 13, East Chicago Roosevelt 3
Munster 27, Calumet 6
Hammond 26, Griffith 23
Sectional 9 Second Round
Hammond Noll 10, Hammond Morton 3
Munster 30, Hammond 0
Sectional 9 Championship
Munster 23, Hammond Noll 7

Sectional 10 First Round
South Bend Clay 44, S.B. Washington 6
Hobart 21, S.B. St. Joseph 0
South Bend Adams 35, Gary Wirt 16
Andrean 38, Gary Mann 16
Sectional 10 Second Round
Hobart 28, South Bend Clay 0
South Bend Adams 14, Andrean 0
Sectional 10 Championship
Hobart 20, South Bend Adams 7

Sectional 11 First Round
Fort Wayne Dwenger 35, East Noble 0
DeKalb 32, Culver Military Academy 7
Concord 18, Columbia City 0
Goshen 12, Homestead 7
Sectional 11 Second Round
Fort Wayne Dwenger 14, DeKalb 7
Concord 6, Goshen 0
Sectional 11 Championship
Fort Wayne Dwenger 42, Concord 7

Sectional 12 First Round
Harding (Fort Wayne) 19, New Haven 7
Fort Wayne South 14, Fort Wayne Elmhurst 12
Logansport 36, Blackford 7
Bellmont 16, Fort Wayne Wayne 13
Sectional 12 Second Round
Harding (Fort Wayne) 24, Fort Wayne South 6
Logansport 7, Bellmont 0
Sectional 12 Championship
Harding (Fort Wayne) 29, Logansport 22

Sectional 13 First Round
Brownsburg 22, Indpls. Washington 9
Northview 26, Pike 20
Plainfield 21, Avon 10
Decatur Central 24, Mooresville 18
Sectional 13 Second Round
Brownsburg 30, Northview 0
Decatur Central 33, Plainfield 21
Sectional 13 Championship
Brownsburg 33, Decatur Central 7

Sectional 14 First Round
Delta 10, Greenfield-Central 0
Muncie South 18, Noblesville 6
Indpls. Chatard 19, Harrison (West Lafayette) 6
McCutcheon 21, Pendleton Heights 6
Sectional 14 Second Round
Muncie South 21, Delta 3
Indpls. Chatard 26, McCutcheon 0
Sectional 14 Championship
Indpls. Chatard 27, Muncie South 0

Sectional 15 First Round
Greenwood 24, Rushville 8
East Central 33, South Dearborn 6

Seymour 24, Shelbyville 14
Franklin Central 21, Madison 7
Sectional 15 Second Round
East Central 21, Greenwood 0
Franklin Central 41, Seymour 16
Sectional 15 Championship
East Central 15, Franklin Central 12

Sectional 16 First Round
Evansville Reitz 2, Boonville 0
Evansville Harrison 42, Evansville Bosse 6
Floyd Central 19, Evansville North 6
Jasper 34, Vincennes Lincoln 31
Sectional 16 Second Round
Evansville Reitz 9, Evansville Harrison 6, OT
Jasper 7, Floyd Central 6
Sectional 16 Championship
Evansville Reitz 21, Jasper 2

Regional Championships
Hobart 41, Munster 0
Harding (Fort Wayne) 14, Fort Wayne Dwenger 6
Brownsburg 3, Indpls. Chatard 0
East Central 18, Evansville Reitz 17

Semi-State Championships
Hobart 26, Harding (Fort Wayne) 7
Brownsburg 34, East Central 7

State Championship
Brownsburg 23, Hobart 17

Class 3A
Sectional 17 First Round
Kankakee Valley 54, Knox 17
Twin Lakes 28, New Prairie 26
Hammond Clark 23, Benton Central 0
Hammond Gavit 33, E.C. Washington 8
Sectional 17 Second Round
Kankakee Valley 21, Twin Lakes 20
Hammond Clark 9, Hammond Gavit 6
Sectional 17 Championship
Kankakee Valley 20, Hammond Clark 19

Sectional 18 First Round
Wawasee 12, Norwell 6
Carroll (Fort Wayne) 30, F.W. Concordia 6
Plymouth 41, Northridge 7
NorthWood 27, Angola 21
Sectional 18 Second Round
Wawasee 22, Carroll (Fort Wayne) 8
Plymouth 14, NorthWood 6
Sectional 18 Championship
Wawasee 7, Plymouth 0

Sectional 19 First Round
Tipton 34, Maconaquah 14
Western 17, Peru 6
Northwestern 10, West Lafayette 7, OT
Hamilton Southeastern 40, Frankfort 20
Sectional 19 Second Round
Tipton 14, Western 7
Hamilton Southeastern 7, Northwestern 0
Sectional 19 Championship
Hamilton Southeastern 7, Tipton 6

Sectional 20 First Round
Yorktown 20, Winchester 6
Elwood 61, Alexandria 0
Mississinewa 51, Eastbrook 24
Madison-Grant 33, Muncie North 24
Sectional 20 Second Round
Elwood 15, Yorktown 8
Mississinewa 8, Madison-Grant 0
Sectional 20 Championship
Mississinewa 32, Elwood 31

Sectional 21 First Round
West Vigo 20, South Vermillion 14
Lebanon 14, Owen Valley 13, 2 OT
Crawfordsville 33, Western Boone 0
Zionsville 26, North Montgomery 21
Sectional 21 Second Round
West Vigo 38, Lebanon 29
Crawfordsville 2, Zionsville 0
Sectional 21 Championship
West Vigo 24, Crawfordsville 23

Sectional 22 First Round
Franklin 42, Whiteland 0
Mount Vernon (Fortville) 36, Indpls. Attucks 14
New Palestine 21, Brookville 0
Roncalli 14, Indpls. Cathedral 12
Sectional 22 Second Round
Mount Vernon (Fortville) 36, Franklin 7
Roncalli 40, New Palestine 6
Sectional 22 Championship
Roncalli 41, Mount Vernon (Fortville) 12

Sectional 23 First Round
Greensburg 27, Edgewood 0
Brown County 30, Charlestown 21
Providence 28, Batesville 7
North Harrison 17, Mitchell 12
Sectional 23 Second Round
Greensburg 21, Brown County 0
Providence 31, North Harrison 0
Sectional 23 Championship
Providence 14, Greensburg 7

Sectional 24 First Round
Evansville Memorial 26, Washington 13
Heritage Hills 40, Mount Vernon 6
Gibson Southern 13, Sullivan 7, 2 OT
Princeton 27, Pike Central 0
Sectional 24 Second Round
Evansville Memorial 20, Heritage Hills 14

Gibson Southern 56, Princeton 6
Sectional 24 Championship
Evansville Memorial 48, Gibson Southern 0

Regional Championships
Wawasee 12, Kankakee Valley 7
Mississinewa 15, Hamilton Southeastern 0
Roncalli 55, West Vigo 0
Evansville Memorial 21, Providence 14

Semi-State Championships
Wawasee 7, Mississinewa 6
Roncalli 28, Evansville Memorial 12

State Championship
Roncalli 37, Wawasee 3

Class 2A
Sectional 25 First Round
Lewis Cass 14, Lake Station 0
Rochester 16, John Glenn 0
Rensselaer Central 25, Mishawaka Marian 12
Delphi 25, North Newton 22
Sectional 25 Second Round
Rochester 48, Lewis Cass 12
Rensselaer Central 18, Delphi 12, 2 OT
Sectional 25 Championship
Rochester 3, Rensselaer Central 0

Sectional 26 First Round
Woodlan 28, Lakeland 21
Garrett 27, West Noble 18
Heritage 21, Leo 19
Fort Wayne Luers 7, Prairie Heights 0
Sectional 26 Second Round
Woodlan 21, Garrett 6
Fort Wayne Luers 34, Heritage 7
Sectional 26 Championship
Fort Wayne Luers 22, Woodlan 7

Sectional 27 First Round
Tippecanoe Valley 35, Oak Hill 26
Bluffton 40, Taylor 15
Whitko 40, Wabash 0
North Miami 44, Manchester 0
Sectional 27 Second Round
Tippecanoe Valley 28, Bluffton 12
North Miami 20, Whitko 14
Sectional 27 Championship
North Miami 22, Tippecanoe Valley 10

Sectional 28 First Round
Shenandoah 32, Union County 12
Knightstown 20, Wes-Del 15
Cambridge City Lincoln 41, Northeastern 13
Hagerstown 49, Centerville 21
Sectional 28 Second Round
Shenandoah 37, Knightstown 0
Hagerstown 34, Cambridge City Lincoln 9

Sectional 28 Championship
Hagerstown 28, Shenandoah 12

Sectional 29 First Round
Tri-West 57, Seeger 0
Danville 26, Southmont 20
Greencastle 20, Monrovia 13
Cascade 13, North Putnam 7
Sectional 29 Second Round
Tri-West 17, Danville 13
Cascade 14, Greencastle 12
Sectional 29 Championship
Tri-West 51, Cascade 6

Sectional 30 First Round
Beech Grove 34, Frankton 15
Indpls. Ritter 25, Brebeuf Jesuit 7
Hamilton Heights 40, Triton Central 38, 6 OT
Speedway 14, Indpls. Scecina 13
Sectional 30 Second Round
Indpls. Ritter 14, Beech Grove 7
Speedway 14, Hamilton Heights 6
Sectional 30 Championship
Indpls. Ritter 9, Speedway 7

Sectional 31 First Round
Lawrenceburg 49, Brownstown Central 6
Salem 35, Paoli 7
Sectional 31 Second Round
Lawrenceburg 43, Salem 0
Indian Creek 34, Corydon Central 7
Sectional 31 Championship
Lawrenceburg 48, Indian Creek 26

Sectional 32 First Round
South Spencer 9, Wood Memorial 3
Tell City 28, Southridge 0
North Knox 13, North Central (Farm.) 6, 2 OT
Evansville Mater Dei 34, North Posey 0
Sectional 32 Second Round
Tell City 14, South Spencer 0
Evansville Mater Dei 23, North Knox 6
Sectional 32 Championship
Tell City 22, Evansville Mater Dei 12

Regional Championships
Fort Wayne Luers 9, Rochester 3
Hagerstown 13, North Miami 7
Indpls. Ritter 20, Tri-West 2
Lawrenceburg 22, Tell City 0

Semi-State Championships
Fort Wayne Luers 22, Hagerstown 6
Lawrenceburg 27, Indpls. Ritter 0

State Championship
Fort Wayne Luers 25, Lawrenceburg 7

Class 1A

Sectional 33 First Round
Triton 30, Culver 16
North Judson 41, Bremen 0
South Central (Union Mills) 42, Whiting 0
LaVille 42, River Forest 14
Sectional 33 Second Round
North Judson 66, Triton 0
South Central (Union Mills) 12, LaVille 7
Sectional 33 Championship
North Judson 63, South Central (Union Mills) 8

Sectional 34 First Round
Churubusco 18, Central Noble 7
Fremont 41, Hamilton 22
Fairfield 20, Eastside 6
Sectional 34 Second Round
Jimtown 32, Churubusco 0
Fairfield 20, Fremont 12
Sectional 34 Championship
Jimtown 34, Fairfield 7

Sectional 35 First Round
Frontier 13, North White 0
South Newton 6, West Central 0
Carroll (Flora) 40, Pioneer 8
Winamac 40, Tri-County 6
Sectional 35 Second Round
South Newton 8, Frontier 7
Winamac 20, Carroll (Flora) 12
Sectional 35 Championship
Winamac 35, South Newton 12

Sectional 36 First Round
Adams Central 21, Southwood 20
South Adams 25, Southern Wells 8
Northfield 46, Caston 6
Sectional 36 Second Round
Adams Central 12, Eastern (Greentown) 7
Northfield 7, South Adams 6
Sectional 36 Championship
Adams Central 13, Northfield 12

Sectional 37 First Round
Covington 58, Cloverdale 0
Attica 17, Rockville 15
Fountain Central 19, Turkey Run 14
South Putnam 41, North Vermillion 6
Sectional 37 Second Round
Attica 10, Covington 7, OT
South Putnam 46, Fountain Central 0
Sectional 37 Championship
South Putnam 26, Attica 15

Sectional 38 First Round
Clinton Prairie 24, Tri-Central 0
Lafayette Central Catholic 7, Clinton Central 0
Westfield 56, South Decatur 0
Sheridan 38, Lapel 14
Sectional 38 Second Round
Lafayette Central Catholic 12, Clinton Prairie 7
Sheridan 8, Westfield 6
Sectional 38 Championship
Sheridan 16, Lafayette Central Catholic 6

Sectional 39 First Round
Eastern Hancock 46, Indiana Deaf 0
Milan 26, Edinburgh 0
Park Tudor 20, Tri 8
Union City 40, North Decatur 19
Sectional 39 Second Round
Eastern Hancock 15, Milan 14
Park Tudor 45, Union City 14
Sectional 39 Championship
Eastern Hancock 34, Park Tudor 7

Sectional 40 First Round
Springs Valley 26, Tecumseh 0
Perry Central 21, North Daviess 6
Linton-Stockton 7, West Washington 0
Clarksville 27, Union (Dugger) 0
Sectional 40 Second Round
Springs Valley 3, Perry Central 0
Clarksville 12, Linton-Stockton 2
Sectional 40 Championship
Clarksville 14, Springs Valley 13

Regional Championships
Jimtown 29, North Judson 22
Adams Central 33, Winamac 20
South Putnam 7, Sheridan 6, OT
Eastern Hancock 27, Clarksville 0

Semi-State Championships
Jimtown 13, Adams Central 6
Eastern Hancock 21, South Putnam 13

State Championship
Eastern Hancock 20, Jimtown 7

1986
Class 5A
Sectional 1 First Round
Gary Wallace 20, Gary Roosevelt 0
Highland 41, Gary West 12
Lake Central 41, Merrillville 14
Crown Point 20, Portage 14
Sectional 1 Second Round
Highland 20, Gary Wallace 18
Lake Central 18, Crown Point 0
Sectional 1 Championship
Highland 20, Lake Central 19

Sectional 2 First Round
Mishawaka 11, South Bend LaSalle 9
Michigan City Rogers 15, South Bend Riley 7
Michigan City Elston 12, Chesterton 10
Valparaiso 34, LaPorte 31, 3 OT
Sectional 2 Second Round

Mishawaka 22, Michigan City Rogers 0
Valparaiso 32, Michigan City Elston 0
Sectional 2 Championship
Valparaiso 28, Mishawaka 7

Sectional 3 First Round
Fort Wayne Snider 36, Fort Wayne North 0
Huntington North 30, Elkhart Memorial 19
Penn 41, Fort Wayne Northrop 7
Elkhart Central 28, Warsaw 13
Sectional 3 Second Round
Fort Wayne Snider 28, Huntington North 19
Penn 35, Elkhart Central 14
Sectional 3 Championship
Fort Wayne Snider 28, Penn 0

Sectional 4 First Round
Lafayette Jefferson 10, Anderson 0
Marion 31, Muncie Central 6
Jay County 38, Anderson Highland 7
Kokomo 47, Anderson Madison-Heights 18
Sectional 4 Second Round
Marion 19, Lafayette Jefferson 14
Kokomo 13, Jay County 9
Sectional 4 Championship
Marion 42, Kokomo 7

Sectional 5 First Round
Carmel 48, Indpls. Broad Ripple 6
North Central (Indpls.) 36, Lawrence North 14
Lawrence Central 20, Indpls. Arlington 6
Sectional 5 Second Round
North Central (Indpls.) 14, Lawrence Central 0
Carmel 41, Indpls. Northwest 8
Sectional 5 Championship
Carmel 19, North Central (Indpls.) 0

Sectional 6 First Round
Richmond 27, New Castle 6
Warren Central 43, Connersville 0
Ben Davis 35, Indpls. Manual 0
Indpls. Howe 26, Indpls. Tech 7
Sectional 6 Second Round
Warren Central 21, Richmond 7
Ben Davis 49, Indpls. Howe 26
Sectional 6 Championship
Warren Central 10, Ben Davis 7

Sectional 7 First Round
Jeffersonville 27, Columbus North 12
New Albany 35, Center Grove 7
Perry Meridian 23, Jennings County 0
Southport 26, Columbus East 21
Sectional 7 Second Round
New Albany 23, Jeffersonville 20
Perry Meridian 28, Southport 7
Sectional 7 Championship
Perry Meridian 28, New Albany 0

Sectional 8 First Round
Terre Haute North 40, Bedford N.L. 0
Terre Haute South 26, Evansville Central 12
Bloomington North 16, Bloomington South 0
Martinsville 12, Castle 10
Sectional 8 Second Round
Terre Haute North 27, Terre Haute South 0
Martinsville 38, Bloomington North 0
Sectional 8 Championship
Terre Haute North 27, Martinsville 20

Regional Championships
Valparaiso 28, Highland 22, OT
Fort Wayne Snider 15, Marion 7
Carmel 8, Warren Central 7
Perry Meridian 34, Terre Haute North 7

Semi-State Championships
Fort Wayne Snider 20, Valparaiso 14
Carmel 37, Perry Meridian 14

State Championship
Carmel 20, Fort Wayne Snider 17

Class 4A
Sectional 9 First Round
Hammond 14, East Chicago Central 0
Munster 27, Hammond Morton 14
Griffith 28, Calumet 7
Hammond Noll 20, Lowell 9
Sectional 9 Second Round
Munster 17, Hammond 14, OT
Hammond Noll 13, Griffith 6
Sectional 9 Championship
Munster 40, Hammond Noll 19

Sectional 10 First Round
Andrean 24, Gary Mann 0
Hobart 30, S.B. Washington 0
S.B. St. Joseph 14, South Bend Clay 0
South Bend Adams 21, Gary Wirt 12
Sectional 10 Second Round
Hobart 42, Andrean 13
S.B. St. Joseph 28, South Bend Adams 13
Sectional 10 Championship
Hobart 27, S.B. St. Joseph 14

Sectional 11 First Round
Goshen 6, Concord 2
DeKalb 35, Columbia City 6
Fort Wayne Dwenger 33, East Noble 14
Culver Military Academy 32, Homestead 17
Sectional 11 Second Round
DeKalb 28, Goshen 7
Culver Military Academy 27, F.W. Dwenger 7
Sectional 11 Championship
DeKalb 14, Culver Military Academy 0

Sectional 12 First Round

Harding (Fort Wayne) 7, Blackford 6
Bellmont 19, Fort Wayne Wayne 0
Logansport 19, Fort Wayne Elmhurst 7
New Haven 22, Fort Wayne South 14
Sectional 12 Second Round
Harding (Fort Wayne) 12, Bellmont 9
Logansport 32, New Haven 29, 2 OT
Sectional 12 Championship
Logansport 12, Harding (Fort Wayne) 6

Sectional 13 First Round
Indpls. Washington 16, Decatur Central 0
Avon 10, Pike 9
Brownsburg 48, Northview 6
Mooresville 15, Plainfield 6
Sectional 13 Second Round
Indpls. Washington 14, Avon 13
Brownsburg 35, Mooresville 12
Sectional 13 Championship
Indpls. Washington 14, Brownsburg 11

Sectional 14 First Round
Indpls. Chatard 25, Pendleton Heights 22
Muncie South 28, McCutcheon 21
Harrison (West Lafayette) 9, Delta 5
Noblesville 17, Greenfield-Central 7
Sectional 14 Second Round
Indpls. Chatard 50, Muncie South 6
Harrison (W.L.) 34, Noblesville 27, 2 OT
Sectional 14 Championship
Indpls. Chatard 21, Harrison (West Lafayette) 7

Sectional 15 First Round
Seymour 40, Rushville 7
East Central 41, South Dearborn 14
Greenwood 14, Madison 6
Franklin Central 56, Shelbyville 14
Sectional 15 Second Round
East Central 45, Seymour 14
Franklin Central 28, Greenwood 7
Sectional 15 Championship
Franklin Central 17, East Central 6

Sectional 16 First Round
Evansville Reitz 40, Vincennes Lincoln 0
Jasper 41, Evansville North 0
Boonville 44, Floyd Central 14
Evansville Harrison 13, Evansville Bosse 0

Sectional 16 Second Round
Jasper 10, Evansville Reitz 7
Evansville Harrison 29, Boonville 14
Sectional 16 Championship
Evansville Harrison 21, Jasper 7

Regional Championships
Munster 24, Hobart 21, 2 OT
DeKalb 43, Logansport 21
Indpls. Chatard 28, Indpls. Washington 12
Franklin Central 17, Evansville Harrison 0

Semi-State Championships
DeKalb 14, Munster 6
Franklin Central 28, Indpls. Chatard 6

State Championship
DeKalb 28, Franklin Central 7

Class 3A
Sectional 17 First Round
Hammond Gavit 22, New Prairie 7
Kankakee Valley 28, Knox 0
Benton Central 25, Hammond Clark 14
Sectional 17 Second Round
Kankakee Valley 27, Benton Central 0
Hammond Gavit 28, Twin Lakes 13
Sectional 17 Championship
Hammond Gavit 9, Kankakee Valley 7

Sectional 18 First Round
Wawasee 28, Fort Wayne Concordia 12
NorthWood 20, Carroll (Fort Wayne) 7
Plymouth 41, Northridge 8
Norwell 36, Angola 6
Sectional 18 Second Round
NorthWood 14, Wawasee 10
Norwell 29, Plymouth 14
Sectional 18 Championship
NorthWood 13, Norwell 7

Sectional 19 First Round
Tipton 9, Hamilton Southeastern 0
Frankfort 31, Maconaquah 23, OT
Northwestern 21, Western 7
West Lafayette 14, Peru 2
Sectional 19 Second Round
Tipton 24, Frankfort 23
West Lafayette 14, Northwestern 10
Sectional 19 Championship
West Lafayette 6, Tipton 2

Sectional 20 First Round
Yorktown 16, Elwood 13
Madison-Grant 20, Eastbrook 17
Mississinewa 27, Alexandria 0
Muncie North 43, Winchester 7
Sectional 20 Second Round
Yorktown 9, Madison-Grant 6, 2 OT
Mississinewa 20, Muncie North 12
Sectional 20 Championship
Mississinewa 20, Yorktown 17

Sectional 21 First Round
Zionsville 35, Lebanon 0
North Montgomery 38, Western Boone 6
Crawfordsville 48, South Vermillion 0
West Vigo 32, Owen Valley 20
Sectional 21 Second Round

Zionsville 20, North Montgomery 19
Crawfordsville 16, West Vigo 8
Sectional 21 Championship
Zionsville 28, Crawfordsville 7

Sectional 22 First Round
Indpls. Cathedral 24, Franklin 6
Roncalli 56, Brookville 0
New Palestine 34, Whiteland 0
Sectional 22 Second Round
Roncalli 28, New Palestine 27, OT
Indpls. Cathedral 21, Mount Vernon (FV) 7
Sectional 22 Championship
Indpls. Cathedral 14, Roncalli 7

Sectional 23 First Round
Batesville 50, Edgewood 12
Providence 29, Mitchell 13
Greensburg 35, Charlestown 14
Brown County 20, North Harrison 0
Sectional 23 Second Round
Batesville 15, Providence 0
Brown County 20, Greensburg 14
Sectional 23 Championship
Batesville 28, Brown County 6

Sectional 24 First Round
Princeton 27, Sullivan 13
Evansville Memorial 7, Washington 0
Heritage Hills 20, Pike Central 0
Gibson Southern 9, Mount Vernon 7
Sectional 24 Second Round
Princeton 35, Evansville Memorial 22
Heritage Hills 13, Gibson Southern 7
Sectional 24 Championship
Princeton 24, Heritage Hills 15

Regional Championships
NorthWood 34, Hammond Gavit 6
West Lafayette 22, Mississinewa 14, OT
Indpls. Cathedral 26, Zionsville 13
Batesville 23, Princeton 21

Semi-State Championships
NorthWood 21, West Lafayette 3
Indpls. Cathedral 42, Batesville 14

State Championship
Indpls. Cathedral 12, NorthWood 0

Class 3A
Sectional 25 First Round
North Newton 24, Lewis Cass 0
Rensselaer Central 22, John Glenn 14
Rochester 28, Mishawaka Marian 14
Lake Station 14, Delphi 13
Sectional 25 Second Round
Rensselaer Central 14, North Newton 7
Rochester 41, Lake Station 14

Sectional 25 Championship
Rensselaer Central 24, Rochester 21, OT

Sectional 26 First Round
Heritage 28, Woodlan 6
Prairie Heights 33, West Noble 0
Fort Wayne Luers 10, Garrett 0
Lakeland 44, Leo 13
Sectional 26 Second Round
Heritage 21, Prairie Heights 6
Fort Wayne Luers 21, Lakeland 14
Sectional 26 Championship
Fort Wayne Luers 27, Heritage 7

Sectional 27 First Round
Whitko 26, Manchester 0
Taylor 14, Bluffton 13
Oak Hill 35, Wabash 20
Tippecanoe Valley 15, North Miami 0
Sectional 27 Second Round
Whitko 47, Taylor 0
Tippecanoe Valley 23, Oak Hill 13
Sectional 27 Championship
Whitko 18, Tippecanoe Valley 0

Sectional 28 First Round
Shenandoah 48, Northeastern 0
Cambridge City Lincoln 32, Hagerstown 28
Knightstown 35, Centerville 6
Union County 20, Wes-Del 14
Sectional 28 Second Round
Shenandoah 10, Cambridge City Lincoln 6
Union County 14, Knightstown 11
Sectional 28 Championship
Shenandoah 34, Union County 6

Sectional 29 First Round
Greencastle 9, North Putnam 7
Danville 35, Cascade 0
Tri-West 31, Monrovia 13
Southmont 33, Seeger 0
Sectional 29 Second Round
Danville 28, Greencastle 0
Tri-West 49, Southmont 0
Sectional 29 Championship
Danville 14, Tri-West 6

Sectional 30 First Round
Indpls. Scecina 39, Speedway 0
Indpls. Ritter 20, Hamilton Heights 0
Brebeuf Jesuit 20, Beech Grove 14
Frankton 14, Triton Central 6
Sectional 30 Second Round
Indpls. Ritter 21, Indpls. Scecina 13
Brebeuf Jesuit 17, Frankton 0
Sectional 30 Championship
Indpls. Ritter 7, Brebeuf Jesuit 0

Sectional 31 First Round

Paoli 33, Corydon Central 0
Lawrenceburg 46, Indian Creek 6
Sectional 31 Second Round
Lawrenceburg 41, Paoli 20
Salem 21, Brownstown Central 13
Sectional 31 Championship
Lawrenceburg 37, Salem 20

Sectional 32 First Round
Evansville Mater Dei 27, Wood Memorial 7
South Spencer 27, North Knox 7
Tell City 20, Southridge 6
North Posey 26, North Central (Farmersburg) 0
Sectional 32 Second Round
Evansville Mater Dei 28, South Spencer 13
Tell City 14, North Posey 13
Sectional 32 Championship
Tell City 14, Evansville Mater Dei 12

Regional Championships
Fort Wayne Luers 31, Rensselaer Central 21
Whitko 21, Shenandoah 20
Danville 12, Indpls. Ritter 8
Tell City 15, Lawrenceburg 14

Semi-State Championships
Whitko 26, Fort Wayne Luers 7
Tell City 21, Danville 8

State Championship
Whitko 26, Tell City 0

Class 2A
Sectional 33 First Round
South Central (Union Mills) 23, Culver 0
North Judson 42, LaVille 0
River Forest 33, Triton 12
Bremen 34, Whiting 0
Sectional 33 Second Round
North Judson 42, South Central (Union Mills) 0
River Forest 40, Bremen 0
Sectional 33 Championship
North Judson 21, River Forest 6

Sectional 34 First Round
Fremont 21, Churubusco 0
Central Noble 30, Eastside 7
Sectional 34 Second Round
Central Noble 13, Fremont 7
Jimtown 36, Fairfield 0
Sectional 34 Championship
Jimtown 21, Central Noble 0

Sectional 35 First Round
South Newton 30, Carroll (Flora) 26
Tri-County 7, North White 6
Frontier 21, West Central 12
Winamac 29, Pioneer 0
Sectional 35 Second Round
Tri-County 7, South Newton 6
Frontier 16, Winamac 6
Sectional 35 Championship
Frontier 28, Tri-County 16

Sectional 36 First Round
Southwood 20, Southern Wells 8
Adams Central 28, Eastern (Greentown) 0
Northfield 22, Caston 0
Sectional 36 Second Round
Adams Central 42, Northfield 14
Southwood 35, South Adams 12
Sectional 36 Championship
Adams Central 28, Southwood 13

Sectional 37 First Round
Fountain Central 14, Turkey Run 0
Attica 31, Cloverdale 12
South Putnam 42, North Vermillion 9
Rockville 7, Covington 0
Sectional 37 Second Round
Attica 12, Fountain Central 6
South Putnam 30, Rockville 6
Sectional 37 Championship
South Putnam 26, Attica 14

Sectional 38 First Round
Westfield 34, Lapel 0
Sheridan 33, Tri-Central 8
Lafayette Central Catholic 41, Clinton Central 7
Sectional 38 Second Round
Lafayette Central Catholic 28, Sheridan 27
Westfield 35, Clinton Prairie 7
Sectional 38 Championship
Westfield 28, Lafayette Central Catholic 0

Sectional 39 First Round
Union City 25, Edinburgh 8
Eastern Hancock 48, North Decatur 14
Milan 28, Indiana Deaf 0
Tri 32, South Decatur 0
Sectional 39 Second Round
Eastern Hancock 21, Union City 6
Tri 22, Milan 0
Sectional 39 Championship
Tri 8, Eastern Hancock 6

Sectional 40 First Round
Linton-Stockton 26, Clarksville 14
Springs Valley 52, North Daviess 6
Union (Dugger) 36, West Washington 12
Tecumseh 7, Perry Central 0
Sectional 40 Second Round
Linton-Stockton 19, Springs Valley 0
Tecumseh 27, Union (Dugger) 0
Sectional 40 Championship
Linton-Stockton 31, Tecumseh 27

Regional Championships

North Judson 14, Jimtown 10
Adams Central 39, Frontier 29
South Putnam 18, Westfield 8
Linton-Stockton 20, Tri 6

Semi-State Championships
North Judson 17, Adams Central 14, OT
South Putnam 14, Linton-Stockton 6

State Championship
South Putnam 29, North Judson 21

1987
Class 5A
Sectional 1 First Round
Highland 44, East Chicago Central 12
Lake Central 28, Gary Wallace 12
Crown Point 17, Gary Roosevelt 0
Merrillville 55, Gary West 8
Sectional 1 Second Round
Highland 16, Lake Central 13
Crown Point 12, Merrillville 10
Sectional 1 Championship
Highland 23, Crown Point 21

Sectional 2 First Round
Chesterton 17, South Bend Adams 6
LaPorte 17, Portage 15
Valparaiso 14, Michigan City Rogers 12
Mishawaka 27, South Bend Riley 7
Sectional 2 Second Round
Chesterton 13, LaPorte 2
Valparaiso 7, Mishawaka 6
Sectional 2 Championship
Valparaiso 24, Chesterton 0

Sectional 3 First Round
Penn 39, Fort Wayne North 32, 2 OT
Fort Wayne Northrop 34, Huntington North 0
Fort Wayne Snider 34, Elkhart Memorial 0
Elkhart Central 63, Warsaw 20
Sectional 3 Second Round
Penn 35, Fort Wayne Northrop 14
Fort Wayne Snider 28, Elkhart Central 7
Sectional 3 Championship
Penn 17, Fort Wayne Snider 7

Sectional 4 First Round
Kokomo 27, Lafayette Jefferson 15
Marion 14, Anderson Highland 3
Anderson 25, Anderson Madison-Heights 13
Carmel 28, Jay County 6
Sectional 4 Second Round
Marion 20, Kokomo 7
Carmel 35, Anderson 6
Sectional 4 Championship
Carmel 41, Marion 7

Sectional 5 First Round
Perry Meridian 9, Indpls. Washington 0
Southport 24, Indpls. Manual 0
Ben Davis 34, North Central (Indpls.) 0
Indpls. Broad Ripple 14, Indpls. Tech 12
Sectional 5 Second Round
Southport 23, Perry Meridian 22, OT
Ben Davis 42, Indpls. Broad Ripple 6
Sectional 5 Championship
Ben Davis 20, Southport 6

Sectional 6 First Round
Lawrence Central 38, New Castle 0
Richmond 45, Connersville 26
Indpls. Howe 7, Indpls. Arlington 6
Warren Central 21, Lawrence North 17
Sectional 6 Second Round
Lawrence Central 12, Richmond 7
Indpls. Howe 20, Warren Central 14
Sectional 6 Championship
Lawrence Central 21, Indpls. Howe 14

Sectional 7 First Round
Martinsville 37, Terre Haute North 22
Terre Haute South 13, Bloomington South 9
Center Grove 17, Columbus North 14
Bloomington North 38, Columbus East 19
Sectional 7 Second Round
Terre Haute South 29, Martinsville 6
Center Grove 23, Bloomington North 18
Sectional 7 Championship
Center Grove 21, Terre Haute South 15

Sectional 8 First Round
Evansville Central 69, Jennings County 7
Evansville Harrison 31, Castle 24, OT
Evansville Reitz 35, Bedford N.L. 19
Jeffersonville 28, New Albany 22
Sectional 8 Second Round
Evansville Central 21, Evansville Harrison 19
Jeffersonville 48, Evansville Reitz 17
Sectional 8 Championship
Jeffersonville 31, Evansville Central 29

Regional Championships
Highland 42, Valparaiso 15
Carmel 28, Penn 14
Ben Davis 13, Lawrence Central 7
Center Grove 17, Jeffersonville 14

Semi-State Championships
Highland 30, Carmel 28
Ben Davis 49, Center Grove 0

State Championship
Ben Davis 14, Highland 7

Class 4A
Sectional 9 First Round
Andrean 28, Griffith 21

Munster 28, Gary Mann 0
Hammond 48, Hammond Noll 7
Hammond Morton 31, Lowell 12
Sectional 9 Second Round
Munster 17, Andrean 0
Hammond 12, Hammond Morton 0
Sectional 9 Championship
Munster 17, Hammond 14, OT

Sectional 10 First Round
Hobart 42, Michigan City Elston 6
South Bend LaSalle 28, S.B. Washington 20
Gary Wirt 28, Kankakee Valley 0
S.B. St. Joseph 42, South Bend Clay 8
Sectional 10 Second Round
Hobart 44, South Bend LaSalle 0
S.B. St. Joseph 33, Gary Wirt 6
Sectional 10 Championship
Hobart 23, S.B. St. Joseph 13

Sectional 11 First Round
East Noble 22, DeKalb 0
Columbia City 21, Wawasee 7
Culver Military Academy 26, Concord 16
Goshen 26, Homestead 7
Sectional 11 Second Round
East Noble 17, Columbia City 14
Goshen 20, Culver Military Academy 7
Sectional 11 Championship
Goshen 19, East Noble 6

Sectional 12 First Round
Blackford 51, Fort Wayne Elmhurst 0
Fort Wayne South 14, Harding (Fort Wayne) 0
Fort Wayne Wayne 26, New Haven 0
Bellmont 21, Peru 6
Sectional 12 Second Round
Fort Wayne South 27, Blackford 14
Fort Wayne Wayne 21, Bellmont 17
Sectional 12 Championship
Fort Wayne Wayne 15, Fort Wayne South 8

Sectional 13 First Round
Logansport 28, Muncie South 12
Delta 20, Muncie Central 11
Harrison (West Lafayette) 28, McCutcheon 21
Noblesville 47, Twin Lakes 14
Sectional 13 Second Round
Logansport 21, Delta 3
Harrison (West Lafayette) 17, Noblesville 14
Sectional 13 Championship
Harrison (West Lafayette) 31, Logansport 14

Sectional 14 First Round
Franklin Central 37, Indpls. Northwest 6
Mooresville 20, Northview 19
Decatur Central 27, Plainfield 0
Pike 31, Brownsburg 0
Sectional 14 Second Round

Franklin Central 35, Mooresville 7
Decatur Central 14, Pike 7
Sectional 14 Championship
Franklin Central 41, Decatur Central 21

Sectional 15 First Round
Pendleton Heights 27, Greenwood 23
East Central 41, Rushville 15
Greenfield-Central 38, South Dearborn 7
Seymour 24, Franklin 13
Sectional 15 Second Round
East Central 51, Pendleton Heights 0
Seymour 29, Greenfield-Central 0
Sectional 15 Championship
East Central 28, Seymour 7

Sectional 16 First Round
Floyd Central 44, Evansville Bosse 20
Mount Vernon 26, Vincennes Lincoln 20, 2 OT
Jasper 42, Evansville North 7
Boonville 29, Madison 14
Sectional 16 Second Round
Floyd Central 29, Mount Vernon 6
Jasper 25, Boonville 0
Sectional 16 Championship
Jasper 21, Floyd Central 20

Regional Championships
Hobart 7, Munster 3
Fort Wayne Wayne 21, Goshen 18
Harrison (W.L.) 31, Franklin Central 28
Jasper 16, East Central 0

Semi-State Championships
Hobart 42, Fort Wayne Wayne 3
Jasper 25, Harrison (West Lafayette) 3

State Championship
Hobart 31, Jasper 0

Class 3A
Sectional 17 First Round
New Prairie 14, Northridge 7
Hammond Gavit 7, Benton Central 0
NorthWood 31, Hammond Clark 0
Plymouth 36, Calumet 0
Sectional 17 Second Round
New Prairie 30, Hammond Gavit 6
NorthWood 21, Plymouth 0
Sectional 17 Championship
NorthWood 19, New Prairie 18

Sectional 18 First Round
Whitko 26, Norwell 14
Carroll (Fort Wayne) 49, Angola 0
Tippecanoe Valley 34, Lakeland 12
Fort Wayne Dwenger 34, F.W. Concordia 7
Sectional 18 Second Round
Carroll (Fort Wayne) 30, Whitko 14

Fort Wayne Dwenger 35, Tippecanoe Valley 26
Sectional 18 Championship
Fort Wayne Dwenger 35, Carroll (F.W.) 18

Sectional 19 First Round
Tipton 35, Frankfort 7
West Lafayette 13, Crawfordsville 9
Maconaquah 33, North Montgomery 20
Western 6, Northwestern 0
Sectional 19 Second Round
West Lafayette 20, Tipton 14
Maconaquah 29, Western 0
Sectional 19 Championship
West Lafayette 43, Maconaquah 23

Sectional 20 First Round
Muncie North 14, Mississinewa 12
Elwood 24, Winchester 20
Alexandria 12, Wabash 7
Yorktown 41, Eastbrook 21
Sectional 20 Second Round
Elwood 39, Muncie North 7
Yorktown 19, Alexandria 0
Sectional 20 Championship
Elwood 25, Yorktown 6

Sectional 21 First Round
Indpls. Cathedral 30, Hamilton Southeastern 6
Mount Vernon (Fortville) 36, Brebeuf Jesuit 0
Indpls. Chatard 14, Hamilton Heights 0
Roncalli 31, Beech Grove 20
Sectional 21 Second Round
Indpls. Cathedral 41, Mount Vernon (FV) 16
Indpls. Chatard 12, Roncalli 9
Sectional 21 Championship
Indpls. Cathedral 18, Indpls. Chatard 12

Sectional 22 First Round
New Palestine 48, Batesville 0
Whiteland 28, Brookville 14
Lawrenceburg 35, Shelbyville 14
Brown County 44, Greensburg 21
Sectional 22 Second Round
New Palestine 42, Whiteland 8
Lawrenceburg 27, Brown County 12
Sectional 22 Championship
New Palestine 36, Lawrenceburg 14

Sectional 23 First Round
Lebanon 17, South Vermillion 0
Zionsville 48, Avon 6
Edgewood 25, West Vigo 6
Sullivan 27, Owen Valley 6
Sectional 23 Second Round
Zionsville 35, Lebanon 0
Edgewood 42, Sullivan 0
Sectional 23 Championship
Zionsville 26, Edgewood 8

Sectional 24 First Round
Heritage Hills 28, Princeton 12
Evansville Memorial 70, Pike Central 0
Washington 20, North Harrison 0
Charlestown 45, Mitchell 6
Sectional 24 Second Round
Evansville Memorial 43, Heritage Hills 28
Charlestown 36, Washington 6
Sectional 24 Championship
Evansville Memorial 21, Charlestown 0

Regional Championships
Fort Wayne Dwenger 28, NorthWood 20
Elwood 21, West Lafayette 14
New Palestine 29, Indpls. Cathedral 28, OT
Zionsville 24, Evansville Memorial 14

Semi-State Championships
Elwood 19, Fort Wayne Dwenger 13
Zionsville 24, New Palestine 6

State Championship
Zionsville 23, Elwood 7

Class 2A
Sectional 25 First Round
North Judson 21, River Forest 20
Rensselaer Central 14, Knox 2
North Newton 48, LaVille 6
John Glenn 14, Lake Station 0
Sectional 25 Second Round
North Judson 6, Rensselaer Central 0
North Newton 42, John Glenn 0
Sectional 25 Championship
North Newton 40, North Judson 0

Sectional 26 First Round
Mishawaka Marian 23, Woodlan 7
Fort Wayne Luers 34, Heritage 7
Prairie Heights 14, West Noble 0
Leo 12, Garrett 6
Sectional 26 Second Round
Fort Wayne Luers 27, Mishawaka Marian 21
Prairie Heights 13, Leo 7
Sectional 26 Championship
Fort Wayne Luers 35, Prairie Heights 0

Sectional 27 First Round
Manchester 26, Eastern (Greentown) 14
Southwood 28, Taylor 21
Rochester 36, Lewis Cass 15
Madison-Grant 31, Oak Hill 0
Sectional 27 Second Round
Manchester 29, Southwood 22
Rochester 24, Madison-Grant 21
Sectional 27 Championship
Rochester 34, Manchester 7

Sectional 28 First Round

Carroll (Flora) 48, Southmont 20
Greencastle 28, Seeger 16
Delphi 43, North Putnam 0
Sectional 28 Second Round
Western Boone 28, Carroll (Flora) 24
Delphi 42, Greencastle 14
Sectional 28 Championship
Western Boone 19, Delphi 16

Sectional 29 First Round
Indpls. Ritter 26, Westfield 6
Danville 35, Monrovia 26
Tri-West 34, Speedway 0
Indpls. Scecina 35, Cascade 7
Sectional 29 Second Round
Indpls. Ritter 29, Danville 6
Tri-West 20, Indpls. Scecina 7
Sectional 29 Championship
Indpls. Ritter 10, Tri-West 3

Sectional 30 First Round
Triton Central 27, Union County 13
Shenandoah 7, Knightstown 6
Hagerstown 20, Centerville 0
Frankton 20, Northeastern 0
Sectional 30 Second Round
Triton Central 26, Shenandoah 6
Hagerstown 20, Frankton 14
Sectional 30 Championship
Triton Central 27, Hagerstown 20

Sectional 31 First Round
Tell City 30, Clarksville 8
Salem 8, Paoli 7
Indian Creek 26, Brownstown Central 6
Providence 33, Corydon Central 16
Sectional 31 Second Round
Tell City 49, Salem 8
Providence 33, Indian Creek 7
Sectional 31 Championship
Tell City 14, Providence 7

Sectional 32 First Round
Wood Memorial 6, North Posey 0
South Spencer 57, North Central (Farm.) 0
Gibson Southern 39, North Knox 8
Evansville Mater Dei 70, Southridge 15
Sectional 32 Second Round
South Spencer 24, Wood Memorial 0
Evansville Mater Dei 48, Gibson Southern 6
Sectional 32 Championship
Evansville Mater Dei 34, South Spencer 16

Regional Championships
North Newton 23, Fort Wayne Luers 13
Rochester 23, Western Boone 20
Indpls. Ritter 34, Triton Central 12
Tell City 12, Evansville Mater Dei 7

Semi-State Championships
Rochester 27, North Newton 0
Indpls. Ritter 14, Tell City 12

State Championship
Rochester 23, Indpls. Ritter 20

Class 1A
Sectional 33 First Round
Winamac 19, Culver 0
Triton 39, West Central 0
Bremen 48, Whiting 0
Sectional 33 Second Round
South Central (Union Mills) 14, Winamac 6
Bremen 44, Triton 0
Sectional 33 Championship
Bremen 33, South Central (Union Mills) 9

Sectional 34 First Round
Churubusco 28, Fairfield 19
Fremont 12, Central Noble 7
Sectional 34 Second Round
Jimtown 29, Eastside 0
Fremont 46, Churubusco 30
Sectional 34 Championship
Jimtown 7, Fremont 6

Sectional 35 First Round
Lafayette Central Catholic 44, Caston 14
Frontier 35, North White 6
Pioneer 24, South Newton 7
Sectional 35 Second Round
Lafayette Central Catholic 44, Tri-County 22
Frontier 39, Pioneer 0
Sectional 35 Championship
Frontier 42, Lafayette Central Catholic 0

Sectional 36 First Round
Wes-Del 29, South Adams 7
North Miami 42, Southern Wells 7
Adams Central 33, Union City 0
Northfield 14, Bluffton 12
Sectional 36 Second Round
Wes-Del 21, North Miami 6
Adams Central 28, Northfield 14
Sectional 36 Championship
Adams Central 27, Wes-Del 14

Sectional 37 First Round
Indiana Deaf 32, Riverton Parke 16
Tri-Central 44, Lapel 0
Sheridan 33, Clinton Central 12
Sectional 37 Second Round
Clinton Prairie 69, Indiana Deaf 0
Sheridan 23, Tri-Central 0
Sectional 37 Championship
Sheridan 20, Clinton Prairie 19

Sectional 38 First Round

South Decatur 15, Edinburgh 12
Milan 27, North Decatur 7
Eastern Hancock 17, Cambridge City Lincoln 0
Sectional 38 Second Round
Tri 28, South Decatur 6
Eastern Hancock 19, Milan 17
Sectional 38 Championship
Eastern Hancock 55, Tri 22

Sectional 39 First Round
Fountain Central 28, Turkey Run 12
North Vermillion 28, Rockville 7
South Putnam 50, Cloverdale 0
Attica 21, Covington 7
Sectional 39 Second Round
North Vermillion 33, Fountain Central 0
South Putnam 47, Attica 0
Sectional 39 Championship
South Putnam 21, North Vermillion 7

Sectional 40 First Round
Tecumseh 47, North Daviess 0
Union (Dugger) 45, West Washington 13
Springs Valley 17, Linton-Stockton 7
Sectional 40 Second Round
Tecumseh 19, Perry Central 3
Springs Valley 33, Union (Dugger) 24
Sectional 40 Championship
Tecumseh 14, Springs Valley 13

Regional Championships
Jimtown 15, Bremen 14
Frontier 20, Adams Central 14, OT
Sheridan 18, Eastern Hancock 8
South Putnam 21, Tecumseh 14

Semi-State Championships
Jimtown 23, Frontier 13
Sheridan 35, South Putnam 7

State Championship
Sheridan 10, Jimtown 0

1988
Class 5A
Sectional 1 First Round
Crown Point 35, Gary West 6
Gary Wallace 53, East Chicago Central 14
Lake Central 21, Highland 17
Merrillville 41, Gary Roosevelt 27
Sectional 1 Second Round
Crown Point 14, Gary Wallace 11
Lake Central 16, Merrillville 7
Sectional 1 Championship
Crown Point 21, Lake Central 0

Sectional 2 First Round
LaPorte 27, Valparaiso 0
Portage 45, South Bend Riley 0

Mishawaka 20, Chesterton 0
S.B. Adams 28, Michigan City Rogers 20
Sectional 2 Second Round
LaPorte 20, Portage 13
Mishawaka 42, South Bend Adams 6
Sectional 2 Championship
Mishawaka 35, LaPorte 15

Sectional 3 First Round
Fort Wayne North 35, Warsaw 13
Fort Wayne Snider 31, Huntington North 13
Penn 20, Elkhart Memorial 0
Elkhart Central 15, Fort Wayne Northrop 12
Sectional 3 Second Round
Fort Wayne North 31, Fort Wayne Snider 0
Penn 20, Elkhart Central 7
Sectional 3 Championship
Fort Wayne North 14, Penn 10

Sectional 4 First Round
Lafayette Jefferson 10, Jay County 0
Marion 45, Anderson Highland 0
Kokomo 48, Anderson 12
Carmel 49, Anderson Madison-Heights 0
Sectional 4 Second Round
Marion 41, Lafayette Jefferson 7
Carmel 28, Kokomo 13
Sectional 4 Championship
Marion 30, Carmel 7

Sectional 5 First Round
North Central (Indpls.) 30, Indpls. Tech 6
Southport 34, Indpls. Washington 33
Indpls. Manual 8, Indpls. Broad Ripple 6
Ben Davis 35, Perry Meridian 0
Sectional 5 Second Round
North Central (Indpls.) 20, Southport 8
Ben Davis 42, Indpls. Manual 18
Sectional 5 Championship
Ben Davis 20, North Central (Indpls.) 6

Sectional 6 First Round
Warren Central 43, Connersville 6
Lawrence North 34, Indpls. Arlington 0
Richmond 31, New Castle 8
Lawrence Central 27, Indpls. Howe 3
Sectional 6 Second Round
Lawrence North 27, Warren Central 22
Lawrence Central 38, Richmond 14
Sectional 6 Championship
Lawrence North 14, Lawrence Central 7

Sectional 7 First Round
Terre Haute North 46, Columbus East 14
Center Grove 27, Bloomington South 0
Terre Haute South 34, Martinsville 18
Bloomington North 21, Columbus North 7
Sectional 7 Second Round
Terre Haute North 12, Center Grove 8

Terre Haute South 25, Bloomington North 7
Sectional 7 Championship
Terre Haute South 27, Terre Haute North 16

Sectional 8 First Round
Bedford North Lawrence 20, Jeffersonville 13
Evansville Central 24, New Albany 0
Evansville Harrison 34, Castle 14
Evansville Reitz 66, Jennings County 6
Sectional 8 Second Round
Evansville Central 26, Bedford N.L. 12
Evansville Harrison 33, Evansville Reitz 0
Sectional 8 Championship
Evansville Central 10, Evansville Harrison 6

Regional Championships
Crown Point 28, Mishawaka 27
Marion 19, Fort Wayne North 0
Ben Davis 31, Lawrence North 0
Terre Haute South 35, Evansville Central 0

Semi-State Championships
Marion 23, Crown Point 7
Ben Davis 51, Terre Haute South 28

State Championship
Ben Davis 43, Marion 0

Class 4A
Sectional 9 First Round
Griffith 38, Gary Mann 6
Hammond Noll 7, Munster 6
Hammond Morton 13, Andrean 7
Hammond 34, Lowell 6
Sectional 9 Second Round
Griffith 21, Hammond Noll 18
Hammond 30, Hammond Morton 0
Sectional 9 Championship
Hammond 27, Griffith 14

Sectional 10 First Round
S.B. Washington 20, Gary Wirt 14
S.B. St. Joseph 24, Michigan City Elston 0
South Bend Clay 26, South Bend LaSalle 0
Hobart 41, Kankakee Valley 0
Sectional 10 Second Round
S.B. Washington 20, S.B. St. Joseph 12
Hobart 42, South Bend Clay 0
Sectional 10 Championship
Hobart 19, S.B. Washington 0

Sectional 11 First Round
Columbia City 20, Concord 6
DeKalb 28, Wawasee 6
Goshen 48, Culver Military Academy 7
Homestead 15, East Noble 6
Sectional 11 Second Round
Columbia City 31, DeKalb 25
Goshen 41, Homestead 13

Sectional 11 Championship
Goshen 39, Columbia City 6

Sectional 12 First Round
New Haven 40, Peru 0
Harding (Fort Wayne) 25, Blackford 6
Fort Wayne Wayne 35, Fort Wayne Elmhurst 8
Fort Wayne South 24, Bellmont 6
Sectional 12 Second Round
New Haven 33, Harding (Fort Wayne) 0
Fort Wayne South 29, Fort Wayne Wayne 21
Sectional 12 Championship
New Haven 14, Fort Wayne South 6

Sectional 13 First Round
Noblesville 33, McCutcheon 0
Logansport 14, Muncie Central 7
Harrison (West Lafayette) 39, Twin Lakes 19
Muncie South 21, Delta 14
Sectional 13 Second Round
Logansport 21, Noblesville 8
Harrison (West Lafayette) 31, Muncie South 0
Sectional 13 Championship
Logansport 11, Harrison (W.L.) 8, 3 OT

Sectional 14 First Round
Indpls. Northwest 16, Plainfield 14
Franklin Central 42, Northview 0
Mooresville 14, Decatur Central 9
Brownsburg 14, Pike 13
Sectional 14 Second Round
Franklin Central 42, Indpls. Northwest 14
Mooresville 28, Brownsburg 14
Sectional 14 Championship
Franklin Central 34, Mooresville 0

Sectional 15 First Round
East Central 17, Pendleton Heights 0
Greenwood 19, Rushville 13
Seymour 41, South Dearborn 7
Franklin 16, Greenfield-Central 0
Sectional 15 Second Round
Greenwood 16, East Central 9
Seymour 47, Franklin 13
Sectional 15 Championship
Greenwood 30, Seymour 3

Sectional 16 First Round
Jasper 23, Mount Vernon 14
Floyd Central 13, Madison 12
Evansville Bosse 28, Vincennes Lincoln 7
Evansville North 10, Boonville 0
Sectional 16 Second Round
Floyd Central 21, Jasper 20
Evansville Bosse 17, Evansville North 14
Sectional 16 Championship
Evansville Bosse 6, Floyd Central 2

Regional Championships

Hammond 31, Hobart 28, OT
Goshen 10, New Haven 8
Franklin Central 42, Logansport 0
Greenwood 13, Evansville Bosse 0

Semi-State Championships
Goshen 39, Hammond 14
Franklin Central 3, Greenwood 0

State Championship
Goshen 24, Franklin Central 10

Class 3A
Sectional 17 First Round
Calumet 18, Benton Central 6
Hammond Clark 36, Northridge 35
NorthWood 34, Plymouth 6
New Prairie 40, Hammond Gavit 0
Sectional 17 Second Round
Hammond Clark 14, Calumet 0
NorthWood 31, New Prairie 0
Sectional 17 Championship
NorthWood 7, Hammond Clark 6

Sectional 18 First Round
Carroll (Fort Wayne) 26, Angola 0
Norwell 36, Fort Wayne Concordia 25
Tippecanoe Valley 20, Whitko 14
Fort Wayne Dwenger 51, Lakeland 8
Sectional 18 Second Round
Carroll (Fort Wayne) 23, Norwell 14
Fort Wayne Dwenger 27, Tippecanoe Valley 6
Sectional 18 Championship
Fort Wayne Dwenger 28, Carroll (F.W.) 20

Sectional 19 First Round
Tipton 44, Northwestern 7
West Lafayette 14, Crawfordsville 9
Western 28, Frankfort 6
North Montgomery 14, Maconaquah 6
Sectional 19 Second Round
Tipton 10, West Lafayette 7
Western 14, North Montgomery 13, 2 OT
Sectional 19 Championship
Tipton 17, Western 14

Sectional 20 First Round
Yorktown 22, Eastbrook 7
Winchester 27, Wabash 6
Elwood 34, Alexandria 12
Sectional 20 Second Round
Mississinewa 48, Yorktown 20
Elwood 47, Winchester 10
Sectional 20 Championship
Mississinewa 20, Elwood 13

Sectional 21 First Round
Hamilton Southeastern 18, Brebeuf Jesuit 14
Indpls. Cathedral 39, Mount Vernon (FV) 0
Roncalli 41, Indpls. Chatard 18
Hamilton Heights 26, Beech Grove 21
Sectional 21 Second Round
Indpls. Cathedral 14, Hamilton Southeastern 0
Roncalli 21, Hamilton Heights 7
Sectional 21 Championship
Roncalli 14, Indpls. Cathedral 0

Sectional 22 First Round
Lawrenceburg 14, Greensburg 0
Whiteland 21, Batesville 14
New Palestine 38, Shelbyville 13
Brookville 20, Brown County 18
Sectional 22 Second Round
Lawrenceburg 13, Whiteland 6
New Palestine 28, Brookville 9
Sectional 22 Championship
Lawrenceburg 20, New Palestine 0

Sectional 23 First Round
Sullivan 50, Avon 15
Zionsville 18, Lebanon 6
West Vigo 44, Owen Valley 6
Edgewood 33, South Vermillion 0
Sectional 23 Second Round
Zionsville 26, Sullivan 0
Edgewood 41, West Vigo 12
Sectional 23 Championship
Zionsville 41, Edgewood 6

Sectional 24 First Round
Mitchell 21, North Harrison 20
Heritage Hills 21, Princeton 12
Evansville Memorial 46, Charlestown 12
Washington 35, Pike Central 0
Sectional 24 Second Round
Heritage Hills 54, Mitchell 13
Evansville Memorial 87, Washington 0
Sectional 24 Championship
Evansville Memorial 20, Heritage Hills 19

Regional Championships
Fort Wayne Dwenger 21, NorthWood 11
Tipton 21, Mississinewa 0
Roncalli 32, Lawrenceburg 28
Evansville Memorial 35, Zionsville 21

Semi-State Championships
Tipton 18, Fort Wayne Dwenger 16
Roncalli 3, Evansville Memorial 0

State Championship
Roncalli 14, Tipton 13

Class 2A
Sectional 25 First Round
North Judson 10, Rensselaer Central 7
LaVille 22, North Newton 21
Knox 6, John Glenn 0

River Forest 14, Lake Station 12
Sectional 25 Second Round
LaVille 26, North Judson 23
River Forest 20, Knox 0
Sectional 25 Championship
River Forest 25, LaVille 12

Sectional 26 First Round
Woodlan 13, Prairie Heights 7
Leo 38, Heritage 14
West Noble 27, Garrett 6
Fort Wayne Luers 30, Mishawaka Marian 13
Sectional 26 Second Round
Woodlan 28, Leo 7
Fort Wayne Luers 41, West Noble 14
Sectional 26 Championship
Woodlan 21, Fort Wayne Luers 0

Sectional 27 First Round
Eastern (Greentown) 27, Madison-Grant 26
Taylor 7, Lewis Cass 3
Manchester 39, Oak Hill 0
Rochester 27, Southwood 0
Sectional 27 Second Round
Taylor 27, Eastern (Greentown) 26
Manchester 21, Rochester 19
Sectional 27 Championship
Manchester 26, Taylor 13

Sectional 28 First Round
Delphi 46, North Putnam 20
Western Boone 34, Carroll (Flora) 0
Greencastle 21, Southmont 20
Sectional 28 Second Round
Delphi 64, Seeger 12
Western Boone 47, Greencastle 32
Sectional 28 Championship
Western Boone 14, Delphi 6

Sectional 29 First Round
Monrovia 47, Cascade 6
Indpls. Scecina 3, Indpls. Ritter 0
Danville 28, Speedway 15
Tri-West 23, Westfield 0
Sectional 29 Second Round
Monrovia 12, Indpls. Scecina 6
Tri-West 21, Danville 14
Sectional 29 Championship
Tri-West 40, Monrovia 0

Sectional 30 First Round
Hagerstown 41, Northeastern 0
Frankton 35, Union County 6
Triton Central 56, Centerville 0
Shenandoah 21, Knightstown 0
Sectional 30 Second Round
Frankton 18, Hagerstown 6
Triton Central 41, Shenandoah 12
Sectional 30 Championship

Triton Central 19, Frankton 16

Sectional 31 First Round
Salem 27, Clarksville 6
Tell City 39, Paoli 0
Providence 31, Brownstown Central 13
Corydon Central 18, Indian Creek 16
Sectional 31 Second Round
Tell City 35, Salem 0
Providence 13, Corydon Central 12
Sectional 31 Championship
Tell City 34, Providence 0

Sectional 32 First Round
Evansville Mater Dei 41, Wood Memorial 10
Gibson Southern 41, North Knox 0
Southridge 34, North Central (Farmersburg) 6
South Spencer 54, North Posey 7
Sectional 32 Second Round
Evansville Mater Dei 17, Gibson Southern 10
South Spencer 25, Southridge 6
Sectional 32 Championship
South Spencer 20, Evansville Mater Dei 0

Regional Championships
Woodlan 27, River Forest 22
Western Boone 41, Manchester 12
Tri-West 17, Triton Central 14
South Spencer 17, Tell City 14

Semi-State Championships
Western Boone 26, Woodlan 21
South Spencer 24, Tri-West 13

State Championship
Western Boone 14, South Spencer 7

Class 1A
Sectional 33 First Round
West Central 45, Culver 20
South Central (Union Mills) 21, Triton 15
Bremen 27, Winamac 7
Sectional 33 Second Round
Whiting 34, West Central 6
Bremen 28, South Central (Union Mills) 0
Sectional 33 Championship
Bremen 35, Whiting 0

Sectional 34 First Round
Fremont 10, Eastside 7
Churubusco 17, Fairfield 0
Sectional 34 Second Round
Churubusco 27, Fremont 16
Jimtown 35, Central Noble 0
Sectional 34 Championship
Churubusco 19, Jimtown 15

Sectional 35 First Round
Frontier 23, Tri-County 3

North White 14, Caston 3
Lafayette Central Catholic 49, Pioneer 13
Sectional 35 Second Round
Frontier 45, South Newton 0
Lafayette Central Catholic 36, North White 18
Sectional 35 Championship
Frontier 14, Lafayette Central Catholic 6

Sectional 36 First Round
Union City 22, South Adams 21
North Miami 53, Southern Wells 7
Bluffton 24, Northfield 6
Adams Central 21, Wes-Del 0
Sectional 36 Second Round
North Miami 42, Union City 0
Bluffton 27, Adams Central 18
Sectional 36 Championship
Bluffton 21, North Miami 7

Sectional 37 First Round
Clinton Prairie 28, Park Tudor 0
Sheridan 83, Lapel 6
Tri-Central 22, Indiana Deaf 0
Clinton Central 37, Riverton Parke 10
Sectional 37 Second Round
Sheridan 85, Clinton Prairie 0
Clinton Central 25, Tri-Central 14
Sectional 37 Championship
Sheridan 53, Clinton Central 6

Sectional 38 First Round
Eastern Hancock 27, Tri 0
South Decatur 28, North Decatur 20
Cambridge City Lincoln 17, Milan 14
Sectional 38 Second Round
Eastern Hancock 42, Edinburgh 0
South Decatur 12, Cambridge City Lincoln 6
Sectional 38 Championship
Eastern Hancock 26, South Decatur 14

Sectional 39 First Round
Rockville 17, Fountain Central 7
South Putnam 39, Cloverdale 6
Covington 14, Attica 0
North Vermillion 23, Turkey Run 7
Sectional 39 Second Round
South Putnam 31, Rockville 6
North Vermillion 22, Covington 13
Sectional 39 Championship
South Putnam 31, North Vermillion 0

Sectional 40 First Round
Linton-Stockton 40, North Daviess 0
Springs Valley 42, West Washington 7
Perry Central 27, Union (Dugger) 26
Sectional 40 Second Round
Linton-Stockton 41, Tecumseh 14
Springs Valley 34, Perry Central 0
Sectional 40 Championship

Springs Valley 13, Linton-Stockton 7

Regional Championships
Bremen 24, Churubusco 0
Bluffton 27, Frontier 18
Sheridan 54, Eastern Hancock 6
South Putnam 13, Springs Valley 10

Semi-State Championships
Bremen 21, Bluffton 14
Sheridan 29, South Putnam 0

State Championship
Sheridan 59, Bremen 0

1989
Class 5A
Sectional 1 First Round
Gary West 16, Hammond 7
Gary Wallace 28, Crown Point 0
Lake Central 42, East Chicago Central 7
Merrillville 14, Gary Roosevelt 3
Sectional 1 Second Round
Gary Wallace 45, Gary West 0
Lake Central 24, Merrillville 21, OT
Sectional 1 Championship
Gary Wallace 56, Lake Central 19

Sectional 2 First Round
Michigan City Rogers 27, South Bend Riley 20
Mishawaka 32, Chesterton 0
Valparaiso 35, South Bend LaSalle 0
Portage 14, LaPorte 7
Sectional 2 Second Round
Mishawaka 36, Michigan City Rogers 12
Valparaiso 29, Portage 0
Sectional 2 Championship
Valparaiso 7, Mishawaka 0

Sectional 3 First Round
Penn 10, Fort Wayne North 3
Fort Wayne Northrop 48, Elkhart Memorial 0
Fort Wayne Snider 13, Fort Wayne Wayne 9
Elkhart Central 7, Warsaw 3
Sectional 3 Second Round
Penn 30, Fort Wayne Northrop 6
Fort Wayne Snider 19, Elkhart Central 7
Sectional 3 Championship
Penn 35, Fort Wayne Snider 0

Sectional 4 First Round
Marion 22, Muncie Central 12
Huntington North 18, Muncie South 13
Anderson Highland 16, Kokomo 13, 2 OT
Lafayette Jefferson 60, And. Madison-Hts. 14
Sectional 4 Second Round
Marion 27, Huntington North 0
Lafayette Jefferson 28, Anderson Highland 15
Sectional 4 Championship

Lafayette Jefferson 18, Marion 13

Sectional 5 First Round
Indpls. Tech 20, Indpls. Manual 0
Indpls. Broad Ripple 25, Decatur Central 8
Ben Davis 21, North Central (Indpls.) 14
Carmel 28, Indpls. Washington 26
Sectional 5 Second Round
Indpls. Broad Ripple 14, Indpls. Tech 8
Carmel 14, Ben Davis 0
Sectional 5 Championship
Carmel 28, Indpls. Broad Ripple 0

Sectional 6 First Round
Lawrence Central 33, Warren Central 9
Lawrence North 31, New Castle 0
Indpls. Arlington 20, Indpls. Howe 19
Richmond 42, Connersville 14
Sectional 6 Second Round
Lawrence North 6, Lawrence Central 0
Richmond 29, Indpls. Arlington 22
Sectional 6 Championship
Lawrence North 19, Richmond 14

Sectional 7 First Round
Southport 41, Terre Haute South 8
Terre Haute North 36, Center Grove 14
Columbus North 30, Martinsville 0
Perry Meridian 21, Bloomington South 14
Sectional 7 Second Round
Terre Haute North 17, Southport 15
Columbus North 28, Perry Meridian 21
Sectional 7 Championship
Columbus North 21, Terre Haute North 20

Sectional 8 First Round
Castle 55, Bedford North Lawrence 0
Evansville Harrison 40, Seymour 14
Evansville Central 35, New Albany 8
Jeffersonville 38, Jennings County 7
Sectional 8 Second Round
Castle 42, Evansville Harrison 7
Evansville Central 40, Jeffersonville 6
Sectional 8 Championship
Castle 7, Evansville Central 6

Regional Championships
Valparaiso 13, Gary Wallace 12
Penn 37, Lafayette Jefferson 12
Carmel 17, Lawrence North 8
Castle 28, Columbus North 14

Semi-State Championships
Penn 20, Valparaiso 6
Carmel 34, Castle 7

State Championship
Carmel 10, Penn 7

Class 4A
Sectional 9 First Round
Munster 20, Gary Mann 3
Lowell 8, Calumet 0
Andrean 9, Highland 0
Hammond Morton 34, Hammond Clark 6
Sectional 9 Second Round
Munster 17, Lowell 0
Andrean 31, Hammond Morton 0
Sectional 9 Championship
Andrean 14, Munster 0

Sectional 10 First Round
South Bend Clay 14, Goshen 13
South Bend Adams 6, Concord 2
S.B. Washington 34, Michigan City Elston 20
Hobart 34, Gary Wirt 0
Sectional 10 Second Round
South Bend Clay 35, South Bend Adams 12
Hobart 21, S.B. Washington 0
Sectional 10 Championship
Hobart 42, South Bend Clay 13

Sectional 11 First Round
DeKalb 25, East Noble 0
Wawasee 20, Fort Wayne South 14
Homestead 6, Fort Wayne Elmhurst 0
Columbia City 26, New Haven 0
Sectional 11 Second Round
DeKalb 23, Wawasee 8
Columbia City 27, Homestead 21
Sectional 11 Championship
DeKalb 24, Columbia City 0

Sectional 12 First Round
Jay County 21, Blackford 7
Bellmont 17, Logansport 13
Harrison (West Lafayette) 35, Peru 0
McCutcheon 13, Plymouth 0
Sectional 12 Second Round
Bellmont 23, Jay County 7
Harrison (West Lafayette) 9, McCutcheon 0
Sectional 12 Championship
Harrison (West Lafayette) 28, Bellmont 21

Sectional 13 First Round
Pike 21, Avon 13
Plainfield 31, Indpls. Northwest 12
Noblesville 23, Lebanon 0
Franklin Central 20, Brownsburg 7
Sectional 13 Second Round
Pike 41, Plainfield 28
Franklin Central 35, Noblesville 13
Sectional 13 Championship
Franklin Central 35, Pike 0

Sectional 14 First Round
Franklin County 21, Greenfield-Central 7
East Central 17, Pendleton Heights 0

Shelbyville 15, Delta 7
Anderson 18, Rushville 0
Sectional 14 Second Round
East Central 28, Franklin County 6
Shelbyville 13, Anderson 12
Sectional 14 Championship
East Central 20, Shelbyville 0

Sectional 15 First Round
Columbus East 41, South Dearborn 20
Madison 28, Bloomington North 0
Greenwood 12, Franklin 3
Mooresville 25, Northview 24, 2 OT
Sectional 15 Second Round
Columbus East 31, Madison 29
Mooresville 33, Greenwood 14
Sectional 15 Championship
Mooresville 12, Columbus East 0

Sectional 16 First Round
Vincennes Lincoln 14, Evansville North 7
Evansville Reitz 10, Washington 6
Floyd Central 13, Boonville 7
Mount Vernon 19, Evansville Bosse 13
Sectional 16 Second Round
Evansville Reitz 17, Vincennes Lincoln 0
Mount Vernon 20, Floyd Central 7
Sectional 16 Championship
Evansville Reitz 32, Mount Vernon 22

Regional Championships
Hobart 14, Andrean 7
Harrison (West Lafayette) 28, DeKalb 17
Franklin Central 20, East Central 3
Mooresville 34, Evansville Reitz 21

Semi-State Championships
Hobart 27, Harrison (West Lafayette) 0
Franklin Central 41, Mooresville 18

State Championship
Hobart 17, Franklin Central 7

Class 3A
Sectional 17 First Round
Hammond Gavit 26, Benton Central 7
Hammond Noll 42, Kankakee Valley 14
Twin Lakes 20, Knox 0
Griffith 36, New Prairie 7
Sectional 17 Second Round
Hammond Noll 20, Hammond Gavit 7
Griffith 26, Twin Lakes 7
Sectional 17 Championship
Hammond Noll 25, Griffith 18

Sectional 18 First Round
S.B. St. Joseph 20, Whitko 6
Lakeland 16, Angola 7
NorthWood 35, Culver Military Academy 0

Sectional 18 Second Round
Northridge 12, S.B. St. Joseph 10
NorthWood 41, Lakeland 16
Sectional 18 Championship
NorthWood 34, Northridge 21

Sectional 19 First Round
Mississinewa 36, Eastbrook 8
Norwell 13, Carroll (Fort Wayne) 0
Harding (Fort Wayne) 28, Fort Wayne Concordia 21
Fort Wayne Dwenger 60, Wabash 0
Sectional 19 Second Round
Norwell 28, Mississinewa 13
Fort Wayne Dwenger 24, Harding (F.W.) 0
Sectional 19 Championship
Fort Wayne Dwenger 54, Norwell 21

Sectional 20 First Round
Western 14, Madison-Grant 8
Crawfordsville 41, Frankfort 0
Tipton 23, Maconaquah 6
Northwestern 27, North Montgomery 12
Sectional 20 Second Round
Crawfordsville 42, Western 0
Tipton 28, Northwestern 20
Sectional 20 Championship
Crawfordsville 16, Tipton 9

Sectional 21 First Round
Roncalli 12, Indpls. Cathedral 6
Brebeuf Jesuit 28, South Vermillion 14
Beech Grove 19, Indpls. Chatard 15
Danville 41, West Vigo 6
Sectional 21 Second Round
Roncalli 42, Brebeuf Jesuit 0
Danville 42, Beech Grove 16
Sectional 21 Championship
Roncalli 32, Danville 6

Sectional 22 First Round
Yorktown 20, Alexandria 12
New Palestine 11, Elwood 10, OT
Hamilton SE 37, Mount Vernon (Fortville) 13
Triton Central 42, Winchester 14
Sectional 22 Second Round
New Palestine 21, Yorktown 0
Hamilton Southeastern 22, Triton Central 21
Sectional 22 Championship
New Palestine 7, Hamilton Southeastern 3

Sectional 23 First Round
Whiteland 18, Indian Creek 13
Salem 17, Brown County 14
Owen Valley 41, Mitchell 0
Greensburg 13, Edgewood 6
Sectional 23 Second Round
Salem 12, Whiteland 10
Greensburg 21, Owen Valley 14

Sectional 23 Championship
Greensburg 9, Salem 7

Sectional 24 First Round
Princeton 41, Pike Central 12
Charlestown 39, North Harrison 0
Evansville Memorial 35, Jasper 7
Tell City 42, Corydon Central 6
Sectional 24 Second Round
Charlestown 30, Princeton 21
Evansville Memorial 7, Tell City 3
Sectional 24 Championship
Charlestown 32, Evansville Memorial 22

Regional Championships
Hammond Noll 42, NorthWood 14
Crawfordsville 41, Fort Wayne Dwenger 17
Roncalli 21, New Palestine 3
Charlestown 37, Greensburg 0

Semi-State Championships
Hammond Noll 32, Crawfordsville 20
Roncalli 14, Charlestown 0

State Championship
Hammond Noll 20, Roncalli 14

Class 2A
Sectional 25 First Round
Rensselaer Central 19, Lake Station 6
John Glenn 3, Mishawaka Marian 0
North Judson 25, River Forest 20
North Newton 18, LaVille 7
Sectional 25 Second Round
Rensselaer Central 48, John Glenn 12
North Judson 42, North Newton 22
Sectional 25 Championship
North Judson 32, Rensselaer Central 0

Sectional 26 First Round
Woodlan 15, Heritage 0
Fort Wayne Luers 28, Prairie Heights 0
West Noble 14, Garrett 0
Fairfield 12, Eastside 0
Sectional 26 Second Round
Fort Wayne Luers 24, Woodlan 0
Fairfield 40, West Noble 14
Sectional 26 Championship
Fort Wayne Luers 42, Fairfield 14

Sectional 27 First Round
Bluffton 22, Winamac 0
Lewis Cass 30, Tippecanoe Valley 12
Rochester 26, Oak Hill 0
Manchester 53, Taylor 22
Sectional 27 Second Round
Lewis Cass 21, Bluffton 14
Manchester 28, Rochester 24
Sectional 27 Championship
Manchester 35, Lewis Cass 34, OT

Sectional 28 First Round
West Lafayette 42, Fountain Central 7
Western Boone 38, Delphi 0
Southmont 7, Hamilton Heights 3
Seeger 20, Westfield 14
Sectional 28 Second Round
Western Boone 34, West Lafayette 10
Southmont 12, Seeger 7
Sectional 28 Championship
Western Boone 40, Southmont 14

Sectional 29 First Round
Batesville 20, Zionsville 0
Indpls. Ritter 42, Speedway 6
Indpls. Scecina 40, Cascade 6
Tri-West 13, Lawrenceburg 7
Sectional 29 Second Round
Indpls. Ritter 24, Batesville 6
Tri-West 28, Indpls. Scecina 15
Sectional 29 Championship
Tri-West 14, Indpls. Ritter 0

Sectional 30 First Round
Union County 32, Shenandoah 23
Centerville 14, Knightstown 12
Frankton 59, Cambridge City Lincoln 0
Hagerstown 26, Northeastern 6
Sectional 30 Second Round
Union County 42, Centerville 0
Frankton 32, Hagerstown 0
Sectional 30 Championship
Frankton 49, Union County 6

Sectional 31 First Round
North Knox 3, Paoli 0
Monrovia 20, Linton-Stockton 0
Greencastle 35, North Central (Farmersburg) 12
Sullivan 26, Brownstown Central 5
Sectional 31 Second Round
Monrovia 27, North Knox 0
Sullivan 51, Greencastle 38
Sectional 31 Championship
Monrovia 3, Sullivan 0, OT

Sectional 32 First Round
South Spencer 40, North Posey 6
Providence 28, Clarksville 14
Heritage Hills 34, Gibson Southern 13
Evansville Mater Dei 26, Southridge 24
Sectional 32 Second Round
South Spencer 28, Providence 27, OT
Evansville Mater Dei 40, Heritage Hills 14
Sectional 32 Championship
Evansville Mater Dei 21, South Spencer 17

Regional Championships
Fort Wayne Luers 39, North Judson 0

Western Boone 53, Manchester 33
Tri-West 28, Frankton 14
Evansville Mater Dei 20, Monrovia 13

Semi-State Championships
Fort Wayne Luers 33, Western Boone 12
Tri-West 35, Evansville Mater Dei 6

State Championship
Fort Wayne Luers 24, Tri-West 22

Class 1A
Sectional 33 First Round
Whiting 14, Triton 0
Jimtown 36, South Central (Union Mills) 7
Bremen 32, Culver 0
Sectional 33 Second Round
Whiting 27, West Central 6
Bremen 17, Jimtown 14
Sectional 33 Championship
Bremen 26, Whiting 12

Sectional 34 First Round
Churubusco 41, Southern Wells 22
Leo 20, Central Noble 0
South Adams 27, Fremont 0
Sectional 34 Second Round
Adams Central 31, Churubusco 15
South Adams 26, Leo 7
Sectional 34 Championship
South Adams 9, Adams Central 7

Sectional 35 First Round
Tri-County 18, Pioneer 6
Carroll (Flora) 34, South Newton 0
Frontier 35, Caston 7
Sectional 35 Second Round
Tri-County 40, North White 12
Carroll (Flora) 6, Frontier 0
Sectional 35 Championship
Tri-County 21, Carroll (Flora) 14

Sectional 36 First Round
Wes-Del 15, Tri-Central 14
North Miami 29, Eastern (Greentown) 8
Southwood 34, Northfield 12
Union City 7, Lapel 6
Sectional 36 Second Round
Wes-Del 14, North Miami 13
Southwood 29, Union City 0
Sectional 36 Championship
Southwood 7, Wes-Del 6

Sectional 37 First Round
Lafayette Central Catholic 41, Park Tudor 0
Sheridan 62, Clinton Prairie 6
Clinton Central 29, Attica 7
Sectional 37 Second Round
Lafayette Central Catholic 42, Covington 0
Sheridan 22, Clinton Central 7
Sectional 37 Championship
Lafayette Central Catholic 17, Sheridan 7

Sectional 38 First Round
Milan 9, North Decatur 8
South Decatur 31, Edinburgh 0
Eastern Hancock 26, Indiana Deaf 6
Sectional 38 Second Round
Tri 48, Milan 19
South Decatur 33, Eastern Hancock 13
Sectional 38 Championship
South Decatur 28, Tri 16

Sectional 39 First Round
South Putnam 19, Rockville 2
Cloverdale 34, Riverton Parke 0
North Putnam 6, Turkey Run 0
Sectional 39 Second Round
South Putnam 31, North Vermillion 20
North Putnam 35, Cloverdale 6
Sectional 39 Championship
South Putnam 21, North Putnam 6

Sectional 40 First Round
Tecumseh 19, North Daviess 12
Springs Valley 40, Wood Memorial 0
West Washington 40, Union (Dugger) 0
Sectional 40 Second Round
Tecumseh 7, Perry Central 6
Springs Valley 47, West Washington 0
Sectional 40 Championship
Springs Valley 41, Tecumseh 0

Regional Championships
Bremen 31, South Adams 13
Southwood 13, Tri-County 7
South Decatur 13, Lafayette Central Catholic 9
Springs Valley 14, South Putnam 0

Semi-State Championships
Bremen 10, Southwood 6
Springs Valley 22, South Decatur 6

State Championship
Bremen 31, Springs Valley 8

1990
Class 5A
Sectional 1 First Round
Gary West 18, Hammond 12
Lake Central 28, Merrillville 10
East Chicago Central 56, Gary Roosevelt 6
Crown Point 21, Gary Wallace 7
Sectional 1 Second Round
Lake Central 19, Gary West 18
Crown Point 21, East Chicago Central 19
Sectional 1 Championship
Lake Central 38, Crown Point 14

Sectional 2 First Round
Valparaiso 28, Portage 14
LaPorte 21, Chesterton 10
Michigan City Rogers 24, South Bend LaSalle 0
Mishawaka 36, South Bend Riley 6
Sectional 2 Second Round
Valparaiso 24, LaPorte 7
Mishawaka 7, Michigan City Rogers 3
Sectional 2 Championship
Mishawaka 16, Valparaiso 14

Sectional 3 First Round
Fort Wayne Snider 21, Fort Wayne Northrop 7
Penn 49, Elkhart Memorial 3
Elkhart Central 3, Fort Wayne Wayne 0
Fort Wayne North 16, Warsaw 0
Sectional 3 Second Round
Fort Wayne Snider 18, Penn 17, OT
Fort Wayne North 28, Elkhart Central 0
Sectional 3 Championship
Fort Wayne North 26, Fort Wayne Snider 7

Sectional 4 First Round
Lafayette Jefferson 28, Kokomo 0
Muncie Central 31, Huntington North 7
Marion 12, Muncie South 7
Anderson Highland 20, And. Madison-Hts. 14
Sectional 4 Second Round
Lafayette Jefferson 21, Muncie Central 0
Marion 40, Anderson Highland 7
Sectional 4 Championship
Marion 24, Lafayette Jefferson 6

Sectional 5 First Round
Ben Davis 61, Indpls. Manual 0
Indpls. Tech 16, Indpls. Washington 8
Carmel 35, Indpls. Broad Ripple 22
North Central (Indpls.) 41, Decatur Central 16
Sectional 5 Second Round
Ben Davis 54, Indpls. Tech 12
North Central (Indpls.) 28, Carmel 7
Sectional 5 Championship
Ben Davis 35, North Central (Indpls.) 14

Sectional 6 First Round
Richmond 21, Indpls. Arlington 7
Lawrence Central 33, Connersville 6
Warren Central 34, Indpls. Howe 18
Lawrence North 46, New Castle 6
Sectional 6 Second Round
Richmond 18, Lawrence Central 16
Lawrence North 14, Warren Central 7
Sectional 6 Championship
Lawrence North 34, Richmond 23

Sectional 7 First Round
Center Grove 20, Bloomington South 12
Southport 14, Terre Haute North 7
Columbus North 20, Perry Meridian 17
Martinsville 21, Terre Haute South 12
Sectional 7 Second Round
Southport 22, Center Grove 0
Columbus North 14, Martinsville 13
Sectional 7 Championship
Southport 36, Columbus North 14

Sectional 8 First Round
Evansville Central 14, Jeffersonville 12
Castle 29, Seymour 22
New Albany 49, Jennings County 0
Evansville Harrison 35, Bedford N.L. 21
Sectional 8 Second Round
Castle 21, Evansville Central 14
Evansville Harrison 45, New Albany 32
Sectional 8 Championship
Evansville Harrison 14, Castle 10

Regional Championships
Lake Central 24, Mishawaka 0
Marion 21, Fort Wayne North 3
Ben Davis 35, Lawrence North 0
Southport 42, Evansville Harrison 0

Semi-State Championships
Marion 10, Lake Central 7
Ben Davis 27, Southport 17

State Championship
Ben Davis 37, Marion 3

Class 4A
Sectional 9 First Round
Calumet 12, Gary Mann 0
Hammond Clark 1, Hammond Morton 0
Highland 14, Munster 12
Andrean 41, Lowell 0
Sectional 9 Second Round
Calumet 13, Hammond Clark 12
Andrean 47, Highland 40, 4 OT
Sectional 9 Championship
Andrean 28, Calumet 0

Sectional 10 First Round
Hobart 47, Goshen 7
Concord 22, South Bend Clay 19
South Bend Adams 23, Michigan City Elston 6
S.B. Washington 24, Gary Wirt 0
Sectional 10 Second Round
Hobart 38, Concord 15
S.B. Washington 28, South Bend Adams 7
Sectional 10 Championship
Hobart 21, S.B. Washington 11

Sectional 11 First Round
Columbia City 12, DeKalb 7
Fort Wayne South 28, East Noble 13
New Haven 35, Wawasee 0

Homestead 30, Fort Wayne Elmhurst 0
Sectional 11 Second Round
Fort Wayne South 20, Columbia City 14
Homestead 28, New Haven 24
Sectional 11 Championship
Fort Wayne South 30, Homestead 20

Sectional 12 First Round
McCutcheon 62, Peru 6
Harrison (West Lafayette) 28, Plymouth 14
Jay County 32, Blackford 16
Bellmont 15, Logansport 14
Sectional 12 Second Round
Harrison (West Lafayette) 28, McCutcheon 26
Bellmont 14, Jay County 6
Sectional 12 Championship
Harrison (West Lafayette) 13, Bellmont 10

Sectional 13 First Round
Noblesville 35, Plainfield 6
Franklin Central 7, Pike 3
Lebanon 34, Indpls. Northwest 12
Brownsburg 21, Avon 14, OT
Sectional 13 Second Round
Franklin Central 44, Noblesville 0
Brownsburg 17, Lebanon 6
Sectional 13 Championship
Franklin Central 48, Brownsburg 13

Sectional 14 First Round
Rushville 21, Delta 7
Franklin County 50, Pendleton Heights 21
Greenfield-Central 20, East Central 6
Anderson 34, Shelbyville 7
Sectional 14 Second Round
Franklin County 46, Rushville 26
Anderson 35, Greenfield-Central 12
Sectional 14 Championship
Franklin County 42, Anderson 37

Sectional 15 First Round
Madison 28, Bloomington North 3
Columbus East 21, Franklin 14
Greenwood 26, South Dearborn 0
Mooresville 20, Northview 14, OT
Sectional 15 Second Round
Columbus East 7, Madison 6
Greenwood 33, Mooresville 0
Sectional 15 Championship
Greenwood 28, Columbus East 0

Sectional 16 First Round
Evansville Bosse 29, Floyd Central 23
Evansville Reitz 26, Vincennes Lincoln 16
Boonville 47, Washington 0
Mount Vernon 28, Evansville North 20
Sectional 16 Second Round
Evansville Bosse 38, Evansville Reitz 7
Mount Vernon 31, Boonville 6

Sectional 16 Championship
Evansville Bosse 28, Mount Vernon 7

Regional Championships
Hobart 14, Andrean 13
Harrison (West Lafayette) 34, F.W. South 15
Franklin Central 26, Franklin County 19
Greenwood 40, Evansville Bosse 12

Semi-State Championships
Hobart 25, Harrison (West Lafayette) 10
Franklin Central 38, Greenwood 0

State Championship
Franklin Central 34, Hobart 14

Class 3A
Sectional 17 First Round
Hammond Gavit 34, Twin Lakes 28, 2 OT
New Prairie 17, Kankakee Valley 7
Hammond Noll 28, Knox 11
Griffith 42, Benton Central 0
Sectional 17 Second Round
Hammond Gavit 39, New Prairie 19
Griffith 40, Hammond Noll 12
Sectional 17 Championship
Griffith 28, Hammond Gavit 6

Sectional 18 First Round
NorthWood 17, Lakeland 7
Culver Military Academy 14, Whitko 13, 2 OT
Northridge 43, Angola 22
Sectional 18 Second Round
S.B. St. Joseph 28, NorthWood 6
Culver Military Academy 49, Northridge 28
Sectional 18 Championship
S.B. St. Joseph 24, Culver Military 21, OT

Sectional 19 First Round
Fort Wayne Concordia 57, Wabash 14
Fort Wayne Dwenger 14, Carroll (F.W.) 3
Mississinewa 28, Harding (Fort Wayne) 15
Eastbrook 28, Norwell 6
Sectional 19 Second Round
Fort Wayne Dwenger 36, F.W. Concordia 16
Eastbrook 21, Mississinewa 8
Sectional 19 Championship
Fort Wayne Dwenger 36, Eastbrook 0

Sectional 20 First Round
Northwestern 35, North Montgomery 7
Western 48, Madison-Grant 22
Crawfordsville 31, Maconaquah 7
Tipton 62, Frankfort 0
Sectional 20 Second Round
Northwestern 27, Western 21
Tipton 20, Crawfordsville 18
Sectional 20 Championship
Northwestern 23, Tipton 14

Sectional 21 First Round
South Vermillion 16, Brebeuf Jesuit 13
Danville 27, Beech Grove 2
Indpls. Chatard 7, Indpls. Cathedral 6
Roncalli 14, West Vigo 7
Sectional 21 Second Round
Danville 38, South Vermillion 10
Indpls. Chatard 36, Roncalli 0
Sectional 21 Championship
Indpls. Chatard 25, Danville 7

Sectional 22 First Round
New Palestine 19, Mount Vernon (Fortville) 7
Alexandria 36, Winchester 6
Hamilton Southeastern 33, Yorktown 12
Elwood 27, Triton Central 12
Sectional 22 Second Round
New Palestine 14, Alexandria 0
Elwood 20, Hamilton Southeastern 12
Sectional 22 Championship
New Palestine 21, Elwood 16

Sectional 23 First Round
Brown County 13, Salem 6
Edgewood 54, Indian Creek 0
Mitchell 7, Whiteland 6
Greensburg 19, Owen Valley 13
Sectional 23 Second Round
Edgewood 32, Brown County 28
Greensburg 34, Mitchell 6
Sectional 23 Championship
Edgewood 49, Greensburg 7

Sectional 24 First Round
Tell City 40, Corydon Central 0
Charlestown 28, North Harrison 13
Jasper 56, Pike Central 6
Sectional 24 Second Round
Tell City 35, Princeton 8
Jasper 14, Charlestown 6
Sectional 24 Championship
Tell City 14, Jasper 13

Regional Championships
S.B. St. Joseph 35, Griffith 6
Fort Wayne Dwenger 41, Northwestern 7
New Palestine 20, Indpls. Chatard 12
Tell City 22, Edgewood 21

Semi-State Championships
Fort Wayne Dwenger 24, S.B. St. Joseph 9
New Palestine 20, Tell City 14

State Championship
Fort Wayne Dwenger 56, New Palestine 14

Class 2A
Sectional 25 First Round
John Glenn 14, Mishawaka Marian 0
Rensselaer Central 28, LaVille 14
Lake Station 43, North Judson 13
River Forest 39, North Newton 6
Sectional 25 Second Round
Rensselaer Central 28, John Glenn 6
River Forest 32, Lake Station 6
Sectional 25 Championship
River Forest 25, Rensselaer Central 16

Sectional 26 First Round
West Noble 21, Heritage 7
Woodlan 19, Prairie Heights 10
Garrett 26, Fairfield 16
Fort Wayne Luers 28, Eastside 14
Sectional 26 Second Round
West Noble 20, Woodlan 14
Fort Wayne Luers 41, Garrett 6
Sectional 26 Championship
Fort Wayne Luers 55, West Noble 20

Sectional 27 First Round
Manchester 30, Oak Hill 14
Lewis Cass 26, Taylor 7
Rochester 30, Bluffton 0
Winamac 18, Tippecanoe Valley 0
Sectional 27 Second Round
Lewis Cass 34, Manchester 0
Rochester 7, Winamac 0
Sectional 27 Championship
Lewis Cass 24, Rochester 23

Sectional 28 First Round
Western Boone 63, Fountain Central 14
Hamilton Heights 47, Delphi 0
West Lafayette 40, Westfield 13
Southmont 35, Seeger 7
Sectional 28 Second Round
Hamilton Heights 36, Western Boone 34, OT
West Lafayette 14, Southmont 7
Sectional 28 Championship
West Lafayette 31, Hamilton Heights 6

Sectional 29 First Round
Speedway 13, Batesville 7
Zionsville 67, Cascade 0
Lawrenceburg 38, Tri-West 20
Indpls. Scecina 28, Indpls. Ritter 16
Sectional 29 Second Round
Zionsville 30, Speedway 8
Indpls. Scecina 29, Lawrenceburg 12
Sectional 29 Championship
Indpls. Scecina 42, Zionsville 14

Sectional 30 First Round
Hagerstown 53, Knightstown 0
Shenandoah 40, Northeastern 6
Centerville 10, Union County 0
Frankton 63, Cambridge City Lincoln 7

Sectional 30 Second Round
Hagerstown 46, Shenandoah 12
Frankton 49, Centerville 9
Sectional 30 Championship
Frankton 36, Hagerstown 6

Sectional 31 First Round
Monrovia 28, Brownstown Central 7
North Knox 32, North Central (Farmersburg) 6
Sullivan 49, Paoli 24
Greencastle 55, Linton-Stockton 0
Sectional 31 Second Round
Monrovia 40, North Knox 0
Greencastle 28, Sullivan 26
Sectional 31 Championship
Greencastle 6, Monrovia 0

Sectional 32 First Round
South Spencer 54, Clarksville 12
Heritage Hills 27, Southridge 20
Evansville Mater Dei 16, Providence 6
Gibson Southern 40, North Posey 29
Sectional 32 Second Round
Heritage Hills 14, South Spencer 6
Evansville Mater Dei 40, Gibson Southern 7
Sectional 32 Championship
Evansville Mater Dei 27, Heritage Hills 13

Regional Championships
River Forest 15, Fort Wayne Luers 12
West Lafayette 17, Lewis Cass 13
Indpls. Scecina 20, Frankton 0
Evansville Mater Dei 40, Greencastle 32

Semi-State Championships
River Forest 22, West Lafayette 15
Indpls. Scecina 34, Evansville Mater Dei 14

State Championship
Indpls. Scecina 28, River Forest 27

Class 1A
Sectional 33 First Round
Bremen 27, South Central (Union Mills) 6
Jimtown 20, Whiting 14
Culver 42, West Central 0
Sectional 33 Second Round
Bremen 70, Triton 0
Jimtown 33, Culver 6
Sectional 33 Championship
Jimtown 25, Bremen 22

Sectional 34 First Round
Churubusco 20, Central Noble 14, OT
South Adams 21, Adams Central 10
Leo 31, Southern Wells 0
Sectional 34 Second Round
Churubusco 29, Fremont 14
South Adams 36, Leo 6

Sectional 34 Championship
South Adams 21, Churubusco 14

Sectional 35 First Round
North White 6, Carroll (Flora) 0
Frontier 34, Tri-County 26
Caston 24, South Newton 7
Sectional 35 Second Round
North White 18, Pioneer 7
Frontier 26, Caston 21
Sectional 35 Championship
Frontier 27, North White 0

Sectional 36 First Round
Eastern (Greentown) 35, Northfield 0
Southwood 46, Union City 0
North Miami 14, Lapel 8
Tri-Central 21, Wes-Del 19
Sectional 36 Second Round
Southwood 41, Eastern (Greentown) 6
Tri-Central 23, North Miami 12
Sectional 36 Championship
Southwood 51, Tri-Central 0

Sectional 37 First Round
Clinton Central 28, Attica 0
Lafayette Central Catholic 28, Park Tudor 0
Clinton Prairie 22, Covington 21, OT
Sectional 37 Second Round
Sheridan 10, Clinton Central 7
Lafayette Central Catholic 20, Clinton Prairie 18
Sectional 37 Championship
Sheridan 19, Lafayette Central Catholic 8

Sectional 38 First Round
Eastern Hancock 17, Indiana Deaf 14
Tri 34, North Decatur 14
Edinburgh 6, Milan 0
Sectional 38 Second Round
South Decatur 60, Eastern Hancock 6
Tri 43, Edinburgh 6
Sectional 38 Championship
South Decatur 42, Tri 18

Sectional 39 First Round
South Putnam 60, Riverton Parke 0
North Putnam 35, Turkey Run 0
North Vermillion 28, Rockville 18
Sectional 39 Second Round
South Putnam 18, Cloverdale 6
North Putnam 39, North Vermillion 8
Sectional 39 Championship
North Putnam 38, South Putnam 0

Sectional 40 First Round
Springs Valley 52, Perry Central 0
West Washington 32, North Daviess 7
Tecumseh 53, Union (Dugger) 0
Sectional 40 Second Round

Springs Valley 61, Wood Memorial 6
Tecumseh 52, West Washington 0
Sectional 40 Championship
Springs Valley 27, Tecumseh 0

Regional Championships
Jimtown 7, South Adams 6
Southwood 20, Frontier 0
South Decatur 6, Sheridan 0, OT
North Putnam 14, Springs Valley 0

Semi-State Championships
Southwood 8, Jimtown 7
South Decatur 16, North Putnam 13

State Championship
South Decatur 44, Southwood 15

1991

Class 5A
Sectional 1 First Round
Crown Point 16, Gary Wallace 15
Lake Central 36, Hammond 0
East Chicago Central 45, Gary Roosevelt 6
Merrillville 53, Gary West 0
Sectional 1 Second Round
Crown Point 14, Lake Central 0
East Chicago Central 26, Merrillville 13
Sectional 1 Championship
Crown Point 22, East Chicago Central 13

Sectional 2 First Round
South Bend Riley 7, LaPorte 3
Valparaiso 38, Michigan City Rogers 8
Portage 12, Chesterton 6
Mishawaka 14, Michigan City Elston 2
Sectional 2 Second Round
Valparaiso 27, South Bend Riley 6
Mishawaka 13, Portage 12
Sectional 2 Championship
Mishawaka 27, Valparaiso 26

Sectional 3 First Round
Fort Wayne Northrop 19, Elkhart Memorial 0
Fort Wayne Snider 7, Huntington North 6
Elkhart Central 20, Fort Wayne North 17
Penn 36, Warsaw 0
Sectional 3 Second Round
Fort Wayne Snider 10, Fort Wayne Northrop 0
Penn 28, Elkhart Central 14
Sectional 3 Championship
Penn 21, Fort Wayne Snider 0

Sectional 4 First Round
Kokomo 38, Anderson 22
Carmel 34, Muncie Central 7
Marion 7, Noblesville 0
Lafayette Jefferson 32, Muncie South 0
Sectional 4 Second Round
Carmel 57, Kokomo 7
Lafayette Jefferson 20, Marion 13
Sectional 4 Championship
Lafayette Jefferson 21, Carmel 7

Sectional 5 First Round
North Central (Indpls.) 9, Pike 0
Perry Meridian 15, Indpls. Tech 6
Ben Davis 61, Indpls. Northwest 7
Southport 38, Indpls. Broad Ripple 14
Sectional 5 Second Round
Perry Meridian 23, North Central (Indpls.) 20
Ben Davis 40, Southport 0
Sectional 5 Championship
Ben Davis 41, Perry Meridian 8

Sectional 6 First Round
Richmond 37, Indpls. Howe 14
Lawrence North 41, Lawrence Central 0
Warren Central 47, Indpls. Arlington 8
Franklin Central 21, Connersville 17
Sectional 6 Second Round
Richmond 19, Lawrence North 6
Franklin Central 29, Warren Central 8
Sectional 6 Championship
Richmond 24, Franklin Central 0

Sectional 7 First Round
Martinsville 28, Terre Haute South 6
Bloomington South 35, Columbus East 13
Decatur Central 14, Center Grove 10
Terre Haute North 37, Columbus North 27
Sectional 7 Second Round
Bloomington South 14, Martinsville 13
Terre Haute North 20, Decatur Central 9
Sectional 7 Championship
Bloomington South 29, Terre Haute North 7

Sectional 8 First Round
Bedford N.L. 28, Evansville Harrison 25
Jeffersonville 32, New Albany 6
Floyd Central 49, Evansville North 14
Evansville Central 61, Castle 7
Sectional 8 Second Round
Jeffersonville 41, Bedford North Lawrence 0
Evansville Central 28, Floyd Central 20
Sectional 8 Championship
Jeffersonville 27, Evansville Central 12

Regional Championships
Mishawaka 14, Crown Point 7
Penn 17, Lafayette Jefferson 6
Ben Davis 30, Richmond 0
Bloomington South 29, Jeffersonville 14

Semi-State Championships
Penn 41, Mishawaka 0
Ben Davis 45, Bloomington South 20

State Championship
Ben Davis 38, Penn 14

Class 4A
Sectional 9 First Round
Andrean 35, Hammond Clark 0
Hammond Morton 19, Lowell 14
Gary Mann 58, Calumet 20
Munster 31, Highland 13
Sectional 9 Second Round
Andrean 15, Hammond Morton 6
Munster 17, Gary Mann 0
Sectional 9 Championship
Andrean 21, Munster 0

Sectional 10 First Round
Hobart 61, Gary Wirt 6
South Bend LaSalle 21, South Bend Clay 7
South Bend Adams 27, Goshen 3
S.B. Washington 18, Concord 6
Sectional 10 Second Round
Hobart 41, South Bend LaSalle 12
South Bend Adams 12, S.B. Washington 0
Sectional 10 Championship
Hobart 59, South Bend Adams 7

Sectional 11 First Round
New Haven 7, DeKalb 0
Plymouth 14, Columbia City 7
Fort Wayne South 28, Wawasee 0
Fort Wayne Concordia 24, East Noble 14
Sectional 11 Second Round
New Haven 26, Plymouth 7
Fort Wayne South 28, Fort Wayne Concordia 7
Sectional 11 Championship
New Haven 15, Fort Wayne South 0

Sectional 12 First Round
Delta 18, Jay County 0
Homestead 45, Logansport 0
Fort Wayne Elmhurst 7, Peru 0
Fort Wayne Wayne 21, Bellmont 0
Sectional 12 Second Round
Homestead 7, Delta 0
Fort Wayne Wayne 7, Fort Wayne Elmhurst 0
Sectional 12 Championship
Fort Wayne Wayne 40, Homestead 6

Sectional 13 First Round
Indpls. Washington 27, Brownsburg 19
Harrison (West Lafayette) 22, Lebanon 13
Plainfield 27, McCutcheon 26
Avon 18, Frankfort 0
Sectional 13 Second Round
Indpls. Washington 20, Harrison (W.L.) 13
Avon 7, Plainfield 6
Sectional 13 Championship
Avon 21, Indpls. Washington 18

Sectional 14 First Round
Indpls. Manual 14, Anderson Madison-Hts. 0
Mooresville 21, Anderson Highland 0
Greenfield-Central 14, Pendleton Heights 0
Greenwood 35, New Castle 8
Sectional 14 Second Round
Mooresville 27, Indpls. Manual 6
Greenwood 25, Greenfield-Central 7
Sectional 14 Championship
Mooresville 21, Greenwood 0

Sectional 15 First Round
Franklin County 69, Jennings County 20
East Central 51, Shelbyville 12
Madison 13, Franklin 7
Rushville 24, South Dearborn 21
Sectional 15 Second Round
Franklin County 33, East Central 13
Madison 30, Rushville 20
Sectional 15 Championship
Franklin County 35, Madison 8

Sectional 16 First Round
Mount Vernon 28, Bloomington North 22
Seymour 27, Boonville 24, 2 OT
Evansville Bosse 42, Northview 14
Vincennes Lincoln 17, Evansville Reitz 14
Sectional 16 Second Round
Seymour 27, Mount Vernon 0
Evansville Bosse 28, Vincennes Lincoln 14
Sectional 16 Championship
Seymour 34, Evansville Bosse 14

Regional Championships
Hobart 38, Andrean 6
Fort Wayne Wayne 19, New Haven 0
Avon 20, Mooresville 0
Seymour 28, Franklin County 14

Semi-State Championships
Hobart 27, Fort Wayne Wayne 15
Seymour 21, Avon 20

State Championship
Hobart 20, Seymour 0

Class 3A
Sectional 17 First Round
Griffith 62, New Prairie 6
Hammond Gavit 24, Knox 7
Hammond Noll 27, Kankakee Valley 13
Benton Central 20, Twin Lakes 19
Sectional 17 Second Round
Griffith 64, Hammond Gavit 0
Hammond Noll 35, Benton Central 6
Sectional 17 Championship
Griffith 34, Hammond Noll 0

Sectional 18 First Round

Northridge 24, Lakeland 7
NorthWood 6, S.B. St. Joseph 3
Angola 21, Culver Military Academy 10
Whitko 23, West Noble 8
Sectional 18 Second Round
NorthWood 23, Northridge 0
Angola 38, Whitko 19
Sectional 18 Championship
Angola 15, NorthWood 7

Sectional 19 First Round
Mississinewa 50, Heritage 27
Norwell 7, Maconaquah 6
Carroll (Fort Wayne) 7, Harding (Fort Wayne) 6
Fort Wayne Dwenger 28, Blackford 7
Sectional 19 Second Round
Norwell 39, Mississinewa 8
Fort Wayne Dwenger 28, Carroll (F.W.) 14
Sectional 19 Championship
Fort Wayne Dwenger 42, Norwell 13

Sectional 20 First Round
Tipton 16, Winchester 14
Hamilton Heights 28, Alexandria 26
Western 28, Elwood 14
Northwestern 14, Yorktown 0
Sectional 20 Second Round
Tipton 27, Hamilton Heights 22
Western 28, Northwestern 7
Sectional 20 Championship
Tipton 30, Western 6

Sectional 21 First Round
West Vigo 28, Owen Valley 20
North Montgomery 46, Brebeuf Jesuit 0
Edgewood 22, Southmont 0
Zionsville 47, South Vermillion 0
Sectional 21 Second Round
West Vigo 25, North Montgomery 20
Zionsville 47, Edgewood 18
Sectional 21 Championship
Zionsville 28, West Vigo 0

Sectional 22 First Round
Hamilton SE 14, Mount Vernon (Fortville) 0
Indpls. Cathedral 35, Beech Grove 0
Roncalli 20, Whiteland 0
New Palestine 7, Indpls. Chatard 6
Sectional 22 Second Round
Indpls. Cathedral 3, Hamilton Southeastern 0
Roncalli 7, New Palestine 0
Sectional 22 Championship
Indpls. Cathedral 35, Roncalli 21

Sectional 23 First Round
Salem 26, Brown County 0
Charlestown 42, Brownstown Central 14
Lawrenceburg 36, Mitchell 25
Batesville 10, Greensburg 0

Sectional 23 Second Round
Charlestown 10, Salem 0
Lawrenceburg 16, Batesville 6
Sectional 23 Championship
Lawrenceburg 27, Charlestown 26, 2 OT

Sectional 24 First Round
Evansville Memorial 42, Jasper 0
Washington 20, Corydon Central 0
Heritage Hills 20, North Harrison 3
Princeton 28, Pike Central 6
Sectional 24 Second Round
Evansville Memorial 48, Washington 0
Heritage Hills 27, Princeton 12
Sectional 24 Championship
Evansville Memorial 50, Heritage Hills 6

Regional Championships
Griffith 21, Angola 8
Fort Wayne Dwenger 28, Tipton 0
Indpls. Cathedral 21, Zionsville 7
Ev. Memorial 42, Lawrenceburg 35, 2 OT

Semi-State Championships
Fort Wayne Dwenger 27, Griffith 21
Indpls. Cathedral 13, Evansville Memorial 12

State Championship
Fort Wayne Dwenger 34, Indpls. Cathedral 27

Class 2A
Sectional 25 First Round
Lake Station 43, John Glenn 0
LaVille 35, North Judson 7
Rensselaer Central 19, River Forest 14
North Newton 21, Mishawaka Marian 20
Sectional 25 Second Round
Lake Station 27, LaVille 0
North Newton 21, Rensselaer Central 0
Sectional 25 Championship
Lake Station 10, North Newton 0

Sectional 26 First Round
Churubusco 7, Woodlan 6
Fort Wayne Luers 9, Eastside 7
Fairfield 8, Leo 7
Garrett 23, Prairie Heights 6
Sectional 26 Second Round
Fort Wayne Luers 47, Churubusco 7
Garrett 46, Fairfield 13
Sectional 26 Championship
Fort Wayne Luers 28, Garrett 6

Sectional 27 First Round
Tippecanoe Valley 14, Rochester 8
Manchester 19, Winamac 6
Carroll (Flora) 20, Lewis Cass 7
Delphi 32, Taylor 6
Sectional 27 Second Round

Manchester 20, Tippecanoe Valley 18
Carroll (Flora) 7, Delphi 6, OT
Sectional 27 Championship
Manchester 34, Carroll (Flora) 21

Sectional 28 First Round
Wabash 30, Bluffton 0
Oak Hill 36, Adams Central 14
South Adams 24, Madison-Grant 7
Southwood 16, Eastbrook 14, 2 OT
Sectional 28 Second Round
Oak Hill 31, Wabash 0
Southwood 13, South Adams 0
Sectional 28 Championship
Southwood 9, Oak Hill 8

Sectional 29 First Round
Speedway 20, North Putnam 2
Westfield 14, Danville 7
West Lafayette 31, Western Boone 6
Crawfordsville 28, Fountain Central 0
Sectional 29 Second Round
Westfield 21, Speedway 0
West Lafayette 21, Crawfordsville 0
Sectional 29 Championship
West Lafayette 14, Westfield 6

Sectional 30 First Round
Frankton 22, Triton Central 21
Hagerstown 41, Union County 20
Indpls. Scecina 40, Centerville 7
Shenandoah 18, Northeastern 0
Sectional 30 Second Round
Frankton 32, Hagerstown 14
Indpls. Scecina 55, Shenandoah 35
Sectional 30 Championship
Indpls. Scecina 31, Frankton 7

Sectional 31 First Round
Paoli 21, North Knox 6
Indian Creek 35, Cascade 33
Greencastle 42, Sullivan 0
Monrovia 41, Linton-Stockton 13
Sectional 31 Second Round
Indian Creek 21, Paoli 12
Greencastle 40, Monrovia 0
Sectional 31 Championship
Greencastle 39, Indian Creek 6

Sectional 32 First Round
Tell City 43, North Posey 14
Gibson Southern 30, Clarksville 13
South Spencer 13, Southridge 0
Providence 7, Evansville Mater Dei 0, OT
Sectional 32 Second Round
Tell City 42, Gibson Southern 16
South Spencer 17, Providence 0
Sectional 32 Championship
Tell City 28, South Spencer 7

Regional Championships
Fort Wayne Luers 14, Lake Station 10
Southwood 9, Manchester 6
Indpls. Scecina 28, West Lafayette 18
Greencastle 21, Tell City 14

Semi-State Championships
Fort Wayne Luers 28, Southwood 18
Indpls. Scecina 19, Greencastle 14

State Championship
Indpls. Scecina 20, Fort Wayne Luers 17

Class 1A
Sectional 33 First Round
Bremen 54, Triton 0
South Central (Union Mills) 21, Culver 0
Pioneer 50, West Central 7
Sectional 33 Second Round
Bremen 61, Whiting 7
Pioneer 24, South Central (Union Mills) 7
Sectional 33 Championship
Bremen 46, Pioneer 0

Sectional 34 First Round
Northfield 20, Southern Wells 6
Fremont 12, Caston 6
North Miami 16, Central Noble 14
Sectional 34 Second Round
Jimtown 41, Northfield 8
North Miami 20, Fremont 0
Sectional 34 Championship
Jimtown 21, North Miami 12

Sectional 35 First Round
North White 37, Attica 2
Frontier 35, Seeger 3
Tri-County 20, South Newton 8
Sectional 35 Second Round
Covington 21, North White 10
Frontier 14, Tri-County 8
Sectional 35 Championship
Frontier 35, Covington 10

Sectional 36 First Round
Lafayette C.C. 30, Eastern (Greent.) 23, 2 OT
Tri-Central 28, Tri-West 6
Sheridan 47, Clinton Prairie 6
Sectional 36 Second Round
Clinton Central 29, Lafayette Central Catholic 3
Tri-Central 17, Sheridan 7
Sectional 36 Championship
Tri-Central 27, Clinton Central 12

Sectional 37 First Round
Knightstown 27, Wes-Del 8
Lapel 18, Eastern Hancock 7
Tri 14, Union City 9

Sectional 37 Second Round
Knightstown 23, Cambridge City Lincoln 22
Tri 28, Lapel 6
Sectional 37 Championship
Tri 20, Knightstown 7

Sectional 38 First Round
Edinburgh 40, Park Tudor 0
Indpls. Ritter 76, Indiana Deaf 20
Milan 21, South Decatur 12
Sectional 38 Second Round
North Decatur 25, Edinburgh 6
Indpls. Ritter 35, Milan 6
Sectional 38 Championship
Indpls. Ritter 42, North Decatur 6

Sectional 39 First Round
South Putnam 29, Riverton Parke 20
Cloverdale 7, Rockville 6, 2 OT
North Vermillion 21, North Central (Farm.) 6
Sectional 39 Second Round
South Putnam 20, Turkey Run 12
Cloverdale 14, North Vermillion 0
Sectional 39 Championship
South Putnam 12, Cloverdale 7

Sectional 40 First Round
Springs Valley 27, Perry Central 0
Wood Memorial 30, West Washington 7
Tecumseh 53, Union (Dugger) 0
Sectional 40 Second Round
Springs Valley 58, North Daviess 0
Tecumseh 33, Wood Memorial 8
Sectional 40 Championship
Tecumseh 19, Springs Valley 14

Regional Championships
Jimtown 8, Bremen 7
Frontier 22, Tri-Central 16
Indpls. Ritter 39, Tri 16
Tecumseh 34, South Putnam 0

Semi-State Championships
Jimtown 35, Frontier 7
Indpls. Ritter 33, Tecumseh 12

State Championship
Jimtown 13, Indpls. Ritter 7

1992
Class 5A
Sectional 1 First Round
Crown Point 27, Hammond 12
Merrillville 35, Lake Central 21
East Chicago Central 42, Gary West 0
Gary Wallace 20, Gary Roosevelt 0
Sectional 1 Second Round
Merrillville 30, Crown Point 6
East Chicago Central 15, Gary Wallace 14

Sectional 1 Championship
Merrillville 17, East Chicago Central 13

Sectional 2 First Round
Michigan City Elston 8, Michigan City Rogers 0
South Bend Riley 27, Portage 13
Mishawaka 13, Chesterton 6
Valparaiso 31, LaPorte 12
Sectional 2 Second Round
South Bend Riley 35, Michigan City Elston 6
Mishawaka 27, Valparaiso 21
Sectional 2 Championship
South Bend Riley 12, Mishawaka 6

Sectional 3 First Round
Fort Wayne North 50, Warsaw 30
Penn 24, Elkhart Central 15
Fort Wayne Snider 63, Huntington North 13
Fort Wayne Northrop 29, Elkhart Memorial 6
Sectional 3 Second Round
Penn 35, Fort Wayne North 16
Fort Wayne Snider 44, Fort Wayne Northrop 0
Sectional 3 Championship
Fort Wayne Snider 28, Penn 14

Sectional 4 First Round
Carmel 42, Lafayette Jefferson 12
Kokomo 28, Noblesville 6
Anderson 21, Muncie Central 16
Muncie South 21, Marion 18
Sectional 4 Second Round
Carmel 28, Kokomo 3
Anderson 27, Muncie South 26
Sectional 4 Championship
Carmel 28, Anderson 7

Sectional 5 First Round
Perry Meridian 28, Indpls. Northwest 7
Ben Davis 35, Pike 7
Indpls. Broad Ripple 42, Indpls. Tech 0
North Central (Indpls.) 42, Southport 25
Sectional 5 Second Round
Ben Davis 44, Perry Meridian 6
North Central (Indpls.) 40, Ind. Broad Ripple 20
Sectional 5 Championship
Ben Davis 55, North Central (Indpls.) 12

Sectional 6 First Round
Franklin Central 13, Connersville 0
Indpls. Howe 41, Indpls. Arlington 20
Richmond 28, Lawrence Central 12
Lawrence North 35, Warren Central 13
Sectional 6 Second Round
Franklin Central 34, Indpls. Howe 7
Richmond 27, Lawrence North 17
Sectional 6 Championship
Richmond 13, Franklin Central 6

Sectional 7 First Round

Martinsville 51, Terre Haute North 37
Decatur Central 23, Center Grove 7
Terre Haute South 30, Columbus East 16
Bloomington South 28, Columbus North 6
Sectional 7 Second Round
Martinsville 28, Decatur Central 25
Bloomington South 24, Terre Haute South 7
Sectional 7 Championship
Bloomington South 28, Martinsville 21

Sectional 8 First Round
Evansville North 49, Bedford North Lawrence 7
Floyd Central 28, Evansville Central 22
Evansville Harrison 28, Jeffersonville 14
New Albany 49, Castle 28
Sectional 8 Second Round
Evansville North 42, Floyd Central 22
Evansville Harrison 38, New Albany 0
Sectional 8 Championship
Evansville North 20, Evansville Harrison 7

Regional Championships
Merrillville 21, South Bend Riley 14, OT
Fort Wayne Snider 42, Carmel 20
Ben Davis 24, Richmond 14
Bloomington South 28, Evansville North 15

Semi-State Championships
Fort Wayne Snider 14, Merrillville 7
Ben Davis 35, Bloomington South 14

State Championship
Fort Wayne Snider 24, Ben Davis 21

Class 4A
Sectional 9 First Round
Hammond Clark 55, Calumet 0
Munster 33, Gary Mann 19
Andrean 36, Highland 14
Lowell 36, Hammond Morton 19
Sectional 9 Second Round
Munster 14, Hammond Clark 7
Lowell 23, Andrean 21
Sectional 9 Championship
Lowell 9, Munster 7

Sectional 10 First Round
South Bend Adams 17, Gary Wirt 8
South Bend Clay 22, Goshen 7
South Bend LaSalle 26, S.B. Washington 25
Hobart 55, Concord 0
Sectional 10 Second Round
South Bend Clay 17, South Bend Adams 7
Hobart 49, South Bend LaSalle 6
Sectional 10 Championship
Hobart 31, South Bend Clay 0

Sectional 11 First Round
Columbia City 38, Wawasee 0
DeKalb 28, New Haven 13
Fort Wayne Concordia 7, East Noble 6
Fort Wayne South 29, Plymouth 22
Sectional 11 Second Round
DeKalb 21, Columbia City 13
Fort Wayne Concordia 28, Fort Wayne South 14
Sectional 11 Championship
DeKalb 35, Fort Wayne Concordia 14

Sectional 12 First Round
Homestead 32, Logansport 14
Jay County 25, Bellmont 7
Fort Wayne Wayne 32, Fort Wayne Elmhurst 0
Peru 32, Delta 14
Sectional 12 Second Round
Homestead 33, Jay County 0
Fort Wayne Wayne 51, Peru 0
Sectional 12 Championship
Fort Wayne Wayne 21, Homestead 14

Sectional 13 First Round
Harrison (West Lafayette) 35, Plainfield 14
Indpls. Washington 28, Lebanon 13
McCutcheon 34, Frankfort 8
Avon 27, Brownsburg 26
Sectional 13 Second Round
Harrison (West Lafayette) 13, Indpls. Washington 12
McCutcheon 29, Avon 19
Sectional 13 Championship
Harrison (West Lafayette) 25, McCutcheon 0

Sectional 14 First Round
Pendleton Heights 28, Mooresville 6
Indpls. Manual 45, New Castle 27
Greenfield-Central 23, And. Madison-Hts. 20
Greenwood 36, Anderson Highland 22
Sectional 14 Second Round
Pendleton Heights 44, Indpls. Manual 14
Greenwood 28, Greenfield-Central 24
Sectional 14 Championship
Greenwood 9, Pendleton Heights 7

Sectional 15 First Round
Jennings County 16, South Dearborn 14
Franklin County 27, Madison 6
Rushville 30, Franklin 10
East Central 42, Shelbyville 14
Sectional 15 Second Round
Franklin County 56, Jennings County 20
East Central 29, Rushville 7
Sectional 15 Championship
East Central 35, Franklin County 13

Sectional 16 First Round
Evansville Bosse 46, Vincennes Lincoln 7
Northview 28, Bloomington North 0
Evansville Reitz 43, Seymour 14
Boonville 34, Mount Vernon 0

Sectional 16 Second Round
Evansville Bosse 17, Northview 0
Evansville Reitz 27, Boonville 10
Sectional 16 Championship
Evansville Reitz 41, Evansville Bosse 0

Regional Championships
Hobart 35, Lowell 7
Fort Wayne Wayne 17, DeKalb 15
Harrison (West Lafayette) 27, Greenwood 6
Evansville Reitz 28, East Central 21, OT

Semi-State Championships
Fort Wayne Wayne 14, Hobart 10
Harrison (West Lafayette) 30, Ev. Reitz 8

State Championship
Harrison (West Lafayette) 21, F.W. Wayne 3

Class 3A
Sectional 17 First Round
Twin Lakes 21, Benton Central 7
Hammond Gavit 35, Knox 7
Kankakee Valley 10, New Prairie 7
Griffith 17, Hammond Noll 0
Sectional 17 Second Round
Twin Lakes 49, Hammond Gavit 18
Griffith 42, Kankakee Valley 6
Sectional 17 Championship
Griffith 40, Twin Lakes 13

Sectional 18 First Round
NorthWood 36, Whitko 0
Lakeland 29, West Noble 6
Culver Military Academy 36, S.B. St. Joseph 15
Angola 35, Northridge 7
Sectional 18 Second Round
NorthWood 43, Lakeland 0
Angola 53, Culver Military Academy 21
Sectional 18 Championship
Angola 34, NorthWood 20

Sectional 19 First Round
Heritage 21, Mississinewa 14
Fort Wayne Dwenger 35, Norwell 14
Maconaquah 6, Blackford 0
Carroll (Fort Wayne) 25, Harding (Fort Wayne) 0
Sectional 19 Second Round
Fort Wayne Dwenger 41, Heritage 2
Carroll (Fort Wayne) 34, Maconaquah 6
Sectional 19 Championship
Fort Wayne Dwenger 28, Carroll (F.W.) 0

Sectional 20 First Round
Western 37, Elwood 36
Northwestern 13, Alexandria 12
Hamilton Heights 42, Yorktown 0
Tipton 36, Winchester 7

Sectional 20 Second Round
Northwestern 35, Western 18
Tipton 26, Hamilton Heights 17
Sectional 20 Championship
Northwestern 21, Tipton 14, OT

Sectional 21 First Round
Zionsville 17, Southmont 6
Owen Valley 56, South Vermillion 0
Edgewood 28, West Vigo 14
North Montgomery 44, Brebeuf Jesuit 7
Sectional 21 Second Round
Owen Valley 14, Zionsville 0
North Montgomery 21, Edgewood 20
Sectional 21 Championship
Owen Valley 14, North Montgomery 13

Sectional 22 First Round
Hamilton Southeastern 35, Whiteland 21
New Palestine 42, Beech Grove 13
Indpls. Cathedral 35, Mount Vernon (FV) 14
Indpls. Chatard 26, Roncalli 19
Sectional 22 Second Round
Hamilton Southeastern 28, New Palestine 14
Indpls. Cathedral 17, Indpls. Chatard 5
Sectional 22 Championship
Indpls. Cathedral 20, Hamilton SE 14, OT

Sectional 23 First Round
Charlestown 29, Brown County 23, 2 OT
Greensburg 38, Mitchell 17
Lawrenceburg 37, Batesville 0
Salem 54, Brownstown Central 0
Sectional 23 Second Round
Greensburg 27, Charlestown 6
Lawrenceburg 35, Salem 6
Sectional 23 Championship
Lawrenceburg 38, Greensburg 21

Sectional 24 First Round
Heritage Hills 27, Washington 7
Evansville Memorial 34, Jasper 7
Corydon Central 35, Pike Central 15
Princeton 49, North Harrison 0
Sectional 24 Second Round
Evansville Memorial 41, Heritage Hills 14
Princeton 53, Corydon Central 14
Sectional 24 Championship
Evansville Memorial 47, Princeton 7

Regional Championships
Angola 12, Griffith 7
Northwestern 13, F.W. Dwenger 10, 2 OT
Indpls. Cathedral 24, Owen Valley 7
Evansville Memorial 29, Lawrenceburg 28, OT

Semi-State Championships
Northwestern 10, Angola 7
Indpls. Cathedral 31, Evansville Memorial 14

State Championship
Indpls. Cathedral 33, Northwestern 14

Class 2A
Sectional 25 First Round
Rensselaer Central 13, North Judson 6
River Forest 27, North Newton 12
LaVille 20, Lake Station 3
Mishawaka Marian 50, John Glenn 0
Sectional 25 Second Round
Rensselaer Central 14, River Forest 0
LaVille 28, Mishawaka Marian 15
Sectional 25 Championship
Rensselaer Central 28, LaVille 19

Sectional 26 First Round
Woodlan 20, Churubusco 10
Fairfield 42, Prairie Heights 22
Leo 27, Eastside 0
Fort Wayne Luers 40, Garrett 0
Sectional 26 Second Round
Woodlan 36, Fairfield 21
Fort Wayne Luers 33, Leo 3
Sectional 26 Championship
Fort Wayne Luers 27, Woodlan 0

Sectional 27 First Round
Carroll (Flora) 12, Winamac 7
Rochester 21, Lewis Cass 14
Manchester 27, Taylor 14
Tippecanoe Valley 23, Delphi 0
Sectional 27 Second Round
Rochester 34, Carroll (Flora) 6
Tippecanoe Valley 49, Manchester 38
Sectional 27 Championship
Tippecanoe Valley 24, Rochester 23

Sectional 28 First Round
Madison-Grant 13, Southwood 7, OT
Wabash 33, Eastbrook 9
South Adams 32, Oak Hill 0
Adams Central 29, Bluffton 3
Sectional 28 Second Round
Madison-Grant 7, Wabash 0
South Adams 21, Adams Central 6
Sectional 28 Championship
South Adams 45, Madison-Grant 14

Sectional 29 First Round
Crawfordsville 28, Speedway 13
West Lafayette 48, Western Boone 6
Danville 50, North Putnam 17
Westfield 42, Fountain Central 0
Sectional 29 Second Round
West Lafayette 27, Crawfordsville 13
Westfield 42, Danville 0
Sectional 29 Championship
Westfield 18, West Lafayette 12

Sectional 30 First Round
Hagerstown 37, Shenandoah 13
Indpls. Scecina 41, Triton Central 0
Union County 41, Centerville 7
Frankton 49, Northeastern 6
Sectional 30 Second Round
Indpls. Scecina 41, Hagerstown 19
Frankton 20, Union County 13
Sectional 30 Championship
Frankton 20, Indpls. Scecina 14

Sectional 31 First Round
Indian Creek 28, Paoli 13
Cascade 45, Linton-Stockton 13
Sullivan 54, North Knox 6
Greencastle 17, Monrovia 7
Sectional 31 Second Round
Cascade 27, Indian Creek 14
Greencastle 13, Sullivan 3
Sectional 31 Championship
Cascade 37, Greencastle 21

Sectional 32 First Round
North Posey 21, Gibson Southern 20, OT
Providence 19, Southridge 0
South Spencer 7, Clarksville 6
Tell City 24, Evansville Mater Dei 0
Sectional 32 Second Round
Providence 32, North Posey 0
Tell City 14, South Spencer 6
Sectional 32 Championship
Tell City 8, Providence 0, OT

Regional Championships
Fort Wayne Luers 42, Rensselaer Central 7
South Adams 21, Tippecanoe Valley 6
Westfield 27, Frankton 6
Tell City 34, Cascade 12

Semi-State Championships
Fort Wayne Luers 21, South Adams 6
Westfield 7, Tell City 0

State Championship
Fort Wayne Luers 17, Westfield 0

Class 1A
Sectional 33 First Round
Pioneer 35, Culver 20
Whiting 7, South Central (Union Mills) 0
West Central 27, Triton 6
Sectional 33 Second Round
Bremen 55, Pioneer 6
Whiting 26, West Central 6
Sectional 33 Championship
Bremen 40, Whiting 14

Sectional 34 First Round

Northfield 46, Caston 24
Jimtown 28, North Miami 6
Southern Wells 19, Fremont 6
Sectional 34 Second Round
Central Noble 24, Northfield 0
Jimtown 53, Southern Wells 0
Sectional 34 Championship
Jimtown 41, Central Noble 6

Sectional 35 First Round
Tri-County 20, Attica 6
Frontier 22, Covington 8
North White 22, Seeger 0
Sectional 35 Second Round
South Newton 12, Tri-County 6
North White 35, Frontier 22
Sectional 35 Championship
South Newton 14, North White 7

Sectional 36 First Round
Clinton Central 28, Tri-Central 14
Sheridan 67, Eastern (Greentown) 6
Clinton Prairie 40, Lafayette Central Catholic 7
Sectional 36 Second Round
Tri-West 22, Clinton Central 0
Sheridan 32, Clinton Prairie 6
Sectional 36 Championship
Sheridan 15, Tri-West 12

Sectional 37 First Round
Knightstown 62, Union City 20
Tri 28, Wes-Del 7
Lapel 20, Eastern Hancock 14, 3 OT
Sectional 37 Second Round
Knightstown 7, Cambridge City Lincoln 6
Tri 61, Lapel 16
Sectional 37 Championship
Knightstown 24, Tri 22, OT

Sectional 38 First Round
South Decatur 25, Indiana Deaf 0
North Decatur 22, Milan 19
Indpls. Ritter 41, Park Tudor 9
Sectional 38 Second Round
Edinburgh 29, South Decatur 7
Indpls. Ritter 34, North Decatur 14
Sectional 38 Championship
Indpls. Ritter 27, Edinburgh 14

Sectional 39 First Round
North Vermillion 22, Rockville 6
Turkey Run 33, North Central (Farmersburg) 0
Cloverdale 43, South Putnam 12
Sectional 39 Second Round
North Vermillion 56, Riverton Parke 0
Cloverdale 42, Turkey Run 14
Sectional 39 Championship
Cloverdale 37, North Vermillion 15

Sectional 40 First Round
Perry Central 19, Tecumseh 10
Springs Valley 59, West Washington 15
North Daviess 27, Union (Dugger) 6
Sectional 40 Second Round
Perry Central 37, Wood Memorial 0
Springs Valley 33, North Daviess 6
Sectional 40 Championship
Springs Valley 34, Perry Central 3

Regional Championships
Bremen 22, Jimtown 21, OT
Sheridan 26, South Newton 20, OT
Indpls. Ritter 21, Knightstown 12
Springs Valley 14, Cloverdale 7

Semi-State Championships
Sheridan 14, Bremen 6
Indpls. Ritter 20, Springs Valley 0

State Championship
Sheridan 6, Indpls. Ritter 0

1993

Class 5A
Sectional 1 First Round
Gary Wallace 48, Gary West 6
Merrillville 19, Crown Point 13
Lake Central 75, Gary Roosevelt 0
Hammond 14, East Chicago Central 12
Sectional 1 Second Round
Merrillville 39, Gary Wallace 24
Lake Central 60, Hammond 7
Sectional 1 Championship
Lake Central 56, Merrillville 13

Sectional 2 First Round
Portage 21, Michigan City Rogers 0
Mishawaka 14, LaPorte 13
Valparaiso 45, Chesterton 7
South Bend Riley 20, South Bend Adams 13
Sectional 2 Second Round
Portage 41, Mishawaka 12
Valparaiso 27, South Bend Riley 14
Sectional 2 Championship
Portage 21, Valparaiso 7

Sectional 3 First Round
Fort Wayne Northrop 34, Warsaw 32
Penn 21, Elkhart Central 0
Fort Wayne North 34, Elkhart Memorial 19
Homestead 23, Fort Wayne Snider 21
Sectional 3 Second Round
Penn 51, Fort Wayne Northrop 3
Homestead 40, Fort Wayne North 7
Sectional 3 Championship
Homestead 32, Penn 29

Sectional 4 First Round

Noblesville 28, Marion 14
Lafayette Jefferson 7, Kokomo 6
Harrison (West Lafayette) 25, Jay County 7
Huntington North 35, Muncie Central 20
Sectional 4 Second Round
Lafayette Jefferson 28, Noblesville 21
Huntington North 35, Harrison (W.L.) 28, OT
Sectional 4 Championship
Huntington North 7, Lafayette Jefferson 6

Sectional 5 First Round
Perry Meridian 31, Indpls. Northwest 26
Indpls. Broad Ripple 18, Southport 14
North Central (Indpls.) 34, Ben Davis 31
Carmel 21, Pike 8
Sectional 5 Second Round
Indpls. Broad Ripple 21, Perry Meridian 14
North Central (Indpls.) 21, Carmel 14
Sectional 5 Championship
North Central (Indpls.) 28, Ind. Broad Ripple 13

Sectional 6 First Round
Warren Central 28, Richmond 27
Lawrence North 29, Indpls. Arlington 6
Franklin Central 14, Lawrence Central 13
Connersville 23, Indpls. Tech 20
Sectional 6 Second Round
Warren Central 10, Lawrence North 9
Franklin Central 39, Connersville 0
Sectional 6 Championship
Franklin Central 14, Warren Central 7

Sectional 7 First Round
Terre Haute North 30, Bloomington North 14
Bloomington South 42, Martinsville 14
Decatur Central 41, Terre Haute South 28
Center Grove 12, Columbus North 7
Sectional 7 Second Round
Bloomington South 35, Terre Haute North 3
Decatur Central 25, Center Grove 7
Sectional 7 Championship
Bloomington South 28, Decatur Central 14

Sectional 8 First Round
Evansville Reitz 38, New Albany 14
Jeffersonville 27, Evansville Central 20
Castle 20, Floyd Central 8
Evansville Harrison 42, Bedford N.L. 20
Sectional 8 Second Round
Evansville Reitz 43, Jeffersonville 36, 2 OT
Evansville Harrison 44, Castle 22
Sectional 8 Championship
Evansville Harrison 28, Evansville Reitz 18

Regional Championships
Lake Central 35, Portage 14
Homestead 35, Huntington North 0
North Central (Indpls.) 34, Franklin Central 0
Bloomington South 49, Evansville Harrison 33

Semi-State Championships
Lake Central 41, Homestead 6
Bloomington South 21, North Central (Ind.) 14

State Championship
Bloomington South 33, Lake Central 27

Class 4A
Sectional 9 First Round
Kankakee Valley 39, Hammond Gavit 13
Lowell 17, Hammond Clark 3
Munster 42, Gary Mann 7
Hammond Morton 24, Highland 7
Sectional 9 Second Round
Lowell 16, Kankakee Valley 14
Munster 15, Hammond Morton 8
Sectional 9 Championship
Munster 28, Lowell 14

Sectional 10 First Round
Goshen 35, South Bend Clay 13
Concord 34, Gary Wirt 0
Hobart 49, Michigan City Elston 6
S.B. Washington 22, South Bend LaSalle 21
Sectional 10 Second Round
Goshen 28, Concord 7
Hobart 49, S.B. Washington 7
Sectional 10 Championship
Hobart 37, Goshen 14

Sectional 11 First Round
Wawasee 17, Plymouth 7
Fort Wayne Concordia 28, East Noble 14
DeKalb 38, Fort Wayne South 15
Columbia City 24, Carroll (Fort Wayne) 0
Sectional 11 Second Round
Fort Wayne Concordia 48, Wawasee 17
Columbia City 29, DeKalb 14
Sectional 11 Championship
Columbia City 28, Fort Wayne Concordia 7

Sectional 12 First Round
Anderson Madison-Hts. 14, F.W. Elmhurst 13
Fort Wayne Wayne 35, Bellmont 19
Delta 15, Muncie South 13
Anderson Highland 42, Anderson 13
Sectional 12 Second Round
Fort Wayne Wayne 20, And. Madison-Hts. 14
Delta 27, Anderson Highland 26
Sectional 12 Championship
Fort Wayne Wayne 19, Delta 7

Sectional 13 First Round
Avon 23, Logansport 0
Indpls. Cathedral 49, Plainfield 12
Brownsburg 14, Lebanon 6
McCutcheon 46, Hamilton Southeastern 3
Sectional 13 Second Round

Indpls. Cathedral 37, Avon 27
Brownsburg 18, McCutcheon 7
Sectional 13 Championship
Indpls. Cathedral 17, Brownsburg 7

Sectional 14 First Round
Franklin 24, Mooresville 3
Greenfield-Central 18, Indpls. Howe 12, 3 OT
Indpls. Manual 28, Pendleton Heights 0
Indpls. Washington 54, Greenwood 7
Sectional 14 Second Round
Greenfield-Central 22, Franklin 14
Indpls. Washington 30, Indpls. Manual 0
Sectional 14 Championship
Indpls. Washington 42, Greenfield-Central 7

Sectional 15 First Round
Columbus East 15, New Castle 14
East Central 42, South Dearborn 0
Rushville 21, Franklin County 7
Jennings County 40, Shelbyville 0
Sectional 15 Second Round
East Central 38, Columbus East 0
Rushville 28, Jennings County 0
Sectional 15 Championship
East Central 42, Rushville 14

Sectional 16 First Round
Mount Vernon 30, Northview 13
Boonville 20, Madison 14
Vincennes Lincoln 34, Evansville Bosse 27, OT
Evansville North 27, Seymour 7
Sectional 16 Second Round
Mount Vernon 8, Boonville 0
Vincennes Lincoln 27, Evansville North 21, OT
Sectional 16 Championship
Vincennes Lincoln 40, Mount Vernon 8

Regional Championships
Hobart 20, Munster 0
Fort Wayne Wayne 26, Columbia City 6
Indpls. Washington 21, Indpls. Cathedral 16
East Central 43, Vincennes Lincoln 7

Semi-State Championships
Hobart 54, Fort Wayne Wayne 0
East Central 7, Indpls. Washington 0

State Championship
Hobart 31, East Central 18

Class 3A
Sectional 17 First Round
Griffith 21, Andrean 7
New Prairie 22, Calumet 14
Twin Lakes 20, Rensselaer Central 12
Benton Central 19, Hammond Noll 7
Sectional 17 Second Round
Griffith 27, New Prairie 14

Twin Lakes 36, Benton Central 8
Sectional 17 Championship
Twin Lakes 20, Griffith 12

Sectional 18 First Round
Angola 42, West Noble 21
S.B. St. Joseph 31, Lakeland 25
NorthWood 62, Culver Military Academy 8
Northridge 40, Whitko 6
Sectional 18 Second Round
S.B. St. Joseph 42, Angola 3
NorthWood 21, Northridge 3
Sectional 18 Championship
NorthWood 28, S.B. St. Joseph 7

Sectional 19 First Round
Fort Wayne Dwenger 53, Harding (F.W.) 8
Manchester 33, Maconaquah 7
Mississinewa 48, Peru 28
Norwell 35, New Haven 14
Sectional 19 Second Round
Fort Wayne Dwenger 35, Manchester 14
Norwell 22, Mississinewa 15
Sectional 19 Championship
Fort Wayne Dwenger 39, Norwell 13

Sectional 20 First Round
Western 26, Madison-Grant 14
Yorktown 21, Elwood 20
Alexandria 40, Hamilton Heights 25
Tipton 56, Blackford 6
Sectional 20 Second Round
Western 35, Yorktown 6
Tipton 35, Alexandria 14
Sectional 20 Championship
Tipton 42, Western 0

Sectional 21 First Round
Danville 54, Owen Valley 21
Edgewood 35, Frankfort 6
North Montgomery 12, West Vigo 6
Crawfordsville 37, South Vermillion 0
Sectional 21 Second Round
Danville 35, Edgewood 0
North Montgomery 32, Crawfordsville 7
Sectional 21 Championship
Danville 35, North Montgomery 18

Sectional 22 First Round
Zionsville 42, Mount Vernon (Fortville) 0
Brebeuf Jesuit 37, Whiteland 0
New Palestine 24, Beech Grove 8
Roncalli 21, Indpls. Chatard 12
Sectional 22 Second Round
Zionsville 31, Brebeuf Jesuit 14
Roncalli 55, New Palestine 6
Sectional 22 Championship
Roncalli 34, Zionsville 28, OT

Sectional 23 First Round
Salem 20, Brown County 12
Batesville 14, Corydon Central 7
Greensburg 49, North Harrison 0
Charlestown 42, Mitchell 14
Sectional 23 Second Round
Salem 14, Batesville 7
Charlestown 56, Greensburg 41
Sectional 23 Championship
Charlestown 35, Salem 7

Sectional 24 First Round
Heritage Hills 35, Sullivan 8
Jasper 42, Washington 0
Tell City 49, Pike Central 20
Evansville Memorial 26, Princeton 13
Sectional 24 Second Round
Heritage Hills 27, Jasper 14
Evansville Memorial 35, Tell City 12
Sectional 24 Championship
Evansville Memorial 16, Heritage Hills 13

Regional Championships
NorthWood 47, Twin Lakes 21
Fort Wayne Dwenger 24, Tipton 12
Roncalli 37, Danville 0
Evansville Memorial 24, Charlestown 0

Semi-State Championships
NorthWood 25, Fort Wayne Dwenger 14
Roncalli 42, Evansville Memorial 0

State Championship
Roncalli 14, NorthWood 12

Class 2A
Sectional 25 First Round
Rochester 35, Lake Station 0
North Newton 14, North Judson 13, OT
John Glenn 22, Winamac 0
Knox 21, River Forest 12
Sectional 25 Second Round
North Newton 27, Rochester 0
Knox 18, John Glenn 13
Sectional 25 Championship
North Newton 46, Knox 6

Sectional 26 First Round
West Lafayette 22, Delphi 13
Western Boone 21, Lewis Cass 12
Northwestern 43, Southmont 18
Carroll (Flora) 14, Seeger 0
Sectional 26 Second Round
West Lafayette 40, Western Boone 6
Carroll (Flora) 17, Northwestern 14
Sectional 26 Championship
West Lafayette 28, Carroll (Flora) 7

Sectional 27 First Round
Mishawaka Marian 25, Northfield 0
Jimtown 53, Wabash 7
Bremen 49, LaVille 0
Tippecanoe Valley 28, Southwood 18
Sectional 27 Second Round
Jimtown 49, Mishawaka Marian 14
Tippecanoe Valley 20, Bremen 19
Sectional 27 Championship
Jimtown 10, Tippecanoe Valley 6

Sectional 28 First Round
Churubusco 28, Prairie Heights 7
Woodlan 34, Leo 14
Heritage 28, Eastside 24
Fort Wayne Luers 26, Garrett 14
Sectional 28 Second Round
Churubusco 22, Woodlan 15
Fort Wayne Luers 28, Heritage 0
Sectional 28 Championship
Fort Wayne Luers 27, Churubusco 0

Sectional 29 First Round
Taylor 26, Shenandoah 20
Eastbrook 21, Eastern (Greentown) 12
Frankton 49, Winchester 0
Bluffton 39, Oak Hill 10
Sectional 29 Second Round
Eastbrook 55, Taylor 0
Bluffton 20, Frankton 14
Sectional 29 Championship
Eastbrook 24, Bluffton 20

Sectional 30 First Round
Indpls. Scecina 27, Greencastle 6
North Putnam 28, Cloverdale 6
Westfield 14, Speedway 6
Cascade 31, Monrovia 23
Sectional 30 Second Round
Indpls. Scecina 30, North Putnam 0
Westfield 33, Cascade 0
Sectional 30 Championship
Westfield 24, Indpls. Scecina 6

Sectional 31 First Round
Triton Central 56, Union County 6
Lawrenceburg 32, Centerville 0
Clarksville 24, Brownstown Central 8
Providence 49, Indian Creek 14
Sectional 31 Second Round
Lawrenceburg 27, Triton Central 7
Providence 34, Clarksville 14
Sectional 31 Championship
Providence 19, Lawrenceburg 7

Sectional 32 First Round
Evansville Mater Dei 39, North Posey 7
Gibson Southern 13, South Spencer 7
Linton-Stockton 32, Paoli 19
North Knox 7, Southridge 0

Sectional 32 Second Round
Evansville Mater Dei 13, Gibson Southern 0
Linton-Stockton 27, North Knox 3
Sectional 32 Championship
Evansville Mater Dei 32, Linton-Stockton 0

Regional Championships
West Lafayette 25, North Newton 14
Fort Wayne Luers 29, Jimtown 26
Westfield 19, Eastbrook 9
Providence 7, Evansville Mater Dei 0

Semi-State Championships
West Lafayette 27, Fort Wayne Luers 7
Providence 28, Westfield 21, OT

State Championship
West Lafayette 22, Providence 7

Class 1A
Sectional 33 First Round
South Central (Union Mills) 12, West Central 8
Whiting 21, North White 7
Tri-County 35, Culver 14
Sectional 33 Second Round
South Newton 44, South Central (Union Mills) 8
Whiting 19, Tri-County 0
Sectional 33 Championship
Whiting 20, South Newton 14, OT

Sectional 34 First Round
Southern Wells 50, Triton 0
Central Noble 21, South Adams 20
Adams Central 14, Fairfield 7
Sectional 34 Second Round
Southern Wells 38, Fremont 0
Adams Central 14, Central Noble 6
Sectional 34 Championship
Adams Central 22, Southern Wells 0

Sectional 35 First Round
Pioneer 28, Clinton Prairie 0
Caston 14, Frontier 6
North Miami 49, Clinton Central 20
Sectional 35 Second Round
Lafayette Central Catholic 21, Pioneer 20
North Miami 35, Caston 0
Sectional 35 Championship
North Miami 22, Lafayette Central Catholic 20

Sectional 36 First Round
Rockville 27, Turkey Run 14
Fountain Central 18, Attica 13
Riverton Parke 14, Covington 12
Sectional 36 Second Round
North Vermillion 41, Rockville 10
Fountain Central 34, Riverton Parke 6
Sectional 36 Championship
North Vermillion 32, Fountain Central 0

Sectional 37 First Round
South Putnam 34, Tri-Central 20
Sheridan 28, Indpls. Ritter 7
Sectional 37 Second Round
Sheridan 33, South Putnam 7
Tri-West 27, Park Tudor 7
Sectional 37 Championship
Tri-West 13, Sheridan 8

Sectional 38 First Round
Tri 40, Union City 14
Hagerstown 44, Northeastern 7
Wes-Del 48, Lapel 24
Sectional 38 Second Round
Tri 46, Cambridge City Lincoln 6
Hagerstown 55, Wes-Del 14
Sectional 38 Championship
Hagerstown 26, Tri 6

Sectional 39 First Round
West Washington 39, Milan 8
North Decatur 22, Eastern Hancock 6
Knightstown 12, South Decatur 0
Sectional 39 Second Round
West Washington 26, Edinburgh 16
North Decatur 32, Knightstown 20
Sectional 39 Championship
West Washington 13, North Decatur 12

Sectional 40 First Round
Springs Valley 14, Tecumseh 0
North Daviess 33, Union (Dugger) 0
North Central (Farm.) 8, Wood Memorial 6
Sectional 40 Second Round
Perry Central 7, Springs Valley 0
North Daviess 47, North Central (Farm.) 0
Sectional 40 Championship
North Daviess 8, Perry Central 6

Regional Championships
Adams Central 17, Whiting 14
North Miami 36, North Vermillion 14
Tri-West 19, Hagerstown 18, OT
West Washington 48, North Daviess 7

Semi-State Championships
North Miami 22, Adams Central 6
West Washington 20, Tri-West 0

State Championship
North Miami 37, West Washington 16

1994
Class 5A
Sectional 1 First Round
Gary Wallace 40, East Chicago Central 9
Hammond 25, Gary Roosevelt 0
Crown Point 16, Gary West 6

Lake Central 35, Merrillville 7
Sectional 1 Second Round
Hammond 7, Gary Wallace 6
Lake Central 44, Crown Point 3
Sectional 1 Championship
Lake Central 15, Hammond 0

Sectional 2 First Round
LaPorte 52, Michigan City Rogers 6
South Bend Riley 23, Mishawaka 17, OT
Valparaiso 21, Chesterton 3
Portage 42, South Bend Adams 0
Sectional 2 Second Round
Portage 37, Valparaiso 8
LaPorte 24, South Bend Riley 21
Sectional 2 Championship
Portage 36, LaPorte 6

Sectional 3 First Round
Fort Wayne Snider 35, Fort Wayne Northrop 14
Penn 42, Warsaw 0
Elkhart Central 34, Homestead 14
Fort Wayne North 36, Elkhart Memorial 12
Sectional 3 Second Round
Fort Wayne Snider 20, Fort Wayne North 14
Penn 14, Elkhart Central 0
Sectional 3 Championship
Fort Wayne Snider 24, Penn 7

Sectional 4 First Round
Harrison (W.L.) 13, Huntington North 7
Muncie Central 17, Marion 16
Lafayette Jefferson 14, Noblesville 10
Kokomo 42, Jay County 6
Sectional 4 Second Round
Harrison (W.L.) 20, Muncie Central 12
Lafayette Jefferson 14, Kokomo 13
Sectional 4 Championship
Harrison (W.L.) 20, Lafayette Jefferson 14, OT

Sectional 5 First Round
Carmel 35, Perry Meridian 13
North Central (Indpls.) 20, Ben Davis 16
Pike 20, Indpls. Broad Ripple 19
Southport 40, Indpls. Northwest 0
Sectional 5 Second Round
Carmel 28, North Central (Indpls.) 21, 2 OT
Southport 35, Pike 17
Sectional 5 Championship
Carmel 34, Southport 20

Sectional 6 First Round
Warren Central 35, Franklin Central 14
Indpls. Tech 12, Connersville 10
Lawrence Central 42, Richmond 0
Lawrence North 41, Indpls. Arlington 20
Sectional 6 Second Round
Warren Central 48, Indpls. Tech 26
Lawrence Central 19, Lawrence North 6

Sectional 6 Championship
Warren Central 21, Lawrence Central 7

Sectional 7 First Round
Martinsville 62, Bloomington South 0
Columbus North 31, Center Grove 13
Decatur Central 38, Terre Haute North 7
Terre Haute South 34, Bloomington North 24
Sectional 7 Second Round
Martinsville 34, Columbus North 27
Decatur Central 42, Terre Haute South 13
Sectional 7 Championship
Martinsville 15, Decatur Central 13

Sectional 8 First Round
Floyd Central 20, Jeffersonville 14
Castle 38, New Albany 7
Evansville Reitz 19, Evansville Harrison 14
Evansville Central 27, Bedford N.L. 20
Sectional 8 Second Round
Castle 42, Floyd Central 17
Evansville Reitz 43, Evansville Central 22
Sectional 8 Championship
Castle 23, Evansville Reitz 10

Regional Championships
Portage 21, Lake Central 7
Fort Wayne Snider 56, Harrison (W.L.) 14
Carmel 14, Warren Central 6
Castle 35, Martinsville 28

Semi-State Championships
Portage 14, Fort Wayne Snider 3
Castle 21, Carmel 20

State Championship
Castle 30, Portage 12

Class 4A
Sectional 9 First Round
Munster 35, Kankakee Valley 28
Lowell 33, Hammond Gavit 7
Hammond Morton 41, Highland 34, OT
Hammond Clark 44, Gary Mann 8
Sectional 9 Second Round
Munster 21, Hammond Morton 12
Lowell 28, Hammond Clark 8
Sectional 9 Championship
Lowell 27, Munster 14

Sectional 10 First Round
Concord 17, Gary Wirt 0
Goshen 28, South Bend LaSalle 14
S.B. Washington 25, South Bend Clay 13
Hobart 29, Michigan City Elston 26
Sectional 10 Second Round
Hobart 42, S.B. Washington 7
Concord 7, Goshen 0
Sectional 10 Championship

Hobart 30, Concord 13

Sectional 11 First Round
Wawasee 43, Fort Wayne South 21
Plymouth 38, Fort Wayne Concordia 14
DeKalb 42, Carroll (Fort Wayne) 22
Columbia City 42, East Noble 13
Sectional 11 Second Round
Plymouth 49, Wawasee 14
DeKalb 49, Columbia City 7
Sectional 11 Championship
DeKalb 21, Plymouth 7

Sectional 12 First Round
Fort Wayne Wayne 35, Fort Wayne Elmhurst 0
Bellmont 69, Anderson 20
Delta 26, Anderson Madison-Heights 0
Muncie South 52, Anderson Highland 32
Sectional 12 Second Round
Fort Wayne Wayne 55, Delta 19
Muncie South 21, Bellmont 17
Sectional 12 Championship
Muncie South 33, Fort Wayne Wayne 12

Sectional 13 First Round
McCutcheon 32, Lebanon 0
Indpls. Cathedral 33, Logansport 14
Avon 20, Hamilton Southeastern 7
Brownsburg 58, Plainfield 0
Sectional 13 Second Round
McCutcheon 14, Brownsburg 0
Indpls. Cathedral 21, Avon 7
Sectional 13 Championship
McCutcheon 17, Indpls. Cathedral 15

Sectional 14 First Round
Indpls. Washington 39, Mooresville 27
Franklin 30, Indpls. Howe 24
Greenfield-Central 46, Pendleton Heights 9
Greenwood 41, Indpls. Manual 6
Sectional 14 Second Round
Indpls. Washington 26, Franklin 18
Greenfield-Central 34, Greenwood 13
Sectional 14 Championship
Indpls. Washington 27, Greenfield-Central 20

Sectional 15 First Round
East Central 45, Jennings County 7
Franklin County 56, New Castle 7
South Dearborn 21, Shelbyville 7
Columbus East 36, Rushville 17
Sectional 15 Second Round
East Central 35, Franklin County 18
South Dearborn 27, Columbus East 26
Sectional 15 Championship
East Central 58, South Dearborn 14

Sectional 16 First Round
Evansville North 35, Evansville Bosse 21
Vincennes Lincoln 35, Madison 0
Seymour 48, Northview 14
Boonville 48, Mount Vernon 14
Sectional 16 Second Round
Evansville North 27, Vincennes Lincoln 20
Seymour 30, Boonville 12
Sectional 16 Championship
Evansville North 37, Seymour 9

Regional Championships
Lowell 28, Hobart 25
DeKalb 38, Muncie South 7
Indpls. Washington 20, McCutcheon 19
East Central 23, Evansville North 0

Semi-State Championships
DeKalb 21, Lowell 0
East Central 56, Indpls. Washington 15

State Championship
East Central 35, DeKalb 0

Class 3A
Sectional 17 First Round
Andrean 32, Benton Central 0
Griffith 47, New Prairie 0
Rensselaer Central 39, Calumet 8
Twin Lakes 28, Hammond Noll 23
Sectional 17 Second Round
Griffith 29, Andrean 14
Twin Lakes 35, Rensselaer Central 21
Sectional 17 Championship
Griffith 21, Twin Lakes 0

Sectional 18 First Round
S.B. St. Joseph 31, Northridge 0
NorthWood 60, Culver Military Academy 6
Angola 16, West Noble 10
Lakeland 7, Whitko 6
Sectional 18 Second Round
S.B. St. Joseph 37, Angola 0
NorthWood 40, Lakeland 21
Sectional 18 Championship
S.B. St. Joseph 20, NorthWood 14

Sectional 19 First Round
Harding (Fort Wayne) 49, Maconaquah 31
Mississinewa 27, Manchester 21
Peru 35, New Haven 22
Norwell 31, Fort Wayne Dwenger 28
Sectional 19 Second Round
Norwell 34, Peru 21
Harding (Fort Wayne) 34, Mississinewa 13
Sectional 19 Championship
Norwell 49, Harding (Fort Wayne) 21

Sectional 20 First Round
Tipton 28, Madison-Grant 20
Western 44, Alexandria 14

Yorktown 30, Elwood 13
Hamilton Heights 35, Blackford 14
Sectional 20 Second Round
Tipton 46, Western 13
Yorktown 34, Hamilton Heights 19
Sectional 20 Championship
Tipton 55, Yorktown 29

Sectional 21 First Round
Danville 37, Crawfordsville 17
Frankfort 50, Owen Valley 0
North Montgomery 27, West Vigo 13
Edgewood 34, South Vermillion 6
Sectional 21 Second Round
Danville 41, Frankfort 26
North Montgomery 41, Edgewood 14
Sectional 21 Championship
Danville 16, North Montgomery 15

Sectional 22 First Round
Roncalli 57, Brebeuf Jesuit 7
Indpls. Chatard 28, Beech Grove 20
Zionsville 28, Mount Vernon (Fortville) 7
Whiteland 35, New Palestine 34, OT
Sectional 22 Second Round
Roncalli 21, Indpls. Chatard 19
Zionsville 41, Whiteland 0
Sectional 22 Championship
Roncalli 28, Zionsville 21

Sectional 23 First Round
Salem 21, Charlestown 8
Greensburg 26, Mitchell 7
Brown County 14, North Harrison 12
Batesville 41, Corydon Central 14
Sectional 23 Second Round
Salem 38, Greensburg 0
Brown County 10, Batesville 6
Sectional 23 Championship
Salem 14, Brown County 12

Sectional 24 First Round
Jasper 34, Evansville Memorial 7
Princeton 41, Washington 20
Heritage Hills 21, Tell City 12
Sullivan 27, Pike Central 0
Sectional 24 Second Round
Jasper 45, Princeton 0
Heritage Hills 23, Sullivan 15
Sectional 24 Championship
Jasper 40, Heritage Hills 7

Regional Championships
Griffith 14, S.B. St. Joseph 7
Tipton 35, Norwell 33
Roncalli 23, Danville 21
Jasper 26, Salem 0

Semi-State Championships

Tipton 25, Griffith 24
Roncalli 10, Jasper 9

State Championship
Roncalli 35, Tipton 14

Class 2A
Sectional 25 First Round
Winamac 27, North Judson 7
Rochester 19, North Newton 16
River Forest 14, Knox 13
John Glenn 20, Lake Station 17
Sectional 25 Second Round
Winamac 26, River Forest 0
Rochester 35, John Glenn 15
Sectional 25 Championship
Rochester 15, Winamac 7

Sectional 26 First Round
Carroll (Flora) 20, Delphi 17
Lewis Cass 24, Southmont 21, 2 OT
Western Boone 7, West Lafayette 6
Seeger 27, Northwestern 17
Sectional 26 Second Round
Lewis Cass 31, Western Boone 0
Carroll (Flora) 14, Seeger 13
Sectional 26 Championship
Lewis Cass 20, Carroll (Flora) 9

Sectional 27 First Round
Southwood 27, Northfield 12
Jimtown 21, Tippecanoe Valley 7
Bremen 68, Wabash 13
LaVille 22, Mishawaka Marian 6
Sectional 27 Second Round
Jimtown 49, Southwood 14
Bremen 54, LaVille 14
Sectional 27 Championship
Bremen 27, Jimtown 0

Sectional 28 First Round
Churubusco 34, Prairie Heights 20
Eastside 16, Fort Wayne Luers 14
Heritage 28, Woodlan 27
Garrett 56, Leo 20
Sectional 28 Second Round
Churubusco 24, Eastside 0
Garrett 14, Heritage 0
Sectional 28 Championship
Garrett 19, Churubusco 3

Sectional 29 First Round
Eastbrook 28, Eastern (Greentown) 6
Frankton 49, Winchester 14
Bluffton 35, Oak Hill 21
Shenandoah 32, Taylor 26
Sectional 29 Second Round
Eastbrook 24, Frankton 20
Bluffton 37, Shenandoah 14

Sectional 29 Championship
Eastbrook 14, Bluffton 12

Sectional 30 First Round
Indpls. Scecina 48, Cascade 14
Westfield 40, Cloverdale 6
Speedway 27, Monrovia 5
North Putnam 28, Greencastle 14
Sectional 30 Second Round
Indpls. Scecina 34, Westfield 20
Speedway 19, North Putnam 7
Sectional 30 Championship
Indpls. Scecina 48, Speedway 14

Sectional 31 First Round
Providence 16, Lawrenceburg 6
Clarksville 27, Centerville 2
Brownstown Central 41, Indian Creek 7
Triton Central 40, Union County 35
Sectional 31 Second Round
Providence 28, Clarksville 14
Brownstown Central 32, Triton Central 12
Sectional 31 Championship
Providence 27, Brownstown Central 21

Sectional 32 First Round
Evansville Mater Dei 41, Southridge 8
South Spencer 48, Paoli 14
North Posey 49, Gibson Southern 21
Linton-Stockton 7, North Knox 6
Sectional 32 Second Round
Evansville Mater Dei 38, South Spencer 28
North Posey 43, Linton-Stockton 0
Sectional 32 Championship
Evansville Mater Dei 34, North Posey 6

Regional Championships
Lewis Cass 7, Rochester 6
Bremen 20, Garrett 0
Indpls. Scecina 42, Eastbrook 7
Evansville Mater Dei 20, Providence 14

Semi-State Championships
Bremen 16, Lewis Cass 7
Evansville Mater Dei 14, Indpls. Scecina 13

State Championship
Bremen 38, Evansville Mater Dei 10

Class 1A
Sectional 33 First Round
South Newton 52, Culver 14
Tri-County 21, Whiting 12
North White 28, South Central (Union Mills) 18
Sectional 33 Second Round
North White 48, West Central 7
South Newton 49, Tri-County 12
Sectional 33 Championship
North White 7, South Newton 0

Sectional 34 First Round
Adams Central 20, Fairfield 14
Southern Wells 36, Fremont 12
South Adams 28, Central Noble 12
Sectional 34 Second Round
South Adams 24, Triton 12
Adams Central 32, Southern Wells 0
Sectional 34 Championship
Adams Central 29, South Adams 0

Sectional 35 First Round
North Miami 38, Caston 0
Lafayette Central Catholic 59, Clinton Prairie 7
Frontier 34, Clinton Central 16
Sectional 35 Second Round
North Miami 22, Lafayette Central Catholic 19
Frontier 34, Pioneer 7
Sectional 35 Championship
North Miami 32, Frontier 6

Sectional 36 First Round
Rockville 14, Covington 6
Fountain Central 13, Turkey Run 8
North Vermillion 38, Attica 19
Sectional 36 Second Round
Rockville 20, Fountain Central 6
North Vermillion 36, Riverton Parke 12
Sectional 36 Championship
Rockville 20, North Vermillion 14

Sectional 37 First Round
Sheridan 49, Park Tudor 7
Tri-West 27, Indpls. Ritter 10
Sectional 37 Second Round
Sheridan 32, Tri-West 19
Tri-Central 6, South Putnam 0
Sectional 37 Championship
Sheridan 7, Tri-Central 6

Sectional 38 First Round
Hagerstown 73, Cambridge City Lincoln 6
Union City 14, Northeastern 6
Tri 30, Wes-Del 10
Sectional 38 Second Round
Hagerstown 53, Union City 6
Tri 26, Lapel 14
Sectional 38 Championship
Hagerstown 36, Tri 12

Sectional 39 First Round
West Washington 34, Milan 8
North Decatur 32, South Decatur 0
Knightstown 33, Eastern Hancock 0
Sectional 39 Second Round
West Washington 14, North Decatur 0
Knightstown 58, Edinburgh 14
Sectional 39 Championship
West Washington 37, Knightstown 6

Sectional 40 First Round
Tecumseh 41, Perry Central 7
Union (Dugger) 7, Wood Memorial 6
North Daviess 13, North Central (Farm.) 0
Sectional 40 Second Round
Tecumseh 55, Union (Dugger) 8
North Daviess 21, Springs Valley 14, OT
Sectional 40 Championship
Tecumseh 12, North Daviess 7

Regional Championships
North White 33, Adams Central 16
North Miami 42, Rockville 7
Sheridan 28, Hagerstown 14
West Washington 22, Tecumseh 14

Semi-State Championships
North White 31, North Miami 20
Sheridan 27, West Washington 6

State Championship
North White 34, Sheridan 7

1995
Class 5A
Sectional 1 First Round
Portage 21, Lake Central 7
Gary Wallace 44, Gary Roosevelt 0
Merrillville 19, Valparaiso 14
Crown Point 35, East Chicago Central 12
Sectional 1 Second Round
Portage 35, Gary Wallace 6
Crown Point 34, Merrillville 7
Sectional 1 Championship
Portage 20, Crown Point 17, OT

Sectional 2 First Round
Chesterton 13, Warsaw 0
Michigan City 15, Elkhart Central 6
Penn 35, South Bend Riley 0
Mishawaka 35, LaPorte 8
Sectional 2 Second Round
Michigan City 20, Chesterton 14
Penn 13, Mishawaka 6
Sectional 2 Championship
Penn 13, Michigan City 7

Sectional 3 First Round
Fort Wayne North 48, Jay County 14
Fort Wayne Snider 41, Homestead 0
Fort Wayne Northrop 20, Huntington North 14
Marion 14, Fort Wayne South 12
Sectional 3 Second Round
Fort Wayne Snider 14, Fort Wayne North 3
Fort Wayne Northrop 34, Marion 12
Sectional 3 Championship
Fort Wayne Snider 23, Fort Wayne Northrop 0

Sectional 4 First Round
Carmel 63, Indpls. Broad Ripple 0
Noblesville 53, Lafayette Jefferson 22
Harrison (West Lafayette) 33, Kokomo 6
North Central (Indpls.) 48, Pike 6
Sectional 4 Second Round
Carmel 35, Noblesville 0
Harrison (W.L.) 32, North Central (Indpls.) 6
Sectional 4 Championship
Carmel 23, Harrison (West Lafayette) 16

Sectional 5 First Round
Ben Davis 42, Southport 6
Indpls. Manual 22, Indpls. Tech 14
Franklin Central 27, Perry Meridian 13
Sectional 5 Second Round
Ben Davis 41, Indpls. Manual 20
Indpls. Northwest 34, Franklin Central 0
Sectional 5 Championship
Ben Davis 49, Indpls. Northwest 6

Sectional 6 First Round
Lawrence Central 34, Richmond 14
Warren Central 34, Lawrence North 3
Connersville 26, Indpls. Arlington 0
Sectional 6 Second Round
Lawrence Central 26, Warren Central 10
Muncie Central 28, Connersville 8
Sectional 6 Championship
Lawrence Central 21, Muncie Central 0

Sectional 7 First Round
Martinsville 25, Terre Haute North 10
Center Grove 41, Terre Haute South 0
Bloomington South 17, Decatur Central 8
Bloomington North 27, Columbus North 0
Sectional 7 Second Round
Martinsville 34, Center Grove 19
Bloomington South 32, Bloomington North 21
Sectional 7 Championship
Martinsville 21, Bloomington South 12

Sectional 8 First Round
Evansville North 36, Bedford N.L. 22
Evansville Reitz 35, Castle 3
Evansville Harrison 35, Jeffersonville 6
Evansville Central 57, New Albany 16
Sectional 8 Second Round
Evansville North 21, Evansville Reitz 17
Evansville Harrison 35, Evansville Central 0
Sectional 8 Championship
Evansville North 28, Evansville Harrison 7

Regional Championships
Penn 21, Portage 8
Carmel 29, Fort Wayne Snider 28, OT
Ben Davis 20, Lawrence Central 14
Evansville North 34, Martinsville 25

Semi-State Championships
Penn 28, Carmel 14
Evansville North 21, Ben Davis 14

State Championship
Penn 35, Evansville North 13

Class 4A
Sectional 9 First Round
Munster 12, Kankakee Valley 0
Lowell 38, Highland 0
Hammond 39, Hammond Gavit 6
Griffith 42, Hammond Morton 7
Sectional 9 Second Round
Munster 16, Lowell 3
Griffith 42, Hammond 0
Sectional 9 Championship
Griffith 19, Munster 7

Sectional 10 First Round
South Bend Clay 34, South Bend LaSalle 6
S.B. Washington 35, Gary West 12
Hobart 60, Gary Wirt 6
South Bend Adams 40, Gary Mann 12
Sectional 10 Second Round
South Bend Clay 6, S.B. Washington 3
Hobart 41, South Bend Adams 7
Sectional 10 Championship
Hobart 31, South Bend Clay 12

Sectional 11 First Round
Plymouth 26, Elkhart Memorial 0
DeKalb 44, Wawasee 0
Concord 34, East Noble 12
Columbia City 38, Goshen 27
Sectional 11 Second Round
DeKalb 42, Plymouth 29
Concord 17, Columbia City 14
Sectional 11 Championship
DeKalb 13, Concord 0

Sectional 12 First Round
Fort Wayne Concordia 47, F.W. Elmhurst 6
Fort Wayne Wayne 16, Bellmont 12
Delta 20, Carroll (Fort Wayne) 19
Peru 17, Logansport 14
Sectional 12 Second Round
Fort Wayne Wayne 38, Fort Wayne Concordia 0
Delta 27, Peru 7
Sectional 12 Championship
Fort Wayne Wayne 42, Delta 0

Sectional 13 First Round
Avon 35, Franklin 0
Mooresville 19, Greenfield-Central 12
Indpls. Cathedral 35, Plainfield 16
Brownsburg 35, Greenwood 0
Sectional 13 Second Round
Avon 28, Mooresville 7
Indpls. Cathedral 32, Brownsburg 16
Sectional 13 Championship
Avon 14, Indpls. Cathedral 7, OT

Sectional 14 First Round
Hamilton Southeastern 13, Muncie South 2
McCutcheon 14, New Castle 13
Pendleton Heights 20, And. Madison-Heights 14
Anderson Highland 33, Anderson 14
Sectional 14 Second Round
Hamilton Southeastern 24, McCutcheon 0
Pendleton Heights 14, Anderson Highland 7, OT
Sectional 14 Championship
Hamilton Southeastern 27, Pendleton Heights 13

Sectional 15 First Round
Franklin County 35, East Central 10
South Dearborn 36, Jennings County 0
Rushville 21, Madison 7
Columbus East 49, Shelbyville 7
Sectional 15 Second Round
Franklin County 48, South Dearborn 14
Rushville 21, Columbus East 18
Sectional 15 Championship
Franklin County 54, Rushville 6

Sectional 16 First Round
Evansville Bosse 31, Owen Valley 6
Mount Vernon 28, Floyd Central 27
Vincennes Lincoln 57, Northview 8
Boonville 26, Seymour 25
Sectional 16 Second Round
Evansville Bosse 56, Mount Vernon 21
Vincennes Lincoln 28, Boonville 14
Sectional 16 Championship
Evansville Bosse 18, Vincennes Lincoln 13

Regional Championships
Hobart 14, Griffith 13
Fort Wayne Wayne 18, DeKalb 12, OT
Avon 14, Hamilton Southeastern 0
Franklin County 45, Evansville Bosse 3

Semi-State Championships
Fort Wayne Wayne 28, Hobart 21
Franklin County 21, Avon 14

State Championship
Fort Wayne Wayne 28, Franklin County 8

Class 3A
Sectional 17 First Round
Andrean 30, Knox 14
Twin Lakes 40, Calumet 0
Benton Central 7, Rensselaer Central 6
Hammond Noll 21, Hammond Clark 13
Sectional 17 Second Round
Twin Lakes 35, Andrean 14
Hammond Noll 26, Benton Central 7

Sectional 17 Championship
Twin Lakes 14, Hammond Noll 12

Sectional 18 First Round
NorthWood 58, Angola 0
Tippecanoe Valley 26, Lakeland 14
S.B. St. Joseph 42, Culver Military Academy 0
Northridge 50, New Prairie 8
Sectional 18 Second Round
NorthWood 12, Tippecanoe Valley 3
S.B. St. Joseph 35, Northridge 6
Sectional 18 Championship
S.B. St. Joseph 31, NorthWood 7

Sectional 19 First Round
Whitko 53, Maconaquah 14
Fort Wayne Dwenger 34, New Haven 0
Norwell 28, Mississinewa 0
Harding (Fort Wayne) 45, Blackford 6
Sectional 19 Second Round
Harding (Fort Wayne) 40, Norwell 13
Whitko 26, Fort Wayne Dwenger 18
Sectional 19 Championship
Harding (Fort Wayne) 23, Whitko 15

Sectional 20 First Round
Hamilton Heights 61, Alexandria 0
Frankfort 19, West Lafayette 13
Yorktown 42, Elwood 20
Western 14, Northwestern 6
Sectional 20 Second Round
Hamilton Heights 28, Frankfort 0
Yorktown 35, Western 22
Sectional 20 Championship
Hamilton Heights 22, Yorktown 19

Sectional 21 First Round
Zionsville 37, Lebanon 3
Southmont 49, South Vermillion 20
Danville 15, Greencastle 8
West Vigo 32, Crawfordsville 13
Sectional 21 Second Round
Zionsville 14, Southmont 9
Danville 42, West Vigo 0
Sectional 21 Championship
Zionsville 17, Danville 8

Sectional 22 First Round
Mount Vernon (Fortville) 7, Beech Grove 6
Roncalli 54, Whiteland 12
New Palestine 20, Brebeuf Jesuit 6
Greensburg 20, Batesville 14
Sectional 22 Second Round
Roncalli 35, Mount Vernon (Fortville) 12
New Palestine 12, Greensburg 7
Sectional 22 Championship
Roncalli 35, New Palestine 21

Sectional 23 First Round
Brown County 21, Edgewood 14
Salem 28, Charlestown 7
Tell City 14, Providence 7
North Harrison 22, Corydon Central 8
Sectional 23 Second Round
Brown County 21, Salem 0
Tell City 26, North Harrison 8
Sectional 23 Championship
Brown County 20, Tell City 19

Sectional 24 First Round
Jasper 62, Pike Central 0
Evansville Mater Dei 24, Evansville Memorial 0
Heritage Hills 37, Washington 21
Princeton 46, Sullivan 0
Sectional 24 Second Round
Jasper 27, Evansville Mater Dei 19
Heritage Hills 42, Princeton 21
Sectional 24 Championship
Jasper 21, Heritage Hills 17

Regional Championships
S.B. St. Joseph 10, Twin Lakes 0
Harding (Fort Wayne) 40, Hamilton Heights 23
Roncalli 8, Zionsville 7
Jasper 27, Brown County 14

Semi-State Championships
S.B. St. Joseph 27, Harding (Fort Wayne) 14
Jasper 32, Roncalli 14

State Championship
S.B. St. Joseph 28, Jasper 0

Class 2A
Sectional 25 First Round
North Judson 62, John Glenn 21
Bremen 56, North Newton 0
Rochester 28, Winamac 14
Lake Station 19, River Forest 11
Sectional 25 Second Round
Bremen 35, North Judson 0
Rochester 19, Lake Station 0
Sectional 25 Championship
Bremen 42, Rochester 0

Sectional 26 First Round
Central Noble 14, Mishawaka Marian 0
Eastside 28, Garrett 0
Jimtown 35, Prairie Heights 0
Fairfield 35, West Noble 7
Sectional 26 Second Round
Central Noble 23, Eastside 8
Jimtown 22, Fairfield 14
Sectional 26 Championship
Jimtown 13, Central Noble 3

Sectional 27 First Round
Fort Wayne Luers 49, Woodlan 6

Churubusco 28, Heritage 24
Leo 28, Northfield 7
Manchester 21, Bluffton 14
Sectional 27 Second Round
Fort Wayne Luers 40, Churubusco 0
Leo 6, Manchester 0
Sectional 27 Championship
Leo 13, Fort Wayne Luers 0

Sectional 28 First Round
Lewis Cass 13, Eastern (Greentown) 6
Eastbrook 31, Taylor 0
Southwood 27, Oak Hill 21
Madison-Grant 14, Wabash 12
Sectional 28 Second Round
Lewis Cass 17, Eastbrook 15
Southwood 22, Madison-Grant 21
Sectional 28 Championship
Southwood 16, Lewis Cass 8

Sectional 29 First Round
Indpls. Chatard 28, Eastern Hancock 0
Westfield 26, Winchester 0
Indpls. Scecina 20, Tipton 7
Centerville 13, Frankton 10
Sectional 29 Second Round
Indpls. Chatard 28, Westfield 13
Indpls. Scecina 35, Centerville 19
Sectional 29 Championship
Indpls. Chatard 35, Indpls. Scecina 21

Sectional 30 First Round
North Montgomery 44, Delphi 18
Speedway 33, Cloverdale 0
Monrovia 12, Western Boone 6
Cascade 35, North Putnam 20
Sectional 30 Second Round
North Montgomery 44, Speedway 7
Monrovia 34, Cascade 6
Sectional 30 Championship
North Montgomery 40, Monrovia 0

Sectional 31 First Round
Brownstown Central 47, Indian Creek 6
Triton Central 56, Union County 6
Lawrenceburg 40, North Decatur 0
Clarksville 38, South Decatur 6
Sectional 31 Second Round
Brownstown Central 21, Triton Central 20
Lawrenceburg 36, Clarksville 26
Sectional 31 Championship
Brownstown Central 33, Lawrenceburg 21

Sectional 32 First Round
North Posey 28, South Spencer 6
Gibson Southern 41, North Knox 0
Southridge 26, Linton-Stockton 14
Paoli 21, Mitchell 6
Sectional 32 Second Round
North Posey 20, Gibson Southern 0
Southridge 38, Paoli 15
Sectional 32 Championship
North Posey 38, Southridge 28

Regional Championships
Bremen 21, Jimtown 0
Southwood 36, Leo 0
North Montgomery 44, Indpls. Chatard 9
North Posey 33, Brownstown Central 6

Semi-State Championships
Bremen 28, Southwood 6
North Montgomery 30, North Posey 23

State Championship
North Montgomery 20, Bremen 17

Class 1A
Sectional 33 First Round
Whiting 20, South Central (Union Mills) 12
Culver 27, North White 26
Tri-County 41, West Central 6
Sectional 33 Second Round
Tri-County 22, South Newton 14
Whiting 17, Culver 14
Sectional 33 Championship
Tri-County 43, Whiting 34

Sectional 34 First Round
North Miami 39, LaVille 0
Southern Wells 44, Fremont 0
Adams Central 28, Triton 14
Sectional 34 Second Round
Adams Central 21, South Adams 20, OT
Southern Wells 14, North Miami 12
Sectional 34 Championship
Adams Central 21, Southern Wells 17

Sectional 35 First Round
Carroll (Flora) 43, Clinton Prairie 0
Clinton Central 8, Lafayette Central Catholic 0
Pioneer 48, Caston 7
Sectional 35 Second Round
Carroll (Flora) 49, Clinton Central 0
Frontier 39, Pioneer 21
Sectional 35 Championship
Carroll (Flora) 28, Frontier 13

Sectional 36 First Round
Turkey Run 28, Fountain Central 20
Covington 26, North Vermillion 7
Rockville 15, Attica 0
Sectional 36 Second Round
Seeger 22, Rockville 0
Turkey Run 28, Covington 0
Sectional 36 Championship
Seeger 20, Turkey Run 14

Sectional 37 First Round
Tri-West 35, Park Tudor 0
Sheridan 36, Riverton Parke 7
Sectional 37 Second Round
Tri-West 34, Sheridan 19
South Putnam 21, Indpls. Ritter 15
Sectional 37 Championship
Tri-West 29, South Putnam 0

Sectional 38 First Round
Shenandoah 49, Northeastern 14
Hagerstown 26, Tri-Central 2
Wes-Del 14, Union City 6
Sectional 38 Second Round
Lapel 30, Wes-Del 6
Shenandoah 47, Hagerstown 8
Sectional 38 Championship
Lapel 18, Shenandoah 13

Sectional 39 First Round
Knightstown 12, West Washington 8
Tri 53, Cambridge City Lincoln 6
Sectional 39 Second Round
Milan 32, Edinburgh 6
Knightstown 26, Tri 12
Sectional 39 Championship
Milan 33, Knightstown 28

Sectional 40 First Round
Springs Valley 34, Union (Dugger) 6
Wood Memorial 34, Perry Central 20
Tecumseh 49, North Daviess 0
Sectional 40 Second Round
Tecumseh 56, North Central (Farmersburg) 7
Springs Valley 34, Wood Memorial 21
Sectional 40 Championship
Tecumseh 54, Springs Valley 0

Regional Championships
Tri-County 8, Adams Central 0
Carroll (Flora) 34, Seeger 6
Tri-West 32, Lapel 8
Tecumseh 28, Milan 0

Semi-State Championships
Carroll (Flora) 35, Tri-County 6
Tri-West 21, Tecumseh 0

State Championship
Carroll (Flora) 26, Tri-West 13

1996
Class 5A
Sectional 1 First Round
Portage 49, Crown Point 7
Valparaiso 44, Gary Wallace 14
Merrillville 21, Lake Central 14
Sectional 1 Second Round
Portage 35, Merrillville 13
Valparaiso 38, East Chicago Central 35
Sectional 1 Championship
Portage 34, Valparaiso 0

Sectional 2 First Round
Chesterton 31, Michigan City 0
Elkhart Central 7, LaPorte 0
Penn 42, Mishawaka 10
South Bend Riley 28, Warsaw 14
Sectional 2 Second Round
Chesterton 21, Elkhart Central 14
Penn 58, South Bend Riley 9
Sectional 2 Championship
Penn 41, Chesterton 14

Sectional 3 First Round
Fort Wayne Snider 42, Fort Wayne South 14
Homestead 33, Huntington North 30, OT
Fort Wayne Northrop 76, Jay County 20
Fort Wayne North 48, Marion 17
Sectional 3 Second Round
Homestead 55, Fort Wayne Northrop 21
Fort Wayne Snider 24, Fort Wayne North 14
Sectional 3 Championship
Fort Wayne Snider 41, Homestead 10

Sectional 4 First Round
Carmel 48, Harrison (West Lafayette) 14
Indpls. Broad Ripple 20, Lafayette Jefferson 15
Kokomo 41, Noblesville 38
North Central (Indpls.) 38, Pike 3
Sectional 4 Second Round
Carmel 70, Indpls. Broad Ripple 6
Kokomo 36, North Central (Indpls.) 34
Sectional 4 Championship
Carmel 46, Kokomo 7

Sectional 5 First Round
Franklin Central 42, Perry Meridian 29
Ben Davis 61, Indpls. Manual 16
Indpls. Northwest 34, Southport 7
Sectional 5 Second Round
Indpls. Northwest 28, Franklin Central 14
Ben Davis 61, Indpls. Tech 20
Sectional 5 Championship
Ben Davis 48, Indpls. Northwest 6

Sectional 6 First Round
Lawrence North 35, Muncie Central 12
Richmond 41, Connersville 22
Lawrence Central 27, Warren Central 21, OT
Sectional 6 Second Round
Richmond 34, Indpls. Arlington 31
Lawrence Central 21, Lawrence North 7
Sectional 6 Championship
Lawrence Central 12, Richmond 0

Sectional 7 First Round
Bloomington South 51, Bloomington North 6

Center Grove 38, Decatur Central 22
Martinsville 56, Columbus North 0
Terre Haute North 40, Terre Haute South 9
Sectional 7 Second Round
Martinsville 34, Bloomington South 7
Terre Haute North 30, Center Grove 8
Sectional 7 Championship
Martinsville 27, Terre Haute North 0

Sectional 8 First Round
Jeffersonville 20, Bedford North Lawrence 6
Castle 18, Evansville Central 14
Evansville Harrison 28, Evansville North 21
Evansville Reitz 30, New Albany 0
Sectional 8 Second Round
Evansville Harrison 45, Evansville Reitz 38
Castle 28, Jeffersonville 17
Sectional 8 Championship
Evansville Harrison 33, Castle 27

Regional Championships
Penn 24, Portage 21
Carmel 20, Fort Wayne Snider 17
Ben Davis 21, Lawrence Central 12
Martinsville 61, Evansville Harrison 28

Semi-State Championships
Penn 28, Carmel 7
Ben Davis 55, Martinsville 35

State Championship
Penn 17, Ben Davis 14

Class 4A
Sectional 9 First Round
Hammond 30, Hammond Morton 0
Highland 15, Kankakee Valley 0
Griffith 33, Lowell 21
Munster 28, Hammond Gavit 0
Sectional 9 Second Round
Griffith 56, Hammond 20
Munster 56, Highland 7
Sectional 9 Championship
Munster 7, Griffith 0

Sectional 10 First Round
South Bend Adams 26, Gary Mann 12
South Bend Clay 40, Gary West 6
S.B. Washington 26, Gary Wirt 20, 2 OT
Hobart 69, South Bend LaSalle 6
Sectional 10 Second Round
Hobart 63, South Bend Adams 8
South Bend Clay 27, S.B. Washington 0
Sectional 10 Championship
Hobart 56, South Bend Clay 0

Sectional 11 First Round
Elkhart Memorial 56, Columbia City 0
Wawasee 35, East Noble 13

Goshen 35, DeKalb 29
Plymouth 19, Concord 6
Sectional 11 Second Round
Plymouth 16, Elkhart Memorial 14
Goshen 28, Wawasee 11
Sectional 11 Championship
Goshen 10, Plymouth 0

Sectional 12 First Round
Fort Wayne Wayne 42, Carroll (Fort Wayne) 3
Bellmont 32, Fort Wayne Elmhurst 6
Fort Wayne Concordia 42, Logansport 0
Delta 43, Peru 7
Sectional 12 Second Round
Delta 42, Bellmont 13
Fort Wayne Wayne 48, Fort Wayne Concordia 7
Sectional 12 Championship
Fort Wayne Wayne 48, Delta 6

Sectional 13 First Round
Avon 20, Mooresville 17
Greenfield-Central 17, Greenwood 14
Indpls. Cathedral 41, Franklin 0
Brownsburg 19, Plainfield 14
Sectional 13 Second Round
Indpls. Cathedral 34, Brownsburg 12
Avon 40, Greenfield-Central 0
Sectional 13 Championship
Indpls. Cathedral 21, Avon 6

Sectional 14 First Round
Pendleton Heights 49, Anderson Highland 9
McCutcheon 21, Anderson 12
Hamilton Southeastern 54, Muncie South 18
Anderson Madison-Heights 26, New Castle 13
Sectional 14 Second Round
McCutcheon 43, Anderson Madison-Heights 13
Hamilton Southeastern 40, Pendleton Heights 10
Sectional 14 Championship
McCutcheon 25, Hamilton Southeastern 13

Sectional 15 First Round
East Central 21, Rushville 6
Franklin County 41, Jennings County 6
Columbus East 35, Madison 0
South Dearborn 62, Shelbyville 15
Sectional 15 Second Round
Franklin County 29, Columbus East 0
East Central 51, South Dearborn 20
Sectional 15 Championship
East Central 14, Franklin County 8

Sectional 16 First Round
Boonville 21, Northview 0
Evansville Bosse 49, Seymour 42
Floyd Central 13, Owen Valley 8
Vincennes Lincoln 41, Mount Vernon 8
Sectional 16 Second Round
Evansville Bosse 40, Floyd Central 26

Vincennes Lincoln 30, Boonville 0
Sectional 16 Championship
Vincennes Lincoln 48, Evansville Bosse 7

Regional Championships
Hobart 10, Munster 0
Goshen 30, Fort Wayne Wayne 21
Indpls. Cathedral 33, McCutcheon 3
Vincennes Lincoln 12, East Central 10

Semi-State Championships
Hobart 45, Goshen 6
Indpls. Cathedral 21, Vincennes Lincoln 19

State Championship
Indpls. Cathedral 27, Hobart 7

Class 3A
Sectional 17 First Round
Andrean 31, Calumet 12
Hammond Noll 25, Benton Central 24
Rensselaer Central 42, Knox 14
Twin Lakes 30, Hammond Clark 6
Sectional 17 Second Round
Andrean 46, Hammond Noll 14
Twin Lakes 25, Rensselaer Central 6
Sectional 17 Championship
Andrean 32, Twin Lakes 15

Sectional 18 First Round
Northridge 21, Angola 14
S.B. St. Joseph 28, Culver Military Academy 12
NorthWood 84, New Prairie 6
Lakeland 10, Tippecanoe Valley 8
Sectional 18 Second Round
Lakeland 35, Northridge 7
NorthWood 16, S.B. St. Joseph 7
Sectional 18 Championship
NorthWood 43, Lakeland 12

Sectional 19 First Round
Whitko 43, Blackford 6
Fort Wayne Dwenger 42, New Haven 0
Maconaquah 27, Norwell 21
Harding (Fort Wayne) 60, Mississinewa 0
Sectional 19 Second Round
Fort Wayne Dwenger 35, Maconaquah 0
Harding (Fort Wayne) 55, Whitko 8
Sectional 19 Championship
Fort Wayne Dwenger 44, Harding (F.W.) 23

Sectional 20 First Round
Northwestern 75, Alexandria 6
West Lafayette 40, Elwood 3
Frankfort 27, Western 20
Yorktown 21, Hamilton Heights 13
Sectional 20 Second Round
Frankfort 12, Northwestern 7
Yorktown 35, West Lafayette 13

Sectional 20 Championship
Frankfort 14, Yorktown 7

Sectional 21 First Round
Danville 48, South Vermillion 7
Lebanon 48, Greencastle 41
Zionsville 48, Southmont 14
West Vigo 35, Crawfordsville 13
Sectional 21 Second Round
West Vigo 8, Lebanon 0
Zionsville 39, Danville 13
Sectional 21 Championship
Zionsville 42, West Vigo 0

Sectional 22 First Round
Roncalli 35, Batesville 0
Beech Grove 49, Whiteland 20
Mount Vernon (Fortville) 49, Brebeuf Jesuit 0
Greensburg 28, New Palestine 27, OT
Sectional 22 Second Round
Mount Vernon (Fortville) 52, Greensburg 12
Roncalli 34, Beech Grove 8
Sectional 22 Championship
Roncalli 35, Mount Vernon (Fortville) 21

Sectional 23 First Round
Edgewood 36, Brown County 26
Providence 28, Corydon Central 6
North Harrison 20, Salem 19, 2 OT
Charlestown 36, Tell City 28, OT
Sectional 23 Second Round
Edgewood 34, Providence 28
Charlestown 65, North Harrison 20
Sectional 23 Championship
Charlestown 32, Edgewood 16

Sectional 24 First Round
Evansville Mater Dei 39, Sullivan 20
Heritage Hills 24, Jasper 21
Evansville Memorial 82, Pike Central 21
Princeton 38, Washington 26
Sectional 24 Second Round
Evansville Memorial 42, Evansville Mater Dei 14
Heritage Hills 47, Princeton 20
Sectional 24 Championship
Heritage Hills 61, Evansville Memorial 21

Regional Championships
NorthWood 42, Andrean 7
Fort Wayne Dwenger 28, Frankfort 7
Zionsville 14, Roncalli 7
Heritage Hills 62, Charlestown 14

Semi-State Championships
Fort Wayne Dwenger 27, NorthWood 13
Zionsville 20, Heritage Hills 19

State Championship

Zionsville 14, Fort Wayne Dwenger 7

Class 2A
Sectional 25 First Round
Bremen 40, Lake Station 24
John Glenn 19, North Newton 6
North Judson 48, River Forest 20
Rochester 48, Winamac 14
Sectional 25 Second Round
North Judson 28, Bremen 14
Rochester 26, John Glenn 10
Sectional 25 Championship
North Judson 20, Rochester 7

Sectional 26 First Round
Garrett 18, Eastside 10
Jimtown 55, West Noble 0
Fairfield 20, Mishawaka Marian 7
Prairie Heights 30, Central Noble 19
Sectional 26 Second Round
Garrett 21, Fairfield 18
Jimtown 42, Prairie Heights 0
Sectional 26 Championship
Jimtown 50, Garrett 8

Sectional 27 First Round
Northfield 24, Bluffton 6
Fort Wayne Luers 45, Churubusco 7
Leo 23, Heritage 7
Woodlan 37, Manchester 26
Sectional 27 Second Round
Fort Wayne Luers 34, Leo 18
Woodlan 20, Northfield 6
Sectional 27 Championship
Fort Wayne Luers 37, Woodlan 8

Sectional 28 First Round
Wabash 41, Eastbrook 35, 2 OT
Eastern (Greentown) 35, Southwood 28
Oak Hill 35, Lewis Cass 8
Madison-Grant 31, Taylor 0
Sectional 28 Second Round
Wabash 20, Madison-Grant 14, OT
Oak Hill 14, Eastern (Greentown) 7
Sectional 28 Championship
Oak Hill 17, Wabash 14

Sectional 29 First Round
Eastern Hancock 39, Centerville 16
Indpls. Chatard 34, Frankton 6
Tipton 18, Winchester 15
Westfield 27, Indpls. Scecina 14
Sectional 29 Second Round
Westfield 26, Eastern Hancock 6
Indpls. Chatard 17, Tipton 14
Sectional 29 Championship
Indpls. Chatard 29, Westfield 13

Sectional 30 First Round
Speedway 50, Cascade 12
Western Boone 24, Delphi 8
North Montgomery 67, Monrovia 18
Cloverdale 41, North Putnam 20
Sectional 30 Second Round
Speedway 42, Cloverdale 6
North Montgomery 48, Western Boone 12
Sectional 30 Championship
North Montgomery 42, Speedway 7

Sectional 31 First Round
Brownstown Central 54, North Decatur 14
Clarksville 36, Indian Creek 2
Lawrenceburg 61, South Decatur 14
Triton Central 61, Union County 27
Sectional 31 Second Round
Brownstown Central 55, Clarksville 35
Triton Central 49, Lawrenceburg 24
Sectional 31 Championship
Brownstown Central 46, Triton Central 20

Sectional 32 First Round
North Posey 42, Mitchell 14
Gibson Southern 34, Paoli 0
South Spencer 21, Linton-Stockton 6
Southridge 32, North Knox 6
Sectional 32 Second Round
Southridge 14, Gibson Southern 0
North Posey 35, South Spencer 0
Sectional 32 Championship
North Posey 35, Southridge 0

Regional Championships
Jimtown 23, North Judson 7
Fort Wayne Luers 49, Oak Hill 28
North Montgomery 41, Indpls. Chatard 13
North Posey 37, Brownstown Central 12

Semi-State Championships
Fort Wayne Luers 17, Jimtown 14
North Montgomery 29, North Posey 22

State Championship
North Montgomery 37, Fort Wayne Luers 34

Class 1A
Sectional 33 First Round
Tri-County 28, North White 7
South Newton 51, Culver 8
South Central (Union Mills) 26, West Central 16
Sectional 33 Second Round
Tri-County 27, South Central (Union Mills) 8
Whiting 7, South Newton 0
Sectional 33 Championship
Whiting 32, Tri-County 21

Sectional 34 First Round
LaVille 45, Adams Central 24
Triton 27, North Miami 0

South Adams 29, Southern Wells 8
Sectional 34 Second Round
LaVille 48, Fremont 13
South Adams 40, Triton 6
Sectional 34 Championship
South Adams 12, LaVille 0

Sectional 35 First Round
Carroll (Flora) 47, Clinton Prairie 0
Caston 13, Lafayette Central Catholic 7
Frontier 21, Clinton Central 6
Sectional 35 Second Round
Frontier 37, Caston 20
Carroll (Flora) 35, Pioneer 21
Sectional 35 Championship
Carroll (Flora) 16, Frontier 13

Sectional 36 First Round
North Vermillion 14, Covington 6
Fountain Central 35, Turkey Run 8
Seeger 54, Attica 14
Sectional 36 Second Round
Fountain Central 39, North Vermillion 6
Seeger 20, Rockville 7
Sectional 36 Championship
Fountain Central 6, Seeger 0

Sectional 37 First Round
Sheridan 49, Park Tudor 14
Tri-West 35, South Putnam 7
Sectional 37 Second Round
Indpls. Ritter 34, Riverton Parke 14
Tri-West 13, Sheridan 7, OT
Sectional 37 Championship
Tri-West 27, Indpls. Ritter 0

Sectional 38 First Round
Lapel 44, Tri-Central 39
Shenandoah 20, Northeastern 15
Hagerstown 27, Union City 21
Sectional 38 Second Round
Shenandoah 38, Lapel 24
Hagerstown 34, Wes-Del 13
Sectional 38 Championship
Hagerstown 30, Shenandoah 13

Sectional 39 First Round
Milan 21, Knightstown 0
Tri 54, Edinburgh 8
Sectional 39 Second Round
Milan 38, Tri 26
West Washington 41, Cambridge City 18
Sectional 39 Championship
Milan 39, West Washington 12

Sectional 40 First Round
Springs Valley 55, North Central (Farm.) 12
North Daviess 15, Union (Dugger) 13
Perry Central 42, Tecumseh 7

Sectional 40 Second Round
Springs Valley 28, Perry Central 13
Wood Memorial 19, North Daviess 7
Sectional 40 Championship
Wood Memorial 34, Springs Valley 12

Regional Championships
Whiting 12, South Adams 7
Carroll (Flora) 34, Fountain Central 3
Tri-West 56, Hagerstown 6
Milan 41, Wood Memorial 12

Semi-State Championships
Carroll (Flora) 48, Whiting 7
Tri-West 28, Milan 0

State Championship
Tri-West 37, Carroll (Flora) 14

1997
Class 5A
Sectional 1 First Round
Crown Point 48, Gary Wallace 6
Lake Central 49, East Chicago Central 42
Portage 54, Gary Roosevelt 6
Valparaiso 21, Merrillville 7
Sectional 1 Second Round
Portage 15, Lake Central 14
Valparaiso 21, Crown Point 0
Sectional 1 Championship
Valparaiso 31, Portage 22

Sectional 2 First Round
Michigan City 26, LaPorte 9
Penn 42, Chesterton 10
South Bend Riley 26, Mishawaka 6
Sectional 2 Second Round
South Bend Riley 13, Elkhart Central 9
Penn 35, Michigan City 0
Sectional 2 Championship
Penn 24, South Bend Riley 13

Sectional 3 First Round
Huntington North 7, Fort Wayne North 0
Fort Wayne South 28, Fort Wayne Northrop 21
Fort Wayne Snider 55, Marion 0
Homestead 49, Warsaw 0
Sectional 3 Second Round
Fort Wayne Snider 42, Homestead 29
Fort Wayne South 47, Huntington North 6
Sectional 3 Championship
Fort Wayne Snider 52, Fort Wayne South 16

Sectional 4 First Round
Kokomo 28, Anderson 20
Harrison (W.L.) 34, Anderson Highland 21
Noblesville 28, Lafayette Jefferson 27, OT
North Central (Indpls.) 34, Carmel 16
Sectional 4 Second Round

North Central (Indpls.) 24, Kokomo 7
Noblesville 45, Harrison (West Lafayette) 14
Sectional 4 Championship
Noblesville 7, North Central (Indpls.) 6

Sectional 5 First Round
Franklin Central 27, Connersville 12
Indpls. Arlington 13, Lawrence North 7
Lawrence Central 35, Indpls. Broad Ripple 14
Richmond 41, Warren Central 19
Sectional 5 Second Round
Franklin Central 42, Richmond 14
Lawrence Central 27, Indpls. Arlington 13
Sectional 5 Championship
Lawrence Central 34, Franklin Central 20

Sectional 6 First Round
Ben Davis 31, Decatur Central 21
Indpls. Northwest 25, Southport 9
Perry Meridian 32, Indpls. Tech 6
Pike 33, Indpls. Manual 20
Sectional 6 Second Round
Ben Davis 28, Indpls. Northwest 6
Perry Meridian 21, Pike 14
Sectional 6 Championship
Ben Davis 34, Perry Meridian 6

Sectional 7 First Round
Bloomington South 37, Terre Haute North 6
Bedford North Lawrence 10, Columbus North 7
Martinsville 22, Terre Haute South 20
Sectional 7 Second Round
Martinsville 38, Bedford North Lawrence 22
Bloomington South 44, Center Grove 0
Sectional 7 Championship
Bloomington South 46, Martinsville 6

Sectional 8 First Round
Evansville Harrison 34, Castle 12
Evansville Central 48, New Albany 23
Evansville North 21, Jeffersonville 20
Sectional 8 Second Round
Evansville Harrison 48, Evansville North 7
Evansville Central 28, Evansville Reitz 7
Sectional 8 Championship
Evansville Harrison 42, Evansville Central 7

Regional Championships
Penn 28, Valparaiso 14
Fort Wayne Snider 63, Noblesville 14
Ben Davis 33, Lawrence Central 13
Bloomington South 31, Evansville Harrison 14

Semi-State Championships
Penn 16, Fort Wayne Snider 13, OT
Bloomington South 28, Ben Davis 7

State Championship
Penn 21, Bloomington South 20

Class 4A
Sectional 9 First Round
Hammond 55, Hammond Morton 3
Highland 35, Hammond Clark 14
Lowell 24, Hammond Gavit 6
Griffith 21, Munster 6
Sectional 9 Second Round
Griffith 63, Highland 6
Hammond 24, Lowell 20
Sectional 9 Championship
Griffith 49, Hammond 7

Sectional 10 First Round
Gary Wirt 25, Kankakee Valley 13
Hobart 28, McCutcheon 20
Plymouth 53, Gary West 14
Sectional 10 Second Round
Hobart 42, Plymouth 6
Gary Wirt 30, Logansport 24
Sectional 10 Championship
Hobart 63, Gary Wirt 18

Sectional 11 First Round
Elkhart Memorial 17, Concord 13
Goshen 56, South Bend Adams 0
South Bend LaSalle 15, Wawasee 14
S.B. Washington 32, South Bend Clay 17
Sectional 11 Second Round
Elkhart Memorial 21, Goshen 19
South Bend LaSalle 22, S.B. Washington 21
Sectional 11 Championship
Elkhart Memorial 35, South Bend LaSalle 0

Sectional 12 First Round
DeKalb 14, Bellmont 0
Carroll (Fort Wayne) 43, F.W. Elmhurst 14
Fort Wayne Dwenger 14, Columbia City 0
Fort Wayne Wayne 43, East Noble 6
Sectional 12 Second Round
Fort Wayne Dwenger 31, Carroll (F.W.) 7
Fort Wayne Wayne 39, DeKalb 6
Sectional 12 Championship
Fort Wayne Dwenger 17, Fort Wayne Wayne 14

Sectional 13 First Round
Hamilton Southeastern 42, New Castle 0
Greenfield-Central 14, Jay County 13
Pendleton Heights 38, Muncie South 0
Sectional 13 Second Round
Pendleton Heights 36, Greenfield-Central 0
Hamilton Southeastern 48, Muncie Central 28
Sectional 13 Championship
Hamilton Southeastern 36, Pendleton Heights 25

Sectional 14 First Round
South Dearborn 28, Bloomington North 0
East Central 35, Jennings County 14
Seymour 35, Columbus East 6

Shelbyville 21, Madison 7
Sectional 14 Second Round
East Central 42, Shelbyville 23
Seymour 17, South Dearborn 10
Sectional 14 Championship
Seymour 24, East Central 22

Sectional 15 First Round
Brownsburg 31, Franklin 14
Avon 38, Greenwood 6
Roncalli 14, Indpls. Cathedral 10
Mooresville 24, Plainfield 14
Sectional 15 Second Round
Avon 37, Mooresville 6
Roncalli 14, Brownsburg 13
Sectional 15 Championship
Avon 27, Roncalli 13

Sectional 16 First Round
Vincennes Lincoln 50, Evansville Bosse 14
Boonville 48, Northview 18
Floyd Central 30, Owen Valley 6
Sectional 16 Second Round
Jasper 26, Boonville 7
Vincennes Lincoln 42, Floyd Central 26
Sectional 16 Championship
Vincennes Lincoln 18, Jasper 14

Regional Championships
Griffith 35, Hobart 21
Fort Wayne Dwenger 26, Elkhart Memorial 6
Hamilton Southeastern 35, Seymour 21
Avon 49, Vincennes Lincoln 14

Semi-State Championships
Griffith 35, Fort Wayne Dwenger 21
Hamilton Southeastern 20, Avon 13

State Championship
Griffith 49, Hamilton Southeastern 7

Class 3A
Sectional 17 First Round
Hammond Noll 40, Calumet 0
Andrean 42, Culver Military Academy 6
Mishawaka Marian 34, New Prairie 0
S.B. St. Joseph 48, Gary Mann 0
Sectional 17 Second Round
Andrean 21, Mishawaka Marian 19
S.B. St. Joseph 49, Hammond Noll 10
Sectional 17 Championship
Andrean 21, S.B. St. Joseph 13

Sectional 18 First Round
Frankfort 41, Crawfordsville 6
Lebanon 38, Benton Central 6
Zionsville 28, West Lafayette 7
Sectional 18 Second Round
Twin Lakes 35, Frankfort 0

Lebanon 21, Zionsville 20, OT
Sectional 18 Championship
Lebanon 14, Twin Lakes 13

Sectional 19 First Round
NorthWood 42, Lakeland 13
Tippecanoe Valley 33, West Noble 22
Angola 21, Whitko 20, OT
Sectional 19 Second Round
NorthWood 27, Angola 21
Northridge 17, Tippecanoe Valley 0
Sectional 19 Championship
NorthWood 28, Northridge 0

Sectional 20 First Round
Fort Wayne Concordia 14, Mississinewa 9
Blackford 19, New Haven 13, OT
Norwell 49, Peru 28
Harding (Fort Wayne) 61, Western 27
Sectional 20 Second Round
Harding (Fort Wayne) 42, Fort Wayne Concordia 6
Norwell 17, Blackford 10
Sectional 20 Championship
Harding (Fort Wayne) 62, Norwell 34

Sectional 21 First Round
Delta 24, New Palestine 6
Hamilton Heights 36, Whiteland 6
Mount Vernon (Fortville) 44, Elwood 3
Yorktown 21, Rushville 0
Sectional 21 Second Round
Delta 20, Hamilton Heights 6
Mount Vernon (Fortville) 6, Yorktown 5
Sectional 21 Championship
Mount Vernon (Fortville) 31, Delta 6

Sectional 22 First Round
Franklin County 10, Providence 0
Greensburg 50, Corydon Central 0
Batesville 42, North Harrison 6
Salem 8, Brown County 6
Sectional 22 Second Round
Franklin County 14, Batesville 7
Salem 25, Greensburg 20
Sectional 22 Championship
Franklin County 38, Salem 6

Sectional 23 First Round
Danville 42, Brebeuf Jesuit 0
Edgewood 52, Sullivan 30
Indpls. Chatard 51, South Vermillion 7
Beech Grove 14, West Vigo 6
Sectional 23 Second Round
Indpls. Chatard 58, Beech Grove 7
Danville 49, Edgewood 18
Sectional 23 Championship
Indpls. Chatard 63, Danville 21

Sectional 24 First Round
Heritage Hills 42, Princeton 7
Evansville Memorial 75, Pike Central 28
Tell City 37, Mount Vernon 0
Gibson Southern 39, Washington 16
Sectional 24 Second Round
Evansville Memorial 46, Gibson Southern 0
Heritage Hills 58, Tell City 0
Sectional 24 Championship
Heritage Hills 28, Evansville Memorial 14

Regional Championships
Andrean 20, Lebanon 6
Harding (Fort Wayne) 28, NorthWood 21
Franklin County 14, Mount Vernon (Fortville) 7
Indpls. Chatard 24, Heritage Hills 21

Semi-State Championships
Andrean 34, Harding (Fort Wayne) 27
Indpls. Chatard 19, Franklin County 8

State Championship
Indpls. Chatard 27, Andrean 23

Class 2A
Sectional 25 First Round
Bremen 49, Knox 0
John Glenn 24, North Judson 13
Lake Station 22, North Newton 12
Winamac 20, Rensselaer Central 17
Sectional 25 Second Round
Bremen 33, Lake Station 3
Winamac 27, John Glenn 21
Sectional 25 Championship
Bremen 27, Winamac 7

Sectional 26 First Round
Rochester 46, Eastern (Greentown) 14
Lewis Cass 34, Maconaquah 23
Northwestern 27, Delphi 26
Tipton 27, Taylor 6
Sectional 26 Second Round
Northwestern 31, Rochester 19
Tipton 41, Lewis Cass 12
Sectional 26 Championship
Northwestern 26, Tipton 23

Sectional 27 First Round
Leo 21, Eastside 7
Fort Wayne Luers 35, Garrett 14
Fairfield 36, Prairie Heights 20
Jimtown 41, Woodlan 12
Sectional 27 Second Round
Leo 31, Fairfield 22
Jimtown 21, Fort Wayne Luers 20
Sectional 27 Championship
Jimtown 31, Leo 14

Sectional 28 First Round
Eastbrook 31, Bluffton 16
Madison-Grant 20, Manchester 7
Heritage 47, Oak Hill 7
Southwood 47, Wabash 7
Sectional 28 Second Round
Southwood 53, Heritage 26
Eastbrook 35, Madison-Grant 21
Sectional 28 Championship
Eastbrook 31, Southwood 19

Sectional 29 First Round
Alexandria 42, Centerville 6
Speedway 35, Eastern Hancock 0
Indpls. Scecina 42, Northeastern 6
Westfield 41, Winchester 6
Sectional 29 Second Round
Speedway 31, Indpls. Scecina 0
Lawrenceburg 38, Union County 13
Sectional 29 Championship
Westfield 53, Speedway 22

Sectional 30 First Round
Clarksville 43, Triton Central 0
Union County 21, Indian Creek 19
Lawrenceburg 35, Charlestown 14
Sectional 30 Second Round
Westfield 30, Alexandria 6
Clarksville 43, Brownstown Central 19
Sectional 30 Championship
Clarksville 39, Lawrenceburg 13

Sectional 31 First Round
North Montgomery 17, South Putnam 14
North Putnam 31, Cascade 13
Southmont 49, Greencastle 0
Western Boone 55, Monrovia 21
Sectional 31 Second Round
North Montgomery 20, North Putnam 18
Western Boone 26, Southmont 20
Sectional 31 Championship
Western Boone 28, North Montgomery 21

Sectional 32 First Round
Evansville Mater Dei 47, Mitchell 8
North Posey 40, North Knox 6
South Spencer 38, Paoli 8
Sectional 32 Second Round
South Spencer 13, North Posey 6
Evansville Mater Dei 35, Southridge 13
Sectional 32 Championship
Evansville Mater Dei 34, South Spencer 6

Regional Championships
Bremen 22, Northwestern 6
Jimtown 21, Eastbrook 7
Clarksville 15, Westfield 14
Western Boone 39, Evansville Mater Dei 7

Semi-State Championships

Jimtown 35, Bremen 0
Clarksville 21, Western Boone 17

State Championship
Jimtown 63, Clarksville 0

Class 1A
Sectional 33 First Round
West Central 36, Culver 7
River Forest 21, Triton 14
Whiting 53, LaVille 0
Sectional 33 Second Round
River Forest 28, South Central (Union Mills) 22
Whiting 64, West Central 0
Sectional 33 Championship
Whiting 42, River Forest 3

Sectional 34 First Round
Carroll (Flora) 16, Tri-County 8
South Newton 35, Caston 0
North White 49, Frontier 0
Pioneer 36, Lafayette Central Catholic 16
Sectional 34 Second Round
Pioneer 34, North White 14
Carroll (Flora) 12, South Newton 7
Sectional 34 Championship
Pioneer 42, Carroll (Flora) 6

Sectional 35 First Round
Churubusco 10, Central Noble 6
Fremont 42, North Miami 8
Adams Central 25, South Adams 15
Southern Wells 27, Northfield 20
Sectional 35 Second Round
Adams Central 28, Churubusco 7
Fremont 27, Southern Wells 18
Sectional 35 Championship
Adams Central 20, Fremont 6

Sectional 36 First Round
Hagerstown 14, Cambridge City Lincoln 0
Frankton 40, Union City 6
Lapel 40, Wes-Del 17
Tri 26, Shenandoah 6
Sectional 36 Second Round
Hagerstown 36, Lapel 20
Frankton 39, Tri 20
Sectional 36 Championship
Hagerstown 20, Frankton 7

Sectional 37 First Round
Clinton Central 41, Cloverdale 12
Clinton Prairie 32, Tri-Central 26
Tri-West 20, Indpls. Ritter 0
Sectional 37 Second Round
Clinton Central 28, Clinton Prairie 7
Tri-West 48, Sheridan 6
Sectional 37 Championship
Clinton Central 44, Tri-West 34

Sectional 38 First Round
Knightstown 21, West Washington 8
Milan 41, Indiana Deaf 6
Park Tudor 21, North Decatur 13
South Decatur 50, Edinburgh 14
Sectional 38 Second Round
Knightstown 28, South Decatur 10
Park Tudor 21, Milan 17
Sectional 38 Championship
Knightstown 14, Park Tudor 13

Sectional 39 First Round
Seeger 6, Covington 3
Fountain Central 14, Attica 0
North Vermillion 26, Riverton Parke 8
Rockville 44, Turkey Run 0
Sectional 39 Second Round
Rockville 25, Fountain Central 7
Seeger 9, North Vermillion 6
Sectional 39 Championship
Rockville 7, Seeger 6

Sectional 40 First Round
North Central (Farm.) 28, Union (Dugger) 12
Perry Central 28, North Daviess 20
Linton-Stockton 16, Springs Valley 13
Tecumseh 31, Wood Memorial 22
Sectional 40 Second Round
Linton-Stockton 28, Tecumseh 7
Perry Central 35, North Central (Farm.) 26
Sectional 40 Championship
Linton-Stockton 35, Perry Central 12

Regional Championships
Pioneer 20, Whiting 17
Adams Central 30, Hagerstown 29
Knightstown 6, Clinton Central 0
Linton-Stockton 31, Rockville 6

Semi-State Championships
Pioneer 42, Adams Central 19
Knightstown 14, Linton-Stockton 7

State Championship
Pioneer 49, Knightstown 21

1998
Class 5A
Sectional 1 First Round
Lake Central 63, Crown Point 34
Valparaiso 44, Gary Roosevelt 0
Merrillville 23, East Chicago Central 8
Portage 54, Gary Wallace 0
Sectional 1 Second Round
Valparaiso 47, Lake Central 21
Portage 31, Merrillville 14
Sectional 1 Championship
Portage 20, Valparaiso 18

Sectional 2 First Round
Chesterton 21, South Bend Riley 15
Mishawaka 27, Michigan City 26
Penn 20, LaPorte 13
Sectional 2 Second Round
Penn 42, Chesterton 21
Elkhart Central 19, Mishawaka 14
Sectional 2 Championship
Penn 42, Elkhart Central 15

Sectional 3 First Round
Fort Wayne Northrop 44, Fort Wayne North 7
Homestead 35, Fort Wayne Snider 21
Huntington North 24, Fort Wayne South 21
Warsaw 46, Marion 20
Sectional 3 Second Round
Fort Wayne Northrop 17, Warsaw 10
Homestead 36, Huntington North 3
Sectional 3 Championship
Homestead 20, Fort Wayne Northrop 7

Sectional 4 First Round
Noblesville 39, Anderson 21
Lafayette Jefferson 27, Anderson Highland 14
Carmel 13, North Central (Indpls.) 10
Harrison (West Lafayette) 43, Kokomo 22
Sectional 4 Second Round
Noblesville 53, Harrison (West Lafayette) 0
Carmel 30, Lafayette Jefferson 14
Sectional 4 Championship
Carmel 35, Noblesville 21

Sectional 5 First Round
Richmond 87, Connersville 46
Lawrence North 14, Franklin Central 7
Indpls. Arlington 34, Indpls. Broad Ripple 26
Warren Central 28, Lawrence Central 25
Sectional 5 Second Round
Indpls. Arlington 58, Richmond 20
Warren Central 30, Lawrence North 0
Sectional 5 Championship
Indpls. Arlington 14, Warren Central 9

Sectional 6 First Round
Pike 33, Indpls. Manual 12
Ben Davis 38, Indpls. Northwest 20
Decatur Central 36, Indpls. Tech 8
Perry Meridian 24, Southport 17
Sectional 6 Second Round
Ben Davis 35, Pike 7
Decatur Central 37, Perry Meridian 23
Sectional 6 Championship
Ben Davis 38, Decatur Central 26

Sectional 7 First Round
Center Grove 35, Columbus North 7
Martinsville 42, Bedford North Lawrence 14
Terre Haute South 35, Terre Haute North 27

Sectional 7 Second Round
Bloomington South 14, Martinsville 7
Center Grove 30, Terre Haute South 28
Sectional 7 Championship
Bloomington South 41, Center Grove 14

Sectional 8 First Round
Evansville Harrison 42, Evansville Central 14
Castle 28, Evansville Reitz 10
Jeffersonville 49, New Albany 14
Sectional 8 Second Round
Jeffersonville 23, Castle 20
Evansville North 22, Evansville Harrison 21
Sectional 8 Championship
Jeffersonville 34, Evansville North 30

Regional Championships
Penn 23, Portage 21
Homestead 27, Carmel 3
Ben Davis 41, Indpls. Arlington 0
Bloomington South 42, Jeffersonville 28

Semi-State Championships
Homestead 9, Penn 7
Bloomington South 52, Ben Davis 21

State Championship
Bloomington South 35, Homestead 14

Class 4A
Sectional 9 First Round
Griffith 49, Hammond Morton 14
Hammond 16, Munster 0
Hammond Clark 21, Lowell 19
Highland 31, Hammond Gavit 6
Sectional 9 Second Round
Griffith 21, Hammond 0
Highland 39, Hammond Clark 14
Sectional 9 Championship
Griffith 35, Highland 0

Sectional 10 First Round
Kankakee Valley 49, Gary Wirt 0
Logansport 35, Gary West 0
Plymouth 37, McCutcheon 0
Sectional 10 Second Round
Plymouth 34, Hobart 6
Logansport 38, Kankakee Valley 0
Sectional 10 Championship
Plymouth 68, Logansport 21

Sectional 11 First Round
Concord 28, Goshen 14
South Bend Clay 20, S.B. Washington 13
Elkhart Memorial 27, South Bend LaSalle 0
South Bend Adams 20, Wawasee 6
Sectional 11 Second Round
Elkhart Memorial 21, South Bend Clay 7
Concord 40, South Bend Adams 20

Sectional 11 Championship
Concord 31, Elkhart Memorial 10

Sectional 12 First Round
Bellmont 12, DeKalb 0
Carroll (Fort Wayne) 51, F.W. Elmhurst 10
Columbia City 30, Fort Wayne Dwenger 24
Fort Wayne Wayne 28, East Noble 13
Sectional 12 Second Round
Carroll (Fort Wayne) 21, Bellmont 20
Columbia City 17, Fort Wayne Wayne 16
Sectional 12 Championship
Carroll (Fort Wayne) 34, Columbia City 7

Sectional 13 First Round
Pendleton Heights 76, Greenfield-Central 14
Muncie Central 49, New Castle 6
Hamilton Southeastern 61, Muncie South 23
Sectional 13 Second Round
Hamilton Southeastern 47, Muncie Central 0
Pendleton Heights 35, Jay County 7
Sectional 13 Championship
Hamilton Southeastern 41, Pendleton Heights 7

Sectional 14 First Round
Bloomington North 42, Columbus East 5
East Central 39, Jennings County 10
South Dearborn 14, Madison 6
Seymour 56, Shelbyville 15
Sectional 14 Second Round
East Central 38, Bloomington North 6
Seymour 38, South Dearborn 21
Sectional 14 Championship
East Central 27, Seymour 14

Sectional 15 First Round
Roncalli 21, Brownsburg 3
Avon 47, Franklin 17
Indpls. Cathedral 68, Greenwood 31
Plainfield 19, Mooresville 0
Sectional 15 Second Round
Avon 10, Roncalli 7
Indpls. Cathedral 28, Plainfield 14
Sectional 15 Championship
Indpls. Cathedral 27, Avon 11

Sectional 16 First Round
Floyd Central 33, Boonville 6
Jasper 13, Owen Valley 0
Evansville Bosse 34, Vincennes Lincoln 13
Sectional 16 Second Round
Jasper 28, Evansville Bosse 7
Floyd Central 61, Northview 7
Sectional 16 Championship
Floyd Central 26, Jasper 24

Regional Championships
Plymouth 32, Griffith 0
Concord 35, Carroll (Fort Wayne) 28, OT
East Central 29, Hamilton Southeastern 26
Indpls. Cathedral 22, Floyd Central 12

Semi-State Championships
Concord 35, Plymouth 14
Indpls. Cathedral 14, East Central 13

State Championship
Indpls. Cathedral 38, Concord 7

Class 3A
Sectional 17 First Round
Andrean 42, Culver Military Academy 14
Mishawaka Marian 42, Gary Mann 0
Calumet 32, Hammond Noll 31
S.B. St. Joseph 49, New Prairie 22
Sectional 17 Second Round
Mishawaka Marian 42, Calumet 0
Andrean 21, S.B. St. Joseph 0
Sectional 17 Championship
Andrean 28, Mishawaka Marian 14

Sectional 18 First Round
Frankfort 23, Crawfordsville 17
Twin Lakes 28, Lebanon 21
Zionsville 13, Benton Central 10
Sectional 18 Second Round
Twin Lakes 35, West Lafayette 25
Zionsville 12, Frankfort 7
Sectional 18 Championship
Twin Lakes 27, Zionsville 6

Sectional 19 First Round
West Noble 27, Lakeland 26
Northridge 13, Tippecanoe Valley 12
NorthWood 42, Angola 21
Sectional 19 Second Round
NorthWood 40, Northridge 7
Whitko 44, West Noble 22
Sectional 19 Championship
NorthWood 49, Whitko 14

Sectional 20 First Round
Mississinewa 47, Blackford 7
Peru 42, Fort Wayne Concordia 28
Harding (Fort Wayne) 45, Norwell 21
New Haven 25, Western 3
Sectional 20 Second Round
Harding (Fort Wayne) 47, Mississinewa 20
Peru 25, New Haven 6
Sectional 20 Championship
Harding (Fort Wayne) 63, Peru 7

Sectional 21 First Round
Delta 48, Whiteland 25
Elwood 10, Hamilton Heights 0
New Palestine 35, Rushville 21
Yorktown 10, Mount Vernon (Fortville) 7
Sectional 21 Second Round

Delta 10, New Palestine 6
Yorktown 22, Elwood 0
Sectional 21 Championship
Yorktown 14, Delta 10

Sectional 22 First Round
Batesville 40, Brown County 14
Greensburg 22, Corydon Central 8
Franklin County 55, North Harrison 12
Providence 35, Salem 20
Sectional 22 Second Round
Franklin County 43, Batesville 8
Providence 59, Greensburg 14
Sectional 22 Championship
Franklin County 14, Providence 0

Sectional 23 First Round
Brebeuf Jesuit 37, Beech Grove 0
Indpls. Chatard 27, South Vermillion 6
Danville 42, Sullivan 21
Edgewood 25, West Vigo 14
Sectional 23 Second Round
Danville 14, Brebeuf Jesuit 0
Indpls. Chatard 16, Edgewood 13, OT
Sectional 23 Championship
Indpls. Chatard 50, Danville 14

Sectional 24 First Round
Evansville Memorial 34, Princeton 6
Tell City 35, Mount Vernon 16
Heritage Hills 62, Pike Central 7
Gibson Southern 8, Washington 6
Sectional 24 Second Round
Evansville Memorial 35, Heritage Hills 28
Gibson Southern 28, Tell City 14
Sectional 24 Championship
Evansville Memorial 55, Gibson Southern 34

Regional Championships
Andrean 13, Twin Lakes 10
NorthWood 18, Harding (Fort Wayne) 7
Franklin County 47, Yorktown 7
Indpls. Chatard 48, Evansville Memorial 14

Semi-State Championships
NorthWood 14, Andrean 12
Indpls. Chatard 24, Franklin County 18

State Championship
Indpls. Chatard 23, NorthWood 6

Class 2A
Sectional 25 First Round
John Glenn 22, Bremen 15
North Judson 41, Knox 20
Lake Station 48, North Newton 12
Winamac 26, Rensselaer Central 20
Sectional 25 Second Round
Lake Station 12, John Glenn 6

North Judson 21, Winamac 6
Sectional 25 Championship
Lake Station 27, North Judson 19

Sectional 26 First Round
Eastern (Greentown) 32, Lewis Cass 7
Maconaquah 28, Northwestern 6
Rochester 31, Tipton 29
Delphi 18, Taylor 16
Sectional 26 Second Round
Rochester 52, Delphi 20
Maconaquah 21, Eastern (Greentown) 13
Sectional 26 Championship
Rochester 40, Maconaquah 7

Sectional 27 First Round
Eastside 33, Garrett 14
Fort Wayne Luers 55, Fairfield 10
Jimtown 38, Woodlan 13
Leo 44, Prairie Heights 6
Sectional 27 Second Round
Fort Wayne Luers 40, Leo 0
Jimtown 45, Eastside 7
Sectional 27 Championship
Jimtown 63, Fort Wayne Luers 21

Sectional 28 First Round
Eastbrook 48, Bluffton 19
Heritage 30, Southwood 24
Manchester 34, Madison-Grant 0
Oak Hill 30, Wabash 0
Sectional 28 Second Round
Heritage 54, Eastbrook 19
Manchester 38, Oak Hill 7
Sectional 28 Championship
Heritage 30, Manchester 23

Sectional 29 First Round
Alexandria 56, Northeastern 21
Indpls. Scecina 28, Eastern Hancock 6
Speedway 37, Centerville 7
Westfield 41, Winchester 12
Sectional 29 Second Round
Speedway 31, Indpls. Scecina 28
Westfield 35, Alexandria 7
Sectional 29 Championship
Speedway 34, Westfield 0

Sectional 30 First Round
Lawrenceburg 43, Brownstown Central 22
Charlestown 36, Clarksville 28
Union County 36, Triton Central 8
Sectional 30 Second Round
Union County 45, Indian Creek 19
Lawrenceburg 47, Charlestown 14
Sectional 30 Championship
Lawrenceburg 21, Union County 6

Sectional 31 First Round

North Montgomery 48, Greencastle 32
North Putnam 32, South Putnam 13
Southmont 28, Cascade 15
Western Boone 70, Monrovia 7
Sectional 31 Second Round
Southmont 34, North Putnam 23
Western Boone 40, North Montgomery 22
Sectional 31 Championship
Western Boone 47, Southmont 14

Sectional 32 First Round
North Posey 54, Mitchell 0
Paoli 34, Southridge 31
Evansville Mater Dei 42, South Spencer 6
Sectional 32 Second Round
Evansville Mater Dei 35, Paoli 7
North Posey 40, North Knox 0
Sectional 32 Championship
Evansville Mater Dei 40, North Posey 20

Regional Championships
Rochester 41, Lake Station 6
Jimtown 35, Heritage 6
Speedway 24, Lawrenceburg 14
Western Boone 28, Evansville Mater Dei 21

Semi-State Championships
Jimtown 23, Rochester 6
Western Boone 33, Speedway 21

State Championship
Jimtown 28, Western Boone 0

Class 1A
Sectional 33 First Round
Culver 35, Triton 14
Whiting 56, River Forest 0
South Central (Union Mills) 48, LaVille 27
Sectional 33 Second Round
West Central 35, Culver 14
Whiting 35, South Central (Union Mills) 6
Sectional 33 Championship
West Central 14, Whiting 10

Sectional 34 First Round
Pioneer 41, Caston 6
Carroll (Flora) 35, Frontier 14
Lafayette Central Catholic 53, Tri-County 49
North White 48, South Newton 8
Sectional 34 Second Round
Lafayette Central Catholic 14, Carroll (Flora) 7
North White 21, Pioneer 0
Sectional 34 Championship
North White 9, Lafayette Central Catholic 6, OT

Sectional 35 First Round
Central Noble 27, Churubusco 13
Fremont 35, North Miami 14
Adams Central 36, Northfield 16

Southern Wells 20, South Adams 14
Sectional 35 Second Round
Adams Central 15, Southern Wells 14
Central Noble 17, Fremont 13
Sectional 35 Championship
Adams Central 26, Central Noble 24

Sectional 36 First Round
Hagerstown 36, Cambridge City Lincoln 6
Wes-Del 35, Lapel 21
Frankton 47, Shenandoah 0
Union City 41, Tri 28
Sectional 36 Second Round
Frankton 48, Wes-Del 6
Union City 8, Hagerstown 7
Sectional 36 Championship
Frankton 28, Union City 12

Sectional 37 First Round
Clinton Central 49, Clinton Prairie 30
Sheridan 55, Cloverdale 0
Tri-West 70, Tri-Central 12
Sectional 37 Second Round
Indpls. Ritter 32, Clinton Central 28
Sheridan 35, Tri-West 0
Sectional 37 Championship
Sheridan 48, Indpls. Ritter 21

Sectional 38 First Round
North Decatur 50, Edinburgh 21
Indiana Deaf 22, South Decatur 21
Knightstown 34, Milan 7
West Washington 50, Park Tudor 20
Sectional 38 Second Round
Knightstown 7, West Washington 6
North Decatur 52, Indiana Deaf 22
Sectional 38 Championship
North Decatur 7, Knightstown 6

Sectional 39 First Round
Attica 40, North Vermillion 0
Covington 33, Turkey Run 0
Fountain Central 47, Riverton Parke 13
Rockville 40, Seeger 0
Sectional 39 Second Round
Attica 20, Covington 0
Fountain Central 16, Rockville 7
Sectional 39 Championship
Fountain Central 29, Attica 6

Sectional 40 First Round
Springs Valley 66, North Central (Farm.) 6
North Daviess 32, Union (Dugger) 0
Tecumseh 21, Perry Central 14
Linton-Stockton 34, Wood Memorial 14
Sectional 40 Second Round
Linton-Stockton 43, Springs Valley 8
North Daviess 35, Tecumseh 7
Sectional 40 Championship

Linton-Stockton 42, North Daviess 27

Regional Championships
North White 3, West Central 0
Adams Central 27, Frankton 20
Sheridan 56, North Decatur 20
Linton-Stockton 21, Fountain Central 18

Semi-State Championships
North White 28, Adams Central 7
Sheridan 43, Linton-Stockton 14

State Championship
Sheridan 56, North White 33

1999

Class 5A
Sectional 1 First Round
Valparaiso 21, Chesterton 17
East Chicago Central 38, Crown Point 35
Lake Central 60, Gary Wallace 0
Portage 17, Merrillville 7
Sectional 1 Second Round
East Chicago Central 14, Valparaiso 3
Lake Central 30, Portage 27
Sectional 1 Championship
Lake Central 56, East Chicago Central 13

Sectional 2 First Round
Michigan City 19, Elkhart Memorial 18
LaPorte 26, South Bend Riley 20
Mishawaka 36, Elkhart Central 33
Penn 51, Warsaw 15
Sectional 2 Second Round
Penn 56, Michigan City 14
LaPorte 24, Mishawaka 12
Sectional 2 Championship
Penn 18, LaPorte 0

Sectional 3 First Round
Marion 35, Fort Wayne North 0
Homestead 20, Fort Wayne South 15
Fort Wayne Northrop 56, Huntington North 10
Sectional 3 Second Round
Fort Wayne Northrop 24, Fort Wayne Snider 14
Marion 35, Homestead 21
Sectional 3 Championship
Fort Wayne Northrop 37, Marion 0

Sectional 4 First Round
Anderson Highland 26, Hamilton SE 14
Carmel 42, Harrison (West Lafayette) 18
Noblesville 35, Kokomo 7
Lafayette Jefferson 59, Anderson 24
Sectional 4 Second Round
Carmel 34, Lafayette Jefferson 7
Anderson Highland 25, Noblesville 22
Sectional 4 Championship
Carmel 38, Anderson Highland 7

Sectional 5 First Round
Indpls. Arlington 35, Richmond 14
Franklin Central 20, Lawrence Central 19
North Central (Indpls.) 28, Lawrence North 19
Warren Central 55, Indpls. Broad Ripple 30
Sectional 5 Second Round
Indpls. Arlington 55, Franklin Central 7
North Central (Ind.) 17, Warren Central 10, OT
Sectional 5 Championship
Indpls. Arlington 39, North Central (Indpls.) 28

Sectional 6 First Round
Ben Davis 66, Indpls. Tech 0
Pike 32, Indpls. Manual 8
Decatur Central 27, Indpls. Northwest 10
Perry Meridian 27, Southport 26, OT
Sectional 6 Second Round
Ben Davis 44, Decatur Central 13
Pike 13, Perry Meridian 10
Sectional 6 Championship
Ben Davis 37, Pike 14

Sectional 7 First Round
Bloomington South 39, Center Grove 20
Martinsville 13, Terre Haute North 10
Terre Haute South 61, Bedford N.L. 0
Sectional 7 Second Round
Martinsville 24, Columbus North 21
Bloomington South 48, Terre Haute South 21
Sectional 7 Championship
Bloomington South 34, Martinsville 6

Sectional 8 First Round
Evansville Central 64, New Albany 10
Castle 10, Evansville Harrison 7
Jeffersonville 34, Floyd Central 17
Sectional 8 Second Round
Evansville Reitz 35, Evansville Central 29, OT
Castle 34, Jeffersonville 20
Sectional 8 Championship
Evansville Reitz 14, Castle 7

Regional Championships
Penn 26, Lake Central 23
Fort Wayne Northrop 37, Carmel 23
Ben Davis 16, Indpls. Arlington 15
Bloomington South 35, Evansville Reitz 20

Semi-State Championships
Penn 28, Fort Wayne Northrop 18
Ben Davis 38, Bloomington South 0

State Championship
Ben Davis 27, Penn 3

Class 4A
Sectional 9 First Round
Griffith 34, Munster 7

Hammond 50, Hammond Clark 13
Hammond Morton 25, Hammond Gavit 7
Lowell 20, Highland 17, OT
Sectional 9 Second Round
Griffith 20, Hammond 14
Lowell 21, Hammond Morton 0
Sectional 9 Championship
Lowell 17, Griffith 14

Sectional 10 First Round
Kankakee Valley 35, Gary West 12
Hobart 21, Logansport 14
McCutcheon 73, Gary Roosevelt 24
Plymouth 44, Gary Wirt 0
Sectional 10 Second Round
Plymouth 44, Hobart 21
McCutcheon 35, Kankakee Valley 12
Sectional 10 Championship
McCutcheon 40, Plymouth 29

Sectional 11 First Round
South Bend Clay 35, South Bend Adams 6
Goshen 63, South Bend LaSalle 6
S.B. Washington 19, Northridge 7
Concord 43, Wawasee 13
Sectional 11 Second Round
South Bend Clay 45, Concord 43
Goshen 42, S.B. Washington 3
Sectional 11 Championship
Goshen 23, South Bend Clay 7

Sectional 12 First Round
Fort Wayne Wayne 18, Columbia City 7
Carroll (Fort Wayne) 25, DeKalb 0
East Noble 37, Fort Wayne Dwenger 14
Sectional 12 Second Round
East Noble 55, Bellmont 6
Carroll (Fort Wayne) 16, F.W. Wayne 13, OT
Sectional 12 Championship
East Noble 30, Carroll (Fort Wayne) 13

Sectional 13 First Round
Connersville 26, Jay County 0
Delta 45, Greenfield-Central 19
Muncie Central 19, New Castle 6
Muncie South 25, Pendleton Heights 24
Sectional 13 Second Round
Muncie Central 35, Connersville 20
Muncie South 28, Delta 7
Sectional 13 Championship
Muncie South 28, Muncie Central 20

Sectional 14 First Round
Columbus East 24, Jennings County 14
Seymour 24, East Central 14
Franklin County 58, Madison 8
Shelbyville 21, South Dearborn 7
Sectional 14 Second Round
Seymour 23, Franklin County 20

Shelbyville 34, Columbus East 21
Sectional 14 Championship
Seymour 65, Shelbyville 19

Sectional 15 First Round
Brownsburg 25, Franklin 21
Indpls. Cathedral 62, Mooresville 20
Plainfield 38, Greenwood 12
Sectional 15 Second Round
Brownsburg 41, Avon 24
Indpls. Cathedral 33, Plainfield 7
Sectional 15 Championship
Indpls. Cathedral 28, Brownsburg 13

Sectional 16 First Round
Evansville North 39, Boonville 19
Jasper 22, Bloomington North 21
Owen Valley 38, Northview 7
Sectional 16 Second Round
Evansville North 18, Owen Valley 12
Vincennes Lincoln 30, Jasper 26
Sectional 16 Championship
Evansville North 32, Vincennes Lincoln 25

Regional Championships
Lowell 38, McCutcheon 20
Goshen 34, East Noble 7
Seymour 31, Muncie South 6
Indpls. Cathedral 37, Evansville North 20

Semi-State Championships
Goshen 24, Lowell 8
Indpls. Cathedral 34, Seymour 13

State Championship
Indpls. Cathedral 24, Goshen 21

Class 3A
Sectional 17 First Round
Andrean 35, S.B. St. Joseph 0
Hammond Noll 28, Calumet 12
Mishawaka Marian 47, Gary Mann 12
Culver Military Academy 49, New Prairie 20
Sectional 17 Second Round
Andrean 20, Culver Military Academy 7
Mishawaka Marian 21, Hammond Noll 6
Sectional 17 Championship
Mishawaka Marian 28, Andrean 7

Sectional 18 First Round
North Montgomery 26, Benton Central 14
Twin Lakes 7, Crawfordsville 6
Zionsville 28, Lebanon 13
West Lafayette 36, Frankfort 35, OT
Sectional 18 Second Round
North Montgomery 26, Twin Lakes 6
Zionsville 34, West Lafayette 15
Sectional 18 Championship
Zionsville 39, North Montgomery 26

Sectional 19 First Round
Fort Wayne Concordia 32, Angola 14
NorthWood 67, Fort Wayne Elmhurst 0
New Haven 24, Lakeland 7
West Noble 23, Whitko 13
Sectional 19 Second Round
New Haven 52, Fort Wayne Concordia 34
NorthWood 47, West Noble 0
Sectional 19 Championship
NorthWood 48, New Haven 3

Sectional 20 First Round
Maconaquah 28, Blackford 6
Peru 21, Mississinewa 20
Norwell 17, Rochester 14
Tippecanoe Valley 35, Western 21
Sectional 20 Second Round
Norwell 48, Tippecanoe Valley 14
Maconaquah 43, Peru 3
Sectional 20 Championship
Norwell 38, Maconaquah 7

Sectional 21 First Round
Elwood 36, New Palestine 24
Mount Vernon (Fortville) 22, Hamilton Hts. 6
Westfield 3, Alexandria 0
Yorktown 24, Rushville 18
Sectional 21 Second Round
Elwood 14, Westfield 10
Mount Vernon (Fortville) 48, Yorktown 25
Sectional 21 Championship
Mount Vernon (Fortville) 18, Elwood 15

Sectional 22 First Round
Beech Grove 22, Sullivan 7
Indpls. Chatard 34, Greencastle 3
Roncalli 49, Brebeuf Jesuit 13
Sectional 22 Second Round
Roncalli 31, Indpls. Chatard 3
Beech Grove 14, West Vigo 7
Sectional 22 Championship
Roncalli 41, Beech Grove 8

Sectional 23 First Round
Batesville 6, Greensburg 0
Edgewood 34, Brown County 7
North Harrison 46, Corydon Central 6
Sectional 23 Second Round
Batesville 21, Edgewood 3
Whiteland 41, North Harrison 0
Sectional 23 Championship
Whiteland 44, Batesville 14

Sectional 24 First Round
Evansville Bosse 51, Princeton 23
Heritage Hills 57, Evansville Memorial 7
Mount Vernon 39, Washington 0
Gibson Southern 40, Pike Central 0

Sectional 24 Second Round
Heritage Hills 25, Evansville Bosse 21
Mount Vernon 42, Gibson Southern 7
Sectional 24 Championship
Mount Vernon 6, Heritage Hills 3

Regional Championships
Mishawaka Marian 15, Zionsville 14
Norwell 35, NorthWood 27
Roncalli 27, Mount Vernon (Fortville) 6
Whiteland 38, Mount Vernon 7

Semi-State Championships
Norwell 19, Mishawaka Marian 18
Roncalli 34, Whiteland 14

State Championship
Roncalli 24, Norwell 14

Class 2A
Sectional 25 First Round
North Judson 10, Bremen 7
John Glenn 20, Rensselaer Central 13
Knox 12, Lake Station 7
Winamac 38, North Newton 0
Sectional 25 Second Round
John Glenn 38, Knox 28
North Judson 14, Winamac 13
Sectional 25 Championship
North Judson 10, John Glenn 7

Sectional 26 First Round
Delphi 34, North Miami 26
Lewis Cass 35, Madison-Grant 14
Northwestern 20, Taylor 0
Eastbrook 56, Oak Hill 28
Sectional 26 Second Round
Eastbrook 31, Delphi 0
Northwestern 40, Lewis Cass 33
Sectional 26 Championship
Eastbrook 26, Northwestern 13

Sectional 27 First Round
Central Noble 27, Churubusco 21
Jimtown 48, Fairfield 0
Eastside 44, Leo 0
Garrett 13, Prairie Heights 7
Sectional 27 Second Round
Central Noble 20, Garrett 0
Jimtown 38, Eastside 3
Sectional 27 Championship
Jimtown 48, Central Noble 0

Sectional 28 First Round
Bluffton 21, Wabash 10
Fort Wayne Luers 35, Heritage 7
Harding (Fort Wayne) 7, Manchester 6
Woodlan 7, South Adams 6, OT
Sectional 28 Second Round

Fort Wayne Luers 14, Harding (Fort Wayne) 6
Woodlan 27, Bluffton 6
Sectional 28 Championship
Fort Wayne Luers 41, Woodlan 13

Sectional 29 First Round
Speedway 26, Centerville 6
Indpls. Scecina 37, Tipton 19
Western Boone 40, Union County 6
Sectional 29 Second Round
Western Boone 20, Speedway 14
Indpls. Scecina 14, Winchester 13
Sectional 29 Championship
Western Boone 21, Indpls. Scecina 20

Sectional 30 First Round
Monrovia 35, South Vermillion 17
Cloverdale 34, North Putnam 6
Southmont 47, Fountain Central 0
Danville 49, Tri-West 0
Sectional 30 Second Round
Monrovia 36, Cloverdale 21
Danville 21, Southmont 17
Sectional 30 Championship
Danville 29, Monrovia 0

Sectional 31 First Round
Lawrenceburg 44, Charlestown 19
Brownstown Central 63, Indian Creek 0
Providence 8, Salem 0
Sectional 31 Second Round
Lawrenceburg 26, Providence 14
Brownstown Central 98, Triton Central 24
Sectional 31 Championship
Lawrenceburg 30, Brownstown Central 21

Sectional 32 First Round
Evansville Mater Dei 61, North Knox 6
Mitchell 20, Paoli 18
Tell City 23, North Posey 14
Southridge 32, South Spencer 7
Sectional 32 Second Round
Evansville Mater Dei 35, Mitchell 14
Southridge 29, Tell City 7
Sectional 32 Championship
Evansville Mater Dei 42, Southridge 21

Regional Championships
Eastbrook 27, North Judson 19
Fort Wayne Luers 7, Jimtown 0
Danville 20, Western Boone 0
Evansville Mater Dei 38, Lawrenceburg 15

Semi-State Championships
Fort Wayne Luers 35, Eastbrook 8
Danville 54, Evansville Mater Dei 47

State Championship
Fort Wayne Luers 38, Danville 6

Class 1A
Sectional 33 First Round
LaVille 35, Caston 6
River Forest 25, South Central (Union Mills) 7
West Central 47, Triton 0
Culver 28, Whiting 0
Sectional 33 Second Round
Culver 34, River Forest 26
LaVille 21, West Central 20
Sectional 33 Championship
Culver 28, LaVille 7

Sectional 34 First Round
North White 50, Carroll (Flora) 0
Pioneer 40, Tri-County 26
Frontier 26, South Newton 7
Sectional 34 Second Round
Lafayette Central Catholic 76, Frontier 7
North White 35, Pioneer 14
Sectional 34 Championship
Lafayette Central Catholic 24, North White 14

Sectional 35 First Round
Eastern (Greentown) 40, Northfield 7
Southern Wells 40, Wes-Del 0
Southwood 35, Fremont 28
Sectional 35 Second Round
Adams Central 29, Southwood 27
Southern Wells 56, Eastern (Greentown) 21
Sectional 35 Championship
Adams Central 18, Southern Wells 13

Sectional 36 First Round
Cambridge City Lincoln 26, Union City 6
Hagerstown 21, Knightstown 7
Eastern Hancock 53, Northeastern 25
Shenandoah 23, Tri 0
Sectional 36 Second Round
Hagerstown 35, Eastern Hancock 13
Shenandoah 30, Cambridge City Lincoln 23
Sectional 36 Championship
Hagerstown 13, Shenandoah 0

Sectional 37 First Round
Cascade 62, Tri-Central 6
Clinton Central 25, Frankton 14
Indpls. Ritter 41, Sheridan 26
Clinton Prairie 20, Lapel 14
Sectional 37 Second Round
Indpls. Ritter 63, Cascade 37
Clinton Central 67, Clinton Prairie 19
Sectional 37 Championship
Indpls. Ritter 40, Clinton Central 35

Sectional 38 First Round
North Vermillion 27, Riverton Parke 0
South Putnam 49, Rockville 8
Seeger 40, Covington 28

Attica 70, Turkey Run 0
Sectional 38 Second Round
Attica 76, North Vermillion 3
Seeger 20, South Putnam 19
Sectional 38 Championship
Seeger 7, Attica 6

Sectional 39 First Round
West Washington 56, Edinburgh 14
Clarksville 47, Indiana Deaf 6
Milan 38, South Decatur 35
North Decatur 35, Park Tudor 15
Sectional 39 Second Round
Milan 35, North Decatur 0
Clarksville 33, West Washington 14
Sectional 39 Championship
Clarksville 35, Milan 20

Sectional 40 First Round
Linton-Stockton 38, North Central (Farm.) 14
Springs Valley 18, North Daviess 7
Perry Central 39, Union (Dugger) 0
Wood Memorial 17, Tecumseh 9
Sectional 40 Second Round
Linton-Stockton 27, Springs Valley 26, OT
Perry Central 72, Wood Memorial 0
Sectional 40 Championship
Perry Central 42, Linton-Stockton 20

Regional Championships
Lafayette Central Catholic 50, Culver 15
Adams Central 45, Hagerstown 24
Indpls. Ritter 33, Seeger 27
Perry Central 42, Clarksville 20

Semi-State Championships
Lafayette Central Catholic 35, Adams Central 0
Perry Central 28, Indpls. Ritter 27

State Championship
Lafayette Central Catholic 59, Perry Central 7

2000

Class 5A
Sectional 1 First Round
Valparaiso 30, Crown Point 0
East Chicago Central 28, Chesterton 21
Lake Central 21, Portage 7
Merrillville 40, Gary Wallace 0
Sectional 1 Second Round
Lake Central 56, East Chicago Central 7
Valparaiso 7, Merrillville 3
Sectional 1 Championship
Valparaiso 28, Lake Central 0

Sectional 2 First Round
Warsaw 55, Elkhart Central 0
Michigan City 24, Elkhart Memorial 21
Mishawaka 28, South Bend Riley 21

Penn 58, LaPorte 10
Sectional 2 Second Round
Mishawaka 34, Michigan City 15
Penn 10, Warsaw 7
Sectional 2 Championship
Penn 54, Mishawaka 14

Sectional 3 First Round
Huntington North 28, Fort Wayne North 27
Fort Wayne Snider 45, Marion 7
Homestead 30, Fort Wayne Northrop 21
Sectional 3 Second Round
Homestead 40, Fort Wayne South 13
Fort Wayne Snider 56, Huntington North 13
Sectional 3 Championship
Fort Wayne Snider 24, Homestead 21

Sectional 4 First Round
Carmel 36, Kokomo 7
Noblesville 41, Hamilton Southeastern 21
Harrison (West Lafayette) 34, Anderson 25
Lafayette Jefferson 64, Anderson Highland 6
Sectional 4 Second Round
Carmel 61, Lafayette Jefferson 18
Noblesville 44, Harrison (West Lafayette) 19
Sectional 4 Championship
Noblesville 27, Carmel 12

Sectional 5 First Round
Franklin Central 35, Lawrence North 28
Warren Central 47, Indpls. Broad Ripple 14
Lawrence Central 24, Indpls. Arlington 0
North Central (Indpls.) 40, Richmond 18
Sectional 5 Second Round
North Central (Indpls.) 26, Franklin Central 21
Warren Central 35, Lawrence Central 14
Sectional 5 Championship
Warren Central 28, North Central (Indpls.) 18

Sectional 6 First Round
Decatur Central 35, Perry Meridian 10
Ben Davis 51, Indpls. Northwest 0
Indpls. Tech 44, Indpls. Manual 6
Pike 50, Southport 26
Sectional 6 Second Round
Ben Davis 34, Pike 19
Decatur Central 44, Indpls. Tech 8
Sectional 6 Championship
Ben Davis 24, Decatur Central 21

Sectional 7 First Round
Bloomington South 19, Martinsville 17
Terre Haute North 21, Columbus North 18
Center Grove 35, Terre Haute South 7
Sectional 7 Second Round
Bloomington South 54, Bedford N.L. 13
Center Grove 55, Terre Haute North 7
Sectional 7 Championship
Center Grove 24, Bloomington South 14

Sectional 8 First Round
New Albany 19, Floyd Central 17
Castle 34, Evansville Reitz 14
Evansville Harrison 21, Jeffersonville 0
Sectional 8 Second Round
Evansville Harrison 13, New Albany 7
Castle 38, Evansville Central 0
Sectional 8 Championship
Castle 38, Evansville Harrison 2

Regional Championships
Penn 28, Valparaiso 7
Noblesville 28, Fort Wayne Snider 25
Ben Davis 65, Warren Central 30
Center Grove 24, Castle 12

Semi-State Championships
Penn 38, Noblesville 15
Center Grove 30, Ben Davis 28

State Championship
Penn 21, Center Grove 0

Class 4A
Sectional 9 First Round
Griffith 49, Hammond Morton 21
Hammond 41, Hammond Clark 20
Munster 24, Highland 7
Lowell 16, Hammond Gavit 9
Sectional 9 Second Round
Hammond 7, Lowell 0
Griffith 34, Munster 10
Sectional 9 Championship
Hammond 30, Griffith 27

Sectional 10 First Round
Hobart 29, Gary Roosevelt 8
McCutcheon 56, Gary West 0
Logansport 22, Gary Wirt 12
Plymouth 53, Kankakee Valley 0
Sectional 10 Second Round
Plymouth 31, Logansport 12
McCutcheon 33, Hobart 27
Sectional 10 Championship
Plymouth 35, McCutcheon 21

Sectional 11 First Round
Concord 34, Northridge 27
Goshen 47, South Bend Clay 7
South Bend Adams 20, South Bend LaSalle 14
Wawasee 34, S.B. Washington 17
Sectional 11 Second Round
Goshen 45, South Bend Adams 6
Concord 30, Wawasee 27
Sectional 11 Championship
Goshen 41, Concord 16

Sectional 12 First Round
Carroll (Fort Wayne) 24, Columbia City 21
East Noble 34, DeKalb 20
Fort Wayne Dwenger 49, Bellmont 6
Sectional 12 Second Round
East Noble 49, Carroll (Fort Wayne) 14
Fort Wayne Wayne 19, Fort Wayne Dwenger 0
Sectional 12 Championship
East Noble 35, Fort Wayne Wayne 7

Sectional 13 First Round
Delta 35, Pendleton Heights 12
Muncie Central 28, Connersville 0
Jay County 25, Greenfield-Central 23
Muncie South 41, New Castle 6
Sectional 13 Second Round
Delta 27, Muncie South 23
Jay County 14, Muncie Central 10
Sectional 13 Championship
Delta 42, Jay County 6

Sectional 14 First Round
Columbus East 32, Seymour 24
East Central 44, Shelbyville 0
Jennings County 31, Madison 26
Franklin County 35, South Dearborn 12
Sectional 14 Second Round
East Central 35, Columbus East 12
Jennings County 16, Franklin County 13
Sectional 14 Championship
East Central 35, Jennings County 0

Sectional 15 First Round
Indpls. Cathedral 41, Avon 0
Franklin 10, Brownsburg 0
Plainfield 48, Greenwood 26
Sectional 15 Second Round
Plainfield 14, Indpls. Cathedral 7
Mooresville 49, Franklin 21
Sectional 15 Championship
Plainfield 34, Mooresville 7

Sectional 16 First Round
Jasper 29, Owen Valley 22
Vincennes Lincoln 46, Northview 7
Evansville North 49, Boonville 6
Sectional 16 Second Round
Evansville North 74, Bloomington North 21
Vincennes Lincoln 31, Jasper 13
Sectional 16 Championship
Evansville North 49, Vincennes Lincoln 36

Regional Championships
Plymouth 21, Hammond 12
East Noble 21, Goshen 14
Delta 28, East Central 14
Plainfield 35, Evansville North 21

Semi-State Championships
East Noble 25, Plymouth 7

Plainfield 19, Delta 14

State Championship
East Noble 28, Plainfield 7

Class 3A
Sectional 17 First Round
Mishawaka Marian 14, Andrean 13
Culver Military Academy 28, Calumet 7
S.B. St. Joseph 30, Hammond Noll 0
New Prairie 51, Gary Mann 6
Sectional 17 Second Round
S.B. St. Joseph 35, Mishawaka Marian 21
Culver Military Academy 26, New Prairie 0
Sectional 17 Championship
Culver Military Academy 35, S.B. St. Joseph 14

Sectional 18 First Round
Benton Central 15, Twin Lakes 13
West Lafayette 48, Crawfordsville 21
Zionsville 44, Frankfort 20
North Montgomery 37, Lebanon 14
Sectional 18 Second Round
Zionsville 38, West Lafayette 14
Benton Central 28, North Montgomery 6
Sectional 18 Championship
Zionsville 43, Benton Central 13

Sectional 19 First Round
Lakeland 34, Fort Wayne Concordia 13
Whitko 47, Fort Wayne Elmhurst 11
NorthWood 34, New Haven 7
Angola 8, West Noble 7
Sectional 19 Second Round
NorthWood 49, Angola 6
Lakeland 47, Whitko 16
Sectional 19 Championship
NorthWood 35, Lakeland 18

Sectional 20 First Round
Mississinewa 28, Maconaquah 7
Norwell 49, Blackford 19
Rochester 39, Western 10
Peru 21, Tippecanoe Valley 17
Sectional 20 Second Round
Peru 28, Mississinewa 10
Rochester 14, Norwell 7
Sectional 20 Championship
Rochester 41, Peru 18

Sectional 21 First Round
New Palestine 16, Alexandria 8
Elwood 22, Westfield 15
Mount Vernon (Fortville) 34, Yorktown 7
Hamilton Heights 40, Rushville 12
Sectional 21 Second Round
Mount Vernon (Fortville) 21, Hamilton Hts. 12
Elwood 79, New Palestine 7
Sectional 21 Championship
Elwood 31, Mount Vernon (Fortville) 9

Sectional 22 First Round
Beech Grove 32, Greencastle 7
Roncalli 29, Indpls. Chatard 28
Brebeuf Jesuit 32, West Vigo 14
Sectional 22 Second Round
Roncalli 31, Brebeuf Jesuit 14
Beech Grove 27, Sullivan 12
Sectional 22 Championship
Roncalli 35, Beech Grove 8

Sectional 23 First Round
Batesville 35, Corydon Central 14
Edgewood 43, Brown County 26
Greensburg 18, North Harrison 13
Sectional 23 Second Round
Whiteland 28, Batesville 21
Edgewood 34, Greensburg 0
Sectional 23 Championship
Whiteland 35, Edgewood 13

Sectional 24 First Round
Mount Vernon 69, Pike Central 7
Evansville Bosse 41, Gibson Southern 14
Evansville Memorial 34, Princeton 14
Heritage Hills 55, Washington 3
Sectional 24 Second Round
Evansville Memorial 26, Evansville Bosse 21
Heritage Hills 36, Mount Vernon 7
Sectional 24 Championship
Heritage Hills 47, Evansville Memorial 7

Regional Championships
Zionsville 35, Culver Military Academy 7
NorthWood 21, Rochester 14
Roncalli 21, Elwood 7
Heritage Hills 32, Whiteland 22

Semi-State Championships
Zionsville 21, NorthWood 20, OT
Heritage Hills 27, Roncalli 0

State Championship
Heritage Hills 27, Zionsville 24, OT

Class 2A
Sectional 25 First Round
Bremen 55, Knox 15
North Newton 40, Lake Station 12
North Judson 30, Rensselaer Central 7
Wheeler 21, John Glenn 20
Sectional 25 Second Round
North Judson 36, North Newton 0
Bremen 60, Wheeler 2
Sectional 25 Championship
North Judson 10, Bremen 7

Sectional 26 First Round

Eastbrook 35, North Miami 8
Delphi 45, Northwestern 20
Oak Hill 47, Taylor 7
Winamac 20, Lewis Cass 18
Sectional 26 Second Round
Delphi 41, Oak Hill 24
Winamac 42, Eastbrook 7
Sectional 26 Championship
Winamac 20, Delphi 0

Sectional 27 First Round
Jimtown 48, Leo 6
Central Noble 45, Churubusco 0
Eastside 49, Prairie Heights 0
Fairfield 27, Garrett 13
Sectional 27 Second Round
Central Noble 41, Fairfield 12
Jimtown 34, Eastside 0
Sectional 27 Championship
Jimtown 28, Central Noble 10

Sectional 28 First Round
Heritage 48, Bluffton 17
Woodlan 19, South Adams 6
Harding (Fort Wayne) 52, Wabash 6
Fort Wayne Luers 56, Manchester 6
Sectional 28 Second Round
Fort Wayne Luers 41, Woodlan 26
Harding (Fort Wayne) 24, Heritage 12
Sectional 28 Championship
Fort Wayne Luers 12, Harding (Fort Wayne) 7

Sectional 29 First Round
Speedway 28, Centerville 6
Western Boone 41, Tipton 7
Union County 46, Madison-Grant 34
Indpls. Scecina 49, Winchester 18
Sectional 29 Second Round
Indpls. Scecina 42, Union County 7
Western Boone 20, Speedway 14
Sectional 29 Championship
Indpls. Scecina 14, Western Boone 7

Sectional 30 First Round
Cloverdale 14, North Putnam 0
Danville 69, South Vermillion 13
Monrovia 47, Fountain Central 0
Southmont 41, Tri-West 18
Sectional 30 Second Round
Danville 63, Cloverdale 0
Monrovia 33, Southmont 10
Sectional 30 Championship
Danville 55, Monrovia 0

Sectional 31 First Round
Brownstown Central 56, Indian Creek 26
Providence 20, Salem 0
Triton Central 39, Lawrenceburg 14
Sectional 31 Second Round
Brownstown Central 57, Triton Central 8
Providence 16, Charlestown 0
Sectional 31 Championship
Brownstown Central 38, Providence 13

Sectional 32 First Round
Mitchell 60, North Knox 21
Tell City 19, North Posey 5
Evansville Mater Dei 70, Paoli 8
South Spencer 8, Southridge 6
Sectional 32 Second Round
Evansville Mater Dei 70, Mitchell 26
Tell City 17, South Spencer 14
Sectional 32 Championship
Evansville Mater Dei 44, Tell City 6

Regional Championships
Winamac 21, North Judson 7
Fort Wayne Luers 35, Jimtown 14
Danville 34, Indpls. Scecina 7
Evansville Mater Dei 24, Brownstown Central 7

Semi-State Championships
Fort Wayne Luers 37, Winamac 20
Evansville Mater Dei 42, Danville 28

State Championship
Evansville Mater Dei 56, Fort Wayne Luers 10

Class 1A
Sectional 33 First Round
LaVille 41, Caston 14
River Forest 48, Triton 13
Culver 50, South Central (Union Mills) 26
Whiting 27, West Central 24
Sectional 33 Second Round
Culver 28, Whiting 21
River Forest 26, LaVille 21
Sectional 33 Championship
Culver 34, River Forest 20

Sectional 34 First Round
Frontier 35, Carroll (Flora) 7
North White 41, Lafayette Central Catholic 14
Pioneer 27, South Newton 20
Sectional 34 Second Round
North White 14, Frontier 2
Pioneer 41, Tri-County 33
Sectional 34 Championship
North White 43, Pioneer 13

Sectional 35 First Round
Adams Central 35, Northfield 6
Southern Wells 38, Fremont 14
Southwood 20, Eastern (Greentown) 14
Sectional 35 Second Round
Adams Central 42, Southwood 7
Southern Wells 48, Wes-Del 14
Sectional 35 Championship

Adams Central 15, Southern Wells 14

Sectional 36 First Round
Eastern Hancock 22, Knightstown 0
Hagerstown 61, Cambridge City Lincoln 0
Shenandoah 37, Tri 0
Union City 26, Northeastern 0
Sectional 36 Second Round
Eastern Hancock 36, Union City 28
Hagerstown 27, Shenandoah 6
Sectional 36 Championship
Hagerstown 30, Eastern Hancock 0

Sectional 37 First Round
Cascade 41, Lapel 26
Frankton 52, Clinton Prairie 30
Sheridan 55, Indpls. Ritter 42
Clinton Central 56, Tri-Central 0
Sectional 37 Second Round
Clinton Central 52, Cascade 21
Frankton 28, Sheridan 21
Sectional 37 Championship
Clinton Central 44, Frankton 13

Sectional 38 First Round
South Putnam 48, Covington 14
North Vermillion 16, Rockville 14
Attica 28, Seeger 13
Turkey Run 41, Riverton Parke 18
Sectional 38 Second Round
Attica 20, Turkey Run 0
South Putnam 34, North Vermillion 0
Sectional 38 Championship
Attica 40, South Putnam 6

Sectional 39 First Round
South Decatur 39, Indiana Deaf 18
Milan 55, Edinburgh 6
West Washington 42, North Decatur 14
Park Tudor 41, Clarksville 21
Sectional 39 Second Round
Milan 7, Park Tudor 0
West Washington 40, South Decatur 16
Sectional 39 Championship
Milan 38, West Washington 22

Sectional 40 First Round
Springs Valley 34, North Central (Farm.) 12
Perry Central 36, Linton-Stockton 12
North Daviess 56, Tecumseh 15
Wood Memorial 38, Union (Dugger) 32
Sectional 40 Second Round
Perry Central 31, North Daviess 8
Springs Valley 26, Wood Memorial 14
Sectional 40 Championship
Perry Central 14, Springs Valley 8

Regional Championships
North White 21, Culver 7

Adams Central 34, Hagerstown 19
Attica 53, Clinton Central 28
Perry Central 20, Milan 14

Semi-State Championships
Adams Central 12, North White 6
Attica 14, Perry Central 6

State Championship
Adams Central 29, Attica 21

2001
Class 5A
Sectional 1 First Round
Chesterton 35, Crown Point 7
Lake Central 33, East Chicago Central 0
Merrillville 41, Gary Wallace 0
Valparaiso 32, Portage 14
Sectional 1 Second Round
Chesterton 19, Merrillville 6
Valparaiso 17, Lake Central 7
Sectional 1 Championship
Valparaiso 42, Chesterton 14

Sectional 2 First Round
Goshen 35, Elkhart Central 12
Elkhart Memorial 41, South Bend Riley 6
Mishawaka 53, LaPorte 28
Penn 52, Michigan City 0
Sectional 2 Second Round
Penn 42, Goshen 0
Elkhart Memorial 24, Mishawaka 12
Sectional 2 Championship
Penn 66, Elkhart Memorial 7

Sectional 3 First Round
Fort Wayne Snider 49, Huntington North 0
Homestead 38, Marion 34
Warsaw 62, Kokomo 0
Sectional 3 Second Round
Homestead 45, Fort Wayne Northrop 6
Fort Wayne Snider 23, Warsaw 20, OT
Sectional 3 Championship
Fort Wayne Snider 31, Homestead 0

Sectional 4 First Round
Lafayette Jefferson 27, Anderson 19
Carmel 24, Hamilton Southeastern 0
Noblesville 40, Harrison (West Lafayette) 14
Sectional 4 Second Round
Carmel 40, Anderson Highland 6
Noblesville 49, Lafayette Jefferson 14
Sectional 4 Championship
Carmel 34, Noblesville 28, OT

Sectional 5 First Round
Lawrence Central 28, Franklin Central 23
Lawrence North 31, Indpls. Arlington 10
North Central (Indpls.) 45, Richmond 28

Warren Central 63, Indpls. Broad Ripple 7
Sectional 5 Second Round
Lawrence Central 37, Lawrence North 13
Warren Central 70, North Central (Indpls.) 14
Sectional 5 Championship
Warren Central 44, Lawrence Central 0

Sectional 6 First Round
Decatur Central 27, Indpls. Manual 0
Indpls. Northwest 29, Indpls. Tech 14
Ben Davis 51, Pike 12
Southport 7, Perry Meridian 6
Sectional 6 Second Round
Ben Davis 48, Southport 0
Decatur Central 18, Indpls. Northwest 0
Sectional 6 Championship
Ben Davis 68, Decatur Central 14

Sectional 7 First Round
Columbus North 33, Bloomington North 26
Center Grove 21, Martinsville 3
Terre Haute North 14, Jennings County 3
Bloomington South 34, Terre Haute South 20
Sectional 7 Second Round
Bloomington South 21, Columbus North 17
Center Grove 35, Terre Haute North 14
Sectional 7 Championship
Bloomington South 28, Center Grove 21

Sectional 8 First Round
Evansville Reitz 28, Bedford N.L. 14
Evansville North 45, Jeffersonville 14
Castle 42, New Albany 12
Sectional 8 Second Round
Castle 48, Evansville North 7
Evansville Reitz 22, Evansville Harrison 21, OT
Sectional 8 Championship
Evansville Reitz 16, Castle 14

Regional Championships
Valparaiso 24, Penn 21, OT
Fort Wayne Snider 49, Carmel 8
Ben Davis 56, Warren Central 21
Evansville Reitz 26, Bloomington South 22

Semi-State Championships
Valparaiso 45, Fort Wayne Snider 13
Ben Davis 61, Evansville Reitz 20

State Championship
Ben Davis 35, Valparaiso 16

Class 4A
Sectional 9 First Round
Highland 48, Gary West 6
Griffith 42, Gary Roosevelt 36
Lowell 35, Hammond 32
Munster 20, Hammond Morton 10
Sectional 9 Second Round
Griffith 35, Highland 6
Lowell 21, Munster 20
Sectional 9 Championship
Griffith 10, Lowell 7

Sectional 10 First Round
Hobart 42, South Bend Adams 28
Plymouth 31, Kankakee Valley 0
S.B. Washington 34, South Bend LaSalle 0
South Bend Clay 38, Logansport 34
Sectional 10 Second Round
Hobart 19, South Bend Clay 13
Plymouth 27, S.B. Washington 6
Sectional 10 Championship
Plymouth 35, Hobart 19

Sectional 11 First Round
DeKalb 13, Columbia City 6
Concord 27, East Noble 25
Carroll (Fort Wayne) 30, Northridge 27
Fort Wayne Dwenger 28, Wawasee 21, OT
Sectional 11 Second Round
Carroll (Fort Wayne) 27, F.W. Dwenger 19
Concord 24, DeKalb 23
Sectional 11 Championship
Carroll (Fort Wayne) 20, Concord 13

Sectional 12 First Round
Delta 24, Fort Wayne South 7
Bellmont 33, Fort Wayne North 20
Fort Wayne Wayne 10, Jay County 7
Muncie Central 27, Muncie South 0
Sectional 12 Second Round
Delta 42, Bellmont 12
Muncie Central 18, Fort Wayne Wayne 3
Sectional 12 Championship
Delta 28, Muncie Central 0

Sectional 13 First Round
Indpls. Cathedral 41, Greenfield-Central 16
Roncalli 50, New Castle 10
Pendleton Heights 43, Connersville 14
Sectional 13 Second Round
Indpls. Cathedral 49, Pendleton Heights 21
Roncalli 21, Shelbyville 7
Sectional 13 Championship
Indpls. Cathedral 17, Roncalli 14, OT

Sectional 14 First Round
Columbus East 44, East Central 38, 2 OT
Greenwood 14, Franklin 10
Seymour 63, Madison 12
Whiteland 20, South Dearborn 0
Sectional 14 Second Round
Whiteland 42, Columbus East 28
Seymour 42, Greenwood 28
Sectional 14 Championship
Seymour 44, Whiteland 41

Sectional 15 First Round
Avon 50, McCutcheon 30
Mooresville 21, Brownsburg 14
Westfield 52, Northview 38
Zionsville 27, Plainfield 21
Sectional 15 Second Round
Zionsville 28, Avon 27
Mooresville 27, Westfield 13
Sectional 15 Championship
Zionsville 35, Mooresville 14

Sectional 16 First Round
Mount Vernon 27, Boonville 26, OT
Owen Valley 12, Evansville Central 0
Floyd Central 10, Vincennes Lincoln 0
Sectional 16 Second Round
Floyd Central 28, Owen Valley 7
Jasper 33, Mount Vernon 0
Sectional 16 Championship
Jasper 21, Floyd Central 7

Regional Championships
Plymouth 41, Griffith 21
Delta 17, Carroll (Fort Wayne) 0
Indpls. Cathedral 34, Seymour 16
Jasper 18, Zionsville 17, 3 OT

Semi-State Championships
Delta 27, Plymouth 7
Jasper 27, Indpls. Cathedral 21

State Championship
Jasper 35, Delta 20

Class 3A
Sectional 17 First Round
Andrean 28, Calumet 7
Hammond Gavit 39, Gary Mann 0
Hammond Noll 33, Hammond Clark 14
New Prairie 54, Gary Wirt 6
Sectional 17 Second Round
Andrean 21, New Prairie 0
Hammond Gavit 21, Hammond Noll 6
Sectional 17 Championship
Andrean 42, Hammond Gavit 6

Sectional 18 First Round
Frankfort 35, Twin Lakes 28
Peru 42, Maconaquah 6
Western 44, Northwestern 0
Benton Central 38, West Lafayette 27
Sectional 18 Second Round
Frankfort 31, Peru 0
Benton Central 21, Western 18
Sectional 18 Championship
Frankfort 13, Benton Central 10

Sectional 19 First Round
NorthWood 49, Whitko 0
Mishawaka Marian 15, S.B. St. Joseph 7
Tippecanoe Valley 14, Culver Military Academy 3
West Noble 17, Lakeland 15
Sectional 19 Second Round
Mishawaka Marian 24, Tippecanoe Valley 3
NorthWood 55, West Noble 0
Sectional 19 Championship
NorthWood 38, Mishawaka Marian 0

Sectional 20 First Round
Fort Wayne Concordia 42, F.W. Elmhurst 3
Harding (Fort Wayne) 14, Angola 12
Norwell 21, Blackford 10
New Haven 48, Leo 31
Sectional 20 Second Round
Fort Wayne Concordia 27, Norwell 20
New Haven 26, Harding (Fort Wayne) 14
Sectional 20 Championship
New Haven 42, Fort Wayne Concordia 14

Sectional 21 First Round
Beech Grove 31, Elwood 6
Mount Vernon (Fortville) 48, Yorktown 0
Tipton 34, New Palestine 7
Sectional 21 Second Round
Hamilton Heights 20, Mount Vernon (FV) 0
Tipton 21, Beech Grove 14
Sectional 21 Championship
Tipton 14, Hamilton Heights 10

Sectional 22 First Round
Southmont 45, Crawfordsville 14
Danville 26, Lebanon 14
Brebeuf Jesuit 28, Edgewood 6
Indpls. Chatard 42, West Vigo 7
Sectional 22 Second Round
Indpls. Chatard 34, Brebeuf Jesuit 7
Danville 42, Southmont 0
Sectional 22 Championship
Indpls. Chatard 27, Danville 0

Sectional 23 First Round
Batesville 21, Corydon Central 0
Brown County 14, Greensburg 6
Franklin County 25, Rushville 20
Sectional 23 Second Round
Batesville 6, Franklin County 0
Brown County 15, North Harrison 14
Sectional 23 Championship
Batesville 55, Brown County 14

Sectional 24 First Round
Evansville Bosse 31, Princeton 28
Evansville Memorial 42, Pike Central 0
Gibson Southern 42, Sullivan 14
Heritage Hills 44, Washington 0
Sectional 24 Second Round
Evansville Bosse 20, Ev. Memorial 14, OT

Heritage Hills 28, Gibson Southern 7
Sectional 24 Championship
Heritage Hills 48, Evansville Bosse 14

Regional Championships
Andrean 10, Frankfort 0
New Haven 21, NorthWood 20
Indpls. Chatard 34, Tipton 28
Heritage Hills 23, Batesville 11

Semi-State Championships
Andrean 35, New Haven 7
Indpls. Chatard 34, Heritage Hills 14

State Championship
Indpls. Chatard 3, Andrean 0

Class 2A
Sectional 25 First Round
Knox 30, Wheeler 20
John Glenn 34, North Newton 0
Rensselaer Central 7, Rochester 0
North Judson 38, Winamac 7
Sectional 25 Second Round
John Glenn 39, Knox 22
Rensselaer Central 20, North Judson 0
Sectional 25 Championship
John Glenn 20, Rensselaer Central 14

Sectional 26 First Round
Mississinewa 22, Alexandria 21
Eastern (Greentown) 22, Delphi 21
Eastbrook 48, North Miami 13
Lewis Cass 21, Oak Hill 7
Sectional 26 Second Round
Eastbrook 27, Lewis Cass 0
Eastern (Greentown) 44, Mississinewa 18
Sectional 26 Championship
Eastbrook 27, Eastern (Greentown) 0

Sectional 27 First Round
Central Noble 34, Prairie Heights 12
Bremen 34, Fairfield 14
Garrett 20, Churubusco 8
Jimtown 21, Eastside 13
Sectional 27 Second Round
Jimtown 38, Bremen 6
Central Noble 13, Garrett 12
Sectional 27 Championship
Jimtown 31, Central Noble 20

Sectional 28 First Round
Woodlan 26, Bluffton 18
Heritage 30, Manchester 8
South Adams 64, Wabash 31
Sectional 28 Second Round
Fort Wayne Luers 42, Heritage 7
Woodlan 30, South Adams 13
Sectional 28 Championship

Fort Wayne Luers 55, Woodlan 6

Sectional 29 First Round
Seeger 61, Cloverdale 0
North Montgomery 19, North Putnam 6
South Vermillion 25, Tri-West 9
Western Boone 44, Greencastle 7
Sectional 29 Second Round
North Montgomery 30, Seeger 13
Western Boone 14, South Vermillion 7
Sectional 29 Championship
Western Boone 35, North Montgomery 8

Sectional 30 First Round
Knightstown 50, Centerville 20
Indpls. Scecina 21, Monrovia 12
Speedway 16, Winchester 6
Triton Central 36, Union County 21
Sectional 30 Second Round
Indpls. Scecina 29, Knightstown 7
Speedway 45, Triton Central 0
Sectional 30 Championship
Speedway 27, Indpls. Scecina 21

Sectional 31 First Round
Indian Creek 48, Charlestown 28
Brownstown Central 68, Clarksville 8
Salem 34, Providence 14
Sectional 31 Second Round
Brownstown Central 41, Indian Creek 20
Salem 29, Lawrenceburg 15
Sectional 31 Championship
Brownstown Central 34, Salem 6

Sectional 32 First Round
Evansville Mater Dei 63, Tell City 28
North Posey 55, Mitchell 45
South Spencer 27, North Knox 0
Southridge 55, Paoli 7
Sectional 32 Second Round
Southridge 37, North Posey 0
Evansville Mater Dei 49, South Spencer 7
Sectional 32 Championship
Evansville Mater Dei 45, Southridge 22

Regional Championships
Eastbrook 8, John Glenn 7
Fort Wayne Luers 24, Jimtown 18
Speedway 16, Western Boone 8
Evansville Mater Dei 55, Brownstown 39

Semi-State Championships
Fort Wayne Luers 58, Eastbrook 13
Evansville Mater Dei 49, Speedway 20

State Championship
Fort Wayne Luers 57, Evansville Mater Dei 29

Class 1A

Sectional 33 First Round
Culver 49, Triton 12
West Central 46, Lake Station 21
Whiting 42, LaVille 0
South Central (Union Mills) 14, River Forest 7
Sectional 33 Second Round
Culver 35, West Central 7
Whiting 16, South Central (Union Mills) 0
Sectional 33 Championship
Culver 26, Whiting 24

Sectional 34 First Round
Adams Central 21, Northfield 0
Southern Wells 48, Madison-Grant 8
Fremont 46, Taylor 7
Sectional 34 Second Round
Fremont 29, Adams Central 8
Southern Wells 27, Southwood 19
Sectional 34 Championship
Southern Wells 43, Fremont 10

Sectional 35 First Round
Frontier 21, Carroll (Flora) 6
North White 26, Caston 2
Pioneer 44, Lafayette Central Catholic 21
South Newton 48, Tri-County 0
Sectional 35 Second Round
Pioneer 24, Frontier 22
South Newton 27, North White 8
Sectional 35 Championship
Pioneer 16, South Newton 12

Sectional 36 First Round
Tri 27, Hagerstown 20
Northeastern 22, Cambridge City Lincoln 19
Shenandoah 42, Wes-Del 6
Eastern Hancock 38, Union City 0
Sectional 36 Second Round
Shenandoah 28, Eastern Hancock 0
Tri 41, Northeastern 6
Sectional 36 Championship
Shenandoah 16, Tri 14, OT

Sectional 37 First Round
Clinton Prairie 35, Sheridan 7
Frankton 14, Lapel 6
Cascade 21, Indpls. Ritter 12
Clinton Central 38, Tri-Central 7
Sectional 37 Second Round
Frankton 46, Cascade 0
Clinton Prairie 50, Clinton Central 8
Sectional 37 Championship
Frankton 32, Clinton Prairie 14

Sectional 38 First Round
Attica 34, Rockville 14
Turkey Run 34, Covington 6
Fountain Central 20, Riverton Parke 13
South Putnam 41, North Vermillion 14

Sectional 38 Second Round
South Putnam 34, Attica 14
Turkey Run 48, Fountain Central 14
Sectional 38 Championship
South Putnam 28, Turkey Run 7

Sectional 39 First Round
Edinburgh 32, Indiana Deaf 14
South Decatur 14, Park Tudor 13
West Washington 38, Milan 21
Sectional 39 Second Round
North Decatur 28, West Washington 16
South Decatur 58, Edinburgh 0
Sectional 39 Championship
South Decatur 26, North Decatur 12

Sectional 40 First Round
Linton-Stockton 53, Union (Dugger) 22
North Central (Farm.) 21, Wood Memorial 14
North Daviess 41, Springs Valley 20
Perry Central 41, Tecumseh 0
Sectional 40 Second Round
North Daviess 14, Linton-Stockton 0
Perry Central 42, North Central (Farmersburg) 0
Sectional 40 Championship
Perry Central 42, North Daviess 0

Regional Championships
Southern Wells 23, Culver 14
Pioneer 24, Shenandoah 7
South Putnam 26, Frankton 22
Perry Central 28, South Decatur 0

Semi-State Championships
Southern Wells 20, Pioneer 8
Perry Central 33, South Putnam 7

State Championship
Southern Wells 30, Perry Central 7

2002
Class 5A
Sectional 1 First Round
Crown Point 34, Chesterton 14
Portage 36, East Chicago Central 18
Lake Central 14, Merrillville 13
Valparaiso 62, Gary Wallace 6
Sectional 1 Second Round
Portage 40, Crown Point 3
Valparaiso 42, Lake Central 14
Sectional 1 Championship
Valparaiso 27, Portage 14

Sectional 2 First Round
Elkhart Central 47, LaPorte 33
Penn 42, Elkhart Memorial 7
Goshen 45, Michigan City 0
Mishawaka 33, South Bend Riley 6
Sectional 2 Second Round

Penn 63, Elkhart Central 0
Goshen 20, Mishawaka 12
Sectional 2 Championship
Penn 31, Goshen 0

Sectional 3 First Round
Homestead 65, Marion 0
Warsaw 14, Fort Wayne Northrop 7
Huntington North 35, Kokomo 21
Sectional 3 Second Round
Fort Wayne Snider 23, Homestead 21
Warsaw 35, Huntington North 14
Sectional 3 Championship
Fort Wayne Snider 52, Warsaw 21

Sectional 4 First Round
Harrison (West Lafayette) 29, Anderson Highland 8
Carmel 37, Anderson 6
Hamilton Southeastern 35, Noblesville 21
Sectional 4 Second Round
Lafayette Jefferson 41, Harrison (W.L.) 28
Carmel 33, Hamilton Southeastern 0
Sectional 4 Championship
Lafayette Jefferson 33, Carmel 29

Sectional 5 First Round
Franklin Central 21, Lawrence Central 7
Richmond 52, Indpls. Arlington 15
Warren Central 42, Lawrence North 7
North Central (Indpls.) 37, Ind. Broad Ripple 18
Sectional 5 Second Round
Franklin Central 51, Richmond 14
Warren Central 68, North Central (Indpls.) 20
Sectional 5 Championship
Warren Central 36, Franklin Central 0

Sectional 6 First Round
Indpls. Northwest 38, Perry Meridian 35
Indpls. Manual 26, Indpls. Tech 6
Pike 28, Decatur Central 0
Ben Davis 63, Southport 0
Sectional 6 Second Round
Indpls. Northwest 48, Indpls. Manual 29
Ben Davis 55, Pike 7
Sectional 6 Championship
Ben Davis 35, Indpls. Northwest 12

Sectional 7 First Round
Bloomington South 21, Bloomington North 6
Columbus North 20, Jennings County 7
Center Grove 26, Martinsville 14
Terre Haute South 14, Terre Haute North 12
Sectional 7 Second Round
Columbus North 38, Bloomington South 28
Center Grove 26, Terre Haute South 7
Sectional 7 Championship
Center Grove 35, Columbus North 0

Sectional 8 First Round
New Albany 59, Evansville Harrison 34
Evansville Reitz 10, Castle 7
Jeffersonville 26, Evansville North 14
Sectional 8 Second Round
New Albany 62, Bedford North Lawrence 14
Evansville Reitz 41, Jeffersonville 19
Sectional 8 Championship
New Albany 32, Evansville Reitz 6

Regional Championships
Valparaiso 16, Penn 15
Fort Wayne Snider 62, Lafayette Jefferson 14
Ben Davis 35, Warren Central 28, OT
Center Grove 42, New Albany 18

Semi-State Championships
Fort Wayne Snider 28, Valparaiso 17
Ben Davis 21, Center Grove 3

State Championship
Ben Davis 31, Fort Wayne Snider 7

Class 4A
Sectional 9 First Round
Lowell 22, Gary Roosevelt 12
Hammond Morton 46, Highland 14
Griffith 21, Munster 18
Hammond 27, Gary West 20
Sectional 9 Second Round
Hammond Morton 24, Lowell 21
Griffith 62, Hammond 6
Sectional 9 Championship
Griffith 62, Hammond Morton 34

Sectional 10 First Round
South Bend Clay 25, Hobart 0
Plymouth 43, South Bend Adams 14
Kankakee Valley 16, S.B. Washington 6
Sectional 10 Second Round
South Bend Clay 39, Logansport 0
Plymouth 57, Kankakee Valley 0
Sectional 10 Championship
South Bend Clay 30, Plymouth 12

Sectional 11 First Round
Fort Wayne Dwenger 31, East Noble 14
Concord 25, Wawasee 15
Columbia City 14, Northridge 7
DeKalb 16, Carroll (Fort Wayne) 12
Sectional 11 Second Round
Fort Wayne Dwenger 40, Concord 12
Columbia City 7, DeKalb 6
Sectional 11 Championship
Fort Wayne Dwenger 35, Columbia City 0

Sectional 12 First Round
Jay County 28, Bellmont 21
Muncie Central 9, Delta 7

Muncie South 39, Fort Wayne North 2
Fort Wayne South 41, Fort Wayne Wayne 0
Sectional 12 Second Round
Muncie Central 20, Jay County 0
Fort Wayne South 42, Muncie South 6
Sectional 12 Championship
Muncie Central 28, Fort Wayne South 24

Sectional 13 First Round
Shelbyville 47, New Castle 23
Roncalli 43, Connersville 0
Indpls. Cathedral 14, Greenfield-Central 7
Sectional 13 Second Round
Shelbyville 41, Pendleton Heights 25
Roncalli 20, Indpls. Cathedral 14
Sectional 13 Championship
Roncalli 28, Shelbyville 7

Sectional 14 First Round
Greenwood 25, South Dearborn 0
East Central 14, Seymour 6
Columbus East 38, Franklin 24
Whiteland 35, Madison 6
Sectional 14 Second Round
East Central 10, Greenwood 7
Whiteland 40, Columbus East 23
Sectional 14 Championship
East Central 38, Whiteland 30

Sectional 15 First Round
Zionsville 3, Mooresville 0
Avon 35, Northview 7
Brownsburg 35, Westfield 28
McCutcheon 18, Plainfield 7
Sectional 15 Second Round
Zionsville 24, Avon 21
McCutcheon 53, Brownsburg 29
Sectional 15 Championship
Zionsville 28, McCutcheon 21

Sectional 16 First Round
Vincennes Lincoln 46, Owen Valley 7
Jasper 24, Evansville Central 7
Floyd Central 26, Mount Vernon 6
Sectional 16 Second Round
Vincennes Lincoln 21, Boonville 17
Jasper 27, Floyd Central 13
Sectional 16 Championship
Jasper 36, Vincennes Lincoln 21

Regional Championships
South Bend Clay 26, Griffith 6
Fort Wayne Dwenger 22, Muncie Central 6
Roncalli 17, East Central 10, OT
Jasper 24, Zionsville 14

Semi-State Championships
Fort Wayne Dwenger 17, South Bend Clay 14, OT

Roncalli 10, Jasper 6

State Championship
Roncalli 24, Fort Wayne Dwenger 21

Class 3A
Sectional 17 First Round
Andrean 54, Gary Wirt 16
Hammond Noll 28, Calumet 8
New Prairie 42, Hammond Clark 7
Hammond Gavit 46, Gary Mann 6
Sectional 17 Second Round
Andrean 35, Hammond Noll 7
New Prairie 13, Hammond Gavit 12, 2 OT
Sectional 17 Championship
Andrean 42, New Prairie 14

Sectional 18 First Round
Twin Lakes 32, Western 20
West Lafayette 23, Benton Central 21
Maconaquah 33, Northwestern 0
Frankfort 55, Peru 14
Sectional 18 Second Round
Twin Lakes 45, West Lafayette 10
Frankfort 41, Maconaquah 0
Sectional 18 Championship
Twin Lakes 29, Frankfort 26

Sectional 19 First Round
Whitko 27, Culver Military Academy 21
S.B. St. Joseph 35, West Noble 14
Tippecanoe Valley 40, Mishawaka Marian 14
NorthWood 42, Lakeland 0
Sectional 19 Second Round
S.B. St. Joseph 28, Whitko 8
NorthWood 47, Tippecanoe Valley 7
Sectional 19 Championship
S.B. St. Joseph 28, NorthWood 12

Sectional 20 First Round
Harding (Fort Wayne) 79, F.W. Elmhurst 18
New Haven 13, Leo 8
Norwell 35, Angola 14
Fort Wayne Concordia 41, Blackford 38, OT
Sectional 20 Second Round
Harding (Fort Wayne) 26, New Haven 14
Fort Wayne Concordia 31, Norwell 21
Sectional 20 Championship
Fort Wayne Concordia 35, Harding (F.W.) 27

Sectional 21 First Round
Tipton 19, Mount Vernon (Fortville) 0
Yorktown 21, Beech Grove 7
Hamilton Heights 63, Elwood 6
Sectional 21 Second Round
New Palestine 31, Tipton 21
Hamilton Heights 49, Yorktown 33
Sectional 21 Championship
Hamilton Heights 26, New Palestine 14

Sectional 22 First Round
Danville 68, Crawfordsville 0
Brebeuf Jesuit 13, Southmont 10
Indpls. Chatard 28, Lebanon 14
West Vigo 39, Edgewood 22
Sectional 22 Second Round
Danville 54, Brebeuf Jesuit 12
Indpls. Chatard 49, West Vigo 13
Sectional 22 Championship
Indpls. Chatard 27, Danville 26

Sectional 23 First Round
Brown County 38, North Harrison 7
Corydon Central 42, Rushville 0
Franklin County 45, Greensburg 14
Sectional 23 Second Round
Batesville 35, Brown County 7
Franklin County 28, Corydon Central 13
Sectional 23 Championship
Batesville 7, Franklin County 6

Sectional 24 First Round
Evansville Bosse 35, Gibson Southern 14
Pike Central 12, Princeton 0
Heritage Hills 14, Evansville Memorial 12
Sullivan 41, Washington 12
Sectional 24 Second Round
Evansville Bosse 48, Pike Central 7
Heritage Hills 50, Sullivan 0
Sectional 24 Championship
Heritage Hills 63, Evansville Bosse 0

Regional Championships
Andrean 29, Twin Lakes 20
Fort Wayne Concordia 30, S.B. St. Joseph 14
Indpls. Chatard 14, Hamilton Heights 0
Heritage Hills 41, Batesville 0

Semi-State Championships
Andrean 28, Fort Wayne Concordia 17
Indpls. Chatard 35, Heritage Hills 28

State Championship
Indpls. Chatard 31, Andrean 12

Class 3A
Sectional 25 First Round
North Judson 44, Rochester 3
Rensselaer Central 28, Wheeler 14
Knox 60, North Newton 27
John Glenn 34, Winamac 22
Sectional 25 Second Round
North Judson 29, Rensselaer Central 10
John Glenn 26, Knox 20
Sectional 25 Championship
North Judson 52, John Glenn 7

Sectional 26 First Round
Alexandria 18, Oak Hill 15
Eastbrook 21, Eastern (Greentown) 13
Lewis Cass 29, Mississinewa 0
Delphi 13, North Miami 6
Sectional 26 Second Round
Eastbrook 49, Alexandria 0
Lewis Cass 9, Delphi 7
Sectional 26 Championship
Eastbrook 7, Lewis Cass 0

Sectional 27 First Round
Jimtown 32, Churubusco 0
Garrett 35, Eastside 14
Prairie Heights 27, Fairfield 0
Central Noble 28, Bremen 10
Sectional 27 Second Round
Jimtown 21, Garrett 20, OT
Central Noble 26, Prairie Heights 7
Sectional 27 Championship
Central Noble 19, Jimtown 14

Sectional 28 First Round
Heritage 20, Manchester 0
Fort Wayne Luers 40, Woodlan 12
Bluffton 30, Wabash 6
Sectional 28 Second Round
Heritage 38, South Adams 0
Fort Wayne Luers 48, Bluffton 21
Sectional 28 Championship
Fort Wayne Luers 48, Heritage 21

Sectional 29 First Round
North Montgomery 40, North Putnam 13
Western Boone 42, South Vermillion 0
Tri-West 39, Greencastle 12
Seeger 49, Cloverdale 12
Sectional 29 Second Round
Western Boone 14, North Montgomery 0
Seeger 35, Tri-West 14
Sectional 29 Championship
Seeger 28, Western Boone 14

Sectional 30 First Round
Triton Central 41, Union County 12
Winchester 28, Monrovia 0
Knightstown 14, Centerville 13
Indpls. Scecina 21, Speedway 7
Sectional 30 Second Round
Winchester 18, Triton Central 12
Indpls. Scecina 37, Knightstown 13
Sectional 30 Championship
Indpls. Scecina 41, Winchester 21

Sectional 31 First Round
Brownstown Central 48, Charlestown 22
Indian Creek 62, Lawrenceburg 0
Salem 23, Providence 22
Sectional 31 Second Round
Brownstown Central 41, Clarksville 14

Indian Creek 22, Salem 14
Sectional 31 Championship
Indian Creek 50, Brownstown Central 6

Sectional 32 First Round
South Spencer 76, North Knox 0
Tell City 37, Paoli 0
Evansville Mater Dei 47, Mitchell 14
Southridge 35, North Posey 0
Sectional 32 Second Round
South Spencer 19, Tell City 13
Southridge 26, Evansville Mater Dei 7
Sectional 32 Championship
Southridge 18, South Spencer 9

Regional Championships
North Judson 26, Eastbrook 0
Fort Wayne Luers 24, Central Noble 7
Indpls. Scecina 28, Seeger 14
Southridge 39, Indian Creek 20

Semi-State Championships
Fort Wayne Luers 29, North Judson 3
Southridge 28, Indpls. Scecina 17

State Championship
Fort Wayne Luers 36, Southridge 30

Class 1A
Sectional 33 First Round
Triton 20, West Central 13
Whiting 27, River Forest 8
South Central (Union Mills) 6, Culver 0
LaVille 45, Lake Station 13
Sectional 33 Second Round
Whiting 18, Triton 7
LaVille 19, South Central (Union Mills) 17
Sectional 33 Championship
LaVille 28, Whiting 0

Sectional 34 First Round
Adams Central 26, Fremont 20, OT
Madison-Grant 42, Northfield 7
Southern Wells 41, Taylor 6
Sectional 34 Second Round
Southwood 24, Adams Central 13
Madison-Grant 39, Southern Wells 38
Sectional 34 Championship
Southwood 35, Madison-Grant 0

Sectional 35 First Round
Lafayette Central Catholic 14, Tri-County 6
Pioneer 48, Caston 7
Frontier 21, Carroll (Flora) 14
North White 14, South Newton 7
Sectional 35 Second Round
Pioneer 27, Lafayette Central Catholic 13
North White 28, Frontier 7
Sectional 35 Championship
Pioneer 33, North White 6

Sectional 36 First Round
Tri 21, Wes-Del 20
Shenandoah 59, Cambridge City Lincoln 0
Hagerstown 28, Union City 13
Eastern Hancock 28, Northeastern 14
Sectional 36 Second Round
Shenandoah 45, Tri 0
Eastern Hancock 30, Hagerstown 0
Sectional 36 Championship
Eastern Hancock 20, Shenandoah 16

Sectional 37 First Round
Clinton Prairie 28, Frankton 19
Sheridan 28, Tri-Central 24
Indpls. Ritter 28, Lapel 0
Clinton Central 54, Cascade 27
Sectional 37 Second Round
Clinton Prairie 20, Sheridan 14
Clinton Central 32, Indpls. Ritter 27
Sectional 37 Championship
Clinton Central 27, Clinton Prairie 12

Sectional 38 First Round
South Putnam 61, Attica 7
Fountain Central 46, Covington 6
Turkey Run 46, North Vermillion 6
Riverton Parke 33, Rockville 0
Sectional 38 Second Round
South Putnam 35, Fountain Central 21
Turkey Run 37, Riverton Parke 22
Sectional 38 Championship
South Putnam 33, Turkey Run 0

Sectional 39 First Round
Heritage Christian 15, Edinburgh 12
Park Tudor 17, Milan 0
West Washington 42, Indiana Deaf 0
South Decatur 20, North Decatur 3
Sectional 39 Second Round
Park Tudor 42, Heritage Christian 15
South Decatur 20, West Washington 14, OT
Sectional 39 Championship
Park Tudor 14, South Decatur 12

Sectional 40 First Round
Perry Central 74, North Central (Farmersburg) 6
Springs Valley 22, Linton-Stockton 12
Tecumseh 53, Union (Dugger) 14
Wood Memorial 34, North Daviess 6
Sectional 40 Second Round
Perry Central 40, Springs Valley 16
Tecumseh 26, Wood Memorial 25
Sectional 40 Championship
Perry Central 38, Tecumseh 8

Regional Championships
Southwood 34, LaVille 0

Pioneer 53, Eastern Hancock 0
South Putnam 53, Clinton Central 20
Perry Central 32, Park Tudor 0

Semi-State Championships
Southwood 34, Pioneer 17
South Putnam 40, Perry Central 21

State Championship
Southwood 17, South Putnam 14

2003
Class 5A
Sectional 1 First Round
Portage 24, Crown Point 14
Valparaiso 41, East Chicago Central 6
Chesterton 16, Michigan City 12
Merrillville 42, Lake Central 12
Sectional 1 Second Round
Portage 24, Valparaiso 14
Merrillville 21, Chesterton 14
Sectional 1 Championship
Portage 43, Merrillville 28

Sectional 2 First Round
South Bend Riley 20, South Bend Adams 7
Elkhart Memorial 23, LaPorte 10
Penn 31, South Bend Clay 13
Elkhart Central 21, Mishawaka 14
Sectional 2 Second Round
Elkhart Memorial 56, South Bend Riley 7
Penn 50, Elkhart Central 22
Sectional 2 Championship
Penn 24, Elkhart Memorial 21, OT

Sectional 3 First Round
Huntington North 21, Warsaw 18
Homestead 34, Marion 21
Fort Wayne Snider 58, Carroll (Fort Wayne) 0
Fort Wayne Northrop 27, Goshen 16
Sectional 3 Second Round
Homestead 31, Huntington North 7
Fort Wayne Snider 35, Fort Wayne Northrop 21
Sectional 3 Championship
Fort Wayne Snider 44, Homestead 21

Sectional 4 First Round
Noblesville 30, Anderson Highland 23
Hamilton Southeastern 35, Kokomo 13
Lafayette Jefferson 56, Anderson 19
Sectional 4 Second Round
Carmel 47, Noblesville 0
Hamilton Southeastern 16, Lafayette Jeff 14
Sectional 4 Championship
Carmel 42, Hamilton Southeastern 10

Sectional 5 First Round
North Central (Indpls.) 53, Ind. Broad Ripple 13
Franklin Central 41, Indpls. Arlington 6

Warren Central 39, Lawrence Central 10
Lawrence North 45, Richmond 13
Sectional 5 Second Round
North Central (Indpls.) 17, Franklin Central 13
Warren Central 19, Lawrence North 7
Sectional 5 Championship
Warren Central 50, North Central (Indpls.) 10

Sectional 6 First Round
Ben Davis 54, Decatur Central 26
Indpls. Manual 24, Indpls. Tech 13
Southport 26, Pike 20
Perry Meridian 42, Indpls. Northwest 8
Sectional 6 Second Round
Ben Davis 48, Indpls. Manual 0
Perry Meridian 23, Southport 7
Sectional 6 Championship
Ben Davis 49, Perry Meridian 0

Sectional 7 First Round
Brownsburg 24, Martinsville 7
Bloomington South 38, Columbus North 27
Terre Haute North 14, Terre Haute South 6
Center Grove 35, Avon 7
Sectional 7 Second Round
Bloomington South 20, Brownsburg 7
Center Grove 14, Terre Haute North 7
Sectional 7 Championship
Center Grove 35, Bloomington South 7

Sectional 8 First Round
New Albany 21, Jeffersonville 12
Evansville North 46, Castle 6
Evansville Reitz 76, Bedford North Lawrence 7
Sectional 8 Second Round
Evansville Harrison 53, New Albany 47
Evansville Reitz 23, Evansville North 6
Sectional 8 Championship
Evansville Reitz 56, Evansville Harrison 18

Regional Championships
Penn 23, Portage 13
Fort Wayne Snider 36, Carmel 17
Warren Central 27, Ben Davis 20
Center Grove 31, Evansville Reitz 20

Semi-State Championships
Penn 62, Fort Wayne Snider 27
Warren Central 30, Center Grove 0

State Championship
Warren Central 57, Penn 7

Class 4A
Sectional 9 First Round
Lowell 58, Gary Wallace 21
Munster 40, Gary West 20
Hobart 27, Highland 25
Kankakee Valley 35, Gary Roosevelt 12

Sectional 9 Second Round
Lowell 21, Munster 7
Hobart 44, Kankakee Valley 9
Sectional 9 Championship
Lowell 34, Hobart 3

Sectional 10 First Round
Plymouth 7, S.B. Washington 3
DeKalb 37, Northridge 21
Wawasee 47, Angola 7
East Noble 35, Concord 0
Sectional 10 Second Round
Plymouth 10, DeKalb 0
East Noble 38, Wawasee 36
Sectional 10 Championship
East Noble 28, Plymouth 14

Sectional 11 First Round
Fort Wayne Dwenger 56, F.W. Elmhurst 19
Logansport 66, Fort Wayne Wayne 29
Bellmont 25, Fort Wayne South 13
Columbia City 55, Fort Wayne North 0
Sectional 11 Second Round
Fort Wayne Dwenger 35, Logansport 7
Columbia City 23, Bellmont 14
Sectional 11 Championship
Fort Wayne Dwenger 35, Columbia City 7

Sectional 12 First Round
Muncie Central 64, New Castle 6
Delta 21, Pendleton Heights 7
Muncie South 42, Greenfield-Central 15
Jay County 34, Connersville 12
Sectional 12 Second Round
Muncie Central 16, Delta 9
Muncie South 36, Jay County 12
Sectional 12 Championship
Muncie Central 36, Muncie South 6

Sectional 13 First Round
Zionsville 9, Indpls. Cathedral 7
Plainfield 43, McCutcheon 18
Harrison (West Lafayette) 25, Lebanon 19
Roncalli 24, Westfield 0
Sectional 13 Second Round
Zionsville 31, Plainfield 6
Roncalli 28, Harrison (West Lafayette) 7
Sectional 13 Championship
Roncalli 24, Zionsville 21

Sectional 14 First Round
Greenwood 47, Whiteland 7
Bloomington North 63, Owen Valley 13
Mooresville 33, Northview 29
Sectional 14 Second Round
Greenwood 37, Franklin 14
Mooresville 32, Bloomington North 28
Sectional 14 Championship
Mooresville 28, Greenwood 7

Sectional 15 First Round
Columbus East 25, Jennings County 10
Shelbyville 42, Madison 7
East Central 47, Franklin County 7
Seymour 43, South Dearborn 32
Sectional 15 Second Round
Columbus East 20, Shelbyville 14
East Central 28, Seymour 7
Sectional 15 Championship
East Central 56, Columbus East 7

Sectional 16 First Round
Floyd Central 33, Evansville Bosse 21
Vincennes Lincoln 52, Mount Vernon 6
Jasper 19, Boonville 0
Sectional 16 Second Round
Floyd Central 38, Evansville Central 24
Vincennes Lincoln 42, Jasper 7
Sectional 16 Championship
Vincennes Lincoln 31, Floyd Central 21

Regional Championships
East Noble 20, Lowell 13
Fort Wayne Dwenger 14, Muncie Central 7
Roncalli 35, Mooresville 14
East Central 35, Vincennes Lincoln 21

Semi-State Championships
East Noble 42, Fort Wayne Dwenger 28
Roncalli 30, East Central 29, OT

State Championship
Roncalli 17, East Noble 0

Class 3A
Sectional 17 First Round
Andrean 48, Gary Wirt 0
Hammond Morton 27, Hammond 8
Hammond Gavit 30, Calumet 14
Griffith 56, Hammond Clark 0
Sectional 17 Second Round
Andrean 35, Hammond Morton 6
Griffith 60, Hammond Gavit 18
Sectional 17 Championship
Andrean 16, Griffith 14

Sectional 18 First Round
Twin Lakes 56, West Lafayette 21
Hamilton Heights 19, Benton Central 7
Frankfort 21, Western 3
Sectional 18 Second Round
Twin Lakes 28, Tipton 8
Hamilton Heights 27, Frankfort 0
Sectional 18 Championship
Hamilton Heights 24, Twin Lakes 15

Sectional 19 First Round
New Prairie 56, Lakeland 14

NorthWood 33, Culver Military Academy 13
Tippecanoe Valley 28, Mishawaka Marian 6
S.B. St. Joseph 48, West Noble 3
Sectional 19 Second Round
NorthWood 32, New Prairie 17
S.B. St. Joseph 35, Tippecanoe Valley 12
Sectional 19 Championship
NorthWood 22, S.B. St. Joseph 21

Sectional 20 First Round
Norwell 47, Peru 14
Fort Wayne Luers 20, Maconaquah 12
Whitko 54, Fort Wayne Concordia 40
New Haven 28, Leo 20
Sectional 20 Second Round
Norwell 31, Fort Wayne Luers 15
Whitko 22, New Haven 19
Sectional 20 Championship
Norwell 28, Whitko 6

Sectional 21 First Round
Yorktown 23, Mount Vernon (Fortville) 14
New Palestine 31, Rushville 6
Blackford 20, Mississinewa 6
Sectional 21 Second Round
Yorktown 35, Elwood 0
Blackford 27, New Palestine 18
Sectional 21 Championship
Blackford 52, Yorktown 23

Sectional 22 First Round
West Vigo 35, Brebeuf Jesuit 21
Indpls. Chatard 40, Danville 0
Crawfordsville 44, Greencastle 18
Sectional 22 Second Round
West Vigo 38, Beech Grove 10
Indpls. Chatard 48, Crawfordsville 0
Sectional 22 Championship
Indpls. Chatard 55, West Vigo 7

Sectional 23 First Round
Edgewood 33, Greensburg 13
Batesville 21, Brown County 9
Salem 16, Corydon Central 0
Sectional 23 Second Round
Edgewood 52, North Harrison 22
Batesville 17, Salem 16
Sectional 23 Championship
Batesville 34, Edgewood 0

Sectional 24 First Round
Sullivan 42, Washington 6
Evansville Memorial 55, Princeton 0
Evansville Mater Dei 40, Gibson Southern 21
Heritage Hills 65, Pike Central 7
Sectional 24 Second Round
Evansville Memorial 40, Sullivan 21
Heritage Hills 21, Evansville Mater Dei 14
Sectional 24 Championship

Heritage Hills 37, Evansville Memorial 12

Regional Championships
Hamilton Heights 22, Andrean 21
NorthWood 58, Norwell 0
Indpls. Chatard 50, Blackford 21
Heritage Hills 16, Batesville 12

Semi-State Championships
NorthWood 19, Hamilton Heights 3
Indpls. Chatard 24, Heritage Hills 3

State Championship
Indpls. Chatard 49, NorthWood 0

Class 2A
Sectional 25 First Round
Winamac 34, Knox 0
Rensselaer Central 21, Wheeler 14
Hammond Noll 34, North Newton 17
North Judson 53, Gary Mann 6
Sectional 25 Second Round
Rensselaer Central 21, Winamac 7
North Judson 23, Hammond Noll 13
Sectional 25 Championship
Rensselaer Central 26, North Judson 14

Sectional 26 First Round
Central Noble 24, John Glenn 7
Garrett 22, Fairfield 0
Jimtown 37, Prairie Heights 0
Eastside 33, Bremen 24
Sectional 26 Second Round
Garrett 19, Central Noble 7
Jimtown 52, Eastside 6
Sectional 26 Championship
Garrett 28, Jimtown 6

Sectional 27 First Round
Harding (Fort Wayne) 47, Churubusco 0
Lewis Cass 33, Heritage 30, 2 OT
Rochester 30, Wabash 7
Woodlan 7, Manchester 6
Sectional 27 Second Round
Harding (Fort Wayne) 48, Lewis Cass 20
Woodlan 26, Rochester 7
Sectional 27 Championship
Harding (Fort Wayne) 47, Woodlan 6

Sectional 28 First Round
Bluffton 21, Madison-Grant 13
Eastbrook 71, Winchester 0
Oak Hill 42, South Adams 14
Centerville 32, Alexandria 26
Sectional 28 Second Round
Eastbrook 39, Bluffton 6
Oak Hill 42, Centerville 21
Sectional 28 Championship
Eastbrook 20, Oak Hill 10

Sectional 29 First Round
Cloverdale 34, South Vermillion 6
North Putnam 30, Southmont 7
Tri-West 48, Cascade 21
North Montgomery 35, South Putnam 13
Sectional 29 Second Round
North Putnam 33, Cloverdale 0
Tri-West 49, North Montgomery 31
Sectional 29 Championship
Tri-West 56, North Putnam 14

Sectional 30 First Round
Western Boone 39, Heritage Christian 7
Indpls. Scecina 21, Eastern (Greentown) 6
Speedway 56, Delphi 14
Northwestern 38, Taylor 3
Sectional 30 Second Round
Western Boone 14, Indpls. Scecina 0
Speedway 55, Northwestern 14
Sectional 30 Championship
Speedway 21, Western Boone 0

Sectional 31 First Round
Indian Creek 28, Lawrenceburg 20
Providence 26, Triton Central 0
Clarksville 42, Union County 8
Brownstown Central 35, Charlestown 0
Sectional 31 Second Round
Indian Creek 24, Providence 21, OT
Brownstown Central 35, Clarksville 12
Sectional 31 Championship
Brownstown Central 34, Indian Creek 21

Sectional 32 First Round
North Posey 47, Tell City 7
Southridge 51, Mitchell 28
South Spencer 48, North Knox 0
Sectional 32 Second Round
North Posey 42, Paoli 6
South Spencer 28, Southridge 0
Sectional 32 Championship
South Spencer 38, North Posey 13

Regional Championships
Garrett 10, Rensselaer Central 7
Harding (Fort Wayne) 15, Eastbrook 7
Tri-West 21, Speedway 18
South Spencer 19, Brownstown Central 6

Semi-State Championships
Harding (Fort Wayne) 45, Garrett 14
Tri-West 28, South Spencer 14

State Championship
Tri-West 41, Harding (Fort Wayne) 36

Class 1A
Sectional 33 First Round
West Central 54, Culver 7
South Newton 48, South Central (U.M.) 21
LaVille 37, River Forest 20
Whiting 30, Lake Station 26
Sectional 33 Second Round
West Central 32, South Newton 12
LaVille 35, Whiting 14
Sectional 33 Championship
LaVille 35, West Central 6

Sectional 34 First Round
Adams Central 34, Fremont 8
Triton 40, Northfield 0
Southwood 37, Southern Wells 18
Sectional 34 Second Round
Adams Central 28, North Miami 7
Southwood 32, Triton 29
Sectional 34 Championship
Adams Central 46, Southwood 7

Sectional 35 First Round
Pioneer 18, Lafayette Central Catholic 14
Seeger 56, Attica 0
Tri-County 21, North White 6
Caston 21, Frontier 7
Sectional 35 Second Round
Seeger 13, Pioneer 6
Caston 17, Tri-County 6
Sectional 35 Championship
Seeger 28, Caston 3

Sectional 36 First Round
Frankton 40, Tri-Central 10
Sheridan 52, Wes-Del 0
Lapel 63, Clinton Prairie 0
Carroll (Flora) 20, Clinton Central 12
Sectional 36 Second Round
Frankton 21, Sheridan 3
Carroll (Flora) 20, Lapel 14
Sectional 36 Championship
Carroll (Flora) 48, Frankton 20

Sectional 37 First Round
Eastern Hancock 55, Union City 14
Shenandoah 34, Tri 27
Northeastern 13, Hagerstown 0
Knightstown 41, Cambridge City Lincoln 7
Sectional 37 Second Round
Eastern Hancock 21, Shenandoah 20
Knightstown 14, Northeastern 13
Sectional 37 Championship
Eastern Hancock 13, Knightstown 7

Sectional 38 First Round
Monrovia 70, Edinburgh 14
Park Tudor 10, Milan 6
South Decatur 21, North Decatur 14
Sectional 38 Second Round
Indpls. Ritter 62, Monrovia 13

Park Tudor 31, South Decatur 14
Sectional 38 Championship
Indpls. Ritter 45, Park Tudor 3

Sectional 39 First Round
Turkey Run 28, Rockville 8
Union (Dugger) 20, Covington 13
Fountain Central 26, North Central (Farm.) 25
Riverton Parke 40, North Vermillion 0
Sectional 39 Second Round
Turkey Run 62, Union (Dugger) 20
Riverton Parke 20, Fountain Central 0
Sectional 39 Championship
Turkey Run 28, Riverton Parke 14

Sectional 40 First Round
Tecumseh 48, Wood Memorial 12
West Washington 44, North Daviess 18
Linton-Stockton 54, Eastern Greene 6
Springs Valley 35, Perry Central 12
Sectional 40 Second Round
Tecumseh 28, West Washington 6
Linton-Stockton 52, Springs Valley 20
Sectional 40 Championship
Tecumseh 12, Linton-Stockton 7

Regional Championships
Adams Central 50, LaVille 13
Seeger 36, Carroll (Flora) 0
Indpls. Ritter 45, Eastern Hancock 3
Tecumseh 41, Turkey Run 19

Semi-State Championships
Seeger 22, Adams Central 21
Indpls. Ritter 40, Tecumseh 20

State Championship
Indpls. Ritter 28, Seeger 0

2004
Class 5A
Sectional 1 First Round
Crown Point 46, Lake Central 3
Merrillville 50, East Chicago Central 19
Portage 35, Chesterton 28
Valparaiso 38, Michigan City 14
Sectional 1 Second Round
Merrillville 34, Crown Point 19
Portage 24, Valparaiso 18
Sectional 1 Championship
Merrillville 44, Portage 38, 3 OT

Sectional 2 First Round
Elkhart Memorial 21, Mishawaka 14
South Bend Clay 56, South Bend Riley 6
LaPorte 31, Elkhart Central 20
Penn 56, South Bend Adams 0
Sectional 2 Second Round
South Bend Clay 14, Elkhart Memorial 0

Penn 28, LaPorte 16
Sectional 2 Championship
Penn 34, South Bend Clay 13

Sectional 3 First Round
Fort Wayne Snider 51, Carroll (Fort Wayne) 0
Huntington North 24, Warsaw 17
Homestead 47, Goshen 0
Fort Wayne Northrop 18, Marion 6
Sectional 3 Second Round
Fort Wayne Snider 63, Huntington North 3
Homestead 23, Fort Wayne Northrop 6
Sectional 3 Championship
Fort Wayne Snider 49, Homestead 21

Sectional 4 First Round
Lafayette Jefferson 56, Kokomo 7
Carmel 35, Anderson Highland 9
Hamilton Southeastern 21, Noblesville 14
Sectional 4 Second Round
Lafayette Jefferson 57, Anderson 21
Carmel 28, Hamilton Southeastern 6
Sectional 4 Championship
Carmel 22, Lafayette Jefferson 19

Sectional 5 First Round
Indpls. Arlington 34, Indpls. Broad Ripple 20
Lawrence Central 14, Franklin Central 7
Warren Central 25, North Central (Indpls.) 10
Lawrence North 40, Richmond 0
Sectional 5 Second Round
Lawrence Central 34, Indpls. Arlington 7
Warren Central 43, Lawrence North 20
Sectional 5 Championship
Warren Central 46, Lawrence Central 14

Sectional 6 First Round
Perry Meridian 19, Indpls. Manual 6
Decatur Central 23, Pike 6
Ben Davis 53, Southport 19
Indpls. Northwest 33, Indpls. Tech 0
Sectional 6 Second Round
Perry Meridian 29, Decatur Central 26
Ben Davis 76, Indpls. Northwest 0
Sectional 6 Championship
Ben Davis 30, Perry Meridian 0

Sectional 7 First Round
Columbus North 56, Terre Haute South 14
Avon 23, Center Grove 21
Terre Haute North 28, Brownsburg 14
Bloomington South 23, Martinsville 14
Sectional 7 Second Round
Columbus North 17, Avon 6
Terre Haute North 21, Bloomington South 14
Sectional 7 Championship
Columbus North 28, Terre Haute North 14

Sectional 8 First Round

Evansville Harrison 21, Evansville Reitz 20
Castle 30, Jeffersonville 7
Evansville North 35, Bedford N.L. 24
Sectional 8 Second Round
Evansville Harrison 42, New Albany 17
Castle 20, Evansville North 17
Sectional 8 Championship
Castle 19, Evansville Harrison 7

Regional Championships
Penn 31, Merrillville 0
Fort Wayne Snider 40, Carmel 22
Warren Central 27, Ben Davis 26
Columbus North 24, Castle 0

Semi-State Championships
Fort Wayne Snider 49, Penn 7
Warren Central 54, Columbus North 17

State Championship
Warren Central 35, Fort Wayne Snider 23

Class 4A
Sectional 9 First Round
Gary West 12, Gary Roosevelt 0
Highland 24, Kankakee Valley 7
Lowell 57, Gary Wallace 12
Hobart 27, Munster 10
Sectional 9 Second Round
Highland 13, Gary West 0
Lowell 13, Hobart 10
Sectional 9 Championship
Lowell 48, Highland 7

Sectional 10 First Round
Plymouth 31, Northridge 3
East Noble 21, Angola 8
DeKalb 35, S.B. Washington 7
Wawasee 48, Concord 9
Sectional 10 Second Round
Plymouth 14, East Noble 0
Wawasee 49, DeKalb 28
Sectional 10 Championship
Wawasee 28, Plymouth 7

Sectional 11 First Round
Bellmont 32, Fort Wayne Dwenger 31, 2 OT
Logansport 28, Fort Wayne Elmhurst 21
Fort Wayne North 48, Fort Wayne Wayne 0
Fort Wayne South 23, Columbia City 14
Sectional 11 Second Round
Logansport 21, Bellmont 20
Fort Wayne South 13, Fort Wayne North 0
Sectional 11 Championship
Logansport 21, Fort Wayne South 14

Sectional 12 First Round
Pendleton Heights 14, Muncie South 7
Greenfield-Central 42, Connersville 28

Delta 55, New Castle 6
Muncie Central 32, Jay County 6
Sectional 12 Second Round
Pendleton Heights 26, Greenfield-Central 0
Muncie Central 7, Delta 6
Sectional 12 Championship
Muncie Central 38, Pendleton Heights 22

Sectional 13 First Round
Zionsville 29, Plainfield 22
Indpls. Cathedral 28, Harrison (W.L.) 21
McCutcheon 35, Lebanon 28
Roncalli 42, Westfield 7
Sectional 13 Second Round
Indpls. Cathedral 21, Zionsville 6
Roncalli 48, McCutcheon 16
Sectional 13 Championship
Roncalli 17, Indpls. Cathedral 16

Sectional 14 First Round
Mooresville 52, Owen Valley 0
Greenwood 14, Whiteland 7
Northview 17, Bloomington North 14
Sectional 14 Second Round
Mooresville 43, Franklin 23
Greenwood 42, Northview 0
Sectional 14 Championship
Mooresville 37, Greenwood 14

Sectional 15 First Round
East Central 28, Madison 17
Columbus East 42, Franklin County 21
Shelbyville 7, South Dearborn 0
Seymour 10, Jennings County 7, OT
Sectional 15 Second Round
Columbus East 24, East Central 16
Shelbyville 13, Seymour 7
Sectional 15 Championship
Columbus East 49, Shelbyville 14

Sectional 16 First Round
Jasper 46, Evansville Bosse 19
Boonville 48, Floyd Central 7
Vincennes Lincoln 15, Mount Vernon 11
Sectional 16 Second Round
Jasper 22, Evansville Central 6
Boonville 35, Vincennes Lincoln 7
Sectional 16 Championship
Boonville 11, Jasper 8

Regional Championships
Wawasee 28, Lowell 21
Logansport 20, Muncie Central 11
Roncalli 20, Mooresville 16
Columbus East 26, Boonville 24
Semi-State Championships
Wawasee 49, Logansport 19
Roncalli 15, Columbus East 14
State Championship

Roncalli 35, Wawasee 10

Sectional 17 First Round
Hammond Morton 44, Gary Wirt 18
Griffith 55, Calumet 0
Andrean 56, Hammond 6
Hammond Gavit 26, Hammond Clark 6
Sectional 17 Second Round
Griffith 43, Hammond Morton 22
Andrean 70, Hammond Gavit 9
Sectional 17 Championship
Andrean 36, Griffith 35

Sectional 18 First Round
Twin Lakes 21, Benton Central 14
Hamilton Heights 68, Western 20
West Lafayette 28, Frankfort 20
Sectional 18 Second Round
Tipton 14, Twin Lakes 7
Hamilton Heights 42, West Lafayette 7
Sectional 18 Championship
Hamilton Heights 22, Tipton 7

Sectional 19 First Round
Culver Military 17, Tippecanoe Valley 14, OT
NorthWood 31, West Noble 7
Mishawaka Marian 41, Lakeland 18
New Prairie 32, S.B. St. Joseph 22
Sectional 19 Second Round
NorthWood 42, Culver Military Academy 7
New Prairie 42, Mishawaka Marian 14
Sectional 19 Championship
New Prairie 14, NorthWood 11

Sectional 20 First Round
Fort Wayne Concordia 37, Maconaquah 18
Norwell 30, Leo 0
Fort Wayne Luers 33, Whitko 10
New Haven 56, Peru 12
Sectional 20 Second Round
Norwell 35, Fort Wayne Concordia 28
Fort Wayne Luers 23, New Haven 6
Sectional 20 Championship
Norwell 20, Fort Wayne Luers 17

Sectional 21 First Round
Yorktown 50, Indpls. Howe 20
Mississinewa 27, Blackford 18
New Palestine 20, Mount Vernon (Fortville) 6
Rushville 13, Elwood 6
Sectional 21 Second Round
Yorktown 28, Mississinewa 6
New Palestine 14, Rushville 13
Sectional 21 Championship
New Palestine 37, Yorktown 20

Sectional 22 First Round
Brebeuf Jesuit 30, Greencastle 14
Danville 67, Beech Grove 21

Indpls. Chatard 72, Indpls. Washington 0
Crawfordsville 35, West Vigo 18
Sectional 22 Second Round
Danville 36, Brebeuf Jesuit 26
Indpls. Chatard 44, Crawfordsville 10
Sectional 22 Championship
Indpls. Chatard 55, Danville 7

Sectional 23 First Round
Corydon Central 19, Greensburg 7
Edgewood 16, Salem 6
Batesville 20, North Harrison 6
Sectional 23 Second Round
Corydon Central 29, Brown County 28
Batesville 38, Edgewood 6
Sectional 23 Championship
Batesville 28, Corydon Central 7

Sectional 24 First Round
Princeton 20, Pike Central 16
Heritage Hills 50, Sullivan 7
Evansville Mater Dei 28, Evansville Memorial 8
Gibson Southern 42, Washington 0
Sectional 24 Second Round
Heritage Hills 58, Princeton 0
Evansville Mater Dei 50, Gibson Southern 0
Sectional 24 Championship
Heritage Hills 24, Evansville Mater Dei 14

Regional Championships
Andrean 48, Hamilton Heights 23
New Prairie 28, Norwell 17
Indpls. Chatard 38, New Palestine 7
Heritage Hills 3, Batesville 0

Semi-State Championships
Andrean 34, New Prairie 21
Heritage Hills 13, Indpls. Chatard 10

State Championship
Andrean 21, Heritage Hills 14

Class 2A
Sectional 25 First Round
North Judson 56, Knox 8
Winamac 35, Wheeler 21
Rensselaer Central 56, Hammond Noll 0
Sectional 25 Second Round
North Judson 41, North Newton 12
Rensselaer Central 37, Winamac 32
Sectional 25 Championship
North Judson 16, Rensselaer Central 13, OT

Sectional 26 First Round
John Glenn 47, Prairie Heights 6
Fairfield 34, Central Noble 7
Eastside 35, Bremen 31
Jimtown 16, Garrett 14
Sectional 26 Second Round

John Glenn 35, Fairfield 0
Eastside 24, Jimtown 19
Sectional 26 Championship
John Glenn 41, Eastside 27

Sectional 27 First Round
Heritage 33, Harding (Fort Wayne) 14
Woodlan 63, Manchester 14
Lewis Cass 49, Wabash 14
Rochester 23, Churubusco 0
Sectional 27 Second Round
Heritage 26, Woodlan 7
Lewis Cass 27, Rochester 25, OT
Sectional 27 Championship
Heritage 30, Lewis Cass 14

Sectional 28 First Round
Eastbrook 34, South Adams 8
Winchester 15, Centerville 8
Oak Hill 21, Alexandria 7
Bluffton 45, Madison-Grant 16
Sectional 28 Second Round
Eastbrook 35, Winchester 0
Bluffton 35, Oak Hill 7
Sectional 28 Championship
Eastbrook 35, Bluffton 10

Sectional 29 First Round
South Vermillion 49, Southmont 27
North Putnam 33, North Montgomery 20
Cascade 14, South Putnam 6
Tri-West 35, Cloverdale 6
Sectional 29 Second Round
South Vermillion 28, North Putnam 27
Tri-West 30, Cascade 0
Sectional 29 Championship
Tri-West 47, South Vermillion 13

Sectional 30 First Round
Delphi 31, Heritage Christian 10
Speedway 23, Indpls. Scecina 20
Eastern (Greentown) 37, Taylor 8
Western Boone 27, Northwestern 12
Sectional 30 Second Round
Speedway 43, Delphi 10
Western Boone 34, Eastern (Greentown) 20
Sectional 30 Championship
Speedway 24, Western Boone 7

Sectional 31 First Round
Lawrenceburg 29, Clarksville 20
Providence 35, Triton Central 0
Brownstown Central 41, Charlestown 9
Indian Creek 42, Union County 8
Sectional 31 Second Round
Providence 38, Lawrenceburg 6
Brownstown Central 26, Indian Creek 13
Sectional 31 Championship
Brownstown Central 27, Providence 24

Sectional 32 First Round
North Posey 62, Paoli 20
Southridge 49, Mitchell 0
South Spencer 47, Tell City 20
Sectional 32 Second Round
North Posey 71, North Knox 14
Southridge 31, South Spencer 25
Sectional 32 Championship
Southridge 55, North Posey 34

Regional Championships
John Glenn 28, North Judson 20
Eastbrook 27, Heritage 19
Tri-West 17, Speedway 14
Brownstown Central 31, Southridge 27

Semi-State Championships
Eastbrook 28, John Glenn 12
Tri-West 55, Brownstown Central 28

State Championship
Tri-West 62, Eastbrook 21

Class 1A
Sectional 33 First Round
South Central (Union Mills) 42, River Forest 23
West Central 35, Lake Station 17
LaVille 34, Culver 7
Whiting 34, South Newton 20
Sectional 33 Second Round
West Central 40, South Central (Union Mills) 6
Whiting 42, LaVille 38
Sectional 33 Championship
West Central 14, Whiting 13

Sectional 34 First Round
Adams Central 49, Northfield 20
Triton 41, North Miami 7
Southern Wells 20, Southwood 6
Sectional 34 Second Round
Adams Central 31, Fremont 28, OT
Southern Wells 27, Triton 19
Sectional 34 Championship
Adams Central 13, Southern Wells 6

Sectional 35 First Round
Lafayette Central Catholic 49, Frontier 6
Attica 21, Tri-County 20, OT
Seeger 49, North White 20
Pioneer 20, Caston 0
Sectional 35 Second Round
Lafayette Central Catholic 41, Attica 20
Seeger 22, Pioneer 0
Sectional 35 Championship
Seeger 50, Lafayette Central Catholic 28

Sectional 36 First Round
Carroll (Flora) 26, Clinton Prairie 8

Frankton 7, Lapel 0
Sheridan 41, Tri-Central 6
Clinton Central 60, Wes-Del 7
Sectional 36 Second Round
Carroll (Flora) 17, Frankton 7
Sheridan 59, Clinton Central 6
Sectional 36 Championship
Sheridan 47, Carroll (Flora) 26

Sectional 37 First Round
Shenandoah 24, Eastern Hancock 14
Hagerstown 42, Northeastern 7
Union City 34, Tri 14
Cambridge City Lincoln 35, Knightstown 28
Sectional 37 Second Round
Shenandoah 35, Hagerstown 7
Cambridge City Lincoln 18, Union City 6
Sectional 37 Championship
Shenandoah 38, Cambridge City Lincoln 0

Sectional 38 First Round
Indpls. Ritter 43, North Decatur 14
Milan 46, Edinburgh 14
Park Tudor 27, Monrovia 7
South Decatur 45, Indiana Deaf 12
Sectional 38 Second Round
Indpls. Ritter 62, Milan 0
Park Tudor 27, South Decatur 6
Sectional 38 Championship
Indpls. Ritter 38, Park Tudor 0

Sectional 39 First Round
North Central (Farmersburg) 33, Covington 0
Rockville 21, Riverton Parke 19
Turkey Run 22, North Vermillion 14
Fountain Central 31, Union (Dugger) 20
Sectional 39 Second Round
Rockville 24, North Central (Farmersburg) 6
Fountain Central 31, Turkey Run 13
Sectional 39 Championship
Fountain Central 17, Rockville 12

Sectional 40 First Round
Linton-Stockton 27, Tecumseh 10
Perry Central 45, Wood Memorial 14
North Daviess 47, Springs Valley 14
West Washington 47, Eastern Greene 14
Sectional 40 Second Round
Linton-Stockton 41, Perry Central 21
West Washington 33, North Daviess 8
Sectional 40 Championship
Linton-Stockton 29, West Washington 22

Regional Championships
West Central 41, Adams Central 14
Seeger 14, Sheridan 7
Indpls. Ritter 26, Shenandoah 15
Linton-Stockton 41, Fountain Central 6

Semi-State Championships
Seeger 18, West Central 0
Indpls. Ritter 21, Linton-Stockton 20, OT

State Championship
Seeger 20, Indpls. Ritter 7

2005
Class 5A
Sectional 1 First Round
Crown Point 45, Valparaiso 20
Chesterton 49, Portage 28
Merrillville 41, Lake Central 3
Michigan City 42, East Chicago Central 14
Sectional 1 Second Round
Crown Point 34, Chesterton 0
Merrillville 49, Michigan City 12
Sectional 1 Championship
Merrillville 16, Crown Point 13

Sectional 2 First Round
Elkhart Memorial 55, South Bend Riley 21
LaPorte 52, South Bend Clay 14
Mishawaka 45, Elkhart Central 6
Penn 56, South Bend Adams 6
Sectional 2 Second Round
Elkhart Memorial 24, LaPorte 14
Penn 28, Mishawaka 7
Sectional 2 Championship
Penn 35, Elkhart Memorial 21

Sectional 3 First Round
Fort Wayne Snider 42, Warsaw 7
Homestead 42, Fort Wayne Northrop 21
Goshen 28, Huntington North 14
Marion 42, Carroll (Fort Wayne) 14
Sectional 3 Second Round
Fort Wayne Snider 41, Homestead 13
Marion 49, Goshen 43
Sectional 3 Championship
Fort Wayne Snider 48, Marion 21

Sectional 4 First Round
Hamilton Southeastern 49, Kokomo 0
Carmel 63, Anderson 10
Anderson Highland 21, Noblesville 19
Sectional 4 Second Round
Hamilton Southeastern 27, Lafayette Jeff 14
Carmel 49, Anderson Highland 7
Sectional 4 Championship
Hamilton Southeastern 17, Carmel 7

Sectional 5 First Round
Lawrence North 28, Richmond 10
North Central (Indpls.) 31, Franklin Central 7
Warren Central 75, Indpls. Broad Ripple 14
Lawrence Central 42, Indpls. Arlington 21
Sectional 5 Second Round
Lawrence North 10, North Central (Ind.) 7, OT

Warren Central 59, Lawrence Central 17
Sectional 5 Championship
Warren Central 55, Lawrence North 3

Sectional 6 First Round
Decatur Central 43, Pike 10
Ben Davis 41, Southport 14
Indpls. Northwest 43, Indpls. Manual 27
Perry Meridian 20, Indpls. Tech 12
Sectional 6 Second Round
Decatur Central 27, Ben Davis 22
Indpls. Northwest 27, Perry Meridian 21
Sectional 6 Championship
Decatur Central 49, Indpls. Northwest 13

Sectional 7 First Round
Columbus North 10, Brownsburg 6
Avon 46, Terre Haute South 0
Center Grove 42, Martinsville 7
Terre Haute North 17, Bloomington South 10
Sectional 7 Second Round
Avon 42, Columbus North 27
Terre Haute North 42, Center Grove 21
Sectional 7 Championship
Avon 38, Terre Haute North 21

Sectional 8 First Round
Evansville North 49, New Albany 25
Jeffersonville 20, Bedford N.L. 17, OT
Evansville Reitz 27, Castle 20
Sectional 8 Second Round
Evansville North 35, Evansville Harrison 6
Evansville Reitz 42, Jeffersonville 14
Sectional 8 Championship
Evansville Reitz 28, Evansville North 7

Regional Championships
Merrillville 7, Penn 0
Hamilton Southeastern 32, F.W. Snider 15
Warren Central 42, Decatur Central 0
Avon 42, Evansville Reitz 35

Semi-State Championships
Hamilton Southeastern 17, Merrillville 7
Warren Central 42, Avon 14

State Championship
Warren Central 55, Hamilton Southeastern 20

Class 4A
Sectional 9 First Round
Hobart 24, Highland 21
Gary West 16, Gary Wallace 8
Kankakee Valley 32, Munster 26
Lowell 41, Gary Roosevelt 6
Sectional 9 Second Round
Hobart 42, Gary West 0
Lowell 41, Kankakee Valley 6
Sectional 9 Championship
Lowell 32, Hobart 6

Sectional 10 First Round
Wawasee 38, S.B. Washington 14
Concord 37, Angola 7
East Noble 35, DeKalb 21
Plymouth 44, Northridge 6
Sectional 10 Second Round
Concord 28, Wawasee 26
Plymouth 7, East Noble 0
Sectional 10 Championship
Concord 42, Plymouth 28

Sectional 11 First Round
Fort Wayne South 34, Fort Wayne North 3
Bellmont 59, Fort Wayne Elmhurst 15
Fort Wayne Dwenger 39, Fort Wayne Wayne 0
Logansport 65, Columbia City 7
Sectional 11 Second Round
Fort Wayne South 42, Bellmont 7
Fort Wayne Dwenger 23, Logansport 20
Sectional 11 Championship
Fort Wayne South 23, Fort Wayne Dwenger 13

Sectional 12 First Round
Jay County 41, Pendleton Heights 28
Delta 42, Connersville 28
New Castle 20, Muncie South 16
Muncie Central 34, Greenfield-Central 6
Sectional 12 Second Round
Delta 28, Jay County 6
Muncie Central 35, New Castle 7
Sectional 12 Championship
Delta 28, Muncie Central 21, 3 OT

Sectional 13 First Round
Indpls. Cathedral 35, McCutcheon 7
Lebanon 18, Harrison (West Lafayette) 6
Roncalli 27, Zionsville 24, OT
Westfield 10, Plainfield 7
Sectional 13 Second Round
Indpls. Cathedral 21, Lebanon 16
Roncalli 28, Westfield 10
Sectional 13 Championship
Roncalli 16, Indpls. Cathedral 12

Sectional 14 First Round
Greenwood 27, Northview 14
Mooresville 33, Bloomington North 12
Whiteland 28, Franklin 12
Sectional 14 Second Round
Greenwood 66, Owen Valley 14
Whiteland 35, Mooresville 28, OT
Sectional 14 Championship
Greenwood 33, Whiteland 14

Sectional 15 First Round
Madison 36, Jennings County 29, 2 OT
South Dearborn 6, Shelbyville 0

Seymour 28, Columbus East 13
East Central 16, Franklin County 8
Sectional 15 Second Round
South Dearborn 41, Madison 13
East Central 34, Seymour 7
Sectional 15 Championship
East Central 17, South Dearborn 0

Sectional 16 First Round
Jasper 27, Evansville Central 16
Boonville 30, Floyd Central 26
Mount Vernon 27, Evansville Bosse 26
Sectional 16 Second Round
Jasper 28, Vincennes Lincoln 23
Mount Vernon 27, Boonville 23
Sectional 16 Championship
Jasper 42, Mount Vernon 28

Regional Championships
Lowell 30, Concord 23
Fort Wayne South 24, Delta 17
Roncalli 17, Greenwood 7
Jasper 18, East Central 9

Semi-State Championships
Lowell 16, Fort Wayne South 14
Roncalli 14, Jasper 9

State Championship
Lowell 28, Roncalli 27

Class 3A
Sectional 17 First Round
Hammond 24, Calumet 17, 3 OT
Hammond Morton 24, Andrean 10
Hammond Gavit 46, Gary Wirt 14
Griffith 57, Hammond Clark 7
Sectional 17 Second Round
Hammond Morton 52, Hammond 18
Griffith 63, Hammond Gavit 0
Sectional 17 Championship
Griffith 24, Hammond Morton 21

Sectional 18 First Round
Western 35, Benton Central 20
Hamilton Heights 33, Tipton 28
Twin Lakes 21, West Lafayette 7
Sectional 18 Second Round
Frankfort 23, Western 14
Hamilton Heights 27, Twin Lakes 21, 2 OT
Sectional 18 Championship
Hamilton Heights 35, Frankfort 21

Sectional 19 First Round
S.B. St. Joseph 30, Mishawaka Marian 13
Tippecanoe Valley 33, New Prairie 6
Culver Military Academy 13, West Noble 6
NorthWood 48, Lakeland 7
Sectional 19 Second Round

S.B. St. Joseph 31, Tippecanoe Valley 20
NorthWood 24, Culver Military Academy 17
Sectional 19 Championship
NorthWood 21, S.B. St. Joseph 7

Sectional 20 First Round
New Haven 40, Maconaquah 7
Fort Wayne Luers 26, Norwell 24
Leo 21, Whitko 13
Fort Wayne Concordia 52, Peru 34
Sectional 20 Second Round
Fort Wayne Luers 23, New Haven 0
Fort Wayne Concordia 45, Leo 20
Sectional 20 Championship
Fort Wayne Luers 24, Fort Wayne Concordia 14

Sectional 21 First Round
Mississinewa 35, Yorktown 6
New Palestine 37, Indpls. Howe 20
Mount Vernon (Fortville) 31, Elwood 7
Rushville 14, Blackford 0
Sectional 21 Second Round
New Palestine 19, Mississinewa 7
Mount Vernon (Fortville) 14, Rushville 0
Sectional 21 Championship
New Palestine 31, Mount Vernon (Fortville) 14

Sectional 22 First Round
Indpls. Washington 26, West Vigo 19
Danville 35, Brebeuf Jesuit 14
Crawfordsville 35, Beech Grove 19
Indpls. Chatard 48, Greencastle 7
Sectional 22 Second Round
Danville 30, Indpls. Washington 12
Indpls. Chatard 21, Crawfordsville 7
Sectional 22 Championship
Indpls. Chatard 34, Danville 23

Sectional 23 First Round
North Harrison 27, Brown County 21
Batesville 30, Greensburg 22
Edgewood 19, Salem 18
Sectional 23 Second Round
North Harrison 20, Corydon Central 7
Batesville 37, Edgewood 0
Sectional 23 Championship
Batesville 49, North Harrison 20

Sectional 24 First Round
Gibson Southern 18, Evansville Memorial 13
Evansville Mater Dei 56, Pike Central 0
Heritage Hills 61, Washington 7
Sullivan 22, Princeton 7
Sectional 24 Second Round
Evansville Mater Dei 42, Gibson Southern 7
Heritage Hills 55, Sullivan 7
Sectional 24 Championship
Heritage Hills 29, Evansville Mater Dei 6
Regional Championships

Griffith 43, Hamilton Heights 14
NorthWood 21, Fort Wayne Luers 14
Indpls. Chatard 14, New Palestine 0
Heritage Hills 46, Batesville 12

Semi-State Championships
NorthWood 17, Griffith 10
Indpls. Chatard 21, Heritage Hills 20, OT

State Championship
NorthWood 7, Indpls. Chatard 0

Class 2A
Sectional 25 First Round
Hammond Noll 43, North Newton 21
North Judson 59, Knox 12
Rensselaer Central 50, Wheeler 0
Sectional 25 Second Round
Winamac 22, Hammond Noll 14
Rensselaer Central 24, North Judson 22
Sectional 25 Championship
Rensselaer Central 56, Winamac 20

Sectional 26 First Round
Jimtown 42, Bremen 0
John Glenn 27, Central Noble 6
Garrett 42, Prairie Heights 6
Eastside 27, Fairfield 20
Sectional 26 Second Round
Jimtown 34, John Glenn 0
Garrett 40, Eastside 33
Sectional 26 Championship
Jimtown 29, Garrett 0

Sectional 27 First Round
Woodlan 14, Rochester 7, OT
Churubusco 62, Wabash 14
Harding (Fort Wayne) 42, Manchester 16
Lewis Cass 21, Heritage 14
Sectional 27 Second Round
Churubusco 21, Woodlan 20, 2 OT
Lewis Cass 15, Harding (Fort Wayne) 8, OT
Sectional 27 Championship
Lewis Cass 34, Churubusco 7

Sectional 28 First Round
Winchester 21, South Adams 14
Oak Hill 21, Centerville 19
Eastbrook 40, Bluffton 19
Madison-Grant 27, Alexandria 0
Sectional 28 Second Round
Oak Hill 10, Winchester 8
Eastbrook 27, Madison-Grant 21
Sectional 28 Championship
Eastbrook 21, Oak Hill 7
Sectional 29 First Round
Tri-West 40, Cascade 14
Cloverdale 43, South Vermillion 35
South Putnam 45, Southmont 33

North Montgomery 21, North Putnam 20
Sectional 29 Second Round
Tri-West 42, Cloverdale 0
South Putnam 49, North Montgomery 35
Sectional 29 Championship
Tri-West 42, South Putnam 21

Sectional 30 First Round
Western Boone 31, Indpls. Scecina 0
Delphi 28, Eastern (Greentown) 18
Heritage Christian 17, Taylor 7
Speedway 43, Northwestern 6
Sectional 30 Second Round
Western Boone 33, Delphi 13
Speedway 33, Heritage Christian 6
Sectional 30 Championship
Speedway 15, Western Boone 6

Sectional 31 First Round
Brownstown Central 14, Providence 10
Indian Creek 46, Union County 16
Clarksville 33, Charlestown 7
Lawrenceburg 29, Triton Central 6
Sectional 31 Second Round
Brownstown Central 22, Indian Creek 15
Lawrenceburg 31, Clarksville 0
Sectional 31 Championship
Lawrenceburg 30, Brownstown Central 24, OT

Sectional 32 First Round
South Spencer 29, Tell City 27
Southridge 36, Mitchell 7
North Posey 62, Paoli 14
Sectional 32 Second Round
South Spencer 41, North Knox 6
North Posey 56, Southridge 35
Sectional 32 Championship
North Posey 28, South Spencer 7

Regional Championships
Jimtown 21, Rensselaer Central 20, OT
Lewis Cass 42, Eastbrook 14
Speedway 30, Tri-West 28
North Posey 31, Lawrenceburg 14

Semi-State Championships
Jimtown 28, Lewis Cass 13
North Posey 21, Speedway 20

State Championship
Jimtown 35, North Posey 7

Class 1A
Sectional 33 First Round
Whiting 43, River Forest 0
LaVille 22, Lake Station 17
South Central (Union Mills) 34, Culver 6
West Central 49, South Newton 21
Sectional 33 Second Round

Whiting 12, LaVille 8
West Central 62, South Central (Union Mills) 32
Sectional 33 Championship
West Central 45, Whiting 21

Sectional 34 First Round
Adams Central 56, North Miami 14
Triton 21, Northfield 13
Southern Wells 47, Fremont 14
Sectional 34 Second Round
Adams Central 34, Southwood 7
Southern Wells 28, Triton 14
Sectional 34 Championship
Adams Central 28, Southern Wells 7

Sectional 35 First Round
Seeger 49, Attica 6
Pioneer 70, Caston 0
Frontier 35, North White 19
Lafayette Central Catholic 24, Tri-County 6
Sectional 35 Second Round
Pioneer 41, Seeger 6
Lafayette Central Catholic 32, Frontier 14
Sectional 35 Championship
Lafayette Central Catholic 35, Pioneer 28

Sectional 36 First Round
Clinton Prairie 69, Tri-Central 22
Sheridan 59, Carroll (Flora) 13
Lapel 48, Wes-Del 6
Clinton Central 42, Frankton 15
Sectional 36 Second Round
Sheridan 45, Clinton Prairie 6
Clinton Central 32, Lapel 28
Sectional 36 Championship
Sheridan 56, Clinton Central 28

Sectional 37 First Round
Union City 34, Tri 30
Knightstown 56, Hagerstown 0
Shenandoah 36, Northeastern 0
Eastern Hancock 35, Cambridge City Lincoln 8
Sectional 37 Second Round
Knightstown 35, Union City 7
Shenandoah 18, Eastern Hancock 14
Sectional 37 Championship
Knightstown 41, Shenandoah 0

Sectional 38 First Round
South Decatur 34, Indiana Deaf 7
Milan 61, Edinburgh 0
Indpls. Ritter 42, North Decatur 20
Park Tudor 40, Monrovia 0
Sectional 38 Second Round
Milan 24, South Decatur 6
Park Tudor 24, Indpls. Ritter 7
Sectional 38 Championship
Park Tudor 40, Milan 8

Sectional 39 First Round
Rockville 49, Covington 21
Union (Dugger) 34, Turkey Run 6
North Vermillion 35, North Central (Farm.) 28
Riverton Parke 36, Fountain Central 21
Sectional 39 Second Round
Rockville 22, Union (Dugger) 6
Riverton Parke 51, North Vermillion 20
Sectional 39 Championship
Riverton Parke 35, Rockville 14

Sectional 40 First Round
Perry Central 28, Linton-Stockton 14
Springs Valley 34, North Daviess 13
West Washington 51, Eastern Greene 14
Tecumseh 8, Wood Memorial 7
Sectional 40 Second Round
Perry Central 38, Springs Valley 0
West Washington 25, Tecumseh 14
Sectional 40 Championship
Perry Central 26, West Washington 7

Regional Championships
Adams Central 21, West Central 14, OT
Sheridan 34, Lafayette Central Catholic 14
Knightstown 13, Park Tudor 6
Perry Central 55, Riverton Parke 13

Semi-State Championships
Sheridan 42, Adams Central 15
Knightstown 22, Perry Central 21

State Championship
Sheridan 21, Knightstown 7

2006
Class 5A
Sectional 1 First Round
Chesterton 18, Michigan City 6
Merrillville 31, East Chicago Central 0
Portage 28, Valparaiso 14
Crown Point 49, Lake Central 0
Sectional 1 Second Round
Merrillville 39, Chesterton 22
Crown Point 14, Portage 13, OT
Sectional 1 Championship
Crown Point 28, Merrillville 7

Sectional 2 First Round
Elkhart Central 13, South Bend Riley 6
LaPorte 51, Mishawaka 21
South Bend Clay 28, Elkhart Memorial 20
Penn 48, South Bend Adams 14
Sectional 2 Second Round
LaPorte 28, Elkhart Central 14
Penn 34, South Bend Clay 13
Sectional 2 Championship
LaPorte 27, Penn 7

Sectional 3 First Round
Fort Wayne Snider 48, Fort Wayne Northrop 21
Marion 43, Huntington North 36
Warsaw 28, Carroll (Fort Wayne) 21
Homestead 35, Goshen 14
Sectional 3 Second Round
Fort Wayne Snider 60, Marion 0
Homestead 26, Warsaw 7
Sectional 3 Championship
Homestead 21, Fort Wayne Snider 16

Sectional 4 First Round
Fishers 33, Kokomo 7
Carmel 64, Anderson 0
Lafayette Jefferson 50, Anderson Highland 14
Hamilton Southeastern 29, Noblesville 9
Sectional 4 Second Round
Carmel 41, Fishers 0
Lafayette Jefferson 14, Hamilton Southeastern 7
Sectional 4 Championship
Carmel 28, Lafayette Jefferson 3

Sectional 5 First Round
Franklin Central 37, Indpls. Arlington 13
Warren Central 61, Richmond 0
Lawrence North 28, Lawrence Central 21, OT
North Central (Indpls.) 70, Ind. Broad Ripple 26
Sectional 5 Second Round
Warren Central 49, Franklin Central 0
North Central (Indpls.) 26, Lawrence North 20
Sectional 5 Championship
Warren Central 28, North Central (Indpls.) 6

Sectional 6 First Round
Indpls. Tech 24, Indpls. Northwest 22
Ben Davis 42, Decatur Central 28
Pike 9, Southport 7
Perry Meridian 56, Indpls. Manual 6
Sectional 6 Second Round
Ben Davis 48, Indpls. Tech 0
Pike 28, Perry Meridian 24
Sectional 6 Championship
Ben Davis 41, Pike 0

Sectional 7 First Round
Avon 42, Brownsburg 14
Columbus North 21, Terre Haute North 14
Bloomington South 31, Terre Haute South 14
Center Grove 20, Martinsville 7
Sectional 7 Second Round
Columbus North 55, Avon 20
Bloomington South 17, Center Grove 14, OT
Sectional 7 Championship
Columbus North 35, Bloomington South 21

Sectional 8 First Round
Bedford North Lawrence 34, New Albany 20
Jeffersonville 27, Castle 13
Evansville Reitz 38, Evansville Harrison 14

Sectional 8 Second Round
Bedford N.L. 13, Evansville North 12
Evansville Reitz 30, Jeffersonville 0
Sectional 8 Championship
Evansville Reitz 40, Bedford N.L. 20

Regional Championships
LaPorte 28, Crown Point 21, OT
Carmel 21, Homestead 0
Warren Central 42, Ben Davis 7
Columbus North 35, Evansville Reitz 28, OT

Semi-State Championships
Carmel 34, LaPorte 0
Warren Central 56, Columbus North 0

State Championship
Warren Central 35, Carmel 14

Class 4A
Sectional 9 First Round
Hobart 28, Munster 17
Highland 44, Gary West 14
Gary Roosevelt 34, Gary Wallace 0
Lowell 24, Kankakee Valley 6
Sectional 9 Second Round
Hobart 49, Highland 0
Lowell 58, Gary Roosevelt 6
Sectional 9 Championship
Lowell 31, Hobart 28

Sectional 10 First Round
Wawasee 45, East Noble 28
Plymouth 28, Northridge 14
DeKalb 27, Angola 6
Concord 61, S.B. Washington 14
Sectional 10 Second Round
Plymouth 21, Wawasee 20, OT
Concord 47, DeKalb 10
Sectional 10 Championship
Concord 42, Plymouth 9

Sectional 11 First Round
Fort Wayne South 56, Fort Wayne North 21
Bellmont 31, Fort Wayne Wayne 28
Columbia City 23, Fort Wayne Elmhurst 20
Fort Wayne Dwenger 14, Logansport 0
Sectional 11 Second Round
Fort Wayne South 34, Bellmont 24
Fort Wayne Dwenger 31, Columbia City 0
Sectional 11 Championship
Fort Wayne Dwenger 40, Fort Wayne South 12

Sectional 12 First Round
Jay County 30, Connersville 6
Muncie Central 32, Greenfield-Central 7
Pendleton Heights 44, Muncie South 14
Delta 35, New Castle 14
Sectional 12 Second Round

Muncie Central 6, Jay County 0
Delta 17, Pendleton Heights 14
Sectional 12 Championship
Muncie Central 24, Delta 3

Sectional 13 First Round
Indpls. Cathedral 28, Roncalli 0
Zionsville 30, Lebanon 27
Westfield 29, Harrison (West Lafayette) 14
Plainfield 24, McCutcheon 21
Sectional 13 Second Round
Indpls. Cathedral 34, Zionsville 0
Plainfield 32, Westfield 7
Sectional 13 Championship
Indpls. Cathedral 35, Plainfield 7

Sectional 14 First Round
Franklin 54, Northview 51
Whiteland 35, Greenwood 20
Mooresville 24, Bloomington North 6
Sectional 14 Second Round
Franklin 35, Owen Valley 15
Whiteland 13, Mooresville 10
Sectional 14 Championship
Whiteland 33, Franklin 27, OT

Sectional 15 First Round
Columbus East 14, East Central 10
Jennings County 25, Madison 19, OT
Seymour 20, South Dearborn 17
Franklin County 30, Shelbyville 22
Sectional 15 Second Round
Columbus East 49, Jennings County 8
Franklin County 20, Seymour 14
Sectional 15 Championship
Columbus East 55, Franklin County 8

Sectional 16 First Round
Vincennes Lincoln 51, Boonville 37
Jasper 40, Mount Vernon 0
Evansville Central 62, Floyd Central 13
Sectional 16 Second Round
Vincennes Lincoln 40, Evansville Bosse 7
Jasper 8, Evansville Central 7
Sectional 16 Championship
Vincennes Lincoln 10, Jasper 7

Regional Championships
Concord 33, Lowell 14
Fort Wayne Dwenger 26, Muncie Central 24
Indpls. Cathedral 31, Whiteland 7
Columbus East 42, Vincennes Lincoln 0

Semi-State Championships
Concord 48, Fort Wayne Dwenger 21
Indpls. Cathedral 37, Columbus East 6

State Championship
Indpls. Cathedral 38, Concord 14

Class 3A
Sectional 17 First Round
Andrean 63, Gary Wirt 14
Griffith 40, Hammond Morton 21
Hammond 22, Hammond Gavit 7
Calumet 48, Hammond Clark 33
Sectional 17 Second Round
Griffith 26, Andrean 7
Hammond 7, Calumet 0
Sectional 17 Championship
Griffith 56, Hammond 20

Sectional 18 First Round
West Lafayette 21, Tipton 12
Western 41, Benton Central 14
Hamilton Heights 21, Twin Lakes 14
Sectional 18 Second Round
Frankfort 28, West Lafayette 0
Hamilton Heights 13, Western 3
Sectional 18 Championship
Frankfort 16, Hamilton Heights 15

Sectional 19 First Round
Culver Military Academy 41, Lakeland 20
NorthWood 55, West Noble 14
New Prairie 34, S.B. St. Joseph 20
Mishawaka Marian 25, Tippecanoe Valley 18
Sectional 19 Second Round
Culver Military Academy 21, NorthWood 13
New Prairie 27, Mishawaka Marian 6
Sectional 19 Championship
New Prairie 26, Culver Military Academy 20

Sectional 20 First Round
Norwell 50, Peru 13
Fort Wayne Luers 33, Whitko 7
New Haven 34, Leo 27
Fort Wayne Concordia 47, Maconaquah 8
Sectional 20 Second Round
Norwell 34, Fort Wayne Luers 0
Fort Wayne Concordia 19, New Haven 16
Sectional 20 Championship
Norwell 49, Fort Wayne Concordia 14

Sectional 21 First Round
New Palestine 48, Indpls. Howe 8
Blackford 6, Yorktown 0
Mount Vernon (Fortville) 37, Rushville 14
Mississinewa 15, Elwood 12
Sectional 21 Second Round
New Palestine 7, Blackford 0
Mount Vernon (Fortville) 41, Mississinewa 0
Sectional 21 Championship
Mount Vernon (Fortville) 17, New Palestine 14

Sectional 22 First Round
Beech Grove 13, Indpls. Washington 6
Indpls. Chatard 54, Crawfordsville 7

Greencastle 14, Brebeuf Jesuit 9
Danville 35, West Vigo 7
Sectional 22 Second Round
Indpls. Chatard 45, Beech Grove 0
Danville 34, Greencastle 7
Sectional 22 Championship
Indpls. Chatard 41, Danville 20

Sectional 23 First Round
Greensburg 55, Salem 12
Edgewood 18, Brown County 0
Batesville 55, Corydon Central 7
Sectional 23 Second Round
Greensburg 47, North Harrison 26
Batesville 34, Edgewood 6
Sectional 23 Championship
Batesville 16, Greensburg 8

Sectional 24 First Round
Washington 30, Sullivan 15
Evansville Memorial 55, Princeton 6
Evansville Mater Dei 30, Heritage Hills 7
Gibson Southern 34, Pike Central 0
Sectional 24 Second Round
Evansville Memorial 13, Washington 0
Evansville Mater Dei 17, Gibson Southern 0
Sectional 24 Championship
Evansville Mater Dei 28, Ev. Memorial 21

Regional Championships
Griffith 35, Frankfort 6
Norwell 49, New Prairie 20
Indpls. Chatard 42, Mount Vernon (Fortville) 14
Evansville Mater Dei 21, Batesville 14

Semi-State Championships
Norwell 35, Griffith 7
Indpls. Chatard 35, Evansville Mater Dei 7

State Championship
Indpls. Chatard 7, Norwell 0

Class 2A
Sectional 25 First Round
North Judson 28, Wheeler 14
Rensselaer Central 23, Knox 0
Hammond Noll 42, North Newton 14
Guerin Catholic 37, Winamac 26
Sectional 25 Second Round
Rensselaer Central 16, North Judson 7
Hammond Noll 35, Guerin Catholic 0
Sectional 25 Championship
Rensselaer Central 20, Hammond Noll 7

Sectional 26 First Round
Eastside 27, Bremen 7
Fairfield 26, Prairie Heights 13
Garrett 27, Central Noble 9
Jimtown 35, John Glenn 12

Sectional 26 Second Round
Fairfield 21, Eastside 0
Jimtown 34, Garrett 6
Sectional 26 Championship
Jimtown 40, Fairfield 7

Sectional 27 First Round
Rochester 22, Churubusco 20
Harding (Fort Wayne) 56, Woodlan 14
Lewis Cass 59, Wabash 18
Heritage 49, Manchester 19
Sectional 27 Second Round
Harding (Fort Wayne) 50, Rochester 0
Heritage 6, Lewis Cass 0
Sectional 27 Championship
Harding (Fort Wayne) 27, Heritage 14

Sectional 28 First Round
South Adams 21, Oak Hill 10
Alexandria 31, Winchester 20
Madison-Grant 22, Centerville 20
Eastbrook 35, Bluffton 14
Sectional 28 Second Round
South Adams 33, Alexandria 6
Madison-Grant 32, Eastbrook 29
Sectional 28 Championship
Madison-Grant 26, South Adams 20, OT

Sectional 29 First Round
Cascade 49, Southmont 0
Cloverdale 34, South Vermillion 20
North Putnam 28, Tri-West 19
North Montgomery 33, South Putnam 12
Sectional 29 Second Round
Cascade 55, Cloverdale 0
North Putnam 13, North Montgomery 6
Sectional 29 Championship
North Putnam 34, Cascade 33

Sectional 30 First Round
Western Boone 24, Heritage Christian 7
Taylor 48, Eastern (Greentown) 0
Northwestern 29, Delphi 19
Speedway 31, Indpls. Scecina 14
Sectional 30 Second Round
Taylor 14, Western Boone 0
Speedway 27, Northwestern 20
Sectional 30 Championship
Speedway 33, Taylor 7

Sectional 31 First Round
Providence 31, Charlestown 8
Clarksville 28, Triton Central 21
Brownstown Central 55, Union County 6
Indian Creek 42, Lawrenceburg 7
Sectional 31 Second Round
Clarksville 16, Providence 0
Brownstown Central 32, Indian Creek 0
Sectional 31 Championship

Brownstown Central 31, Clarksville 30, 2 OT

Sectional 32 First Round
North Knox 14, Mitchell 13
Southridge 28, Tell City 7
South Spencer 48, Paoli 0
Sectional 32 Second Round
North Posey 48, North Knox 0
Southridge 14, South Spencer 0
Sectional 32 Championship
Southridge 52, North Posey 20

Regional Championships
Jimtown 13, Rensselaer Central 9
Harding (Fort Wayne) 33, Madison-Grant 13
North Putnam 23, Speedway 18
Southridge 32, Brownstown Central 7

Semi-State Championships
Harding (Fort Wayne) 28, Jimtown 0
Southridge 22, North Putnam 7

State Championship
Harding (Fort Wayne) 20, Southridge 7

Class 1A
Sectional 33 First Round
Whiting 35, Culver 14
West Central 45, Lake Station 28
South Newton 51, LaVille 20
South Central (Union Mills) 55, River Forest 12
Sectional 33 Second Round
West Central 10, Whiting 7
South Newton 28, South Central (U.M.) 12
Sectional 33 Championship
South Newton 37, West Central 13

Sectional 34 First Round
Southwood 28, Triton 6
Adams Central 39, North Miami 7
Indpls. Lutheran 57, Northfield 22
Southern Wells 40, Fremont 27
Sectional 34 Second Round
Adams Central 21, Southwood 12
Southern Wells 20, Indpls. Lutheran 7
Sectional 34 Championship
Adams Central 21, Southern Wells 6

Sectional 35 First Round
Pioneer 61, Attica 7
Frontier 22, Caston 0
Seeger 50, North White 14
Lafayette Central Catholic 24, Tri-County 0
Sectional 35 Second Round
Pioneer 50, Frontier 0
Seeger 30, Lafayette Central Catholic 22
Sectional 35 Championship
Pioneer 14, Seeger 7

Sectional 36 First Round
Carroll (Flora) 39, Wes-Del 27
Frankton 34, Clinton Central 26
Sheridan 47, Lapel 8
Clinton Prairie 54, Tri-Central 14
Sectional 36 Second Round
Frankton 47, Carroll (Flora) 12
Sheridan 35, Clinton Prairie 6
Sectional 36 Championship
Sheridan 40, Frankton 6

Sectional 37 First Round
Eastern Hancock 64, Union City 13
Shenandoah 19, Hagerstown 3
Tri 29, Cambridge City Lincoln 25
Knightstown 29, Northeastern 6
Sectional 37 Second Round
Eastern Hancock 14, Shenandoah 13
Knightstown 32, Tri 29
Sectional 37 Championship
Eastern Hancock 35, Knightstown 7

Sectional 38 First Round
Indpls. Ritter 61, Indiana Deaf 30
Milan 51, Edinburgh 0
Monrovia 18, North Decatur 15
Park Tudor 13, South Decatur 7
Sectional 38 Second Round
Indpls. Ritter 42, Milan 7
Park Tudor 28, Monrovia 0
Sectional 38 Championship
Indpls. Ritter 35, Park Tudor 0

Sectional 39 First Round
North Vermillion 28, Turkey Run 24
Fountain Central 35, Union (Dugger) 15
North Central (Farmersburg) 43, Covington 20
Riverton Parke 20, Rockville 14
Sectional 39 Second Round
Fountain Central 42, North Vermillion 0
Riverton Parke 41, North Central (Farm.) 14
Sectional 39 Championship
Fountain Central 31, Riverton Parke 6

Sectional 40 First Round
Linton-Stockton 40, Wood Memorial 6
Perry Central 41, Eastern Greene 0
Springs Valley 9, West Washington 6
North Daviess 14, Tecumseh 8, OT
Sectional 40 Second Round
Perry Central 21, Linton-Stockton 14
Springs Valley 28, North Daviess 6
Sectional 40 Championship
Perry Central 41, Springs Valley 0

Regional Championships
South Newton 38, Adams Central 35
Sheridan 40, Pioneer 6
Indpls. Ritter 42, Eastern Hancock 14

Perry Central 24, Fountain Central 21, 2 OT

Semi-State Championships
Sheridan 63, South Newton 33
Indpls. Ritter 21, Perry Central 20

State Championship
Sheridan 34, Indpls. Ritter 28, OT

2007
Class 5A
Sectional 1 First Round
Crown Point 35, Munster 9
Merrillville 21, Chesterton 0
Lake Central 10, Michigan City 7
Valparaiso 28, Portage 25
Sectional 1 Second Round
Merrillville 13, Crown Point 7
Lake Central 14, Valparaiso 7
Sectional 1 Championship
Merrillville 30, Lake Central 6

Sectional 2 First Round
Goshen 23, South Bend Riley 8
South Bend Adams 48, Elkhart Memorial 35
Penn 28, Elkhart Central 14
Mishawaka 26, LaPorte 21
Sectional 2 Second Round
Goshen 35, South Bend Adams 21
Penn 28, Mishawaka 0
Sectional 2 Championship
Penn 13, Goshen 3

Sectional 3 First Round
Huntington North 31, Homestead 14
Fort Wayne Snider 51, Fort Wayne North 0
Fort Wayne South 24, Carroll (Fort Wayne) 7
Warsaw 48, Fort Wayne Northrop 16
Sectional 3 Second Round
Fort Wayne Snider 52, Huntington North 9
Warsaw 14, Fort Wayne South 7
Sectional 3 Championship
Fort Wayne Snider 52, Warsaw 14

Sectional 4 First Round
McCutcheon 32, Anderson Highland 22
Harrison (West Lafayette) 49, Lafayette Jeff 28
Carmel 49, Anderson 6
Noblesville 42, Kokomo 14
Sectional 4 Second Round
Harrison (West Lafayette) 43, McCutcheon 7
Carmel 28, Noblesville 7
Sectional 4 Championship
Carmel 49, Harrison (West Lafayette) 7

Sectional 5 First Round
Lawrence Central 28, Fishers 17
Hamilton Southeastern 51, Richmond 21
North Central (Indpls.) 21, Indpls. Arlington 20
Warren Central 49, Lawrence North 28
Sectional 5 Second Round
Hamilton Southeastern 22, Lawrence Central 0
Warren Central 20, North Central (Indpls.) 14
Sectional 5 Championship
Hamilton Southeastern 31, Warren Central 10

Sectional 6 First Round
Avon 42, Perry Meridian 28
Franklin Central 31, Southport 17
Pike 41, Indpls. Tech 0
Ben Davis 35, Brownsburg 13
Sectional 6 Second Round
Franklin Central 30, Avon 14
Pike 20, Ben Davis 12
Sectional 6 Championship
Pike 17, Franklin Central 14, OT

Sectional 7 First Round
Decatur Central 17, Bloomington South 14
Terre Haute North 28, Martinsville 21
Columbus North 47, Terre Haute South 0
Center Grove 70, Bloomington North 21
Sectional 7 Second Round
Decatur Central 40, Terre Haute North 21
Columbus North 23, Center Grove 7
Sectional 7 Championship
Columbus North 31, Decatur Central 7

Sectional 8 First Round
Evansville North 28, Jennings County 7
Castle 39, Floyd Central 20
Jeffersonville 14, Bedford North Lawrence 0
Sectional 8 Second Round
Evansville North 42, New Albany 13
Jeffersonville 40, Castle 21
Sectional 8 Championship
Jeffersonville 28, Evansville North 14

Regional Championships
Merrillville 21, Penn 20
Carmel 20, Fort Wayne Snider 3
Pike 13, Hamilton Southeastern 7
Columbus North 42, Jeffersonville 6

Semi-State Championships
Carmel 35, Merrillville 13
Pike 20, Columbus North 14

State Championship
Carmel 16, Pike 7

Class 4A
Sectional 9 First Round
Griffith 37, Hammond Morton 34
Highland 30, Gary Wallace 18
Hammond 41, Gary West 0
Hobart 35, East Chicago Central 6
Sectional 9 Second Round

Griffith 41, Highland 0
Hobart 21, Hammond 13
Sectional 9 Championship
Griffith 17, Hobart 14

Sectional 10 First Round
Lowell 54, Logansport 13
Plymouth 34, Northridge 6
Kankakee Valley 20, S.B. Washington 18
Concord 49, South Bend Clay 27
Sectional 10 Second Round
Lowell 14, Plymouth 8
Concord 21, Kankakee Valley 6
Sectional 10 Championship
Lowell 31, Concord 21

Sectional 11 First Round
DeKalb 21, Wawasee 3
Fort Wayne Wayne 24, New Haven 23
Columbia City 24, East Noble 21
Fort Wayne Dwenger 42, F.W. Elmhurst 8
Sectional 11 Second Round
DeKalb 31, Fort Wayne Wayne 24
Fort Wayne Dwenger 42, Columbia City 7
Sectional 11 Championship
Fort Wayne Dwenger 52, DeKalb 20

Sectional 12 First Round
Delta 21, Marion 13
Muncie South 27, Mount Vernon (Fortville) 24
Jay County 49, Muncie Central 29
New Castle 42, Pendleton Heights 36, OT
Sectional 12 Second Round
Muncie South 38, Delta 20
Jay County 23, New Castle 16
Sectional 12 Championship
Jay County 34, Muncie South 21

Sectional 13 First Round
Plainfield 24, Frankfort 6
Lebanon 25, Indpls. Northwest 6
Zionsville 21, Mooresville 7
Westfield 42, Indpls. Broad Ripple 14
Sectional 13 Second Round
Plainfield 42, Lebanon 3
Westfield 21, Zionsville 12
Sectional 13 Championship
Westfield 14, Plainfield 7

Sectional 14 First Round
Indpls. Cathedral 42, Roncalli 7
Greenwood 35, New Palestine 27
Franklin 35, Greenfield-Central 14
Whiteland 37, Indpls. Manual 0
Sectional 14 Second Round
Indpls. Cathedral 35, Greenwood 10
Whiteland 55, Franklin 20
Sectional 14 Championship
Indpls. Cathedral 42, Whiteland 14

Sectional 15 First Round
South Dearborn 36, Madison 7
Shelbyville 45, Franklin County 14
East Central 35, Seymour 7
Columbus East 54, Connersville 13
Sectional 15 Second Round
Shelbyville 41, South Dearborn 13
Columbus East 35, East Central 20
Sectional 15 Championship
Columbus East 28, Shelbyville 7

Sectional 16 First Round
Evansville Reitz 48, Owen Valley 13
Jasper 13, Northview 10
Evansville Central 42, Evansville Harrison 7
Sectional 16 Second Round
Evansville Reitz 47, Boonville 0
Jasper 13, Evansville Central 10
Sectional 16 Championship
Evansville Reitz 34, Jasper 8

Regional Championships
Lowell 20, Griffith 13
Fort Wayne Dwenger 42, Jay County 14
Indpls. Cathedral 34, Westfield 0
Evansville Reitz 61, Columbus East 60

Semi-State Championships
Lowell 10, Fort Wayne Dwenger 7
Evansville Reitz 35, Indpls. Cathedral 34

State Championship
Evansville Reitz 33, Lowell 14

Class 3A
Sectional 17 First Round
Knox 52, Hammond Gavit 0
Andrean 14, New Prairie 7
Hammond Clark 54, Gary Roosevelt 14
Calumet 19, Gary Wirt 14
Sectional 17 Second Round
Andrean 26, Knox 7
Hammond Clark 44, Calumet 18
Sectional 17 Championship
Andrean 49, Hammond Clark 34

Sectional 18 First Round
Culver Military Academy 24, Peru 16
S.B. St. Joseph 35, Tippecanoe Valley 6
John Glenn 62, Maconaquah 10
NorthWood 37, Mishawaka Marian 35
Sectional 18 Second Round
S.B. St. Joseph 41, Culver Military Academy 7
NorthWood 22, John Glenn 19
Sectional 18 Championship
S.B. St. Joseph 41, NorthWood 27

Sectional 19 First Round

Bellmont 23, Lakeland 6
Norwell 67, West Noble 13
Heritage 17, Leo 14
Fort Wayne Concordia 41, Angola 14
Sectional 19 Second Round
Bellmont 14, Norwell 7
Fort Wayne Concordia 42, Heritage 14
Sectional 19 Championship
Fort Wayne Concordia 34, Bellmont 7

Sectional 20 First Round
Western 42, Yorktown 21
Eastbrook 21, West Lafayette 14
Twin Lakes 7, Benton Central 6
Mississinewa 14, Blackford 6
Sectional 20 Second Round
Western 17, Eastbrook 14
Twin Lakes 32, Mississinewa 8
Sectional 20 Championship
Western 12, Twin Lakes 7

Sectional 21 First Round
Crawfordsville 36, West Vigo 0
Danville 42, Greencastle 10
North Montgomery 34, Southmont 14
Brebeuf Jesuit 59, Western Boone 44
Sectional 21 Second Round
Danville 31, Crawfordsville 14
Brebeuf Jesuit 28, North Montgomery 26
Sectional 21 Championship
Danville 40, Brebeuf Jesuit 20

Sectional 22 First Round
Rushville 28, Beech Grove 21
Indpls. Chatard 34, Greensburg 8
Batesville 36, Indpls. Howe 14
Sectional 22 Second Round
Hamilton Heights 20, Rushville 19
Indpls. Chatard 16, Batesville 6
Sectional 22 Championship
Indpls. Chatard 13, Hamilton Heights 10

Sectional 23 First Round
Heritage Hills 42, Salem 14
Charlestown 49, Brown County 20
Corydon Central 26, Crawford County 6
Edgewood 36, North Harrison 29
Sectional 23 Second Round
Heritage Hills 42, Charlestown 24
Edgewood 47, Corydon Central 7
Sectional 23 Championship
Heritage Hills 51, Edgewood 15

Sectional 24 First Round
Evansville Memorial 34, Gibson Southern 7
Washington 39, Pike Central 0
Evansville Bosse 27, Vincennes Lincoln 14
Mount Vernon 45, Princeton 14
Sectional 24 Second Round
Evansville Memorial 44, Washington 23
Mount Vernon 42, Evansville Bosse 14
Sectional 24 Championship
Mount Vernon 21, Evansville Memorial 14

Regional Championships
S.B. St. Joseph 35, Andrean 21
Fort Wayne Concordia 20, Western 13
Indpls. Chatard 52, Danville 6
Heritage Hills 36, Mount Vernon 14

Semi-State Championships
S.B. St. Joseph 28, Fort Wayne Concordia 10
Indpls. Chatard 28, Heritage Hills 17

State Championship
S.B. St. Joseph 31, Indpls. Chatard 7

Class 2A
Sectional 25 First Round
Winamac 36, Seeger 32
Delphi 55, North Newton 12
Rensselaer Central 44, Hammond Noll 19
Wheeler 34, North Judson 11
Sectional 25 Second Round
Delphi 24, Winamac 12
Wheeler 12, Rensselaer Central 0
Sectional 25 Championship
Wheeler 28, Delphi 7

Sectional 26 First Round
Whitko 34, Wabash 28, OT
Manchester 21, Bluffton 7
Bremen 34, Oak Hill 7
Lewis Cass 28, Rochester 14
Sectional 26 Second Round
Manchester 20, Whitko 0
Lewis Cass 27, Bremen 13
Sectional 26 Championship
Lewis Cass 42, Manchester 14

Sectional 27 First Round
Fairfield 16, Harding (Fort Wayne) 8
Jimtown 42, Woodlan 13
Central Noble 27, Garrett 13
Fort Wayne Luers 31, Prairie Heights 6
Sectional 27 Second Round
Jimtown 35, Fairfield 27
Fort Wayne Luers 31, Central Noble 7
Sectional 27 Championship
Fort Wayne Luers 24, Jimtown 17

Sectional 28 First Round
Tipton 37, Madison-Grant 14
Northwestern 26, Winchester 0
Taylor 64, Alexandria 22
Elwood 40, Frankton 13
Sectional 28 Second Round
Northwestern 17, Tipton 0

Elwood 20, Taylor 7
Sectional 28 Championship
Northwestern 20, Elwood 17

Sectional 29 First Round
Centerville 22, Shenandoah 12
Lawrenceburg 32, Indpls. Washington 8
Heritage Christian 55, Union County 12
Triton Central 60, Knightstown 20
Sectional 29 Second Round
Lawrenceburg 30, Centerville 7
Heritage Christian 31, Triton Central 3
Sectional 29 Championship
Heritage Christian 35, Lawrenceburg 0

Sectional 30 First Round
Speedway 20, Tri-West 0
North Putnam 53, South Vermillion 0
Cascade 35, Cloverdale 32
Monrovia 7, South Putnam 0
Sectional 30 Second Round
North Putnam 27, Speedway 14
Monrovia 43, Cascade 10
Sectional 30 Championship
North Putnam 26, Monrovia 7

Sectional 31 First Round
Paoli 23, Clarksville 20
Brownstown Central 55, Indian Creek 28
Providence 62, Eastern (Pekin) 15
Mitchell 20, Eastern Greene 16
Sectional 31 Second Round
Brownstown Central 26, Paoli 7
Providence 28, Mitchell 0
Sectional 31 Championship
Providence 35, Brownstown Central 26

Sectional 32 First Round
Evansville Mater Dei 35, South Spencer 13
Southridge 36, North Knox 20
Tell City 60, Sullivan 22
Sectional 32 Second Round
Evansville Mater Dei 34, North Posey 0
Southridge 26, Tell City 12
Sectional 32 Championship
Southridge 14, Evansville Mater Dei 13, OT

Regional Championships
Lewis Cass 41, Wheeler 0
Fort Wayne Luers 42, Northwestern 14
Heritage Christian 14, North Putnam 7
Southridge 35, Providence 28

Semi-State Championships
Fort Wayne Luers 14, Lewis Cass 0
Heritage Christian 24, Southridge 14

State Championship
Fort Wayne Luers 21, Heritage Christian 6

Class 1A
Sectional 33 First Round
South Newton 61, Lake Station 20
LaVille 26, West Central 17
Triton 63, River Forest 0
Whiting 40, South Central (Union Mills) 13
Sectional 33 Second Round
South Newton 47, LaVille 20
Triton 41, Whiting 13
Sectional 33 Championship
Triton 36, South Newton 21

Sectional 34 First Round
Churubusco 28, Southwood 7
Eastside 7, Fremont 0
Adams Central 28, Northfield 3
South Adams 37, Southern Wells 18
Sectional 34 Second Round
Churubusco 48, Eastside 6
Adams Central 28, South Adams 0
Sectional 34 Championship
Churubusco 17, Adams Central 14

Sectional 35 First Round
Tri-County 41, North White 0
Pioneer 62, Caston 13
North Miami 34, Carroll (Flora) 8
Culver 25, Frontier 10
Sectional 35 Second Round
Tri-County 23, Pioneer 21
North Miami 41, Culver 13
Sectional 35 Championship
Tri-County 16, North Miami 14

Sectional 36 First Round
Sheridan 54, Eastern (Greentown) 6
Clinton Central 28, Lafayette C.C. 27
Clinton Prairie 28, Park Tudor 6
Guerin Catholic 35, Tri-Central 13
Sectional 36 Second Round
Sheridan 49, Clinton Central 0
Guerin Catholic 15, Clinton Prairie 12
Sectional 36 Championship
Sheridan 48, Guerin Catholic 7

Sectional 37 First Round
Indpls. Lutheran 31, Edinburgh 14
Indiana Deaf 44, North Decatur 16
Indpls. Scecina 14, Milan 0
Indpls. Ritter 42, South Decatur 14
Sectional 37 Second Round
Indiana Deaf 36, Indpls. Lutheran 3
Indpls. Ritter 50, Indpls. Scecina 29
Sectional 37 Championship
Indpls. Ritter 27, Indiana Deaf 8

Sectional 38 First Round
Hagerstown 27, Cambridge City Lincoln 8

Northeastern 20, Eastern Hancock 6
Tri 35, Union City 6
Lapel 33, Wes-Del 24
Sectional 38 Second Round
Northeastern 40, Hagerstown 26
Tri 12, Lapel 6
Sectional 38 Championship
Tri 17, Northeastern 14

Sectional 39 First Round
Covington 21, Riverton Parke 6
Rockville 34, Turkey Run 7
Fountain Central 14, Attica 7
North Central (Farm.) 52, North Vermillion 12
Sectional 39 Second Round
Rockville 55, Covington 13
Fountain Central 20, North Central (Farm.) 14
Sectional 39 Championship
Rockville 41, Fountain Central 14

Sectional 40 First Round
Tecumseh 34, Union (Dugger) 13
Perry Central 29, North Daviess 23, OT
Wood Memorial 27, West Washington 26
Linton-Stockton 22, Springs Valley 6
Sectional 40 Second Round
Perry Central 43, Tecumseh 6
Linton-Stockton 30, Wood Memorial 0
Sectional 40 Championship
Linton-Stockton 35, Perry Central 14

Regional Championships
Churubusco 28, Triton 14
Sheridan 36, Tri-County 0
Indpls. Ritter 35, Tri 13
Rockville 25, Linton-Stockton 13

Semi-State Championships
Sheridan 48, Churubusco 13
Rockville 35, Indpls. Ritter 17

State Championship
Sheridan 34, Rockville 28

2008
Class 5A
Sectional 1 First Round
Merrillville 42, Crown Point 6
Munster 23, Lake Central 0
Chesterton 28, Michigan City 19
Valparaiso 42, Portage 19
Sectional 1 Second Round
Merrillville 37, Munster 7
Chesterton 10, Valparaiso 6
Sectional 1 Championship
Merrillville 14, Chesterton 7

Sectional 2 First Round
LaPorte 49, Elkhart Memorial 42

South Bend Adams 42, Goshen 30
Penn 38, Elkhart Central 0
Mishawaka 35, South Bend Riley 14
Sectional 2 Second Round
LaPorte 37, South Bend Adams 27
Penn 17, Mishawaka 7
Sectional 2 Championship
Penn 33, LaPorte 18

Sectional 3 First Round
Fort Wayne South 34, Fort Wayne Northrop 7
Huntington North 24, Warsaw 21
Fort Wayne Snider 41, Homestead 14
Fort Wayne North 35, Carroll (Fort Wayne) 13
Sectional 3 Second Round
Fort Wayne South 21, Huntington North 20
Fort Wayne Snider 28, Fort Wayne North 27
Sectional 3 Championship
Fort Wayne Snider 21, Fort Wayne South 6

Sectional 4 First Round
Kokomo 40, Anderson Highland 14
Harrison (West Lafayette) 42, McCutcheon 14
Lafayette Jefferson 42, Anderson 14
Carmel 41, Noblesville 0
Sectional 4 Second Round
Harrison (West Lafayette) 23, Kokomo 20
Carmel 44, Lafayette Jefferson 21
Sectional 4 Championship
Carmel 48, Harrison (West Lafayette) 3

Sectional 5 First Round
Richmond 48, Indpls. Arlington 46
Lawrence Central 44, North Central (Indpls.) 17
Fishers 31, Lawrence North 20
Warren Central 49, Hamilton Southeastern 21
Sectional 5 Second Round
Lawrence Central 73, Richmond 41
Warren Central 56, Fishers 27
Sectional 5 Championship
Warren Central 32, Lawrence Central 23

Sectional 6 First Round
Avon 49, Indpls. Tech 3
Southport 56, Perry Meridian 35
Ben Davis 34, Pike 14
Brownsburg 21, Franklin Central 18
Sectional 6 Second Round
Avon 35, Southport 21
Ben Davis 45, Brownsburg 10
Sectional 6 Championship
Ben Davis 26, Avon 14

Sectional 7 First Round
Bloomington North 23, Decatur Central 21
Terre Haute North 40, Martinsville 36
Center Grove 49, Terre Haute South 14
Bloomington South 40, Columbus North 37
Sectional 7 Second Round

Bloomington North 50, T.H. North 49, 2 OT
Center Grove 56, Bloomington South 14
Sectional 7 Championship
Center Grove 55, Bloomington North 16

Sectional 8 First Round
Castle 41, Evansville North 12
Jeffersonville 41, Jennings County 8
Floyd Central 23, Bedford North Lawrence 14
Sectional 8 Second Round
Castle 56, New Albany 14
Jeffersonville 42, Floyd Central 17
Sectional 8 Championship
Castle 49, Jeffersonville 39

Regional Championships
Penn 19, Merrillville 0
Carmel 24, Fort Wayne Snider 21
Ben Davis 45, Warren Central 23
Center Grove 49, Castle 7

Semi-State Championships
Carmel 38, Penn 3
Center Grove 49, Ben Davis 21

State Championship
Center Grove 36, Carmel 33

Class 4A
Sectional 9 First Round
Hammond Morton 30, Gary Wallace 0
Hammond 8, Highland 6
Griffith 42, East Chicago Central 0
Hobart 59, Gary West 12
Sectional 9 Second Round
Hammond Morton 42, Hammond 0
Griffith 35, Hobart 14
Sectional 9 Championship
Griffith 21, Hammond Morton 7

Sectional 10 First Round
Northridge 26, Logansport 20
South Bend Clay 28, Kankakee Valley 7
Lowell 24, S.B. Washington 7
Plymouth 25, Concord 24
Sectional 10 Second Round
South Bend Clay 14, Northridge 7
Lowell 20, Plymouth 14, OT
Sectional 10 Championship
Lowell 49, South Bend Clay 20

Sectional 11 First Round
Fort Wayne Dwenger 21, East Noble 17
Columbia City 24, Wawasee 9
New Haven 24, Fort Wayne Elmhurst 13
Fort Wayne Wayne 14, DeKalb 13
Sectional 11 Second Round
Fort Wayne Dwenger 42, Columbia City 0
Fort Wayne Wayne 35, New Haven 17

Sectional 11 Championship
Fort Wayne Dwenger 47, Fort Wayne Wayne 7

Sectional 12 First Round
Delta 49, Pendleton Heights 28
Mount Vernon (Fortville) 28, Muncie Central 7
Muncie South 42, New Castle 28
Marion 47, Jay County 33
Sectional 12 Second Round
Delta 49, Mount Vernon (Fortville) 13
Muncie South 43, Marion 35
Sectional 12 Championship
Delta 42, Muncie South 6

Sectional 13 First Round
Indpls. Broad Ripple 23, Indpls. Northwest 8
Plainfield 28, Frankfort 7
Mooresville 35, Lebanon 0
Zionsville 24, Westfield 0
Sectional 13 Second Round
Plainfield 28, Indpls. Broad Ripple 0
Zionsville 28, Mooresville 15
Sectional 13 Championship
Zionsville 42, Plainfield 13

Sectional 14 First Round
Indpls. Cathedral 21, Roncalli 8
Greenfield-Central 14, Indpls. Manual 8
Greenwood 9, Franklin 7
Whiteland 40, New Palestine 7
Sectional 14 Second Round
Indpls. Cathedral 45, Greenfield-Central 7
Whiteland 44, Greenwood 17
Sectional 14 Championship
Indpls. Cathedral 24, Whiteland 0

Sectional 15 First Round
Shelbyville 49, Franklin County 7
East Central 59, Connersville 7
Columbus East 42, Seymour 14
Madison 35, South Dearborn 0
Sectional 15 Second Round
East Central 38, Shelbyville 28
Columbus East 42, Madison 6
Sectional 15 Championship
Columbus East 28, East Central 12

Sectional 16 First Round
Evansville Central 7, Boonville 6
Evansville Reitz 40, Northview 8
Jasper 50, Owen Valley 8
Sectional 16 Second Round
Evansville Central 35, Evansville Harrison 17
Jasper 38, Evansville Reitz 35
Sectional 16 Championship
Jasper 42, Evansville Central 28

Regional Championships
Lowell 19, Griffith 13

Fort Wayne Dwenger 49, Delta 20
Indpls. Cathedral 27, Zionsville 11
Columbus East 24, Jasper 7

Semi-State Championships
Fort Wayne Dwenger 38, Lowell 22
Indpls. Cathedral 41, Columbus East 10

State Championship
Indpls. Cathedral 10, Fort Wayne Dwenger 7

Class 3A
Sectional 17 First Round
Knox 32, Gary Wirt 18
Hammond Clark 22, Hammond Gavit 12
New Prairie 49, Gary Roosevelt 14
Andrean 46, Calumet 6
Sectional 17 Second Round
Knox 32, Hammond Clark 13
Andrean 37, New Prairie 14
Sectional 17 Championship
Andrean 52, Knox 14

Sectional 18 First Round
NorthWood 49, Peru 14
Culver Military Academy 24, Maconaquah 8
Mishawaka Marian 39, Tippecanoe Valley 25
S.B. St. Joseph 35, John Glenn 0
Sectional 18 Second Round
NorthWood 40, Culver Military Academy 7
S.B. St. Joseph 45, Mishawaka Marian 0
Sectional 18 Championship
NorthWood 34, S.B. St. Joseph 28

Sectional 19 First Round
Bellmont 54, Angola 20
Fort Wayne Concordia 35, Norwell 14
Leo 42, West Noble 0
Heritage 13, Lakeland 10
Sectional 19 Second Round
Bellmont 30, Fort Wayne Concordia 20
Leo 26, Heritage 7
Sectional 19 Championship
Bellmont 41, Leo 7

Sectional 20 First Round
West Lafayette 33, Benton Central 14
Eastbrook 42, Blackford 0
Western 37, Mississinewa 3
Yorktown 50, Twin Lakes 20
Sectional 20 Second Round
West Lafayette 34, Eastbrook 16
Yorktown 22, Western 21
Sectional 20 Championship
Yorktown 34, West Lafayette 26

Sectional 21 First Round
Southmont 21, Greencastle 14
Western Boone 33, Danville 32

North Montgomery 22, Brebeuf Jesuit 0
West Vigo 14, Crawfordsville 0
Sectional 21 Second Round
Southmont 32, Western Boone 11
North Montgomery 42, West Vigo 18
Sectional 21 Championship
North Montgomery 24, Southmont 8

Sectional 22 First Round
Greensburg 34, Batesville 28
Hamilton Heights 46, Beech Grove 14
Rushville 49, Indpls. Howe 0
Sectional 22 Second Round
Indpls. Chatard 42, Greensburg 0
Rushville 21, Hamilton Heights 14
Sectional 22 Championship
Indpls. Chatard 41, Rushville 13

Sectional 23 First Round
Heritage Hills 28, Salem 0
Charlestown 33, North Harrison 15
Edgewood 49, Corydon Central 20
Brown County 35, Crawford County 20
Sectional 23 Second Round
Heritage Hills 32, Charlestown 6
Edgewood 49, Brown County 7
Sectional 23 Championship
Heritage Hills 44, Edgewood 0

Sectional 24 First Round
Vincennes Lincoln 33, Pike Central 7
Evansville Memorial 42, Gibson Southern 20
Evansville Bosse 42, Princeton 26
Washington 20, Mount Vernon 12
Sectional 24 Second Round
Evansville Memorial 35, Vincennes Lincoln 7
Washington 56, Evansville Bosse 13
Sectional 24 Championship
Evansville Memorial 37, Washington 15

Regional Championships
NorthWood 35, Andrean 28
Bellmont 25, Yorktown 21
Indpls. Chatard 42, North Montgomery 20
Evansville Memorial 6, Heritage Hills 3

Semi-State Championships
Bellmont 35, NorthWood 21
Evansville Memorial 27, Indpls. Chatard 14

State Championship
Bellmont 28, Evansville Memorial 14

Class 2A
Sectional 25 First Round
Winamac 21, North Newton 6
Rensselaer Central 52, Hammond Noll 22
Seeger 35, Delphi 7
North Judson 31, Wheeler 28

Sectional 25 Second Round
Rensselaer Central 55, Winamac 27
North Judson 62, Seeger 34
Sectional 25 Championship
Rensselaer Central 9, North Judson 0

Sectional 26 First Round
Rochester 30, Manchester 20
Oak Hill 42, Bluffton 6
Lewis Cass 29, Bremen 27
Whitko 16, Wabash 10
Sectional 26 Second Round
Oak Hill 34, Rochester 13
Lewis Cass 27, Whitko 0
Sectional 26 Championship
Lewis Cass 53, Oak Hill 27

Sectional 27 First Round
Jimtown 42, Central Noble 8
Harding (Fort Wayne) 43, Woodlan 7
Fairfield 35, Garrett 7
Fort Wayne Luers 49, Prairie Heights 0
Sectional 27 Second Round
Jimtown 18, Harding (Fort Wayne) 8
Fort Wayne Luers 44, Fairfield 14
Sectional 27 Championship
Jimtown 21, Fort Wayne Luers 14, OT

Sectional 28 First Round
Tipton 53, Alexandria 0
Northwestern 20, Taylor 14
Elwood 44, Winchester 20
Madison-Grant 35, Frankton 6
Sectional 28 Second Round
Tipton 26, Northwestern 13
Madison-Grant 28, Elwood 26
Sectional 28 Championship
Madison-Grant 14, Tipton 0

Sectional 29 First Round
Heritage Christian 53, Union County 7
Shenandoah 28, Triton Central 14
Lawrenceburg 56, Indpls. Washington 13
Centerville 21, Knightstown 0
Sectional 29 Second Round
Heritage Christian 31, Shenandoah 14
Lawrenceburg 21, Centerville 3
Sectional 29 Championship
Heritage Christian 27, Lawrenceburg 7

Sectional 30 First Round
South Vermillion 30, Cascade 7
Monrovia 52, Cloverdale 7
North Putnam 35, South Putnam 0
Speedway 27, Tri-West 7
Sectional 30 Second Round
Monrovia 67, South Vermillion 20
Speedway 28, North Putnam 27
Sectional 30 Championship
Speedway 34, Monrovia 16

Sectional 31 First Round
Mitchell 16, Eastern (Pekin) 14
Paoli 49, Eastern Greene 24
Indian Creek 42, Clarksville 8
Brownstown Central 17, Providence 7
Sectional 31 Second Round
Paoli 58, Mitchell 0
Brownstown Central 30, Indian Creek 28
Sectional 31 Championship
Brownstown Central 28, Paoli 21

Sectional 32 First Round
Southridge 21, Evansville Mater Dei 7
North Knox 49, Tell City 27
South Spencer 15, Forest Park 7
North Posey 49, Sullivan 18
Sectional 32 Second Round
Southridge 44, North Knox 13
North Posey 42, South Spencer 21
Sectional 32 Championship
Southridge 42, North Posey 28

Regional Championships
Lewis Cass 30, Rensselaer Central 14
Jimtown 21, Madison-Grant 0
Heritage Christian 27, Speedway 21
Brownstown Central 26, Southridge 6

Semi-State Championships
Lewis Cass 28, Jimtown 7
Heritage Christian 24, Brownstown Central 16

State Championship
Heritage Christian 17, Lewis Cass 14

Class 1A
Sectional 33 First Round
Triton 35, Whiting 14
LaVille 40, South Central (Union Mills) 12
South Newton 19, West Central 16
Lake Station 12, River Forest 6
Sectional 33 Second Round
Triton 14, LaVille 6
South Newton 48, Lake Station 0
Sectional 33 Championship
Triton 23, South Newton 21

Sectional 34 First Round
Southern Wells 59, Northfield 14
Adams Central 21, Fremont 7
Churubusco 35, South Adams 14
Southwood 52, Eastside 20
Sectional 34 Second Round
Southern Wells 34, Adams Central 6
Southwood 24, Churubusco 13
Sectional 34 Championship
Southern Wells 35, Southwood 0

Sectional 35 First Round
Pioneer 50, Carroll (Flora) 7
Tri-County 14, Culver 12
Frontier 23, North White 15
North Miami 42, Caston 26
Sectional 35 Second Round
Pioneer 43, Tri-County 8
North Miami 21, Frontier 19
Sectional 35 Championship
Pioneer 28, North Miami 7

Sectional 36 First Round
Guerin Catholic 50, Eastern (Greentown) 39
Clinton Central 61, Clinton Prairie 0
Sheridan 55, Tri-Central 6
Lafayette Central Catholic 40, Park Tudor 14
Sectional 36 Second Round
Clinton Central 55, Guerin Catholic 0
Sheridan 34, Lafayette Central Catholic 28
Sectional 36 Championship
Sheridan 34, Clinton Central 0

Sectional 37 First Round
Indpls. Ritter 49, Indiana Deaf 0
Indpls. Scecina 28, Indpls. Lutheran 0
South Decatur 52, Edinburgh 0
Milan 48, North Decatur 14
Sectional 37 Second Round
Indpls. Ritter 28, Indpls. Scecina 7
South Decatur 17, Milan 14, 2 OT
Sectional 37 Championship
Indpls. Ritter 42, South Decatur 7

Sectional 38 First Round
Tri 20, Wes-Del 0
Lapel 22, Eastern Hancock 0
Northeastern 34, Union City 20
Hagerstown 38, Cambridge City Lincoln 6
Sectional 38 Second Round
Lapel 39, Tri 20
Hagerstown 42, Northeastern 6
Sectional 38 Championship
Lapel 40, Hagerstown 21

Sectional 39 First Round
Riverton Parke 21, Turkey Run 8
Attica 28, North Central (Farmersburg) 0
Rockville 29, Fountain Central 0
North Vermillion 19, Covington 7
Sectional 39 Second Round
Attica 54, Riverton Parke 25
Rockville 50, North Vermillion 7
Sectional 39 Championship
Rockville 35, Attica 7

Sectional 40 First Round
North Daviess 68, Springs Valley 0
Perry Central 45, Wood Memorial 0
West Washington 40, Union (Dugger) 20
Linton-Stockton 13, Tecumseh 6
Sectional 40 Second Round
North Daviess 7, Perry Central 6
Linton-Stockton 20, West Washington 8
Sectional 40 Championship
Linton-Stockton 18, North Daviess 16

Regional Championships
Southern Wells 32, Triton 0
Sheridan 21, Pioneer 19
Indpls. Ritter 47, Lapel 9
Linton-Stockton 28, Rockville 14

Semi-State Championships
Sheridan 48, Southern Wells 14
Indpls. Ritter 30, Linton-Stockton 26

State Championship
Indpls. Ritter 34, Sheridan 27

2009
Class 5A
Sectional 1 First Round
Portage 42, East Chicago Central 0
Chesterton 16, Crown Point 13
Merrillville 31, Valparaiso 0
Lake Central 7, Munster 3
Sectional 1 Second Round
Portage 14, Chesterton 0
Merrillville 20, Lake Central 13
Sectional 1 Championship
Merrillville 9, Portage 3

Sectional 2 First Round
Elkhart Memorial 23, Michigan City 0
Mishawaka 27, LaPorte 14
South Bend Adams 29, Elkhart Central 26
Penn 28, Goshen 7
Sectional 2 Second Round
Mishawaka 32, Elkhart Memorial 26
Penn 14, South Bend Adams 7
Sectional 2 Championship
Mishawaka 24, Penn 21

Sectional 3 First Round
Fort Wayne North 20, Huntington North 17
Fort Wayne Snider 42, Kokomo 7
Homestead 26, Carroll (Fort Wayne) 3
Warsaw 21, Fort Wayne Northrop 0
Sectional 3 Second Round
Fort Wayne Snider 35, Fort Wayne North 0
Warsaw 10, Homestead 7
Sectional 3 Championship
Fort Wayne Snider 33, Warsaw 20

Sectional 4 First Round
Hamilton Southeastern 19, Harrison (W.L.) 0
Noblesville 58, Lafayette Jefferson 30

Carmel 21, Westfield 7
Fishers 37, McCutcheon 7
Sectional 4 Second Round
Hamilton Southeastern 34, Noblesville 0
Carmel 7, Fishers 0
Sectional 4 Championship
Carmel 17, Hamilton Southeastern 9

Sectional 5 First Round
Perry Meridian 27, Richmond 7
Warren Central 14, Franklin Central 13
Lawrence Central 33, Lawrence North 21
North Central (Indpls.) 37, Southport 22
Sectional 5 Second Round
Warren Central 42, Perry Meridian 7
Lawrence Central 34, North Central (Indpls.) 6
Sectional 5 Championship
Warren Central 28, Lawrence Central 14

Sectional 6 First Round
Brownsburg 65, Indpls. Tech 0
Zionsville 17, Terre Haute South 14
Avon 28, Ben Davis 24
Pike 31, Terre Haute North 15
Sectional 6 Second Round
Brownsburg 20, Zionsville 14
Avon 10, Pike 7
Sectional 6 Championship
Brownsburg 42, Avon 14

Sectional 7 First Round
Center Grove 49, Bloomington South 6
Columbus East 27, Columbus North 26
Bloomington North 50, Decatur Central 49, OT
Whiteland 58, Martinsville 33
Sectional 7 Second Round
Center Grove 21, Columbus East 14
Bloomington North 49, Whiteland 42
Sectional 7 Championship
Center Grove 48, Bloomington North 7

Sectional 8 First Round
Castle 21, Jeffersonville 14
New Albany 33, Evansville North 21
Floyd Central 62, Jennings County 27
Sectional 8 Second Round
Castle 21, Bedford North Lawrence 6
Floyd Central 34, New Albany 27
Sectional 8 Championship
Floyd Central 42, Castle 32

Regional Championships
Merrillville 28, Mishawaka 27
Carmel 10, Fort Wayne Snider 7
Warren Central 14, Brownsburg 6
Center Grove 42, Floyd Central 7

Semi-State Championships
Carmel 42, Merrillville 0

Warren Central 28, Center Grove 10

State Championship
Warren Central 42, Carmel 36

Class 4A
Sectional 9 First Round
Griffith 66, Gary West 6
Hammond Morton 14, Highland 0
Hammond 40, Gary Wallace 14
Hobart 57, Gary Roosevelt 6
Sectional 9 Second Round
Hammond Morton 34, Griffith 20
Hobart 35, Hammond 6
Sectional 9 Championship
Hammond Morton 42, Hobart 0

Sectional 10 First Round
South Bend Riley 15, Kankakee Valley 13
Concord 45, Logansport 13
Lowell 14, Plymouth 6
S.B. Washington 21, South Bend Clay 20
Sectional 10 Second Round
Concord 42, South Bend Riley 8
Lowell 24, S.B. Washington 7
Sectional 10 Championship
Lowell 60, Concord 23

Sectional 11 First Round
East Noble 32, Wawasee 0
Columbia City 21, Fort Wayne Elmhurst 6
Northridge 35, Angola 6
Fort Wayne Dwenger 54, DeKalb 0
Sectional 11 Second Round
Columbia City 17, East Noble 13
Fort Wayne Dwenger 28, Northridge 0
Sectional 11 Championship
Fort Wayne Dwenger 56, Columbia City 0

Sectional 12 First Round
New Haven 28, Jay County 10
Fort Wayne Wayne 30, Marion 0
Delta 21, Fort Wayne South 7
Muncie South 41, Muncie Central 7
Sectional 12 Second Round
Fort Wayne Wayne 14, New Haven 2
Delta 7, Muncie South 6
Sectional 12 Championship
Delta 18, Fort Wayne Wayne 6

Sectional 13 First Round
Mount Vernon (Fortville) 48, New Castle 0
Anderson Highland 36, Greenfield-Central 6
Indpls. Arlington 21, Anderson 14
New Palestine 41, Pendleton Heights 21
Sectional 13 Second Round
And. Highland 21, Mt. Vernon (FV) 20, 2 OT
New Palestine 33, Indpls. Arlington 0
Sectional 13 Championship

New Palestine 48, Anderson Highland 22

Sectional 14 First Round
Roncalli 39, Indpls. Broad Ripple 14
Plainfield 49, Indpls. Northwest 12
Mooresville 61, Indpls. Manual 18
Indpls. Cathedral 47, Lebanon 15
Sectional 14 Second Round
Plainfield 21, Roncalli 14
Indpls. Cathedral 24, Mooresville 9
Sectional 14 Championship
Indpls. Cathedral 48, Plainfield 21

Sectional 15 First Round
South Dearborn 24, Madison 10
Shelbyville 34, Franklin County 14
East Central 56, Connersville 18
Greenwood 17, Franklin 0
Sectional 15 Second Round
Shelbyville 13, South Dearborn 12
East Central 14, Greenwood 0
Sectional 15 Championship
East Central 21, Shelbyville 17

Sectional 16 First Round
Boonville 35, Owen Valley 6
Jasper 50, Northview 0
Evansville Reitz 35, Seymour 0
Evansville Central 37, Evansville Harrison 7
Sectional 16 Second Round
Jasper 28, Boonville 0
Evansville Reitz 35, Evansville Central 7
Sectional 16 Championship
Evansville Reitz 42, Jasper 6

Regional Championships
Lowell 42, Hammond Morton 0
Fort Wayne Dwenger 49, Delta 12
Indpls. Cathedral 45, New Palestine 6
Evansville Reitz 52, East Central 28

Semi-State Championships
Lowell 24, Fort Wayne Dwenger 21
Evansville Reitz 31, Indpls. Cathedral 10

State Championship
Evansville Reitz 23, Lowell 9

Class 3A
Sectional 17 First Round
New Prairie 52, Hammond Gavit 6
Culver Military Academy 21, Hammond Clark 0
Andrean 53, Calumet 7
Knox 31, John Glenn 15
Sectional 17 Second Round
Culver Military Academy 14, New Prairie 0
Andrean 28, Knox 7
Sectional 17 Championship
Andrean 48, Culver Military Academy 7

Sectional 18 First Round
NorthWood 25, Lakeland 6
S.B. St. Joseph 54, Tippecanoe Valley 7
Rochester 42, West Noble 20
Jimtown 17, Mishawaka Marian 14
Sectional 18 Second Round
NorthWood 12, S.B. St. Joseph 6
Jimtown 14, Rochester 0
Sectional 18 Championship
Jimtown 16, NorthWood 7

Sectional 19 First Round
Harding (Fort Wayne) 28, Norwell 21
Eastbrook 33, Leo 26
Heritage 31, Fort Wayne Concordia 28
Bellmont 50, Blackford 0
Sectional 19 Second Round
Eastbrook 21, Harding (Fort Wayne) 14
Bellmont 30, Heritage 0
Sectional 19 Championship
Eastbrook 34, Bellmont 0

Sectional 20 First Round
Peru 31, Mississinewa 0
Frankfort 32, Twin Lakes 7
Western 41, Maconaquah 0
West Lafayette 28, Benton Central 8
Sectional 20 Second Round
Frankfort 30, Peru 0
West Lafayette 21, Western 6
Sectional 20 Championship
West Lafayette 54, Frankfort 22

Sectional 21 First Round
Indpls. Chatard 38, Crawfordsville 21
Southmont 23, West Vigo 0
North Montgomery 31, Western Boone 28
Brebeuf Jesuit 49, Danville 7
Sectional 21 Second Round
Indpls. Chatard 35, Southmont 0
Brebeuf Jesuit 21, North Montgomery 7
Sectional 21 Championship
Indpls. Chatard 21, Brebeuf Jesuit 7

Sectional 22 First Round
Rushville 15, Greensburg 11
Hamilton Heights 20, Yorktown 14
Beech Grove 35, Indpls. Howe 8
Sectional 22 Second Round
Batesville 28, Rushville 6
Hamilton Heights 27, Beech Grove 7
Sectional 22 Championship
Batesville 27, Hamilton Heights 6

Sectional 23 First Round
Corydon Central 27, Edgewood 7
Indian Creek 20, Charlestown 0
Salem 28, Brown County 0

Heritage Hills 43, North Harrison 7
Sectional 23 Second Round
Indian Creek 13, Corydon Central 8
Heritage Hills 29, Salem 0
Sectional 23 Championship
Heritage Hills 7, Indian Creek 0

Sectional 24 First Round
Gibson Southern 24, Vincennes Lincoln 9
Washington 38, Princeton 0
Evansville Memorial 44, Mount Vernon 21
Evansville Bosse 31, Pike Central 26
Sectional 24 Second Round
Washington 40, Gibson Southern 13
Evansville Memorial 49, Evansville Bosse 26
Sectional 24 Championship
Evansville Memorial 42, Washington 20

Regional Championships
Jimtown 10, Andrean 7
West Lafayette 35, Eastbrook 14
Indpls. Chatard 31, Batesville 14
Evansville Memorial 28, Heritage Hills 20

Semi-State Championships
West Lafayette 28, Jimtown 14
Evansville Memorial 37, Indpls. Chatard 21

State Championship
West Lafayette 24, Evansville Memorial 10

Class 2A
Sectional 25 First Round
North Judson 64, River Forest 14
Wheeler 41, North Newton 7
Rensselaer Central 20, Seeger 14
Bowman Academy 36, Hammond Noll 20
Sectional 25 Second Round
Wheeler 48, North Judson 7
Rensselaer Central 64, Bowman Academy 6
Sectional 25 Championship
Rensselaer Central 21, Wheeler 18

Sectional 26 First Round
Garrett 32, Woodlan 0
Bremen 44, Eastside 0
Central Noble 29, Whitko 26
Fairfield 79, Prairie Heights 6
Sectional 26 Second Round
Bremen 3, Garrett 0
Fairfield 14, Central Noble 6
Sectional 26 Championship
Fairfield 28, Bremen 27

Sectional 27 First Round
Madison-Grant 55, Wabash 21
Winchester 14, Oak Hill 6
Eastern (Greentown) 38, Bluffton 12
Fort Wayne Luers 45, Manchester 21

Sectional 27 Second Round
Winchester 30, Madison-Grant 22
Fort Wayne Luers 35, Eastern (Greentown) 22
Sectional 27 Championship
Fort Wayne Luers 68, Winchester 0

Sectional 28 First Round
Tipton 41, Delphi 13
Lewis Cass 31, Frankton 0
Taylor 35, Alexandria 21
Northwestern 61, Elwood 0
Sectional 28 Second Round
Lewis Cass 15, Tipton 0
Northwestern 25, Taylor 0
Sectional 28 Championship
Lewis Cass 28, Northwestern 7

Sectional 29 First Round
Indpls. Ritter 55, Union County 13
Heritage Christian 27, Park Tudor 14
Speedway 59, Indpls. Washington 0
Centerville 41, Shenandoah 24
Sectional 29 Second Round
Indpls. Ritter 6, Heritage Christian 0
Speedway 35, Centerville 6
Sectional 29 Championship
Indpls. Ritter 41, Speedway 17

Sectional 30 First Round
South Putnam 33, South Vermillion 28
Monrovia 53, Cloverdale 0
Tri-West 7, Greencastle 2
North Putnam 40, Cascade 0
Sectional 30 Second Round
Monrovia 6, South Putnam 3, OT
North Putnam 4, Tri-West 0
Sectional 30 Championship
Monrovia 7, North Putnam 6

Sectional 31 First Round
Lawrenceburg 30, Eastern (Pekin) 6
Brownstown Central 55, Mitchell 24
Providence 21, Triton Central 14
Paoli 48, Clarksville 16
Sectional 31 Second Round
Brownstown Central 14, Lawrenceburg 7
Paoli 8, Providence 7
Sectional 31 Championship
Paoli 21, Brownstown Central 13

Sectional 32 First Round
Tell City 47, Crawford County 7
North Posey 12, Southridge 9
Evansville Mater Dei 61, Forest Park 21
South Spencer 30, Sullivan 20
Sectional 32 Second Round
North Posey 21, Tell City 0
Evansville Mater Dei 12, South Spencer 0
Sectional 32 Championship

Evansville Mater Dei 28, North Posey 7

Regional Championships
Rensselaer Central 35, Fairfield 0
Fort Wayne Luers 54, Lewis Cass 53, 2 OT
Monrovia 20, Indpls. Ritter 15
Paoli 14, Evansville Mater Dei 7

Semi-State Championships
Fort Wayne Luers 52, Rensselaer Central 21
Monrovia 30, Paoli 13

State Championship
Fort Wayne Luers 24, Monrovia 17

Class 1A
Sectional 33 First Round
Culver 22, LaVille 16
Triton 27, Winamac 14
Whiting 48, Lake Station 0
South Central (Union Mills) 32, West Central 12
Sectional 33 Second Round
Culver 20, Triton 13
Whiting 14, South Central (Union Mills) 12
Sectional 33 Championship
Culver 48, Whiting 21

Sectional 34 First Round
Lafayette Central Catholic 20, Pioneer 0
Frontier 34, Tri-County 0
Caston 35, North White 20
South Newton 30, Carroll (Flora) 7
Sectional 34 Second Round
Lafayette Central Catholic 33, Frontier 6
Caston 14, South Newton 7
Sectional 34 Championship
Lafayette Central Catholic 58, Caston 13

Sectional 35 First Round
Adams Central 20, Churubusco 6
Southwood 14, North Miami 3
Fremont 29, Northfield 6
Southern Wells 28, South Adams 15
Sectional 35 Second Round
Southwood 24, Adams Central 0
Southern Wells 28, Fremont 0
Sectional 35 Championship
Southern Wells 17, Southwood 3

Sectional 36 First Round
Hagerstown 42, Union City 6
Knightstown 55, Cambridge City Lincoln 13
Northeastern 62, Wes-Del 12
Tri 48, Monroe Central 0
Sectional 36 Second Round
Knightstown 33, Hagerstown 0
Northeastern 7, Tri 0
Sectional 36 Championship
Knightstown 34, Northeastern 8

Sectional 37 First Round
Guerin Catholic 30, Sheridan 13
Clinton Prairie 38, Indiana Deaf 14
Clinton Central 66, Tri-Central 7
Lapel 20, Eastern Hancock 14
Sectional 37 Second Round
Guerin Catholic 28, Clinton Prairie 17
Clinton Central 42, Lapel 13
Sectional 37 Championship
Clinton Central 27, Guerin Catholic 6

Sectional 38 First Round
Indpls. Lutheran 30, West Washington 6
North Decatur 41, Edinburgh 14
Milan 27, South Decatur 13
Indpls. Scecina 43, Eastern Greene 26
Sectional 38 Second Round
Indpls. Lutheran 21, North Decatur 0
Indpls. Scecina 21, Milan 13
Sectional 38 Championship
Indpls. Lutheran 13, Indpls. Scecina 7

Sectional 39 First Round
Rockville 46, Turkey Run 0
North Vermillion 41, North Central (Farm.) 14
Fountain Central 55, Attica 6
Riverton Parke 26, Covington 0
Sectional 39 Second Round
Rockville 41, North Vermillion 0
Fountain Central 52, Riverton Parke 7
Sectional 39 Championship
Fountain Central 39, Rockville 0

Sectional 40 First Round
Perry Central 55, Springs Valley 0
North Daviess 64, Wood Memorial 0
North Knox 28, Union (Dugger) 8
Linton-Stockton 68, Tecumseh 13
Sectional 40 Second Round
North Daviess 14, Perry Central 7
Linton-Stockton 44, North Knox 0
Sectional 40 Championship
Linton-Stockton 28, North Daviess 24

Regional Championships
Lafayette Central Catholic 56, Culver 0
Southern Wells 41, Knightstown 14
Clinton Central 14, Indpls. Lutheran 0
Fountain Central 21, Linton-Stockton 7

Semi-State Championships
Lafayette Central Catholic 47, So. Wells 13
Fountain Central 42, Clinton Central 14

State Championship
Lafayette Central Catholic 52, Fountain Cent. 0

2010
Class 5A
Sectional 1 First Round
Crown Point 23, Portage 21
Munster 21, Lake Central 14
Valparaiso 61, East Chicago Central 22
Merrillville 48, Chesterton 27
Sectional 1 Second Round
Crown Point 28, Munster 10
Valparaiso 20, Merrillville 14
Sectional 1 Championship
Valparaiso 16, Crown Point 6

Sectional 2 First Round
Mishawaka 55, Elkhart Central 14
Goshen 49, Michigan City 31
Penn 44, South Bend Adams 0
Elkhart Memorial 21, LaPorte 6
Sectional 2 Second Round
Mishawaka 35, Goshen 7
Penn 27, Elkhart Memorial 6
Sectional 2 Championship
Mishawaka 14, Penn 7, OT

Sectional 3 First Round
Homestead 43, Huntington North 13
Carroll (Fort Wayne) 35, Fort Wayne Northrop 34, OT
Fort Wayne North 27, Warsaw 16
Fort Wayne Snider 44, Kokomo 14
Sectional 3 Second Round
Homestead 51, Carroll (Fort Wayne) 21
Fort Wayne Snider 41, Fort Wayne North 21
Sectional 3 Championship
Fort Wayne Snider 37, Homestead 29

Sectional 4 First Round
Hamilton Southeastern 38, Noblesville 0
Lafayette Jefferson 34, Harrison (W.L.) 33
Fishers 38, Westfield 7
Carmel 30, McCutcheon 14
Sectional 4 Second Round
Hamilton Southeastern 49, Lafayette Jeff 14
Fishers 17, Carmel 14
Sectional 4 Championship
Fishers 28, Hamilton Southeastern 0

Sectional 5 First Round
Perry Meridian 41, Richmond 27
Lawrence Central 35, Warren Central 14
Lawrence North 21, Franklin Central 13
Southport 16, North Central (Indpls.) 12
Sectional 5 Second Round
Lawrence Central 39, Perry Meridian 14
Southport 34, Lawrence North 20
Sectional 5 Championship
Lawrence Central 31, Southport 27

Sectional 6 First Round
Pike 45, Ben Davis 38, OT
Terre Haute North 28, Zionsville 24
Brownsburg 28, Terre Haute South 21, OT
Avon 56, Indpls. Tech 12
Sectional 6 Second Round
Pike 17, Terre Haute North 7
Avon 25, Brownsburg 21
Sectional 6 Championship
Avon 30, Pike 27

Sectional 7 First Round
Whiteland 37, Bloomington South 14
Columbus East 27, Center Grove 13
Bloomington North 31, Martinsville 24
Columbus North 66, Decatur Central 28
Sectional 7 Second Round
Whiteland 59, Columbus East 22
Bloomington North 45, Columbus North 35
Sectional 7 Championship
Bloomington North 28, Whiteland 21

Sectional 8 First Round
Castle 42, Bedford North Lawrence 35, 2 OT
New Albany 32, Jeffersonville 13
Floyd Central 41, Evansville North 13
Sectional 8 Second Round
Castle 69, Jennings County 27
Floyd Central 48, New Albany 47
Sectional 8 Championship
Castle 45, Floyd Central 44, OT

Regional Championships
Valparaiso 21, Mishawaka 14
Fishers 47, Fort Wayne Snider 34
Lawrence Central 46, Avon 39
Bloomington North 21, Castle 17

Semi-State Championships
Fishers 30, Valparaiso 12
Lawrence Central 41, Bloomington North 17

State Championship
Fishers 38, Lawrence Central 19

Class 4A
Sectional 9 First Round
Hammond Morton 56, Gary Roosevelt 8
Hobart 35, Griffith 14
Hammond 60, Gary Wallace 6
Gary West 28, Highland 22
Sectional 9 Second Round
Hammond Morton 58, Hobart 21
Gary West 41, Hammond 20
Sectional 9 Championship
Hammond Morton 54, Gary West 20

Sectional 10 First Round
Logansport 39, Kankakee Valley 0
South Bend Clay 42, South Bend Riley 12

Concord 44, Lowell 13
S.B. Washington 31, Plymouth 29
Sectional 10 Second Round
South Bend Clay 55, Logansport 10
Concord 35, S.B. Washington 13
Sectional 10 Championship
Concord 28, South Bend Clay 21

Sectional 11 First Round
Fort Wayne Dwenger 56, Northridge 0
Angola 19, Wawasee 18
Columbia City 41, DeKalb 21
Sectional 11 Second Round
Fort Wayne Dwenger 52, East Noble 42
Columbia City 41, Angola 27
Sectional 11 Championship
Fort Wayne Dwenger 50, Columbia City 7

Sectional 12 First Round
Delta 28, Fort Wayne Wayne 7
Muncie South 35, Marion 14
Fort Wayne South 56, Muncie Central 14
New Haven 73, Jay County 14
Sectional 12 Second Round
Delta 28, Muncie South 6
New Haven 64, Fort Wayne South 31
Sectional 12 Championship
New Haven 28, Delta 7

Sectional 13 First Round
Pendleton Heights 27, Mount Vernon (FV) 10
New Palestine 51, Anderson 21
Greenfield-Central 45, Indpls. Arlington 14
Sectional 13 Second Round
Pendleton Heights 49, New Castle 7
Greenfield-Central 7, New Palestine 0
Sectional 13 Championship
Pendleton Heights 14, Greenfield-Central 0

Sectional 14 First Round
Indpls. Cathedral 53, Indpls. Broad Ripple 6
Mooresville 31, Lebanon 27
Roncalli 24, Plainfield 21
Sectional 14 Second Round
Indpls. Cathedral 78, Indpls. Northwest 14
Roncalli 45, Mooresville 14
Sectional 14 Championship
Indpls. Cathedral 48, Roncalli 7

Sectional 15 First Round
Shelbyville 24, South Dearborn 21
Franklin County 48, Madison 14
Greenwood 47, Connersville 8
East Central 36, Franklin 8
Sectional 15 Second Round
Franklin County 22, Shelbyville 14, OT
East Central 17, Greenwood 16
Sectional 15 Championship
East Central 35, Franklin County 6

Sectional 16 First Round
Northview 40, Boonville 7
Evansville Reitz 47, Jasper 20
Evansville Central 21, Seymour 7
Owen Valley 28, Evansville Harrison 22
Sectional 16 Second Round
Evansville Reitz 42, Northview 13
Evansville Central 34, Owen Valley 7
Sectional 16 Championship
Evansville Reitz 38, Evansville Central 20

Regional Championships
Hammond Morton 46, Concord 13
Fort Wayne Dwenger 42, New Haven 26
Indpls. Cathedral 56, Pendleton Heights 24
Evansville Reitz 43, East Central 26

Semi-State Championships
Fort Wayne Dwenger 48, Hammond Morton 12
Indpls. Cathedral 56, Evansville Reitz 28

State Championship
Indpls. Cathedral 31, Fort Wayne Dwenger 20

Class 3A
Sectional 17 First Round
John Glenn 41, Calumet 6
New Prairie 34, Hammond Gavit 14
Andrean 28, Hammond Clark 6
Culver Military Academy 28, Knox 13
Sectional 17 Second Round
John Glenn 34, New Prairie 0
Andrean 41, Culver Military Academy 0
Sectional 17 Championship
Andrean 56, John Glenn 14

Sectional 18 First Round
NorthWood 34, Rochester 7
Jimtown 54, Tippecanoe Valley 0
S.B. St. Joseph 27, Mishawaka Marian 6
Lakeland 35, West Noble 14
Sectional 18 Second Round
Jimtown 21, NorthWood 7
S.B. St. Joseph 49, Lakeland 0
Sectional 18 Championship
S.B. St. Joseph 24, Jimtown 22

Sectional 19 First Round
Leo 31, Norwell 7
Heritage 35, Blackford 7
Harding (Fort Wayne) 38, Fort Wayne Concordia 0
Eastbrook 42, Bellmont 13
Sectional 19 Second Round
Leo 35, Heritage 14
Eastbrook 44, Harding (Fort Wayne) 12
Sectional 19 Championship
Leo 49, Eastbrook 40

Sectional 20 First Round
West Lafayette 38, Twin Lakes 7
Frankfort 63, Peru 19
Mississinewa 25, Maconaquah 21
Western 49, Benton Central 26
Sectional 20 Second Round
West Lafayette 35, Frankfort 14
Western 35, Mississinewa 14
Sectional 20 Championship
West Lafayette 29, Western 9

Sectional 21 First Round
Western Boone 17, Brebeuf Jesuit 14
West Vigo 24, Crawfordsville 7
Indpls. Chatard 49, North Montgomery 14
Southmont 27, Danville 13
Sectional 21 Second Round
Western Boone 41, West Vigo 3
Indpls. Chatard 42, Southmont 7
Sectional 21 Championship
Indpls. Chatard 41, Western Boone 14

Sectional 22 First Round
Batesville 25, Greensburg 20
Yorktown 7, Indpls. Howe 0
Hamilton Heights 41, Beech Grove 0
Sectional 22 Second Round
Batesville 45, Rushville 39, 2 OT
Hamilton Heights 22, Yorktown 14
Sectional 22 Championship
Hamilton Heights 37, Batesville 14

Sectional 23 First Round
Brown County 35, Salem 10
Charlestown 28, Edgewood 21
Indian Creek 15, Corydon Central 8
Heritage Hills 49, North Harrison 7
Sectional 23 Second Round
Charlestown 54, Brown County 20
Indian Creek 35, Heritage Hills 17
Sectional 23 Championship
Indian Creek 48, Charlestown 28

Sectional 24 First Round
Evansville Memorial 83, Princeton 21
Mount Vernon 35, Gibson Southern 21
Evansville Bosse 83, Pike Central 23
Washington 70, Vincennes Lincoln 15
Sectional 24 Second Round
Evansville Memorial 48, Mount Vernon 33
Evansville Bosse 35, Washington 28
Sectional 24 Championship
Evansville Bosse 21, Evansville Memorial 14

Regional Championships
S.B. St. Joseph 28, Andrean 21
Leo 14, West Lafayette 10
Indpls. Chatard 49, Hamilton Heights 7
Indian Creek 45, Evansville Bosse 35

Semi-State Championships
S.B. St. Joseph 27, Leo 7
Indpls. Chatard 21, Indian Creek 3

State Championship
Indpls. Chatard 28, S.B. St. Joseph 14

Class 2A
Sectional 25 First Round
Wheeler 71, Hammond Noll 21
North Newton 54, Bowman Academy 34
Seeger 73, River Forest 14
Rensselaer Central 48, North Judson 16
Sectional 25 Second Round
Wheeler 46, North Newton 2
Rensselaer Central 49, Seeger 0
Sectional 25 Championship
Rensselaer Central 28, Wheeler 0

Sectional 26 First Round
Bremen 20, Whitko 17, OT
Fairfield 45, Woodlan 0
Garrett 42, Central Noble 14
Eastside 18, Prairie Heights 12
Sectional 26 Second Round
Bremen 42, Fairfield 14
Garrett 28, Eastside 13
Sectional 26 Championship
Bremen 35, Garrett 21

Sectional 27 First Round
Manchester 47, Winchester 20
Fort Wayne Luers 63, Eastern (Greentown) 14
Bluffton 52, Wabash 35
Madison-Grant 35, Oak Hill 0
Sectional 27 Second Round
Fort Wayne Luers 69, Manchester 0
Madison-Grant 61, Bluffton 45
Sectional 27 Championship
Fort Wayne Luers 49, Madison-Grant 14

Sectional 28 First Round
Tipton 23, Elwood 6
Frankton 53, Taylor 14
Lewis Cass 41, Delphi 13
Northwestern 41, Alexandria 14
Sectional 28 Second Round
Tipton 13, Frankton 7
Northwestern 23, Lewis Cass 22, OT
Sectional 28 Championship
Tipton 20, Northwestern 7

Sectional 29 First Round
Shenandoah 35, Heritage Christian 14
Speedway 43, Park Tudor 0
Indpls. Ritter 49, Centerville 21
Sectional 29 Second Round

Shenandoah 54, Union County 13
Speedway 24, Indpls. Ritter 21
Sectional 29 Championship
Speedway 28, Shenandoah 25

Sectional 30 First Round
North Putnam 40, South Putnam 7
Monrovia 17, Tri-West 14
Cascade 28, South Vermillion 14
Greencastle 27, Cloverdale 24
Sectional 30 Second Round
North Putnam 37, Monrovia 0
Greencastle 24, Cascade 0
Sectional 30 Championship
North Putnam 54, Greencastle 21

Sectional 31 First Round
Lawrenceburg 43, Eastern (Pekin) 42
Paoli 34, Mitchell 7
Brownstown Central 49, Clarksville 20
Triton Central 29, Providence 25
Sectional 31 Second Round
Paoli 39, Lawrenceburg 6
Brownstown Central 30, Triton Central 20
Sectional 31 Championship
Brownstown Central 45, Paoli 6

Sectional 32 First Round
Evansville Mater Dei 62, Sullivan 0
Forest Park 42, Tell City 27
Southridge 44, Crawford County 0
North Posey 28, South Spencer 21
Sectional 32 Second Round
Evansville Mater Dei 48, Forest Park 14
Southridge 17, North Posey 6
Sectional 32 Championship
Evansville Mater Dei 28, Southridge 21

Regional Championships
Rensselaer Central 35, Bremen 28, OT
Fort Wayne Luers 55, Tipton 14
North Putnam 25, Speedway 14
Evansville Mater Dei 42, Brownstown 14

Semi-State Championships
Fort Wayne Luers 42, Rensselaer Central 21
North Putnam 6, Evansville Mater Dei 0

State Championship
Fort Wayne Luers 26, North Putnam 14

Class 1A
Sectional 33 First Round
South Central (Union Mills) 52, Winamac 0
Triton 34, West Central 19
Whiting 42, LaVille 13
Culver 39, Lake Station 7
Sectional 33 Second Round
South Central (Union Mills) 47, Triton 20
Culver 42, Whiting 35
Sectional 33 Championship
South Central (Union Mills) 20, Culver 7

Sectional 34 First Round
Carroll (Flora) 19, Caston 13
Pioneer 51, South Newton 6
North White 28, Frontier 24
Lafayette Central Catholic 58, Tri-County 0
Sectional 34 Second Round
Pioneer 59, Carroll (Flora) 0
Lafayette Central Catholic 52, North White 0
Sectional 34 Championship
Lafayette Central Catholic 40, Pioneer 12

Sectional 35 First Round
Churubusco 50, Adams Central 6
Southern Wells 21, Southwood 14
Northfield 56, Fremont 20
South Adams 20, North Miami 14
Sectional 35 Second Round
Churubusco 12, Southern Wells 6
South Adams 33, Northfield 23
Sectional 35 Championship
Churubusco 43, South Adams 21

Sectional 36 First Round
Union City 36, Cambridge City Lincoln 14
Hagerstown 70, Wes-Del 14
Northeastern 36, Tri 7
Knightstown 56, Monroe Central 18
Sectional 36 Second Round
Hagerstown 14, Union City 10
Knightstown 46, Northeastern 13
Sectional 36 Championship
Hagerstown 37, Knightstown 20

Sectional 37 First Round
Sheridan 53, Lapel 13
Guerin Catholic 35, Indiana Deaf 12
Clinton Central 48, Eastern Hancock 22
Clinton Prairie 40, Tri-Central 20
Sectional 37 Second Round
Guerin Catholic 42, Sheridan 13
Clinton Prairie 21, Clinton Central 0
Sectional 37 Championship
Guerin Catholic 7, Clinton Prairie 6

Sectional 38 First Round
Milan 39, North Decatur 21
Indpls. Lutheran 57, Edinburgh 22
Indpls. Scecina 56, Eastern Greene 12
West Washington 27, South Decatur 26, OT
Sectional 38 Second Round
Milan 28, Indpls. Lutheran 25
West Washington 27, Indpls. Scecina 13
Sectional 38 Championship
Milan 28, West Washington 14

Sectional 39 First Round
Rockville 42, Turkey Run 7
Attica 57, Riverton Parke 14
Fountain Central 57, North Central (Farm.) 21
North Vermillion 33, Covington 32
Sectional 39 Second Round
Rockville 43, Attica 28
Fountain Central 59, North Vermillion 6
Sectional 39 Championship
Fountain Central 42, Rockville 7

Sectional 40 First Round
North Daviess 56, Union (Dugger) 0
Perry Central 40, Wood Memorial 18
North Knox 41, Tecumseh 8
Linton-Stockton 21, Springs Valley 14
Sectional 40 Second Round
Perry Central 14, North Daviess 13
Linton-Stockton 42, North Knox 12
Sectional 40 Championship
Perry Central 28, Linton-Stockton 17

Regional Championships
Lafayette C.C. 35, South Central (U.M.) 14
Churubusco 58, Hagerstown 14
Guerin Catholic 28, Milan 7
Fountain Central 31, Perry Central 15

Semi-State Championships
Lafayette Central Catholic 42, Churubusco 14
Fountain Central 22, Guerin Catholic 20
State Championship
Lafayette C.C. 31, Fountain Central 6

2011
Class 5A
Sectional 1 First Round
Valparaiso 28, Portage 17
Crown Point 21, Munster 10
Chesterton 28, Michigan City 7
Merrillville 30, Lake Central 24
Sectional 1 Second Round
Crown Point 12, Valparaiso 10
Merrillville 48, Chesterton 45, OT
Sectional 1 Championship
Crown Point 42, Merrillville 21

Sectional 2 First Round
Elkhart Memorial 31, Elkhart Central 27
Penn 42, South Bend Adams 0
Goshen 21, LaPorte 20, OT
Carroll (Fort Wayne) 27, Warsaw 0
Sectional 2 Second Round
Penn 58, Elkhart Memorial 28
Carroll (Fort Wayne) 28, Goshen 10
Sectional 2 Championship
Penn 31, Carroll (Fort Wayne) 8

Sectional 3 First Round
Fort Wayne Snider 43, Fort Wayne South 0
Fort Wayne North 39, Fort Wayne Northrop 35
Kokomo 52, Fort Wayne Wayne 0
Homestead 68, Huntington North 17
Sectional 3 Second Round
Fort Wayne Snider 35, Fort Wayne North 14
Kokomo 44, Homestead 41
Sectional 3 Championship
Fort Wayne Snider 52, Kokomo 28

Sectional 4 First Round
Fishers 29, McCutcheon 23
Lafayette Jefferson 21, Anderson 7
Hamilton Southeastern 49, Harrison (W.L.) 0
Westfield 26, Noblesville 8
Sectional 4 Second Round
Fishers 50, Lafayette Jefferson 19
Hamilton Southeastern 42, Westfield 24
Sectional 4 Championship
Hamilton Southeastern 35, Fishers 10

Sectional 5 First Round
Indpls. Tech 34, Lawrence North 24
Warren Central 29, North Central (Indpls.) 0
Lawrence Central 56, Southport 7
Carmel 59, Perry Meridian 20
Sectional 5 Second Round
Warren Central 61, Indpls. Tech 14
Carmel 35, Lawrence Central 14
Sectional 5 Championship
Carmel 34, Warren Central 30

Sectional 6 First Round
Brownsburg 28, Terre Haute South 0
Ben Davis 34, Zionsville 10
Avon 35, Terre Haute North 26
Pike 63, Decatur Central 23
Sectional 6 Second Round
Ben Davis 38, Brownsburg 31, OT
Avon 24, Pike 21
Sectional 6 Championship
Ben Davis 64, Avon 41

Sectional 7 First Round
Martinsville 35, Whiteland 28
Columbus North 37, Bloomington South 6
Center Grove 35, Franklin 14
Bloomington North 26, Franklin Central 19
Sectional 7 Second Round
Columbus North 48, Martinsville 20
Center Grove 28, Bloomington North 26
Sectional 7 Championship
Center Grove 38, Columbus North 24

Sectional 8 First Round
Castle 56, New Albany 7
Floyd Central 47, Jeffersonville 20
Bedford N.L. 53, Jennings County 27
Sectional 8 Second Round

Castle 35, Evansville North 14
Bedford North Lawrence 36, Floyd Central 32
Sectional 8 Championship
Bedford North Lawrence 25, Castle 21

Regional Championships
Penn 20, Crown Point 3
Fort Wayne Snider 38, Hamilton SE 21
Carmel 11, Ben Davis 9
Center Grove 48, Bedford North Lawrence 19

Semi-State Championships
Penn 28, Fort Wayne Snider 10
Carmel 21, Center Grove 17

State Championship
Carmel 54, Penn 0

Class 4A
Sectional 9 First Round
Hammond 62, Gary Roosevelt 0
Griffith 63, Hammond Clark 7
East Chicago Central 48, Highland 40
Hammond Morton 40, Gary West 20
Sectional 9 Second Round
Griffith 56, Hammond 27
Hammond Morton 35, East Chicago Central 21
Sectional 9 Championship
Hammond Morton 27, Griffith 26

Sectional 10 First Round
South Bend Riley 27, New Prairie 12
Mishawaka 35, Lowell 14
S.B. Washington 40, Kankakee Valley 14
Hobart 24, South Bend Clay 20
Sectional 10 Second Round
Mishawaka 42, South Bend Riley 15
S.B. Washington 35, Hobart 10
Sectional 10 Championship
S.B. Washington 37, Mishawaka 19

Sectional 11 First Round
Concord 35, DeKalb 7
East Noble 35, Northridge 13
NorthWood 14, Wawasee 10
Plymouth 49, Angola 21
Sectional 11 Second Round
Concord 43, East Noble 16
NorthWood 49, Plymouth 16
Sectional 11 Championship
NorthWood 26, Concord 13

Sectional 12 First Round
Fort Wayne Dwenger 27, Columbia City 10
New Haven 51, Logansport 30
Leo 48, Norwell 7
Marion 56, Jay County 19
Sectional 12 Second Round
Fort Wayne Dwenger 31, New Haven 21

Leo 42, Marion 22
Sectional 12 Championship
Leo 35, Fort Wayne Dwenger 14

Sectional 13 First Round
New Palestine 62, Muncie Central 0
Delta 62, Frankfort 0
Greenfield-Central 48, Muncie South 22
Pendleton Heights 31, Mount Vernon (FV) 7
Sectional 13 Second Round
New Palestine 27, Delta 14
Pendleton Heights 45, Greenfield-Central 14
Sectional 13 Championship
Pendleton Heights 24, New Palestine 13

Sectional 14 First Round
Lebanon 40, Owen Valley 20
Greenwood 28, Northview 3
Indpls. Cathedral 61, Mooresville 14
Roncalli 35, Plainfield 7
Sectional 14 Second Round
Greenwood 38, Lebanon 14
Indpls. Cathedral 20, Roncalli 13
Sectional 14 Championship
Indpls. Cathedral 38, Greenwood 14

Sectional 15 First Round
Franklin County 28, Richmond 7
Connersville 14, New Castle 7
East Central 31, South Dearborn 0
Columbus East 49, Shelbyville 21
Sectional 15 Second Round
Franklin County 21, Connersville 7
Columbus East 27, East Central 17
Sectional 15 Championship
Columbus East 34, Franklin County 12

Sectional 16 First Round
Evansville Harrison 27, Madison 24
Evansville Central 28, Seymour 14
Evansville Reitz 55, Boonville 21
Sectional 16 Second Round
Jasper 35, Evansville Harrison 7
Evansville Central 37, Evansville Reitz 35
Sectional 16 Championship
Evansville Central 23, Jasper 14

Regional Championships
S.B. Washington 33, Hammond Morton 20
Leo 24, NorthWood 12
Indpls. Cathedral 35, Pendleton Heights 0
Columbus East 49, Evansville Central 0

Semi-State Championships
S.B. Washington 13, Leo 3
Indpls. Cathedral 62, Columbus East 7

State Championship
Indpls. Cathedral 42, S.B. Washington 7

Class 3A
Sectional 17 First Round
S.B. St. Joseph 50, Gary Wallace 6
Culver Military Academy 44, Knox 12
John Glenn 51, Hammond Gavit 6
Mishawaka Marian 49, Calumet 12
Sectional 17 Second Round
S.B. St. Joseph 35, Culver Military Academy 15
Mishawaka Marian 22, John Glenn 14
Sectional 17 Championship
S.B. St. Joseph 21, Mishawaka Marian 0

Sectional 18 First Round
Whitko 18, Fort Wayne Concordia 15
Garrett 27, Tippecanoe Valley 14
Lakeland 50, West Noble 28
Jimtown 36, Heritage 19
Sectional 18 Second Round
Garrett 42, Whitko 14
Jimtown 42, Lakeland 0
Sectional 18 Championship
Jimtown 34, Garrett 14

Sectional 19 First Round
Yorktown 38, Eastbrook 24
Bellmont 63, Blackford 7
Mississinewa 28, Maconaquah 24
Western 34, Peru 0
Sectional 19 Second Round
Bellmont 22, Yorktown 7
Western 58, Mississinewa 21
Sectional 19 Championship
Bellmont 21, Western 20, OT

Sectional 20 First Round
Hamilton Heights 49, Southmont 12
Western Boone 48, Twin Lakes 7
West Lafayette 30, Crawfordsville 7
Sectional 20 Second Round
Hamilton Heights 30, North Montgomery 7
West Lafayette 30, Western Boone 10
Sectional 20 Championship
West Lafayette 20, Hamilton Heights 19

Sectional 21 First Round
Indpls. Chatard 30, Greencastle 0
Danville 34, Indpls. Arlington 12
Brebeuf Jesuit 23, Tri-West 7
West Vigo 45, Indpls. Northwest 34
Sectional 21 Second Round
Indpls. Chatard 42, Danville 0
Brebeuf Jesuit 48, West Vigo 13
Sectional 21 Championship
Indpls. Chatard 34, Brebeuf Jesuit 13

Sectional 22 First Round
Edgewood 18, Indpls. Howe 6
Greensburg 20, Batesville 18
Brown County 15, Rushville 8
Indian Creek 40, Beech Grove 6
Sectional 22 Second Round
Greensburg 35, Edgewood 20
Indian Creek 31, Brown County 21
Sectional 22 Championship
Indian Creek 20, Greensburg 13

Sectional 23 First Round
Salem 29, Silver Creek 21
Heritage Hills 61, Mitchell 0
Corydon Central 35, Brownstown Central 13
Charlestown 56, North Harrison 0
Sectional 23 Second Round
Heritage Hills 53, Salem 0
Corydon Central 33, Charlestown 28
Sectional 23 Championship
Corydon Central 13, Heritage Hills 12

Sectional 24 First Round
Washington 28, Mount Vernon 0
Evansville Memorial 42, Evansville Bosse 26
Gibson Southern 48, Princeton 14
Vincennes Lincoln 49, Pike Central 14
Sectional 24 Second Round
Evansville Memorial 49, Washington 35
Vincennes Lincoln 28, Gibson Southern 7
Sectional 24 Championship
Evansville Memorial 49, Vincennes Lincoln 28

Regional Championships
S.B. St. Joseph 21, Jimtown 0
West Lafayette 14, Bellmont 7
Indpls. Chatard 62, Indian Creek 22
Corydon Central 47, Ev. Memorial 41, OT

Semi-State Championships
S.B. St. Joseph 21, West Lafayette 13
Indpls. Chatard 38, Corydon Central 6

State Championship
Indpls. Chatard 21, S.B. St. Joseph 7

Class 2A
Sectional 25 First Round
Rensselaer Central 52, Bowman Academy 28
Wheeler 12, Andrean 7
North Newton 16, Boone Grove 8
River Forest 49, Lake Station 14
Sectional 25 Second Round
Wheeler 14, Rensselaer Central 7
North Newton 34, River Forest 21
Sectional 25 Championship
Wheeler 48, North Newton 6

Sectional 26 First Round
Bremen 57, Prairie Heights 7
Manchester 46, Wabash 14
Rochester 34, North Judson 20

Lewis Cass 41, Fairfield 17
Sectional 26 Second Round
Bremen 47, Manchester 14
Lewis Cass 28, Rochester 7
Sectional 26 Championship
Bremen 28, Lewis Cass 6

Sectional 27 First Round
Madison-Grant 51, Oak Hill 27
Churubusco 38, Woodlan 0
Fort Wayne Luers 49, Elwood 19
Eastside 16, Bluffton 13, OT
Sectional 27 Second Round
Churubusco 28, Madison-Grant 20
Fort Wayne Luers 42, Eastside 7
Sectional 27 Championship
Fort Wayne Luers 34, Churubusco 7

Sectional 28 First Round
Delphi 17, Taylor 14, OT
Northwestern 42, Fountain Central 41
Benton Central 40, Seeger 6
Tipton 28, Eastern (Greentown) 27
Sectional 28 Second Round
Northwestern 55, Delphi 7
Tipton 35, Benton Central 7
Sectional 28 Championship
Tipton 41, Northwestern 22

Sectional 29 First Round
Guerin Catholic 51, Alexandria 10
Heritage Christian 66, Winchester 6
Centerville 35, Union County 3
Shenandoah 45, Frankton 6
Sectional 29 Second Round
Guerin Catholic 41, Heritage Christian 38, OT
Shenandoah 31, Centerville 13
Sectional 29 Championship
Guerin Catholic 36, Shenandoah 20

Sectional 30 First Round
Park Tudor 45, Cascade 30
South Putnam 61, South Vermillion 0
Indpls. Ritter 34, Indpls. Broad Ripple 0
North Putnam 48, Speedway 10
Sectional 30 Second Round
South Putnam 35, Park Tudor 7
North Putnam 41, Indpls. Ritter 34
Sectional 30 Championship
South Putnam 40, North Putnam 22

Sectional 31 First Round
Paoli 41, Clarksville 14
Monrovia 40, Crawford County 0
Lawrenceburg 34, Eastern (Pekin) 19
Triton Central 31, Providence 17
Sectional 31 Second Round
Paoli 34, Monrovia 20
Triton Central 41, Lawrenceburg 21

Sectional 31 Championship
Triton Central 36, Paoli 27

Sectional 32 First Round
Evansville Mater Dei 45, North Posey 20
Southridge 49, Tell City 7
South Spencer 14, Forest Park 0
Sectional 32 Second Round
Evansville Mater Dei 41, Sullivan 7
Southridge 28, South Spencer 10
Sectional 32 Championship
Evansville Mater Dei 39, Southridge 21

Regional Championships
Bremen 35, Wheeler 21
Fort Wayne Luers 44, Tipton 23
Guerin Catholic 41, South Putnam 27
Evansville Mater Dei 48, Triton Central 14

Semi-State Championships
Fort Wayne Luers 35, Bremen 21
Evansville Mater Dei 27, Guerin Catholic 16

State Championship
Fort Wayne Luers 41, Evansville Mater Dei 17

Class 1A
Sectional 33 First Round
Winamac 27, South Central (Union Mills) 14
South Newton 32, Hammond Noll 27
West Central 39, Whiting 7
Culver 44, Tri-County 6
Sectional 33 Second Round
South Newton 43, Winamac 6
Culver 24, West Central 14
Sectional 33 Championship
South Newton 27, Culver 21

Sectional 34 First Round
Caston 17, Carroll (Flora) 7
Clinton Central 20, Clinton Prairie 13
North White 42, Frontier 36
Lafayette Central Catholic 47, Pioneer 6
Sectional 34 Second Round
Caston 38, Clinton Central 13
Lafayette Central Catholic 56, North White 6
Sectional 34 Championship
Lafayette Central Catholic 69, Caston 8

Sectional 35 First Round
Northfield 47, LaVille 6
North Miami 28, Southwood 21
Fremont 62, Central Noble 26
Adams Central 38, Triton 18
Sectional 35 Second Round
North Miami 13, Northfield 7
Adams Central 55, Fremont 6
Sectional 35 Championship
Adams Central 30, North Miami 6

Sectional 36 First Round
South Adams 46, Monroe Central 0
Union City 42, Wes-Del 20
Lapel 25, Tri-Central 14
Sheridan 49, Southern Wells 12
Sectional 36 Second Round
South Adams 40, Union City 26
Sheridan 48, Lapel 16
Sectional 36 Championship
Sheridan 41, South Adams 40, OT

Sectional 37 First Round
Northeastern 47, Indiana Deaf 0
Cambridge City 42, Eastern Hancock 21
Knightstown 27, Hagerstown 18
Indpls. Scecina 44, Tri 8
Sectional 37 Second Round
Northeastern 27, Cambridge City Lincoln 13
Indpls. Scecina 43, Knightstown 22
Sectional 37 Championship
Indpls. Scecina 49, Northeastern 0

Sectional 38 First Round
Cloverdale 53, Riverton Parke 0
North Vermillion 9, Attica 7
Rockville 56, North Central (Farmersburg) 40
Covington 42, Turkey Run 14
Sectional 38 Second Round
North Vermillion 52, Cloverdale 12
Rockville 40, Covington 14
Sectional 38 Championship
North Vermillion 27, Rockville 20, OT

Sectional 39 First Round
Edinburgh 20, South Decatur 14
Indpls. Lutheran 35, West Washington 6
Milan 21, Springs Valley 6
Sectional 39 Second Round
North Decatur 41, Edinburgh 14
Milan 24, Indpls. Lutheran 20
Sectional 39 Championship
Milan 32, North Decatur 27

Sectional 40 First Round
North Daviess 27, Tecumseh 20
Wood Memorial 41, Union (Dugger) 20
Eastern Greene 22, North Knox 20
Linton-Stockton 48, Perry Central 7
Sectional 40 Second Round
North Daviess 21, Wood Memorial 14
Linton-Stockton 47, Eastern Greene 0
Sectional 40 Championship
Linton-Stockton 61, North Daviess 8

Regional Championships
Lafayette Central Catholic 54, South Newton 0
Sheridan 56, Adams Central 0
Indpls. Scecina 35, North Vermillion 8
Linton-Stockton 28, Milan 0

Semi-State Championships
Lafayette Central Catholic 17, Sheridan 0
Indpls. Scecina 17, Linton-Stockton 0

State Championship
Lafayette Central Catholic 38, Indpls. Scecina 7

2012
Class 5A
Sectional 1 First Round
Crown Point 23, Valparaiso 15
Lake Central 16, Portage 0
Merrillville 28, Munster 21
Chesterton 37, Michigan City 7
Sectional 1 Second Round
Crown Point 21, Lake Central 14
Merrillville 45, Chesterton 21
Sectional 1 Championship
Merrillville 24, Crown Point 14

Sectional 2 First Round
Elkhart Central 17, Elkhart Memorial 13
South Bend Adams 39, Goshen 7
Carroll (Fort Wayne) 49, LaPorte 7
Penn 42, Warsaw 21
Sectional 2 Second Round
South Bend Adams 49, Elkhart Central 28
Carroll (Fort Wayne) 14, Penn 13
Sectional 2 Championship
Carroll (Fort Wayne) 44, South Bend Adams 35

Sectional 3 First Round
Fort Wayne North 42, Fort Wayne Northrop 21
Fort Wayne South 14, Huntington North 6
Fort Wayne Wayne 31, Kokomo 28
Fort Wayne Snider 30, Homestead 20
Sectional 3 Second Round
Fort Wayne North 26, Fort Wayne South 22
Fort Wayne Snider 45, Fort Wayne Wayne 9
Sectional 3 Championship
Fort Wayne Snider 24, Fort Wayne North 14

Sectional 4 First Round
McCutcheon 34, Harrison (W.L.) 0
Noblesville 24, Westfield 20
Fishers 27, Anderson 14
Hamilton Southeastern 41, Lafayette Jeff 13
Sectional 4 Second Round
McCutcheon 26, Noblesville 10
Fishers 42, Hamilton Southeastern 7
Sectional 4 Championship
Fishers 38, McCutcheon 13

Sectional 5 First Round
Lawrence Central 34, Southport 13
Warren Central 31, Carmel 24, 3 OT
Indpls. Tech 30, Perry Meridian 27

North Central (Indpls.) 50, Lawrence North 21
Sectional 5 Second Round
Lawrence Central 21, Warren Central 14
North Central (Indpls.) 20, Indpls. Tech 7
Sectional 5 Championship
Lawrence Central 21, North Central (Indpls.) 7

Sectional 6 First Round
Pike 35, Ben Davis 25
Zionsville 19, Brownsburg 17
Avon 38, Decatur Central 14
Terre Haute North 28, Terre Haute South 10
Sectional 6 Second Round
Pike 24, Zionsville 23
Avon 16, Terre Haute North 14
Sectional 6 Championship
Pike 55, Avon 24

Sectional 7 First Round
Franklin Central 41, Bloomington South 14
Columbus North 35, Whiteland 33
Center Grove 41, Martinsville 12
Franklin 22, Bloomington North 19
Sectional 7 Second Round
Columbus North 17, Franklin Central 14
Center Grove 62, Franklin 6
Sectional 7 Championship
Center Grove 42, Columbus North 7

Sectional 8 First Round
Jeffersonville 62, New Albany 35
Castle 56, Floyd Central 12
Bedford North Lawrence 34, Jennings County 6
Sectional 8 Second Round
Jeffersonville 37, Evansville North 27
Castle 49, Bedford North Lawrence 14
Sectional 8 Championship
Castle 50, Jeffersonville 29

Regional Championships
Merrillville 50, Carroll (Fort Wayne) 21
Fort Wayne Snider 36, Fishers 35, OT
Lawrence Central 49, Pike 21
Center Grove 58, Castle 34

Semi-State Championships
Fort Wayne Snider 42, Merrillville 39
Lawrence Central 28, Center Grove 15

State Championship
Lawrence Central 39, Fort Wayne Snider 14

Class 4A
Sectional 9 First Round
Hammond Morton 54, Hammond Clark 22
East Chicago Central 28, Hammond 7
Highland 20, Griffith 18
Gary West 54, Gary Roosevelt 12
Sectional 9 Second Round
Hammond Morton 50, East Chicago Central 28
Highland 41, Gary West 34
Sectional 9 Championship
Hammond Morton 34, Highland 0

Sectional 10 First Round
Hobart 38, Kankakee Valley 0
Mishawaka 27, Lowell 0
New Prairie 21, South Bend Clay 6
S.B. Washington 28, South Bend Riley 18
Sectional 10 Second Round
Mishawaka 49, Hobart 28
S.B. Washington 36, New Prairie 14
Sectional 10 Championship
Mishawaka 36, S.B. Washington 34, OT

Sectional 11 First Round
NorthWood 17, Plymouth 13
Wawasee 27, DeKalb 14
Northridge 18, Angola 13
Concord 38, East Noble 35
Sectional 11 Second Round
Wawasee 31, NorthWood 28
Concord 35, Northridge 8
Sectional 11 Championship
Concord 24, Wawasee 10

Sectional 12 First Round
Fort Wayne Dwenger 42, Jay County 40
Columbia City 14, Leo 7
Norwell 22, Logansport 0
New Haven 43, Marion 20
Sectional 12 Second Round
Fort Wayne Dwenger 36, Columbia City 14
Norwell 22, New Haven 20
Sectional 12 Championship
Fort Wayne Dwenger 14, Norwell 7

Sectional 13 First Round
Greenfield-Central 21, Muncie Central 14
Delta 20, Frankfort 0
Pendleton Heights 41, Muncie South 21
Mount Vernon (Fortville) 40, New Palestine 21
Sectional 13 Second Round
Delta 28, Greenfield-Central 3
Mount Vernon (Fortville) 54, Pendleton Hts. 34
Sectional 13 Championship
Mount Vernon (Fortville) 28, Delta 13

Sectional 14 First Round
Roncalli 24, Plainfield 7
Greenwood 44, Owen Valley 7
Indpls. Cathedral 62, Northview 0
Lebanon 19, Mooresville 0
Sectional 14 Second Round
Roncalli 35, Greenwood 14
Indpls. Cathedral 49, Lebanon 19
Sectional 14 Championship
Indpls. Cathedral 34, Roncalli 7

Sectional 15 First Round
Richmond 14, Shelbyville 0
Franklin County 20, New Castle 19
Columbus East 26, East Central 7
Connersville 21, South Dearborn 13
Sectional 15 Second Round
Franklin County 14, Richmond 13
Columbus East 48, Connersville 6
Sectional 15 Championship
Columbus East 36, Franklin County 14

Sectional 16 First Round
Evansville Reitz 56, Madison 7
Seymour 65, Evansville Harrison 58
Jasper 50, Boonville 13
Sectional 16 Second Round
Evansville Reitz 43, Evansville Central 42, OT
Jasper 45, Seymour 13
Sectional 16 Championship
Evansville Reitz 31, Jasper 30

Regional Championships
Mishawaka 39, Hammond Morton 7
Concord 35, Fort Wayne Dwenger 21
Indpls. Cathedral 41, Mount Vernon (FV) 7
Columbus East 35, Evansville Reitz 21

Semi-State Championships
Mishawaka 24, Concord 21
Indpls. Cathedral 49, Columbus East 14

State Championship
Indpls. Cathedral 56, Mishawaka 29

Class 3A
Sectional 17 First Round
S.B. St. Joseph 42, Knox 8
Calumet 30, Hammond Gavit 24
John Glenn 35, Culver Military Academy 14
Mishawaka Marian 42, Gary Wallace 8
Sectional 17 Second Round
S.B. St. Joseph 35, Calumet 0
Mishawaka Marian 42, John Glenn 20
Sectional 17 Championship
Mishawaka Marian 21, S.B. St. Joseph 7

Sectional 18 First Round
Whitko 21, Garrett 16
Jimtown 42, Fort Wayne Concordia 20
Tippecanoe Valley 44, West Noble 0
Heritage 42, Lakeland 16
Sectional 18 Second Round
Jimtown 55, Whitko 7
Heritage 49, Tippecanoe Valley 8
Sectional 18 Championship
Heritage 40, Jimtown 29

Sectional 19 First Round
Eastbrook 41, Peru 7
Yorktown 31, Bellmont 20
Mississinewa 60, Blackford 7
Western 28, Maconaquah 7
Sectional 19 Second Round
Eastbrook 35, Yorktown 20
Western 47, Mississinewa 26
Sectional 19 Championship
Eastbrook 31, Western 28

Sectional 20 First Round
Southmont 48, Crawfordsville 7
Hamilton Heights 18, West Lafayette 0
Twin Lakes 12, North Montgomery 8
Sectional 20 Second Round
Western Boone 12, Southmont 8
Hamilton Heights 38, Twin Lakes 0
Sectional 20 Championship
Hamilton Heights 52, Western Boone 16

Sectional 21 First Round
Tri-West 37, Indpls. Arlington 0
Greencastle 35, West Vigo 0
Indpls. Chatard 48, Danville 20
Brebeuf Jesuit 54, Indpls. Northwest 16
Sectional 21 Second Round
Greencastle 20, Tri-West 14
Indpls. Chatard 28, Brebeuf Jesuit 0
Sectional 21 Championship
Indpls. Chatard 50, Greencastle 7

Sectional 22 First Round
Batesville 31, Edgewood 7
Greensburg 36, Brown County 0
Beech Grove 48, Indpls. Howe 6
Indian Creek 28, Rushville 6
Sectional 22 Second Round
Greensburg 14, Batesville 0
Indian Creek 28, Beech Grove 8
Sectional 22 Championship
Greensburg 27, Indian Creek 19

Sectional 23 First Round
Salem 27, North Harrison 6
Brownstown Central 27, Heritage Hills 24
Corydon Central 42, Silver Creek 8
Charlestown 82, Mitchell 0
Sectional 23 Second Round
Brownstown Central 35, Salem 7
Charlestown 49, Corydon Central 6
Sectional 23 Championship
Charlestown 62, Brownstown Central 10

Sectional 24 First Round
Vincennes Lincoln 28, Evansville Bosse 7
Gibson Southern 49, Mount Vernon 21
Washington 43, Pike Central 9
Evansville Memorial 47, Princeton 3
Sectional 24 Second Round

Gibson Southern 37, Vincennes Lincoln 31, OT
Evansville Memorial 49, Washington 7
Sectional 24 Championship
Gibson Southern 27, Ev. Memorial 24, OT

Regional Championships
Mishawaka Marian 42, Heritage 20
Hamilton Heights 19, Eastbrook 14
Indpls. Chatard 49, Greensburg 9
Gibson Southern 57, Charlestown 49

Semi-State Championships
Hamilton Heights 42, Mishawaka Marian 13
Indpls. Chatard 59, Gibson Southern 7

State Championship
Indpls. Chatard 30, Hamilton Heights 13

Class 2A
Sectional 25 First Round
Bowman Academy 28, River Forest 26
Rensselaer Central 40, North Newton 13
Boone Grove 47, Lake Station 6
Andrean 63, Wheeler 13
Sectional 25 Second Round
Rensselaer Central 56, Bowman Academy 6
Andrean 62, Boone Grove 0
Sectional 25 Championship
Andrean 28, Rensselaer Central 21

Sectional 26 First Round
Lewis Cass 34, Bremen 28, 2 OT
Fairfield 28, Prairie Heights 13
Rochester 43, Wabash 0
North Judson 26, Manchester 6
Sectional 26 Second Round
Lewis Cass 46, Fairfield 14
North Judson 20, Rochester 16
Sectional 26 Championship
Lewis Cass 35, North Judson 7

Sectional 27 First Round
Elwood 22, Madison-Grant 14
Churubusco 38, Oak Hill 14
Fort Wayne Luers 23, Woodlan 8
Eastside 52, Bluffton 12
Sectional 27 Second Round
Churubusco 35, Elwood 13
Fort Wayne Luers 42, Eastside 7
Sectional 27 Championship
Fort Wayne Luers 21, Churubusco 0

Sectional 28 First Round
Tipton 60, Seeger 12
Northwestern 20, Taylor 0
Benton Central 28, Fountain Central 27
Delphi 8, Eastern (Greentown) 7
Sectional 28 Second Round
Tipton 53, Northwestern 26

Benton Central 34, Delphi 14
Sectional 28 Championship
Tipton 35, Benton Central 17

Sectional 29 First Round
Guerin Catholic 55, Centerville 0
Heritage Christian 69, Alexandria 8
Winchester 41, Frankton 20
Shenandoah 37, Union County 0
Sectional 29 Second Round
Heritage Christian 28, Guerin Catholic 14
Shenandoah 58, Winchester 24
Sectional 29 Championship
Shenandoah 41, Heritage Christian 35

Sectional 30 First Round
Speedway 21, North Putnam 6
Indpls. Ritter 62, South Vermillion 14
Park Tudor 24, Cascade 7
Indpls. Broad Ripple 34, South Putnam 21
Sectional 30 Second Round
Indpls. Ritter 49, Speedway 21
Indpls. Broad Ripple 34, Park Tudor 27
Sectional 30 Championship
Indpls. Ritter 48, Indpls. Broad Ripple 8

Sectional 31 First Round
Clarksville 32, Eastern (Pekin) 0
Lawrenceburg 55, Crawford County 0
Triton Central 33, Monrovia 12
Paoli 40, Providence 0
Sectional 31 Second Round
Lawrenceburg 56, Clarksville 7
Paoli 22, Triton Central 21, OT
Sectional 31 Championship
Lawrenceburg 52, Paoli 34

Sectional 32 First Round
South Spencer 6, Sullivan 0, OT
Evansville Mater Dei 22, Southridge 15
North Posey 35, Tell City 7
Sectional 32 Second Round
South Spencer 38, Forest Park 17
Evansville Mater Dei 31, North Posey 28
Sectional 32 Championship
Evansville Mater Dei 42, South Spencer 0

Regional Championships
Andrean 67, Lewis Cass 66, 5 OT
Fort Wayne Luers 22, Tipton 12
Indpls. Ritter 49, Shenandoah 7
Evansville Mater Dei 33, Lawrenceburg 14

Semi-State Championships
Fort Wayne Luers 35, Andrean 21
Indpls. Ritter 49, Evansville Mater Dei 14

State Championship
Fort Wayne Luers 40, Indpls. Ritter 28

Class 1A
Sectional 33 First Round
Hammond Noll 35, South Newton 6
Winamac 40, Tri-County 15
West Central 26, Culver 7
Whiting 33, South Central (Union Mills) 12
Sectional 33 Second Round
Winamac 14, Hammond Noll 10
West Central 43, Whiting 3
Sectional 33 Championship
Winamac 49, West Central 13

Sectional 34 First Round
Carroll (Flora) 28, Clinton Prairie 6
Pioneer 55, Frontier 0
Lafayette Central Catholic 35, North White 0
Caston 42, Clinton Central 7
Sectional 34 Second Round
Pioneer 35, Carroll (Flora) 21
Lafayette Central Catholic 42, Caston 7
Sectional 34 Championship
Lafayette Central Catholic 38, Pioneer 7

Sectional 35 First Round
Southwood 20, Fremont 12
Adams Central 38, Triton 14
Northfield 60, Central Noble 22
North Miami 52, LaVille 0
Sectional 35 Second Round
Adams Central 42, Southwood 7
North Miami 35, Northfield 12
Sectional 35 Championship
North Miami 33, Adams Central 15

Sectional 36 First Round
Tri-Central 54, Wes-Del 6
Lapel 14, South Adams 13, OT
Sheridan 51, Southern Wells 12
Union City 52, Monroe Central 7
Sectional 36 Second Round
Tri-Central 35, Lapel 10
Sheridan 40, Union City 6
Sectional 36 Championship
Sheridan 38, Tri-Central 28

Sectional 37 First Round
Indpls. Scecina 40, Cambridge City Lincoln 13
Knightstown 74, Indiana Deaf 52
Eastern Hancock 42, Hagerstown 14
Northeastern 22, Tri 0
Sectional 37 Second Round
Indpls. Scecina 55, Knightstown 13
Eastern Hancock 34, Northeastern 6
Sectional 37 Championship
Indpls. Scecina 35, Eastern Hancock 19

Sectional 38 First Round
North Vermillion 58, Covington 6
North Central (Farmersburg) 20, Turkey Run 7
Cloverdale 44, Riverton Parke 22
Attica 28, Rockville 0
Sectional 38 Second Round
North Vermillion 27, North Central (Farm.) 14
Attica 54, Cloverdale 0
Sectional 38 Championship
North Vermillion 27, Attica 7

Sectional 39 First Round
West Washington 42, Indpls. Lutheran 12
Milan 31, Edinburgh 0
Springs Valley 40, North Decatur 35
Sectional 39 Second Round
West Washington 29, South Decatur 14
Milan 27, Springs Valley 12
Sectional 39 Championship
West Washington 24, Milan 7

Sectional 40 First Round
North Daviess 40, Union (Dugger) 12
Tecumseh 57, Wood Memorial 0
Linton-Stockton 46, North Knox 0
Perry Central 47, Eastern Greene 20
Sectional 40 Second Round
North Daviess 33, Tecumseh 13
Linton-Stockton 45, Perry Central 7
Sectional 40 Championship
Linton-Stockton 48, North Daviess 6

Regional Championships
Lafayette Central Catholic 49, Winamac 14
Sheridan 35, North Miami 14
Indpls. Scecina 27, North Vermillion 0
Linton-Stockton 28, West Washington 0

Semi-State Championships
Lafayette Central Catholic 13, Sheridan 3
Indpls. Scecina 17, Linton-Stockton 14, OT

State Championship
Lafayette Central Catholic 14, Indpls. Scecina 0

2013
NOTE: 2013 saw the expansion of the state tournament from five classes to six. In effect, Class 5A was split in two (6A & 5A), with those sectionals containing 4-5 teams.

Class 6A
Sectional 1 Semifinals
Merrillville 39, Lafayette Jefferson 18
Lake Central 9, Crown Point 6
Sectional 1 Championship
Lake Central 31, Merrillville 0

Sectional 2 Semifinals
Penn 28, Portage 7
Chesterton 31, Valparaiso 3

Sectional 2 Championship
Penn 30, Chesterton 0

Sectional 3 Semifinals
Warsaw 40, Fort Wayne Northrop 20
Carroll (Fort Wayne) 49, Homestead 7
Sectional 3 Championship
Carroll (Fort Wayne) 42, Warsaw 7

Sectional 4 Semifinals
Fishers 17, Noblesville 13
Carmel 40, Hamilton Southeastern 7
Sectional 4 Championship
Carmel 35, Fishers 20

Sectional 5 Semifinals
Pike 57, Brownsburg 7
Ben Davis 35, Avon 14
Sectional 5 Championship
Pike 34, Ben Davis 32

Sectional 6 Semifinals
Warren Central 14, Lawrence Central 0
North Central (Indpls.) 32, Lawrence North 16
Sectional 6 Championship
Warren Central 14, North Central (Indpls.) 7

Sectional 7 Semifinals
Indpls. Tech 28, Franklin Central 14
Southport 45, Perry Meridian 15
Sectional 7 Championship
Southport 27, Indpls. Tech 10

Sectional 8 Semifinals
Center Grove 70, New Albany 14
Jeffersonville 30, Columbus North 22
Sectional 8 Championship
Center Grove 35, Jeffersonville 0

Regional Championships
Penn 33, Lake Central 6
Carmel 38, Carroll (Fort Wayne) 7
Warren Central 24, Pike 21
Center Grove 56, Southport 14

Semi-State Championships
Carmel 28, Penn 13
Warren Central 12, Center Grove 7

State Championship
Warren Central 7, Carmel 6

Class 5A
Sectional 9 First Round
Mishawaka 38, LaPorte 14
Sectional 9 Second Round
Mishawaka 27, South Bend Adams 0
Munster 21, Michigan City 13
Sectional 9 Championship
Mishawaka 24, Munster 17

Sectional 10 Semifinals
Elkhart Central 35, Goshen 21
Concord 23, Elkhart Memorial 7
Sectional 10 Championship
Concord 34, Elkhart Central 0

Sectional 11 Semifinals
McCutcheon 42, Kokomo 13
Westfield 42, Harrison (West Lafayette) 14
Sectional 11 Championship
Westfield 45, McCutcheon 21

Sectional 12 Semifinals
Fort Wayne Snider 15, Fort Wayne Wayne 7
Fort Wayne North 42, Huntington North 20
Sectional 12 Championship
Fort Wayne Snider 17, F.W. North 14, OT

Sectional 13 First Round
Indpls. Cathedral 54, Decatur Central 26
Sectional 13 Second Round
Indpls. Cathedral 35, Zionsville 21
Anderson 35, Richmond 24
Sectional 13 Championship
Indpls. Cathedral 56, Anderson 13

Sectional 14 Semifinals
Floyd Central 27, Jennings County 0
Whiteland 24, Franklin 22
Sectional 14 Championship
Whiteland 41, Floyd Central 20

Sectional 15 Semifinals
Bloomington North 49, Bedford N.L. 7
Bloomington South 55, Martinsville 22
Sectional 15 Championship
Bloomington North 24, Bloomington South 21

Sectional 16 Semifinals
Terre Haute North 38, Castle 13
Evansville North 33, Terre Haute South 28
Sectional 16 Championship
Terre Haute North 42, Evansville North 7

Regional Championships
Concord 34, Mishawaka 14
Westfield 36, Fort Wayne Snider 7
Indpls. Cathedral 56, Whiteland 28
Terre Haute North 56, Bloomington North 21

Semi-State Championships
Westfield 35, Concord 3
Indpls. Cathedral 42, Terre Haute North 20

State Championship
Indpls. Cathedral 42, Westfield 18

Class 4A
Sectional 17 First Round
Griffith 50, Hammond Clark 36
East Chicago Central 26, Hammond Morton 21
Gary West 30, Lowell 9
Highland 55, Hammond Gavit 6
Sectional 17 Second Round
East Chicago Central 51, Griffith 19
Gary West 46, Highland 27
Sectional 17 Championship
East Chicago Central 46, Gary West 44

Sectional 18 First Round
S.B. St. Joseph 42, Hobart 28
S.B. Washington 40, South Bend Clay 34
New Prairie 62, Kankakee Valley 0
Plymouth 28, South Bend Riley 21, OT
Sectional 18 Second Round
S.B. St. Joseph 49, S.B. Washington 27
New Prairie 42, Plymouth 21
Sectional 18 Championship
New Prairie 28, S.B. St. Joseph 6

Sectional 19 First Round
East Noble 55, NorthWood 21
Leo 35, Wawasee 7
Angola 21, DeKalb 7
Fort Wayne Dwenger 28, Northridge 3
Sectional 19 Second Round
East Noble 10, Leo 7
Fort Wayne Dwenger 45, Angola 7
Sectional 19 Championship
Fort Wayne Dwenger 33, East Noble 13

Sectional 20 First Round
Norwell 45, Columbia City 28
Jay County 50, Marion 16
Frankfort 31, Logansport 13
Fort Wayne South 49, New Haven 6
Sectional 20 Second Round
Norwell 42, Jay County 12
New Haven 47, Frankfort 0
Sectional 20 Championship
New Haven 37, Norwell 7

Sectional 21 First Round
New Palestine 62, Pendleton Heights 40
Muncie South 35, New Castle 27
Mount Vernon (Fortville) 49, Beech Grove 14
Greenfield-Central 33, Muncie Central 22
Sectional 21 Second Round
New Palestine 53, Muncie South 0
Mount Vernon (FV) 16, Greenfield-Central 13
Sectional 21 Championship
New Palestine 33, Mount Vernon (Fortville) 0

Sectional 22 First Round
Roncalli 48, Mooresville 6
Lebanon 35, Plainfield 24
Danville 77, Indpls. Northwest 12
Indpls. Chatard 48, Northview 7
Sectional 22 Second Round
Roncalli 28, Lebanon 0
Indpls. Chatard 49, Danville 6
Sectional 22 Championship
Indpls. Chatard 28, Roncalli 8

Sectional 23 First Round
Shelbyville 33, Franklin County 7
East Central 28, Connersville 8
Columbus East 55, Madison 6
Greenwood 48, South Dearborn 32
Sectional 23 Second Round
Shelbyville 25, East Central 22
Columbus East 49, Greenwood 14
Sectional 23 Championship
Columbus East 42, Shelbyville 7

Sectional 24 First Round
Evansville Reitz 38, Owen Valley 0
Silver Creek 48, Boonville 41
Evansville Central 77, Seymour 28
Jasper 40, Evansville Harrison 7
Sectional 24 Second Round
Evansville Reitz 49, Silver Creek 15
Jasper 28, Evansville Central 7
Sectional 24 Championship
Jasper 17, Evansville Reitz 9

Regional Championships
East Chicago Central 38, New Prairie 37, OT
Fort Wayne Dwenger 42, New Haven 7
New Palestine 27, Indpls. Chatard 14
Columbus East 42, Jasper 0

Semi-State Championships
F.W. Dwenger 38, East Chicago Central 0
Columbus East 49, New Palestine 14

State Championship
Columbus East 28, Fort Wayne Dwenger 27

Class 3A
Sectional 25 First Round
Calumet 27, Gary Wallace 12
Andrean 58, Knox 6
John Glenn 37, Mishawaka Marian 21
Hammond 41, Gary Roosevelt 0
Sectional 25 Second Round
Andrean 52, Calumet 12
John Glenn 43, Hammond 0
Sectional 25 Championship
Andrean 42, John Glenn 0

Sectional 26 First Round
Twin Lakes 14, Culver Military Academy 13
Fairfield 42, Maconaquah 28
Jimtown 53, Tippecanoe Valley 18

Rochester 52, Peru 21
Sectional 26 Second Round
Twin Lakes 27, Fairfield 21
Jimtown 35, Rochester 24
Sectional 26 Championship
Jimtown 42, Twin Lakes 21

Sectional 27 First Round
Fort Wayne Concordia 28, Lakeland 14
Bellmont 35, Whitko 13
Fort Wayne Luers 41, West Noble 3
Heritage 41, Garrett 38
Sectional 27 Second Round
Fort Wayne Concordia 48, Bellmont 15
Fort Wayne Luers 18, Heritage 13
Sectional 27 Championship
Fort Wayne Concordia 42, Fort Wayne Luers 21

Sectional 28 First Round
Western 41, Mississinewa 28
West Lafayette 50, Delta 12
Yorktown 21, Eastbrook 20
Northwestern 42, Blackford 17
Sectional 28 Second Round
West Lafayette 34, Western 7
Yorktown 49, Northwestern 7
Sectional 28 Championship
West Lafayette 54, Yorktown 41

Sectional 29 First Round
Edgewood 41, Crawfordsville 7
Tri-West 47, Greencastle 41
Brebeuf Jesuit 48, North Montgomery 14
Western Boone 40, West Vigo 22
Sectional 29 Second Round
Tri-West 32, Edgewood 18
Brebeuf Jesuit 24, Western Boone 0
Sectional 29 Championship
Brebeuf Jesuit 42, Tri-West 21

Sectional 30 First Round
Indpls. Marshall 32, Greensburg 27
Guerin Catholic 31, Rushville 0
Indian Creek 17, Batesville 14
Hamilton Heights 55, Lawrenceburg 7
Sectional 30 Second Round
Guerin Catholic 27, Indpls. Marshall 0
Indian Creek 34, Hamilton Heights 27
Sectional 30 Championship
Guerin Catholic 24, Indian Creek 20

Sectional 31 First Round
Brownstown Central 62, Washington 30
North Harrison 42, Mitchell 14
Brown County 42, Salem 13
Charlestown 28, Corydon Central 7
Sectional 31 Second Round
Brownstown Central 52, North Harrison 13
Charlestown 41, Brown County 24

Sectional 31 Championship
Brownstown Central 62, Charlestown 6

Sectional 32 First Round
Princeton 34, Mount Vernon 21
Evansville Bosse 25, Pike Central 20
Gibson Southern 42, Vincennes Lincoln 21
Evansville Memorial 34, Heritage Hills 14
Sectional 32 Second Round
Evansville Bosse 41, Princeton 27
Gibson Southern 29, Evansville Memorial 23
Sectional 32 Championship
Gibson Southern 39, Evansville Bosse 35

Regional Championships
Andrean 27, Jimtown 7
West Lafayette 25, Fort Wayne Concordia 21
Brebeuf Jesuit 38, Guerin Catholic 17
Gibson Southern 44, Brownstown Central 29

Semi-State Championships
Andrean 52, West Lafayette 7
Brebeuf Jesuit 35, Gibson Southern 14

State Championship
Andrean 35, Brebeuf Jesuit 27

Class 2A
Sectional 33 First Round
North Judson 50, North Newton 6
Rensselaer Central 52, Hammond Noll 19
Boone Grove 7, Wheeler 6
Bowman Academy 26, River Forest 20, OT
Sectional 33 Second Round
Rensselaer Central 43, North Judson 14
Bowman Academy 28, Boone Grove 21
Sectional 33 Championship
Rensselaer Central 40, Bowman Academy 12

Sectional 34 First Round
Churubusco 28, Eastside 13
Bremen 49, Manchester 21
Woodlan 57, Central Noble 26
Prairie Heights 15, Wabash 7
Sectional 34 Second Round
Bremen 35, Churubusco 28
Woodlan 33, Prairie Heights 6
Sectional 34 Championship
Bremen 20, Woodlan 13

Sectional 35 First Round
Southmont 56, Taylor 6
Delphi 21, Benton Central 7
Lafayette Central Catholic 51, North Putnam 0
Tipton 38, Lewis Cass 13
Sectional 35 Second Round
Delphi 40, Southmont 21
Tipton 28, Lafayette Central Catholic 24
Sectional 35 Championship

Tipton 37, Delphi 21

Sectional 36 First Round
Elwood 58, Lapel 50
Alexandria 61, Frankton 34
Oak Hill 40, Madison-Grant 14
Bluffton 62, Eastern (Greentown) 34
Sectional 36 Second Round
Alexandria 27, Elwood 26
Oak Hill 55, Bluffton 22
Sectional 36 Championship
Oak Hill 35, Alexandria 14

Sectional 37 First Round
Speedway 35, Park Tudor 9
Cascade 33, Cloverdale 14
Indpls. Ritter 58, Indpls. Washington 20
Monrovia 25, South Vermillion 6
Sectional 37 Second Round
Speedway 39, Cascade 0
Indpls. Ritter 48, Monrovia 12
Sectional 37 Championship
Indpls. Ritter 35, Speedway 10

Sectional 38 First Round
Indpls. Scecina 49, Centerville 13
Winchester 61, Heritage Christian 20
Knightstown 39, Union County 14
Shenandoah 49, Indpls. Broad Ripple 6
Sectional 38 Second Round
Indpls. Scecina 48, Winchester 8
Shenandoah 40, Knightstown 20
Sectional 38 Championship
Indpls. Scecina 46, Shenandoah 14

Sectional 39 First Round
Paoli 54, Eastern (Pekin) 16
Clarksville 42, Crawford County 38
Triton Central 35, Milan 0
Providence 56, Indpls. Manual 6
Sectional 39 Second Round
Paoli 54, Clarksville 12
Triton Central 28, Providence 7
Sectional 39 Championship
Paoli 21, Triton Central 14

Sectional 40 First Round
Sullivan 48, South Spencer 21
Evansville Mater Dei 49, Forest Park 7
North Posey 55, Eastern Greene 14
Southridge 28, Tell City 27
Sectional 40 Second Round
Evansville Mater Dei 35, Sullivan 20
Southridge 27, North Posey 21
Sectional 40 Championship
Southridge 21, Evansville Mater Dei 19

Regional Championships
Rensselaer Central 24, Bremen 0

Tipton 56, Oak Hill 2
Indpls. Ritter 28, Indpls. Scecina 14
Paoli 24, Southridge 20

Semi-State Championships
Tipton 27, Rensselaer Central 0
Indpls. Ritter 49, Paoli 16

State Championship
Indpls. Ritter 56, Tipton 6

Class 1A
Sectional 41 First Round
West Central 66, Triton 6
Culver 36, South Central (Union Mills) 33
Whiting 29, LaVille 17
Winamac 73, Lake Station 14
Sectional 41 Second Round
West Central 54, Culver 38
Winamac 41, Whiting 20
Sectional 41 Championship
Winamac 33, West Central 7

Sectional 42 First Round
Carroll (Flora) 40, North White 22
Pioneer 59, Seeger 6
Frontier 38, South Newton 12
Caston 48, Tri-County 14
Sectional 42 Second Round
Pioneer 41, Carroll (Flora) 6
Frontier 27, Caston 0
Sectional 42 Championship
Pioneer 32, Frontier 0

Sectional 43 First Round
Adams Central 34, North Miami 7
South Adams 28, Northfield 14
Southwood 58, Fremont 19
Southern Wells 67, Howe Military 0
Sectional 43 Second Round
South Adams 14, Adams Central 13
Southwood 42, Southern Wells 22
Sectional 43 Championship
South Adams 40, Southwood 39, OT

Sectional 44 First Round
Indpls. Shortridge 43, Indpls. Tindley 6
Clinton Prairie 43, Indiana Deaf 6
Tri-Central 37, Clinton Central 6
Sheridan 66, Indpls. Arlington 0
Sectional 44 Second Round
Clinton Prairie 52, Indpls. Shortridge 50
Tri-Central 35, Sheridan 7
Sectional 44 Championship
Tri-Central 32, Clinton Prairie 0

Sectional 45 First Round
Monroe Central 36, Wes-Del 16
Northeastern 64, Tri 36

Cambridge City Lincoln 49, Hagerstown 28
Eastern Hancock 78, Union City 27
Sectional 45 Second Round
Northeastern 28, Monroe Central 7
Eastern Hancock 62, Cambridge City Lincoln 0
Sectional 45 Championship
Eastern Hancock 57, Northeastern 36

Sectional 46 First Round
South Putnam 64, Trinity Lutheran 0
West Washington 21, South Decatur 12
Edinburgh 42, North Decatur 20
Indpls. Lutheran 14, Indpls. Howe 8
Sectional 46 Second Round
South Putnam 26, West Washington 13
Indpls. Lutheran 50, Edinburgh 28
Sectional 46 Championship
South Putnam 42, Indpls. Lutheran 28

Sectional 47 First Round
Attica 54, Covington 0
North Vermillion 27, Rockville 6
Fountain Central 68, Riverton Parke 12
North Central (Farmersburg) 46, Turkey Run 0
Sectional 47 Second Round
Attica 13, North Vermillion 7
Fountain Central 34, North Central (Farm.) 20
Sectional 47 Championship
Fountain Central 48, Attica 12

Sectional 48 First Round
Tecumseh 71, Wood Memorial 12
Linton-Stockton 71, Union (Dugger) 0
North Daviess 50, Springs Valley 18
Perry Central 37, North Knox 35
Sectional 48 Second Round
Linton-Stockton 28, Tecumseh 24
Perry Central 28, North Daviess 12
Sectional 48 Championship
Linton-Stockton 42, Perry Central 9

Regional Championships
Winamac 28, Pioneer 14
Tri-Central 28, South Adams 7
Eastern Hancock 29, South Putnam 14
Linton-Stockton 47, Fountain Central 28

Semi-State Championships
Tri-Central 20, Winamac 14
Eastern Hancock 37, Linton-Stockton 16

State Championship
Tri-Central 20, Eastern Hancock 10

2014
Class 6A
Sectional 1 Semifinals
Merrillville 45, Crown Point 42
Lake Central 41, Lafayette Jefferson 6

Sectional 1 Championship
Merrillville 21, Lake Central 19

Sectional 2 Semifinals
Penn 43, Portage 7
Chesterton 17, Valparaiso 7
Sectional 2 Championship
Penn 41, Chesterton 6

Sectional 3 Semifinals
Homestead 56, Fort Wayne Northrop 21
Carroll (Fort Wayne) 40, Warsaw 3
Sectional 3 Championship
Carroll (Fort Wayne) 28, Homestead 0

Sectional 4 Semifinals
Carmel 28, Noblesville 6
Fishers 21, Hamilton Southeastern 0
Sectional 4 Championship
Carmel 14, Fishers 7

Sectional 5 Semifinals
Ben Davis 49, Pike 38
Avon 41, Brownsburg 10
Sectional 5 Championship
Ben Davis 34, Avon 27

Sectional 6 Semifinals
Warren Central 43, North Central (Indpls.) 0
Lawrence Central 39, Lawrence North 0
Sectional 6 Championship
Warren Central 16, Lawrence Central 0

Sectional 7 Semifinals
Franklin Central 42, Indpls. Tech 26
Southport 31, Perry Meridian 21
Sectional 7 Championship
Southport 28, Franklin Central 18

Sectional 8 Semifinals
Columbus North 30, Jeffersonville 20
Center Grove 56, New Albany 6
Sectional 8 Championship
Center Grove 54, Columbus North 7

Regional Championships
Penn 42, Merrillville 6
Carmel 56, Carroll (Fort Wayne) 6
Ben Davis 40, Warren Central 36
Center Grove 35, Southport 22

Semi-State Championships
Carmel 14, Penn 13
Ben Davis 49, Center Grove 45

State Championship
Ben Davis 42, Carmel 24

Class 5A

Sectional 9 First Round
Mishawaka 45, South Bend Adams 15
Sectional 9 Second Round
Mishawaka 35, Munster 21
LaPorte 24, Michigan City 0
Sectional 9 Championship
LaPorte 28, Mishawaka 21

Sectional 10 Semifinals
Elkhart Central 47, Goshen 8
Concord 29, Elkhart Memorial 0
Sectional 10 Championship
Elkhart Central 23, Concord 14

Sectional 11 Semifinals
Harrison (West Lafayette) 17, Kokomo 14
Westfield 28, McCutcheon 7
Sectional 11 Championship
Westfield 45, Harrison (West Lafayette) 24

Sectional 12 Semifinals
Fort Wayne Wayne 40, Fort Wayne North 35
Fort Wayne Snider 30, Huntington North 21
Sectional 12 Championship
Fort Wayne Snider 24, Fort Wayne Wayne 13

Sectional 13 First Round
Indpls. Cathedral 49, Richmond 13
Sectional 13 Second Round
Indpls. Cathedral 70, Anderson 0
Decatur Central 24, Zionsville 20
Sectional 13 Championship
Indpls. Cathedral 59, Decatur Central 14

Sectional 14 Semifinals
Whiteland 19, Franklin 6
Floyd Central 8, Jennings County 7
Sectional 14 Championship
Whiteland 42, Floyd Central 13

Sectional 15 Semifinals
Bloomington South 51, Bedford N.L. 7
Martinsville 32, Bloomington North 28
Sectional 15 Championship
Bloomington South 59, Martinsville 21

Sectional 16 Semifinals
Terre Haute North 45, Evansville North 9
Terre Haute South 28, Castle 27
Sectional 16 Championship
Terre Haute South 34, Terre Haute North 24

Regional Championships
LaPorte 55, Elkhart Central 21
Fort Wayne Snider 32, Westfield 24
Indpls. Cathedral 48, Whiteland 14
Bloomington South 36, Terre Haute South 22

Semi-State Championships

LaPorte 35, Fort Wayne Snider 7
Ind. Cathedral 27, Bloomington South 24, OT

State Championship
Indpls. Cathedral 56, LaPorte 7

Class 4A
Sectional 17 First Round
Lowell 48, Griffith 7
Gary West 18, East Chicago Central 12, 2 OT
Hammond Morton 42, Hammond Gavit 0
Highland 47, Hammond Clark 16
Sectional 17 Second Round
Lowell 41, Gary West 0
Hammond Morton 28, Highland 21
Sectional 17 Championship
Lowell 28, Hammond Morton 3

Sectional 18 First Round
Kankakee Valley 61, South Bend Riley 14
New Prairie 50, South Bend Clay 7
Plymouth 46, S.B. Washington 24
S.B. St. Joseph 27, Hobart 24
Sectional 18 Second Round
New Prairie 67, Kankakee Valley 3
Plymouth 28, S.B. St. Joseph 21
Sectional 18 Championship
New Prairie 37, Plymouth 35

Sectional 19 First Round
Leo 20, Wawasee 16
NorthWood 48, Angola 6
Northridge 21, Fort Wayne Dwenger 0
East Noble 48, DeKalb 22
Sectional 19 Second Round
Leo 28, NorthWood 7
Northridge 51, East Noble 6
Sectional 19 Championship
Northridge 9, Leo 7

Sectional 20 First Round
Columbia City 39, Fort Wayne South 0
New Haven 38, Logansport 14
Norwell 35, Frankfort 14
Marion 38, Jay County 20
Sectional 20 Second Round
Columbia City 7, New Haven 3
Norwell 41, Marion 7
Sectional 20 Championship
Norwell 35, Columbia City 7

Sectional 21 First Round
New Palestine 61, Muncie Central 7
Beech Grove 36, Mount Vernon (Fortville) 21
Pendleton Heights 21, Greenfield-Central 20
Sectional 21 Second Round
New Palestine 74, New Castle 0
Beech Grove 46, Pendleton Heights 0
Sectional 21 Championship

New Palestine 83, Beech Grove 20

Sectional 22 First Round
Indpls. Chatard 34, Lebanon 0
Roncalli 42, Indpls. Northwest 0
Northview 28, Mooresville 19
Plainfield 31, Danville 8
Sectional 22 Second Round
Roncalli 31, Indpls. Chatard 6
Plainfield 28, Northview 13
Sectional 22 Championship
Roncalli 24, Plainfield 17

Sectional 23 First Round
East Central 41, Greenwood 26
Shelbyville 48, Connersville 27
Madison 16, Franklin County 14
Columbus East 82, South Dearborn 13
Sectional 23 Second Round
East Central 48, Shelbyville 12
Columbus East 48, Madison 10
Sectional 23 Championship
Columbus East 28, East Central 9

Sectional 24 First Round
Jasper 46, Silver Creek 26
Evansville Central 42, Evansville Harrison 0
Owen Valley 28, Boonville 21
Evansville Reitz 59, Seymour 35
Sectional 24 Second Round
Jasper 35, Evansville Central 20
Evansville Reitz 35, Owen Valley 10
Sectional 24 Championship
Evansville Reitz 45, Jasper 38

Regional Championships
New Prairie 28, Lowell 27
Northridge 17, Norwell 10
New Palestine 44, Roncalli 13
Columbus East 42, Evansville Reitz 14

Semi-State Championships
New Prairie 28, Northridge 10
New Palestine 30, Columbus East 28

State Championship
New Palestine 77, New Prairie 42

Class 3A
Sectional 25 First Round
Calumet 41, Gary Roosevelt 6
Mishawaka Marian 35, John Glenn 14
Andrean 61, Hammond 7
Sectional 25 Second Round
Calumet 20, Knox 18
Andrean 56, Mishawaka Marian 21
Sectional 25 Championship
Andrean 62, Calumet 6

Sectional 26 First Round
Peru 28, Maconaquah 20
Culver Military 27, Tippecanoe Valley 26
Rochester 31, Twin Lakes 24
Jimtown 42, Fairfield 6
Sectional 26 Second Round
Peru 19, Culver Military Academy 7
Jimtown 21, Rochester 0
Sectional 26 Championship
Jimtown 48, Peru 0

Sectional 27 First Round
Garrett 40, Lakeland 7
Bellmont 24, Whitko 20
Fort Wayne Luers 40, Fort Wayne Concordia 26
Heritage 41, West Noble 34
Sectional 27 Second Round
Garrett 34, Bellmont 12
Fort Wayne Luers 33, Heritage 9
Sectional 27 Championship
Fort Wayne Luers 54, Garrett 6

Sectional 28 First Round
Mississinewa 69, Eastbrook 13
Delta 52, Northwestern 7
Yorktown 48, West Lafayette 35
Western 38, Blackford 0
Sectional 28 Second Round
Delta 42, Mississinewa 0
Yorktown 44, Western 8
Sectional 28 Championship
Yorktown 35, Delta 12

Sectional 29 First Round
Brebeuf Jesuit 73, Crawfordsville 20
Tri-West 58, West Vigo 7
Edgewood 36, Greencastle 13
Western Boone 27, North Montgomery 26
Sectional 29 Second Round
Tri-West 14, Brebeuf Jesuit 7
Western Boone 35, Edgewood 0
Sectional 29 Championship
Tri-West 54, Western Boone 28

Sectional 30 First Round
Rushville 34, Indpls. Marshall 24
Hamilton Heights 28, Indian Creek 27
Guerin Catholic 28, Lawrenceburg 13
Batesville 24, Greensburg 10
Sectional 30 Second Round
Hamilton Heights 31, Rushville 6
Guerin Catholic 21, Batesville 13
Sectional 30 Championship
Guerin Catholic 28, Hamilton Heights 20

Sectional 31 First Round
Mitchell 48, Brown County 8
North Harrison 16, Salem 0
Brownstown Central 74, Washington 0

Charlestown 15, Corydon Central 6
Sectional 31 Second Round
North Harrison 40, Mitchell 0
Charlestown 27, Brownstown Central 16
Sectional 31 Championship
Charlestown 18, North Harrison 7

Sectional 32 First Round
Mount Vernon 27, Princeton 17
Gibson Southern 50, Evansville Memorial 17
Evansville Bosse 41, Pike Central 20
Heritage Hills 27, Vincennes Lincoln 20
Sectional 32 Second Round
Gibson Southern 57, Mount Vernon 13
Heritage Hills 49, Evansville Bosse 0
Sectional 32 Championship
Heritage Hills 14, Gibson Southern 13

Regional Championships
Andrean 38, Jimtown 7
Fort Wayne Luers 26, Yorktown 25
Tri-West 23, Guerin Catholic 15
Heritage Hills 28, Charlestown 7

Semi-State Championships
Andrean 17, Fort Wayne Luers 15
Tri-West 14, Heritage Hills 6

State Championship
Tri-West 49, Andrean 27

Class 2A
Sectional 33 First Round
Boone Grove 39, North Newton 14
Wheeler 49, North Judson 26
Bowman Academy 46, River Forest 14
Rensselaer Central 67, Hammond Noll 6
Sectional 33 Second Round
Wheeler 27, Boone Grove 7
Rensselaer Central 60, Bowman Academy 14
Sectional 33 Championship
Rensselaer Central 51, Wheeler 7

Sectional 34 First Round
Bremen 48, Prairie Heights 27
Wabash 21, Manchester 7
Eastside 41, Central Noble 7
Woodlan 42, Churubusco 14
Sectional 34 Second Round
Bremen 42, Wabash 28
Woodlan 29, Eastside 26
Sectional 34 Championship
Bremen 35, Woodlan 14

Sectional 35 First Round
Lewis Cass 35, Tipton 25
Benton Central 21, North Putnam 15
Lafayette Central Catholic 72, Taylor 6
Delphi 34, Southmont 21

Sectional 35 Second Round
Lewis Cass 51, Benton Central 7
Lafayette Central Catholic 56, Delphi 6
Sectional 35 Championship
Lafayette Central Catholic 42, Lewis Cass 0

Sectional 36 First Round
Lapel 67, Elwood 16
Alexandria 42, Eastern (Greentown) 35
Bluffton 46, Madison-Grant 40
Oak Hill 47, Frankton 0
Sectional 36 Second Round
Lapel 20, Alexandria 12
Oak Hill 44, Bluffton 6
Sectional 36 Championship
Lapel 24, Oak Hill 20

Sectional 37 First Round
Indpls. Ritter 62, Indpls. Washington 0
Park Tudor 56, Cloverdale 20
South Vermillion 40, Cascade 14
Monrovia 22, Speedway 20
Sectional 37 Second Round
Indpls. Ritter 41, Park Tudor 0
Monrovia 41, South Vermillion 7
Sectional 37 Championship
Monrovia 62, Indpls. Ritter 14

Sectional 38 First Round
Shenandoah 30, Indpls. Scecina 14
Heritage Christian 44, Union County 0
Centerville 34, Indpls. Broad Ripple 32
Winchester 48, Knightstown 34
Sectional 38 Second Round
Shenandoah 28, Heritage Christian 0
Winchester 33, Centerville 12
Sectional 38 Championship
Shenandoah 27, Winchester 7

Sectional 39 First Round
Triton Central 57, Indpls. Manual 0
Providence 46, Clarksville 30
Eastern (Pekin) 28, Crawford County 0
Milan 36, Paoli 15
Sectional 39 Second Round
Triton Central 51, Providence 0
Milan 34, Eastern (Pekin) 3
Sectional 39 Championship
Triton Central 31, Milan 6

Sectional 40 First Round
Southridge 28, Sullivan 27
Evansville Mater Dei 48, Forest Park 6
Tell City 47, Eastern Greene 32
North Posey 49, South Spencer 16
Sectional 40 Second Round
Evansville Mater Dei 35, Southridge 7
North Posey 42, Tell City 21
Sectional 40 Championship

Evansville Mater Dei 28, North Posey 9

Regional Championships
Rensselaer Central 48, Bremen 13
Lafayette Central Catholic 54, Lapel 12
Monrovia 24, Shenandoah 14
Evansville Mater Dei 28, Triton Central 14

Semi-State Championships
Rensselaer Central 17, Lafayette C.C. 14
Evansville Mater Dei 42, Monrovia 18

State Championship
Rensselaer Central 45, Evansville Mater Dei 21

Class 1A
Sectional 41 First Round
Triton 34, South Central (Union Mills) 20
LaVille 41, Lake Station 0
Whiting 21, Culver 13
Winamac 64, West Central 0
Sectional 41 Second Round
LaVille 15, Triton 0
Winamac 34, Whiting 14
Sectional 41 Championship
Winamac 33, LaVille 3

Sectional 42 First Round
Caston 38, Seeger 22
Carroll (Flora) 45, South Newton 29
North White 45, Frontier 0
Pioneer 69, Tri-County 14
Sectional 42 Second Round
Carroll (Flora) 52, Caston 0
Pioneer 63, North White 14
Sectional 42 Championship
Pioneer 44, Carroll (Flora) 0

Sectional 43 First Round
South Adams 9, Adams Central 6
Southern Wells 29, North Miami 14
Southwood 62, Fremont 14
Sectional 43 Second Round
South Adams 26, Northfield 7
Southern Wells 33, Southwood 7
Sectional 43 Championship
South Adams 31, Southern Wells 14

Sectional 44 First Round
Sheridan 75, Indpls. Tindley 20
Tri-Central 1, Clinton Prairie 0
Indpls. Shortridge 46, Indiana Deaf 17
Sectional 44 Second Round
Sheridan 60, Clinton Central 24
Tri-Central 47, Indpls. Shortridge 6
Sectional 44 Championship
Tri-Central 34, Sheridan 14

Sectional 45 First Round
Eastern Hancock 41, Cambridge City 12
Tri 41, Monroe Central 0
Hagerstown 30, Union City 25
Northeastern 42, Wes-Del 0
Sectional 45 Second Round
Eastern Hancock 35, Monroe Central 18
Northeastern 50, Hagerstown 13
Sectional 45 Championship
Eastern Hancock 21, Northeastern 20

Sectional 46 First Round
South Putnam 45, West Washington 29
Indpls. Lutheran 55, Edinburgh 7
Indpls. Howe 60, Trinity Lutheran 14
South Decatur 41, North Decatur 0
Sectional 46 Second Round
Indpls. Lutheran 47, South Putnam 0
Indpls. Howe 20, South Decatur 13
Sectional 46 Championship
Indpls. Lutheran 49, Indpls. Howe 14

Sectional 47 First Round
Rockville 28, North Central (Farmersburg) 6
Fountain Central 49, Attica 21
Covington 40, Riverton Parke 6
North Vermillion 61, Turkey Run 6
Sectional 47 Second Round
Fountain Central 19, Rockville 7
North Vermillion 48, Covington 0
Sectional 47 Championship
North Vermillion 48, Fountain Central 20

Sectional 48 First Round
North Knox 53, Springs Valley 14
Linton-Stockton 67, Wood Memorial 6
Perry Central 41, North Daviess 21
Sectional 48 Second Round
North Knox 28, Tecumseh 8
Linton-Stockton 63, Perry Central 13
Sectional 48 Championship
Linton-Stockton 41, North Knox 0

Regional Championships
Pioneer 28, Winamac 6
South Adams 14, Tri-Central 6
Indpls. Lutheran 21, Eastern Hancock 19
North Vermillion 31, Linton-Stockton 8

Semi-State Championships
Pioneer 62, South Adams 7
North Vermillion 37, Indpls. Lutheran 19

State Championship
North Vermillion 27, Pioneer 26

2015
Class 6A
Sectional 1 Semifinals
Portage 36, Lake Central 14

Merrillville 22, Crown Point 12
Sectional 1 Championship
Merrillville 28, Portage 21

Sectional 2 Semifinals
Chesterton 23, Valparaiso 7
Penn 49, LaPorte 21
Sectional 2 Championship
Penn 49, Chesterton 14

Sectional 3 Semifinals
Carroll (Fort Wayne) 49, Warsaw 21
Homestead 48, Fort Wayne Northrop 14
Sectional 3 Championship
Homestead 35, Carroll (Fort Wayne) 26

Sectional 4 Semifinals
Fishers 38, Hamilton Southeastern 22
Carmel 45, Noblesville 29
Sectional 4 Championship
Carmel 28, Fishers 7

Sectional 5 Semifinals
Ben Davis 55, Pike 27
Avon 61, Brownsburg 14
Sectional 5 Championship
Avon 27, Ben Davis 22

Sectional 6 Semifinals
Indpls. Cathedral 43, Lawrence Central 22
Lawrence North 42, North Central (Indpls.) 7
Sectional 6 Championship
Indpls. Cathedral 35, Lawrence North 14

Sectional 7 Semifinals
Warren Central 49, Perry Meridian 7
Southport 34, Franklin Central 14
Sectional 7 Championship
Warren Central 54, Southport 17

Sectional 8 Semifinals
Jeffersonville 35, New Albany 34
Center Grove 34, Columbus North 7
Sectional 8 Championship
Center Grove 56, Jeffersonville 6

Regional Championships
Penn 56, Merrillville 38
Carmel 41, Homestead 7
Avon 37, Indpls. Cathedral 34, 2 OT
Center Grove 24, Warren Central 13

Semi-State Championships
Penn 16, Carmel 10
Center Grove 35, Avon 34, 2 OT

State Championship
Center Grove 28, Penn 16

Class 5A
Sectional 9 First Round
South Bend Adams 51, Elkhart Memorial 21
Sectional 9 Second Round
South Bend Adams 41, Michigan City 28
Mishawaka 51, Elkhart Central 7
Sectional 9 Championship
Mishawaka 27, South Bend Adams 6

Sectional 10 Semifinals
Concord 28, Fort Wayne North 19
Fort Wayne Snider 42, Goshen 10
Sectional 10 Championship
Fort Wayne Snider 47, Concord 21

Sectional 11 Semifinals
Lafayette Jefferson 41, McCutcheon 29
Westfield 42, Harrison (West Lafayette) 22
Sectional 11 Championship
Westfield 45, Lafayette Jefferson 27

Sectional 12 Semifinals
Huntington North 33, Anderson 29
Kokomo 20, Muncie Central 15
Sectional 12 Championship
Kokomo 57, Huntington North 0

Sectional 13 Semifinals
Decatur Central 30, Plainfield 27
Zionsville 37, Indpls. Tech 7
Sectional 13 Championship
Zionsville 50, Decatur Central 32

Sectional 14 First Round
Columbus East 56, Franklin 28
Sectional 14 Second Round
Columbus East 28, Whiteland 14
New Palestine 70, Martinsville 6
Sectional 14 Championship
New Palestine 24, Columbus East 14

Sectional 15 Semifinals
Terre Haute North 17, Terre Haute South 7
Bloomington South 44, Bloomington North 13
Sectional 15 Championship
Bloomington South 35, Terre Haute North 7

Sectional 16 Semifinals
Castle 44, Evansville North 0
Bedford North Lawrence 17, Floyd Central 0
Sectional 16 Championship
Castle 49, Bedford North Lawrence 13

Regional Championships
Fort Wayne Snider 42, Mishawaka 32
Kokomo 21, Westfield 19
New Palestine 49, Zionsville 21
Castle 45, Bloomington South 26

Semi-State Championships
Fort Wayne Snider 56, Kokomo 20
New Palestine 56, Castle 6

State Championship
Fort Wayne Snider 64, New Palestine 61

Class 4A
Sectional 17 First Round
Hammond Morton 40, Highland 25
Lowell 31, Munster 0
East Chicago Central 28, Gary West 22
Hammond Gavit 33, Hammond Clark 14
Sectional 17 Second Round
Lowell 35, Hammond Morton 14
East Chicago Central 26, Hammond Gavit 21
Sectional 17 Championship
Lowell 34, East Chicago Central 16

Sectional 18 First Round
South Bend Riley 12, Kankakee Valley 8
S.B. St. Joseph 19, Hobart 17
Andrean 40, New Prairie 32
S.B. Washington 45, South Bend Clay 0
Sectional 18 Second Round
S.B. St. Joseph 42, South Bend Riley 6
S.B. Washington 35, Andrean 34
Sectional 18 Championship
S.B. St. Joseph 21, S.B. Washington 13

Sectional 19 First Round
NorthWood 42, East Noble 28
Northridge 14, Columbia City 0
Plymouth 66, Wawasee 7
DeKalb 39, Angola 13
Sectional 19 Second Round
NorthWood 43, Northridge 21
Plymouth 56, DeKalb 14
Sectional 19 Championship
Plymouth 37, NorthWood 29

Sectional 20 First Round
Fort Wayne South 38, Marion 12
Leo 56, Logansport 19
Fort Wayne Dwenger 42, Fort Wayne Wayne 6
New Haven 40, Mississinewa 0
Sectional 20 Second Round
Leo 41, Fort Wayne South 8
Fort Wayne Dwenger 37, New Haven 6
Sectional 20 Championship
Fort Wayne Dwenger 24, Leo 22

Sectional 21 First Round
Lebanon 40, Western 6
Roncalli 28, Frankfort 0
Greenwood 42, Beech Grove 25
Northview 41, Mooresville 30
Sectional 21 Second Round
Roncalli 28, Lebanon 14
Greenwood 29, Northview 17
Sectional 21 Championship
Roncalli 35, Greenwood 19

Sectional 22 First Round
Mount Vernon (Fortville) 42, Jay County 14
Pendleton Heights 48, Connersville 32
Delta 14, Greenfield-Central 12
New Castle 21, Richmond 20
Sectional 22 Second Round
Pendleton Heights 41, Mount Vernon (FV) 7
Delta 49, New Castle 7
Sectional 22 Championship
Delta 46, Pendleton Heights 32

Sectional 23 First Round
Silver Creek 42, Madison 31
Seymour 46, Franklin County 30
East Central 40, South Dearborn 0
Shelbyville 49, Jennings County 26
Sectional 23 Second Round
Seymour 40, Silver Creek 21
East Central 36, Shelbyville 25
Sectional 23 Championship
East Central 58, Seymour 6

Sectional 24 First Round
Evansville Reitz 35, Evansville Central 28
Jasper 38, Owen Valley 0
Boonville 53, Evansville Bosse 40
Evansville Harrison 43, Edgewood 3
Sectional 24 Second Round
Jasper 24, Evansville Reitz 22
Evansville Harrison 54, Boonville 14
Sectional 24 Championship
Evansville Harrison 48, Jasper 13

Regional Championships
S.B. St. Joseph 7, Lowell 6
Fort Wayne Dwenger 8, Plymouth 0
Roncalli 49, Delta 12
East Central 42, Evansville Harrison 28

Semi-State Championships
Fort Wayne Dwenger 41, S.B. St. Joseph 7
East Central 21, Roncalli 0

State Championship
Fort Wayne Dwenger 27, East Central 3

Class 3A
Sectional 25 First Round
Griffith 15, Rensselaer Central 14
Hammond 52, Calumet 8
Wheeler 41, Hanover Central 14
Mishawaka Marian 48, John Glenn 0
Sectional 25 Second Round
Hammond 17, Griffith 14
Mishawaka Marian 41, Wheeler 21

Sectional 25 Championship
Mishawaka Marian 49, Hammond 9

Sectional 26 First Round
Lakeland 42, Heritage 35
Culver Military Academy 24, Fairfield 21
Garrett 43, West Noble 14
Jimtown 53, Tippecanoe Valley 0
Sectional 26 Second Round
Culver Military Academy 57, Lakeland 28
Garrett 24, Jimtown 7
Sectional 26 Championship
Culver Military Academy 23, Garrett 21

Sectional 27 First Round
Bellmont 57, Maconaquah 0
Fort Wayne Concordia 51, Norwell 0
Yorktown 35, Peru 28
Fort Wayne Luers 82, Northwestern 52
Sectional 27 Second Round
Bellmont 38, Fort Wayne Concordia 7
Fort Wayne Luers 40, Yorktown 7
Sectional 27 Championship
Bellmont 21, Fort Wayne Luers 7

Sectional 28 First Round
Twin Lakes 33, Tipton 12
North Montgomery 51, Benton Central 7
Hamilton Heights 63, Crawfordsville 7
West Lafayette 41, Western Boone 23
Sectional 28 Second Round
North Montgomery 37, Twin Lakes 0
West Lafayette 34, Hamilton Heights 21
Sectional 28 Championship
West Lafayette 35, North Montgomery 28

Sectional 29 First Round
Guerin Catholic 68, Greencastle 0
Indpls. Chatard 20, Brebeuf Jesuit 14
Tri-West 48, Danville 7
West Vigo 35, Indpls. Northwest 27
Sectional 29 Second Round
Indpls. Chatard 14, Guerin Catholic 7
Tri-West 56, West Vigo 13
Sectional 29 Championship
Indpls. Chatard 42, Tri-West 10

Sectional 30 First Round
Greensburg 47, Indpls. Marshall 8
Lawrenceburg 67, Rushville 7
Batesville 45, Indpls. Manual 0
Indian Creek 62, Indpls. Washington 14
Sectional 30 Second Round
Lawrenceburg 35, Greensburg 27
Batesville 49, Indian Creek 22
Sectional 30 Championship
Batesville 29, Lawrenceburg 17

Sectional 31 First Round
Corydon Central 49, Brown County 7
Southridge 28, North Harrison 21
Brownstown Central 43, Salem 18
Charlestown 39, Heritage Hills 37
Sectional 31 Second Round
Southridge 44, Corydon Central 12
Brownstown Central 44, Charlestown 19
Sectional 31 Championship
Brownstown Central 37, Southridge 0

Sectional 32 First Round
Princeton 22, Evansville Memorial 19
Mount Vernon 42, Pike Central 0
Gibson Southern 64, Vincennes Lincoln 20
Sullivan 36, Washington 14
Sectional 32 Second Round
Princeton 20, Mount Vernon 12
Gibson Southern 48, Sullivan 7
Sectional 32 Championship
Gibson Southern 49, Princeton 21

Regional Championships
Mishawaka Marian 21, Culver Military 14
West Lafayette 28, Bellmont 21
Indpls. Chatard 33, Batesville 0
Gibson Southern 56, Brownstown Central 7

Semi-State Championships
West Lafayette 14, Mishawaka Marian 10
Indpls. Chatard 29, Gibson Southern 20

State Championship
Indpls. Chatard 31, West Lafayette 7

Class 2A
Sectional 33 First Round
Knox 30, River Forest 20
North Newton 50, Hammond Noll 0
Gary Roosevelt 52, Bowman Academy 22
Whiting 20, Boone Grove 0
Sectional 33 Second Round
Knox 41, North Newton 6
Whiting 59, Gary Roosevelt 14
Sectional 33 Championship
Whiting 31, Knox 21

Sectional 34 First Round
Bremen 41, Rochester 7
Oak Hill 51, Delphi 14
Lewis Cass 31, Wabash 20
Winamac 34, Manchester 0
Sectional 34 Second Round
Bremen 48, Oak Hill 0
Lewis Cass 21, Winamac 14, OT
Sectional 34 Championship
Bremen 48, Lewis Cass 21

Sectional 35 First Round
Churubusco 34, South Adams 3

Whitko 45, Prairie Heights 0
Eastside 40, Bluffton 0
Woodlan 42, Central Noble 7
Sectional 35 Second Round
Whitko 34, Churubusco 27
Woodlan 14, Eastside 13
Sectional 35 Championship
Woodlan 22, Whitko 19

Sectional 36 First Round
Eastbrook 55, Alexandria 6
Taylor 38, Blackford 7
Elwood 26, Madison-Grant 20
Winchester 62, Eastern (Greentown) 6
Sectional 36 Second Round
Eastbrook 69, Taylor 14
Winchester 28, Elwood 0
Sectional 36 Championship
Winchester 44, Eastbrook 28

Sectional 37 First Round
Heritage Christian 50, Indpls. Broad Ripple 0
Speedway 49, Frankton 38
Indpls. Scecina 14, Lapel 13
Indpls. Ritter 50, Park Tudor 6
Sectional 37 Second Round
Heritage Christian 23, Speedway 7
Indpls. Scecina 26, Indpls. Ritter 22
Sectional 37 Championship
Indpls. Scecina 40, Heritage Christian 7

Sectional 38 First Round
Triton Central 45, Union County 6
Centerville 21, Switzerland County 0
Eastern Hancock 35, Northeastern 0
Indpls. Howe 57, Milan 35
Sectional 38 Second Round
Triton Central 56, Centerville 0
Indpls. Howe 34, Eastern Hancock 13
Sectional 38 Championship
Indpls. Howe 50, Triton Central 10

Sectional 39 First Round
Monrovia 55, Mitchell 0
Southmont 46, South Vermillion 20
Paoli 53, Cascade 18
North Putnam 42, Cloverdale 6
Sectional 39 Second Round
Monrovia 42, Southmont 7
North Putnam 40, Paoli 32
Sectional 39 Championship
Monrovia 50, North Putnam 0

Sectional 40 First Round
North Posey 35, Forest Park 12
Eastern (Pekin) 15, Clarksville 0
Evansville Mater Dei 63, South Spencer 22
Providence 41, Crawford County 18
Sectional 40 Second Round
North Posey 41, Eastern (Pekin) 14
Evansville Mater Dei 41, Providence 7
Sectional 40 Championship
Evansville Mater Dei 49, North Posey 7

Regional Championships
Whiting 28, Bremen 21
Woodlan 29, Winchester 26
Indpls. Howe 26, Indpls. Scecina 7
Monrovia 40, Evansville Mater Dei 20

Semi-State Championships
Whiting 14, Woodlan 7
Monrovia 37, Indpls. Howe 31

State Championship
Monrovia 33, Whiting 6

Class 1A
Sectional 41 First Round
Pioneer 56, North White 12
South Newton 21, South Central (Union Mills) 7
Lake Station 13, West Central 7
North Judson 57, Tri-County 0
Sectional 41 Second Round
Pioneer 77, South Newton 20
North Judson 56, Lake Station 0
Sectional 41 Championship
Pioneer 56, North Judson 18

Sectional 42 First Round
Attica 35, Covington 20
Lafayette Central Catholic 70, Clinton Central 8
Carroll (Flora) 35, Seeger 14
Clinton Prairie 40, Frontier 12
Sectional 42 Second Round
Lafayette Central Catholic 70, Attica 7
Clinton Prairie 50, Carroll (Flora) 0
Sectional 42 Championship
Lafayette Central Catholic 51, Clinton Prairie 0

Sectional 43 First Round
LaVille 48, Fremont 0
North Miami 35, Culver 17
Southwood 53, Triton 20
Northfield 48, Caston 0
Sectional 43 Second Round
LaVille 41, North Miami 7
Northfield 43, Southwood 13
Sectional 43 Championship
Northfield 24, LaVille 21

Sectional 44 First Round
Southern Wells 56, Union City 20
Adams Central 40, Wes-Del 0
Tri-Central 24, Shenandoah 22
Monroe Central 60, Anderson Prep Academy 14
Sectional 44 Second Round
Adams Central 35, Southern Wells 7

Monroe Central 20, Tri-Central 6
Sectional 44 Championship
Adams Central 28, Monroe Central 12

Sectional 45 First Round
North Vermillion 62, Turkey Run 25
Riverton Parke 29, Covenant Christian 13
South Putnam 56, Sheridan 22
Fountain Central 15, Rockville 12
Sectional 45 Second Round
North Vermillion 56, Riverton Parke 0
South Putnam 26, Fountain Central 9
Sectional 45 Championship
North Vermillion 48, South Putnam 20

Sectional 46 First Round
Tri 28, Hagerstown 27
Cambridge City 51, Indpls. Shortridge 14
Indpls. Lutheran 56, Knightstown 42
Indiana Deaf 20, Indpls. Tindley 16
Sectional 46 Second Round
Cambridge City Lincoln 35, Tri 24
Indpls. Lutheran 53, Indiana Deaf 0
Sectional 46 Championship
Indpls. Lutheran 56, Cambridge City Lincoln 26

Sectional 47 First Round
Eastern Greene 41, South Decatur 21
Oldenburg Academy 47, Edinburgh 12
North Decatur 13, Springs Valley 10
Sectional 47 Second Round
West Washington 34, Eastern Greene 21
North Decatur 32, Oldenburg Academy 14
Sectional 47 Championship
West Washington 14, North Decatur 6

Sectional 48 First Round
Linton-Stockton 76, Tell City 8
Perry Central 49, Wood Memorial 14
Tecumseh 16, North Daviess 14
North Central (Farmersburg) 34, North Knox 27
Sectional 48 Second Round
Linton-Stockton 63, Perry Central 7
North Central (Farmersburg) 55, Tecumseh 22
Sectional 48 Championship
Linton-Stockton 74, North Central (Farm.) 0

Regional Championships
Lafayette Central Catholic 31, Pioneer 14
Northfield 21, Adams Central 13
North Vermillion 55, Indpls. Lutheran 37
Linton-Stockton 35, West Washington 13

Semi-State Championships
Lafayette Central Catholic 45, Northfield 6
Linton-Stockton 56, North Vermillion 27

State Championship
Lafayette Central Catholic 34, Linton 7

2016
Class 6A
Sectional 1 Semifinals
Crown Point 10, Lake Central 6
Merrillville 22, Portage 21
Championship
Crown Point 24, Merrillville 19

Sectional 2 Semifinals
LaPorte 17, Chesterton 7
Penn 35, Valparaiso 7
Championship
Penn 42, LaPorte 21

Sectional 3 Semifinals
Homestead 66, Fort Wayne Northrop 31
Warsaw 23, Carroll (Fort Wayne) 13
Championship
Homestead 52, Warsaw 27

Sectional 4 Semifinals
Carmel 17, Hamilton Southeastern 14
Fishers 28, Noblesville 14
Championship
Carmel 23, Fishers 10

Sectional 5 Semifinals
Avon 39, Pike 20
Ben Davis 49, Brownsburg 13
Championship
Ben Davis 47, Avon 40

Sectional 6 Semifinals
Lawrence Central 43, North Central (Indpls.) 13
Indpls. Cathedral 41, Lawrence North 38, OT
Championship
Indpls. Cathedral 20, Lawrence Central 17, OT

Sectional 7 Semifinals
Warren Central 49, Franklin Central 17
Southport 20, Perry Meridian 13
Championship
Warren Central 50, Southport 20

Sectional 8 Semifinals
Columbus North 56, New Albany 6
Center Grove 62, Jeffersonville 6
Championship
Center Grove 41, Columbus North 14

Regional Championships
Penn 23, Crown Point 0
Carmel 42, Homestead 7
Ben Davis 51, Indpls. Cathedral 21
Center Grove 28, Warren Central 7

Semi-State Championship
Carmel 21, Penn 10

Center Grove 42, Ben Davis 22

State Championship
Carmel 16, Center Grove 13

Class 5A
Sectional 9 First Round
Mishawaka 42, Elkhart Memorial 13
Second Round
Mishawaka 43, South Bend Adams 14
Michigan City 49, Elkhart Central 33
Championship
Mishawaka 18, Michigan City 7

Sectional 10 Semifinals
Goshen 49, Fort Wayne North 7
Fort Wayne Snider 56, Concord 3
Championship
Fort Wayne Snider 56, Goshen 16

Sectional 11 Semifinals
McCutcheon 29, Harrison (West Lafayette) 12
Westfield 38, Lafayette Jefferson 14
Championship
Westfield 34, McCutcheon 7

Sectional 12 Semifinals
Muncie Central 46, Anderson 14
Kokomo 24, Huntington North 0
Championship
Kokomo 48, Muncie Central 33

Sectional 13 Semifinals
Plainfield 24, Indpls. Tech 8
Zionsville 48, Decatur Central 23
Championship
Zionsville 33, Plainfield 28

Sectional 14 First Round
Columbus East 35, New Palestine 7
Second Round
Columbus East 49, Martinsville 9
Whiteland 34, Franklin 0
Championship
Columbus East 56, Whiteland 31

Sectional 15 Semifinals
Bloomington South 38, Bloomington North 0
Terre Haute North 6, Terre Haute South 0
Championship
Bloomington South 45, Terre Haute North 14

Sectional 16 Semifinals
Castle 21, Evansville North 14
Floyd Central 40, Bedford North Lawrence 34
Championship
Castle 42, Floyd Central 28

Regional Championships
Fort Wayne Snider 31, Mishawaka 7
Westfield 45, Kokomo 7
Columbus East 42, Zionsville 35
Bloomington South 44, Castle 23

Semi-State Championships
Westfield 23, Fort Wayne Snider 17
Columbus East 35, Bloomington South 15

State Championship
Westfield 16, Columbus East 13

Class 4A
Sectional 17 First Round
Lowell 65, Gary West 6
Hammond Morton 18, Hammond Gavit 12, OT
Munster 28, East Chicago Central 22
Highland 57, Hammond Clark 6
Second Round
Lowell 49, Hammond Morton 2
Munster 36, Highland 15
Championship
Lowell 42, Munster 14

Sectional 18 First Round
Kankakee Valley 49, South Bend Clay 8
Hobart 33, S.B. Washington 14
Andrean 30, S.B. St. Joseph 13
New Prairie 42, South Bend Riley 14
Second Round
Hobart 55, Kankakee Valley 21
New Prairie 28, Andrean 14
Championship
Hobart 35, New Prairie 14

Sectional 19 First Round
Plymouth 26, Angola 23
East Noble 45, DeKalb 0
Northridge 21, Wawasee 20
NorthWood 52, Columbia City 13
Second Round
East Noble 40, Plymouth 22
NorthWood 44, Northridge 13
Championship
NorthWood 52, East Noble 24

Sectional 20 First Round
Mississinewa 49, Logansport 6
Fort Wayne Dwenger 22, Marion 14
New Haven 49, Fort Wayne Wayne 7
Fort Wayne South 33, Leo 9
Second Round
Fort Wayne Dwenger 56, Mississinewa 2
New Haven 51, Fort Wayne South 19
Championship
New Haven 28, Fort Wayne Dwenger 23

Sectional 21 First Round
Roncalli 35, Northview 14

Lebanon 62, Beech Grove 48
Mooresville 26, Western 23
Greenwood 42, Frankfort 12
Second Round
Roncalli 34, Lebanon 33
Greenwood 27, Mooresville 0
Championship
Roncalli 42, Greenwood 6

Sectional 22 First Round
Pendleton Heights 31, Connersville 7
Mount Vernon (Fortville) 46, Richmond 14
Greenfield-Central 41, Jay County 21
Delta 27, New Castle 7
Second Round
Mount Vernon (Fortville) 13, Pendleton Hts. 0
Delta 42, Greenfield-Central 21
Championship
Delta 12, Mount Vernon (Fortville) 6

Sectional 23 First Round
East Central 41, Shelbyville 27
Franklin County 42, South Dearborn 7
Seymour 24, Silver Creek 6
Jennings County 17, Madison 7
Second Round
East Central 30, Franklin County 20
Seymour 43, Jennings County 0
Championship
East Central 52, Seymour 8

Sectional 24 First Round
Evansville Reitz 48, Evansville Bosse 8
Evansville Central 41, Owen Valley 13
Boonville 42, Edgewood 6
Evansville Harrison 38, Jasper 27
Second Round
Evansville Reitz 34, Evansville Central 7
Evansville Harrison 48, Boonville 0
Championship
Evansville Reitz 52, Evansville Harrison 7

Regional Championships
Lowell 44, Hobart 23
NorthWood 52, New Haven 28
Roncalli 42, Delta 7
East Central 33, Evansville Reitz 27 (Nov. 12)

Semi-State Championships
NorthWood 21, Lowell 14
Roncalli 24, East Central 21

State Championship
Roncalli 34, NorthWood 22

Class 3A
Sectional 25 First Round
Griffith 48, John Glenn 7
Rensselaer Central 38, Calumet 7
Hanover Central 49, Hammond 12
Mishawaka Marian 57, Wheeler 8
Second Round
Griffith 28, Rensselaer Central 21
Mishawaka Marian 43, Hanover Central 6
Championship
Mishawaka Marian 49, Griffith 14

Sectional 26 First Round
Garrett 42, Fairfield 16
Culver Military Academy 45, Lakeland 34
Jimtown 49, Heritage 6
West Noble 30, Tippecanoe Valley 28
Second Round
Garrett 28, Culver Military Academy 0
Jimtown 27, West Noble 3
Championship
Garrett 29, Jimtown 26
Sectional 27 First Round
Fort Wayne Luers 42, Northwestern 15

Sectional 27 First Round
Peru 40, Maconaquah 21
Bellmont 39, Norwell 20
Fort Wayne Concordia 54, Yorktown 14
Second Round
Fort Wayne Luers 48, Peru 12
Fort Wayne Concordia 47, Bellmont 7
Sectional 27 Championship
Fort Wayne Concordia 45, Fort Wayne Luers 22

Sectional 28 First Round
West Lafayette 48, Tipton 7
Western Boone 56, Benton Central 21
North Montgomery 14, Crawfordsville 0
Twin Lakes 28, Hamilton Heights 14
Second Round
West Lafayette 43, Western Boone 12
Twin Lakes 31, North Montgomery 6
Championship
West Lafayette 56, Twin Lakes 24

Sectional 29 First Round
Danville 53, Indpls. Northwest 12
Greencastle 33, West Vigo 30
Indpls. Chatard 28, Brebeuf Jesuit 7
Tri-West 35, Guerin Catholic 3
Second Round
Danville 21, Greencastle 14
Indpls. Chatard 28, Tri-West 14
Championship
Danville 40, Indpls. Chatard 35

Sectional 30 First Round
Greensburg 40, Batesville 14
Rushville 35, Indpls. Marshall 6
Indian Creek 49, Indpls. Washington 6
Lawrenceburg 68, Indpls. Manual 6
Second Round

The Complete History of the the Indiana High School Football State Tournament

Greensburg 63, Rushville 41
Lawrenceburg 44, Indian Creek 13
Championship
Lawrenceburg 47, Greensburg 20

Sectional 31 First Round
Brownstown Central 62, Brown County 0
Salem 49, Corydon Central 20
Southridge 37, Heritage Hills 34, 2 OT
North Harrison 17, Charlestown 14
Second Round
Brownstown Central 46, Salem 10
Southridge 24, North Harrison 7
Championship
Brownstown Central 50, Southridge 14

Sectional 32 First Round
Washington 48, Pike Central 18
Evansville Memorial 29, Gibson Southern 20
Vincennes Lincoln 49, Mount Vernon 28
Sullivan 35, Princeton 29
Second Round
Evansville Memorial 48, Washington 23
Sullivan 42, Vincennes Lincoln 14
Championship
Evansville Memorial 63, Sullivan 35

Regional Championships
Garrett 31, Mishawaka Marian 28
Fort Wayne Concordia 62, West Lafayette 27
Lawrenceburg 37, Danville 20
Brownstown Central 30, Evansville Memorial 7

Semi-State Championships
Fort Wayne Concordia 56, Garrett 42
Lawrenceburg 41, Brownstown Central 40

State Championship
Fort Wayne Concordia 56, Lawrenceburg 14

Class 2A
Sectional 33 First Round
Whiting 36, Boone Grove 6
North Newton 42, Bowman Academy 0
Knox 42, Gary Roosevelt 6
River Forest 41, Hammond Noll 6
Sectional 33 Second Round
Whiting 21, North Newton 12
Knox 12, River Forest 7
Sectional 33 Championship
Whiting 17, Knox 14

Sectional 34 First Round
Winamac 28, Lewis Cass 8
Oak Hill 48, Rochester 0
Manchester 28, Delphi 19
Bremen 35, Wabash 14
Sectional 34 Second Round
Winamac 35, Oak Hill 14

Bremen 41, Manchester 6
Sectional 34 Championship
Winamac 21, Bremen 14

Sectional 35 First Round
Whitko 28, Central Noble 24
Churubusco 21, Eastside 16
South Adams 54, Prairie Heights 7
Woodlan 54, Bluffton 6
Sectional 35 Second Round
Churubusco 20, Whitko 6
South Adams 20, Woodlan 14
Sectional 35 Championship
South Adams 29, Churubusco 27

Sectional 36 First Round
Winchester 30, Madison-Grant 0
Eastbrook 44, Eastern (Greentown) 3
Elwood 33, Alexandria 20
Blackford 28, Taylor 6
Sectional 36 Second Round
Eastbrook 31, Winchester 21
Elwood 60, Blackford 24
Sectional 36 Championship
Eastbrook 37, Elwood 0

Sectional 37 First Round
Park Tudor 39, Indpls. Broad Ripple 14
Lapel 28, Frankton 12
Indpls. Ritter 35, Heritage Christian 13
Indpls. Scecina 28, Speedway 6
Sectional 37 Second Round
Lapel 49, Park Tudor 18
Indpls. Ritter 20, Indpls. Scecina 0
Sectional 37 Championship
Indpls. Ritter 26, Lapel 21

Sectional 38 First Round
Milan 63, Union County 0
Indpls. Howe 32, Northeastern 26
Eastern Hancock 27, Centerville 0
Triton Central 42, Switzerland County 6
Sectional 38 Second Round
Milan 63, Indpls. Howe 35
Triton Central 7, Eastern Hancock 0
Sectional 38 Championship
Milan 52, Triton Central 28

Sectional 39 First Round
Cascade 27, Cloverdale 6
Mitchell 48, South Vermillion 27
North Putnam 42, Paoli 20
Monrovia 44, Southmont 6
Sectional 39 Second Round
Mitchell 44, Cascade 12
Monrovia 56, North Putnam 13
Sectional 39 Championship
Monrovia 63, Mitchell 0

Sectional 40 First Round
South Spencer 34, Forest Park 18
Eastern (Pekin) 49, Crawford County 18
Evansville Mater Dei 45, North Posey 28
Providence 63, Clarksville 14
Sectional 40 Second Round
South Spencer 53, Eastern (Pekin) 15
Evansville Mater Dei 42, Providence 7
Sectional 40 Championship
Evansville Mater Dei 56, South Spencer 20

Regional Championships
Whiting 55, Winamac 14
Eastbrook 28, South Adams 21
Indpls. Ritter 40, Milan 6
Monrovia 35, Evansville Mater Dei 28

Semi-State Championships
Eastbrook 20, Whiting 13
Indpls. Ritter 14, Monrovia 13

State Championship
Indpls. Ritter 28, Eastbrook 6

Class 1A
Sectional 41 First Round
Pioneer 49, Tri-County 13
Lake Station 28, North White 12
North Judson 27, South Newton 14
South Central (Union Mills) 28, West Central 0
Sectional 41 Second Round
Pioneer 62, Lake Station 0
North Judson 27, South Central (U.M.) 22
Sectional 41 Championship
Pioneer 47, North Judson 17

Sectional 42 First Round
Lafayette Central Catholic 55, Frontier 7
Carroll (Flora) 56, Seeger 0
Clinton Central 16, Covington 8, OT
Attica 70, Clinton Prairie 46
Sectional 42 Second Round
Lafayette Central Catholic 27, Carroll (Flora) 7
Attica 36, Clinton Central 30
Sectional 42 Championship
Lafayette Central Catholic 57, Attica 29

Sectional 43 First Round
Culver 32, North Miami 14
LaVille 41, Fremont 13
Triton 50, Caston 0
Southwood 28, Northfield 14
Sectional 43 Second Round
LaVille 42, Culver 14
Southwood 39, Triton 20
Sectional 43 Championship
Southwood 43, LaVille 40

Sectional 44 First Round
Adams Central 35, Wes-Del 7
Shenandoah 64, Union City 12
Monroe Central 62, Southern Wells 7
Tri-Central 60, Anderson Prep Academy 7
Sectional 44 Second Round
Adams Central 35, Shenandoah 24
Monroe Central 42, Tri-Central 0
Sectional 44 Championship
Adams Central 15, Monroe Central 12

Sectional 45 First Round
Covenant Christian 55, Turkey Run 6
North Vermillion 55, Rockville 7
Fountain Central 72, Riverton Parke 20
Sheridan 49, South Putnam 12
Sectional 45 Second Round
North Vermillion 37, Covenant Christian 21
Fountain Central 38, Sheridan 7
Sectional 45 Championship
Fountain Central 54, North Vermillion 8

Sectional 46 First Round
Tri 43, Indiana Deaf 6
Indpls. Lutheran 63, Cambridge City Lincoln 8
Knightstown 63, Indpls. Tindley 12
Hagerstown 55, Indpls. Shortridge 8
Sectional 46 Second Round
Indpls. Lutheran 63, Tri 8
Hagerstown 55, Knightstown 10
Sectional 46 Championship
Indpls. Lutheran 48, Hagerstown 27

Sectional 47 First Round
Eastern Greene 41, Springs Valley 7
West Washington 49, Oldenburg Academy 0
North Decatur 40, Edinburgh 0
Sectional 47 Second Round
Eastern Greene 54, South Decatur 37
West Washington 64, North Decatur 14
Sectional 47 Championship
Eastern Greene 34, West Washington 32

Sectional 48 First Round
Linton-Stockton 56, Tecumseh 15
North Central (Farmersburg) 30, Tell City 0
Perry Central 34, North Daviess 14
Sectional 48 Second Round
Linton-Stockton 56, North Knox 7
North Central (Farm.) 36, Perry Central 29
Sectional 48 Championship
Linton-Stockton 48, North Central (Farm.) 14

Regional Championships
Pioneer 28, Lafayette Central Catholic 27
Adams Central 23, Southwood 7
Indpls. Lutheran 48, Fountain Central 19
Linton-Stockton 56, Eastern Greene 7

Semi-State Championships

Pioneer 22, Adams Central 8
Linton-Stockton 43, Indpls. Lutheran 14

State Championship
Linton-Stockton 34, Pioneer 20

2017
Class 6A
Sectional 1 Semifinals
Crown Point 23, Merrillville 14
Portage 34, Lake Central 14
Sectional 1 Championship
Crown Point 14, Portage 7

Sectional 2 Semifinals
Warsaw 26, Chesterton 16
Penn 13, Valparaiso 0
Sectional 2 Championship
Penn 40, Warsaw 0

Sectional 3 Semifinals
Carroll (Fort Wayne) 42, F.W. Northrop 34
Fort Wayne Snider 37, Homestead 0
Sectional 3 Championship
Fort Wayne Snider 52, Carroll (Fort Wayne) 14

Sectional 4 Semifinals
Lafayette Jefferson 27, Westfield 24
Carmel 25, Noblesville 7
Sectional 4 Championship
Carmel 41, Lafayette Jefferson 20

Sectional 5 Semifinals
Fishers 9, Hamilton Southeastern 6
Pike 42, North Central (Indianapolis) 21
Sectional 5 Championship
Fishers 28, Pike 7

Sectional 6 Semifinals
Warren Central 41, Lawrence North 16
Ben Davis 33, Lawrence Central 20
Sectional 6 Championship
Ben Davis 36, Warren Central 29

Sectional 7 Semifinals
Avon 33, Southport 2
Brownsburg 56, Perry Meridian 3
Sectional 7 Championship
Avon 47, Brownsburg 25

Sectional 8 Semifinals
Columbus North 56, Jeffersonville 14
Center Grove 35, Franklin Central 3
Sectional 8 Championship
Center Grove 20, Columbus North 14

Regional Championship
Penn 33, Crown Point 3
Carmel 22, Fort Wayne Snider 21

Ben Davis 50, Fishers 7
Avon 32, Center Grove 21

Semi-State Championship
Penn 34, Carmel 7
Ben Davis 57, Avon 20

State Championship
Ben Davis 63, Penn 14

Class 5A
Sectional 9 Semifinals
LaPorte 40, South Bend Adams 19
Michigan City 28, Munster 14
Sectional 9 Championship
Michigan City 38, LaPorte 10

Sectional 10 First Round
Elkhart Memorial 14, Fort Wayne North 6
Sectional 10 Second Round
Concord 16, Elkhart Memorial 9
Goshen 15, Elkhart Central 14
Sectional 10 Championship
Concord 28, Goshen 12

Sectional 11 Semifinals
Kokomo 13, Harrison (West Lafayette) 8
McCutcheon 42, Huntington North 7
Sectional 11 Championship
Kokomo 37, McCutcheon 7

Sectional 12 First Round
Zionsville 40, Greenfield-Central 14
Sectional 12 Second Round
Zionsville 35, Anderson 0
New Palestine 54, Muncie Central 14
Sectional 12 Championship
Zionsville 26, New Palestine 24

Sectional 13 First Round
Decatur Central 41, Plainfield 20
Sectional 13 Second Round
Decatur Central 47, Indianapolis Tech 8
Indianapolis Cathedral 28, Roncalli 23
Sectional 13 Championship
Indianapolis Cathedral 42, Decatur Central 21

Sectional 14 First Round
Bloomington South 42, Whiteland 37
Sectional 14 Second Round
Bloomington South 34, Bloomington North 6
Martinsville 24, Franklin 21
Sectional 14 Championship
Bloomington South 56, Martinsville 21

Sectional 15 First Round
Columbus East 63, Seymour 0
Sectional 15 Second Round
Columbus East 56, Bedford North Lawrence 14

Floyd Central 31, New Albany 13
Sectional 15 Championship
Columbus East 42, Floyd Central 14

Sectional 16 Semifinals
Terre Haute North 31, Evansville North 0
Terre Haute South 31, Castle 28
Sectional 16 Championship
Terre Haute North 34, Terre Haute South 10

Regional Championship
Michigan City 21, Concord 7
Kokomo 33, Zionsville 21
Indpls. Cathedral 35, Bloomington South 21
Columbus East 49, Terre Haute North 18

Semi-State Championship
Kokomo 21, Michigan City 14
Columbus East 42, Indianapolis Cathedral 13

State Championship
Columbus East 42, Kokomo 28

Class 4A
Sectional 17 First Round
Hammond Morton 27, East Chicago Central 0
Griffith 55, Hammond 0
Lowell 41, Gary West 0
Highland 27, Hammond Gavit 0
Sectional 17 Second Round
Griffith 35, Hammond Morton 21
Lowell 35, Highland 0
Sectional 17 Championship
Lowell 42, Griffith 7

Sectional 18 First Round
New Prairie 56, South Bend Washington 0
Mishawaka 71, South Bend Clay 0
South Bend Riley 49, Kankakee Valley 10
South Bend St. Joseph 19, Hobart 7
Sectional 18 Second Round
New Prairie 42, Mishawaka 21
South Bend St. Joseph 39, South Bend Riley 27
Sectional 18 Championship
New Prairie 42, South Bend St. Joseph 7

Sectional 19 First Round
Angola 38, Wawasee 7
NorthWood 54, DeKalb 3
Culver Military Academy 35, Northridge 12
East Noble 14, Plymouth 13
Sectional 19 Second Round
Angola 28, NorthWood 21, OT
Culver Military Academy 33, East Noble 28
Sectional 19 Championship
Angola 31, Culver Military Academy 30, OT

Sectional 20 First Round
Jay County 22, Logansport 21
Fort Wayne Wayne 62, Columbia City 20
New Haven 20, Leo 7
Fort Wayne Dwenger 41, Fort Wayne South 7
Sectional 20 Second Round
Fort Wayne Wayne 9, Jay County 6
Fort Wayne Dwenger 13, New Haven 6
Sectional 20 Championship
Fort Wayne Dwenger 41, Fort Wayne Wayne 20

Sectional 21 First Round
Western 35, Yorktown 34
Pendleton Heights 30, Lebanon 22
Marion 35, Delta 21
Mississinewa 65, Frankfort 20
Sectional 21 Second Round
Western 35, Pendleton Heights 7
Mississinewa 21, Marion 14
Sectional 21 Championship
Mississinewa 41, Western 39

Sectional 22 First Round
Mooresville 61, Connersville 13
New Castle 41, Richmond 0
Greenwood 43, Beech Grove 7
Mount Vernon (Fortville) 30, Shelbyville 14
Sectional 22 Second Round
Mooresville 42, New Castle 35
Greenwood 50, Mount Vernon (Fortville) 6
Sectional 22 Championship
Greenwood 59, Mooresville 32

Sectional 23 First Round
Franklin County 46, Jennings County 34
Silver Creek 42, Madison 7
East Central 48, Edgewood 6
South Dearborn 22, Scottsburg 21
Sectional 23 Second Round
Silver Creek 7, Franklin County 6
East Central 51, South Dearborn 0
Sectional 23 Championship
East Central 24, Silver Creek 0

Sectional 24 First Round
Owen Valley 14, Evansville Harrison 10
Evansville Bosse 20, Boonville 14
Jasper 41, Northview 17
Evansville Central 34, Evansville Reitz 6
Sectional 24 Second Round
Evansville Bosse 26, Owen Valley 0
Evansville Central 26, Jasper 15
Sectional 24 Championship
Evansville Central 28, Evansville Bosse 0

Regional Championship
Lowell 25, New Prairie 20
Fort Wayne Dwenger 34, Angola 0
Greenwood 34, Mississinewa 27
East Central 35, Evansville Central 13

Semi-State Championship
Lowell 21, Fort Wayne Dwenger 7
East Central 27, Greenwood 14

State Championship
East Central 14, Lowell 7

Class 3A
Sectional 25 First Round
Wheeler 45, Hammond Clark 14
Andrean 24, Hanover Central 9
Twin Lakes 43, Calumet 20
West Lafayette 79, Benton Central 7
Sectional 25 Second Round
Andrean 69, Wheeler 6
West Lafayette 56, Twin Lakes 6
Sectional 25 Championship
West Lafayette 56, Andrean 10

Sectional 26 First Round
Hamilton Heights 37, North Montgomery 23
Southmont 49, Crawfordsville 7
Brebeuf Jesuit 21, Guerin Catholic 6
Blackford 28, Northwestern 27
Sectional 26 Second Round
Southmont 35, Hamilton Heights 14
Brebeuf Jesuit 42, Blackford 14
Sectional 26 Championship
Brebeuf Jesuit 48, Southmont 14

Sectional 27 First Round
Mishawaka Marian 8, John Glenn 0
Knox 49, Fairfield 7
Peru 33, Tippecanoe Valley 14
Jimtown 20, Maconaquah 7
Sectional 27 Second Round
Mishawaka Marian 17, Knox 13
Jimtown 24, Peru 7
Sectional 27 Championship
Mishawaka Marian 21, Jimtown 7

Sectional 28 First Round
Lakeland 38, Heritage 26
Fort Wayne Concordia 20, Garrett 6
Norwell 24, Bellmont 7
Fort Wayne Luers 42, West Noble 14
Sectional 28 Second Round
Fort Wayne Concordia 32, Lakeland 0
Fort Wayne Luers 40, Norwell 17
Sectional 28 Championship
Fort Wayne Luers 20, Fort Wayne Concordia 14

Sectional 29 First Round
Indianapolis Chatard 62, Indpls. Northwest 6
Indian Creek 44, Indianapolis Manual 8
Indianapolis Ritter 55, Rushville 14
Sectional 29 Second Round
Indianapolis Chatard 48, Indpls. Broad Ripple 0
Indianapolis Ritter 41, Indian Creek 22

Sectional 29 Championship
Indianapolis Chatard 56, Indianapolis Ritter 27

Sectional 30 First Round
Sullivan 34, West Vigo 0
Greencastle 34, Brown County 7
Tri-West 41, Monrovia 21
Danville 55, South Vermillion 28
Sectional 30 Second Round
Greencastle 14, Sullivan 0
Danville 32, Tri-West 20
Sectional 30 Championship
Danville 44, Greencastle 0

Sectional 31 First Round
Lawrenceburg 33, Brownstown Central 14
Greensburg 33, Salem 30
Batesville 38, Charlestown 22
North Harrison 50, Corydon Central 14
Sectional 31 Second Round
Lawrenceburg 43, Greensburg 14
North Harrison 20, Batesville 19
Sectional 31 Championship
Lawrenceburg 35, North Harrison 29

Sectional 32 First Round
Washington 32, Princeton 15
Evansville Memorial 41, Heritage Hills 21
Gibson Southern 63, Pike Central 6
Vincennes Lincoln 60, Mount Vernon 28
Sectional 32 Second Round
Evansville Memorial 49, Washington 15
Gibson Southern 39, Vincennes Lincoln 28
Sectional 32 Championship
Evansville Memorial 26, Gibson Southern 17

Regional Championship
Brebeuf Jesuit 13, West Lafayette 10
Mishawaka Marian 30, Fort Wayne Luers 7
Danville 38, Indianapolis Chatard 7
Evansville Memorial 56, Lawrenceburg 35

Semi-State Championship
Brebeuf Jesuit 17, Mishawaka Marian 0
Evansville Memorial 28, Danville 7

State Championship
Evansville Memorial 29, Brebeuf Jesuit 17

Class 2A
Sectional 33 First Round
North Newton 20, Whiting 14
Boone Grove 21, River Forest 0
Gary Roosevelt 52, Hammond Noll 6
Sectional 33 Second Round
North Newton 36, Lake Station 6
Boone Grove 47, Gary Roosevelt 20
Sectional 33 Championship
North Newton 38, Boone Grove 14

Sectional 34 First Round
Central Noble 56, Whitko 8
Bluffton 27, Bremen 19
Wabash 30, Manchester 27
Woodlan 68, Prairie Heights 0
Sectional 34 Second Round
Central Noble 54, Bluffton 14
Woodlan 32, Wabash 8
Sectional 34 Championship
Woodlan 44, Central Noble 19

Sectional 35 First Round
Eastbrook 56, Eastern (Greentown) 7
Rensselaer Central 66, Taylor 0
Lewis Cass 7, Rochester 6
Delphi 35, Oak Hill 7
Sectional 35 Second Round
Eastbrook 21, Rensselaer Central 3
Lewis Cass 33, Delphi 6
Sectional 35 Championship
Eastbrook 28, Lewis Cass 7

Sectional 36 First Round
Alexandria 56, Elwood 42
Lapel 38, Winchester 22
Frankton 67, Madison-Grant 8
Shenandoah 60, Northeastern 8
Sectional 36 Second Round
Lapel 31, Alexandria 14
Shenandoah 49, Frankton 18
Sectional 36 Championship
Lapel 34, Shenandoah 20

Sectional 37 First Round
Milan 28, Heritage Christian 14
Triton Central 21, Knightstown 0
Eastern Hancock 35, Centerville 21
Indianapolis Scecina 49, Union County 24
Sectional 37 Second Round
Triton Central 21, Milan 15
Indianapolis Scecina 41, Eastern Hancock 7
Sectional 37 Championship
Indianapolis Scecina 14, Triton Central 0

Sectional 38 First Round
Western Boone 48, Cascade 20
Tipton 49, North Putnam 7
Cloverdale 25, Speedway 20
Park Tudor 52, Indianapolis Washington 0
Sectional 38 Second Round
Western Boone 21, Tipton 14
Park Tudor 28, Cloverdale 6
Sectional 38 Championship
Western Boone 46, Park Tudor 7

Sectional 39 First Round
Eastern (Pekin) 59, Switzerland County 21
Paoli 42, Clarksville 0
Providence 48, Perry Central 15
Mitchell 26, Crawford County 20, OT
Sectional 39 Second Round
Paoli 52, Eastern (Pekin) 20
Providence 14, Mitchell 12
Sectional 39 Championship
Providence 41, Paoli 25

Sectional 40 First Round
Linton-Stockton 36, North Posey 35
Southridge 46, South Spencer 7
Evansville Mater Dei 49, Tell City 6
Forest Park 27, North Knox 14
Sectional 40 Second Round
Southridge 20, Linton-Stockton 0
Evansville Mater Dei 55, Forest Park 14
Sectional 40 Championship
Southridge 38, Evansville Mater Dei 31, OT

Regional Championship
Woodlan 40, North Newton 28
Eastbrook 56, Lapel 26
Indianapolis Scecina 48, Western Boone 33
Southridge 47, Providence 7

Semi-State Championship
Woodlan 15, Eastbrook 14
Southridge 24, Indianapolis Scecina 7

State Championship
Southridge 15, Woodlan 14

Class 1A
Sectional 41 First Round
Winamac 28, South Central (Union Mills) 20
Triton 42, Caston 13
Culver 49, West Central 14
LaVille 30, North Judson 0
Sectional 41 Second Round
Triton 48, Winamac 29
LaVille 19, Culver 16
Sectional 41 Championship
LaVille 10, Triton 7

Sectional 42 First Round
North Miami 57, South Newton 16
Lafayette Central Catholic 35, Tri-County 28
Pioneer 55, Carroll (Flora) 21
North White 8, Frontier 0
Sectional 42 Second Round
Lafayette Central Catholic 38, North Miami 28
Pioneer 46, North White 0
Sectional 42 Championship
Pioneer 48, Lafayette Central Catholic 20

Sectional 43 First Round
Adams Central 28, South Adams 7
Churubusco 31, Northfield 15
Eastside 41, Southern Wells 14

Southwood 70, Fremont 14
Sectional 43 Second Round
Adams Central 17, Churubusco 14
Southwood 51, Eastside 19
Sectional 43 Championship
Southwood 50, Adams Central 27

Sectional 44 First Round
Clinton Prairie 74, Anderson Prep Academy 20
Monroe Central 57, Clinton Central 6
Sheridan 50, Tri-Central 8
Wes-Del 24, Union City 8
Sectional 44 Second Round
Monroe Central 42, Clinton Prairie 12
Sheridan 35, Wes-Del 8
Sectional 44 Championship
Monroe Central 26, Sheridan 7

Sectional 45 First Round
Indianapolis Tindley 28, Indpls. Shortridge 7
Indianapolis Howe 22, Indiana Deaf 6
South Putnam 40, Covenant Christian 15
Sectional 45 Second Round
Indianapolis Arlington 52, Indpls. Tindley 0
South Putnam 19, Indianapolis Howe 12
Sectional 45 Championship
Indianapolis Arlington 46, South Putnam 6

Sectional 46 First Round
Hagerstown 40, North Decatur 12
Tri 60, Oldenburg Academy 14
Indianapolis Lutheran 54, Cambridge City 16
South Decatur 57, Edinburgh 34
Sectional 46 Second Round
Hagerstown 33, Tri 14
Indianapolis Lutheran 55, South Decatur 12
Sectional 46 Championship
Indianapolis Lutheran 19, Hagerstown 12

Sectional 47 First Round
Attica 22, North Vermillion 16
Rockville 38, Turkey Run 8
Fountain Central 54, Covington 13
Seeger 40, Riverton Parke 20
Sectional 47 Second Round
Attica 40, Rockville 6
Fountain Central 40, Seeger 14
Sectional 47 Championship
Fountain Central 43, Attica 0

Sectional 48 First Round
Eastern Greene 57, North Daviess 0
Tecumseh 54, Wood Memorial 0
North Central (Farm.) 17, Springs Valley 14
Sectional 48 Second Round
Eastern Greene 41, West Washington 0
North Central (Farmersburg) 34, Tecumseh 20
Sectional 48 Championship
Eastern Greene 33, North Central (Farm.) 14

Regional Championship
Pioneer 38, LaVille 0
Monroe Central 28, Southwood 21
Indianapolis Lutheran 50, Indpls. Arlington 15
Eastern Greene 42, Fountain Central 19

Semi-State Championship
Pioneer 42, Monroe Central 14
Eastern Greene 12, Indianapolis Lutheran 8

State Championship
Pioneer 42, Eastern Greene 14

2018
Class 6A
Sectional 1 Semifinals
Crown Point 12, Portage 7
Merrillville 42, Lake Central 14
Sectional 1 Championship
Crown Point 17, Merrillville 13

Sectional 2 Semifinals
Valparaiso 55, Chesterton 7
Penn 16, Warsaw 7
Sectional 2 Championship
Valparaiso 21, Penn 0

Sectional 3 Semifinals
Fort Wayne Snider 49, Carroll (Fort Wayne) 30
Homestead 24, Fort Wayne Northrop 7
Sectional 3 Championship
Fort Wayne Snider 49, Homestead 35

Sectional 4 Semifinals
Carmel 28, Westfield 7
Lafayette Jefferson 35, Noblesville 24
Sectional 4 Championship
Carmel 41, Lafayette Jefferson 21

Sectional 5 Semifinals
North Central (Indpls.) 41, Hamilton SE 12
Fishers 33, Pike 20
Sectional 5 Championship
North Central (Indianapolis) 42, Fishers 7

Sectional 6 Semifinals
Warren Central 49, Ben Davis 28
Lawrence Central 27, Lawrence North 20
Sectional 6 Championship
Warren Central 55, Lawrence Central 7

Sectional 7 Semifinals
Brownsburg 42, Southport 20
Avon 42, Perry Meridian 7
Sectional 7 Championship
Avon 38, Brownsburg 0

Sectional 8 Semifinals

Franklin Central 42, Jeffersonville 3
Center Grove 42, Columbus North 0
Sectional 8 Championship
Center Grove 23, Franklin Central 6

Regional Championships
Valparaiso 23, Crown Point 6
Carmel 20, Fort Wayne Snider 6
Warren Central 42, North Central (Indpls.) 32
Center Grove 17, Avon 0

Semi-State Championships
Carmel 14, Valparaiso 10
Warren Central 27, Center Grove 20

State Championship
Warren Central 27, Carmel 7

Class 5A
Sectional 9 Semifinals
LaPorte 33, South Bend Adams 19
Michigan City 72, Munster 19
Sectional 9 Championship
Michigan City 49, LaPorte 7

Sectional 10 First Round
Elkhart Central 46, Fort Wayne North 22
Sectional 10 Second Round
Elkhart Central 19, Goshen 0
Concord 28, Elkhart Memorial 20
Sectional 10 Championship
Concord 17, Elkhart Central 14

Sectional 11 Semifinals
Kokomo 22, McCutcheon 20
Harrison (W.L.) 54, Huntington North 20
Sectional 11 Championship
Harrison (West Lafayette) 19, Kokomo 16

Sectional 12 First Round
Zionsville 52, Muncie Central 0
Sectional 12 Second Round
New Palestine 29, Zionsville 17
Anderson 33, Greenfield-Central 12
Sectional 12 Championship
New Palestine 78, Anderson 0

Sectional 13 First Round
Indianapolis Cathedral 51, Plainfield 14
Sectional 13 Second Round
Indianapolis Cathedral 30, Roncalli 10
Decatur Central 49, Indianapolis Tech 14
Sectional 13 Championship
Decatur Central 21, Indianapolis Cathedral 14

Sectional 14 First Round
Whiteland 40, Franklin 28
Sectional 14 Second Round
Bloomington South 34, Whiteland 24

Martinsville 31, Bloomington North 9
Sectional 14 Championship
Bloomington South 28, Martinsville 25, 2 OT

Sectional 15 First Round
Columbus East 31, New Albany 16
Sectional 15 Second Round
Columbus East 49, Seymour 13
Bedford North Lawrence 35, Floyd Central 7
Sectional 15 Championship
Columbus East 51, Bedford North Lawrence 14

Sectional 16 Semifinals
Terre Haute South 37, T.H. North 31, 2 OT
Castle 55, Evansville North 7
Sectional 16 Championship
Castle 55, Terre Haute South 34

Regional Championships
Michigan City 62, Concord 21
New Palestine 31, Harrison (West Lafayette) 7
Decatur Central 28, Bloomington South 0
Columbus East 20, Castle 13

Semi-State Championships
New Palestine 35, Michigan City 10
Decatur Central 27, Columbus East 24

State Championship
New Palestine 28, Decatur Central 14

Class 4A
Sectional 17 First Round
East Chicago Central 28, Hammond 12
Hammond Morton 55, Hammond Gavit 20
Lowell 34, Highland 14
Griffith 53, Gary West 0
Sectional 17 Second Round
Hammond Morton 0, East Chicago Central 0
Lowell 45, Griffith 14
Sectional 17 Championship
Lowell 20, Hammond Morton 14

Sectional 18 First Round
New Prairie 56, South Bend Washington 7
South Bend St. Joseph 38, Kankakee Valley 21
South Bend Riley 40, South Bend Clay 6
Mishawaka 35, Hobart 7
Sectional 18 Second Round
South Bend St. Joseph 42, New Prairie 30
Mishawaka 35, South Bend Riley 28
Sectional 18 Championship
Mishawaka 27, South Bend St. Joseph 23

Sectional 19 First Round
NorthWood 40, Plymouth 7
East Noble 33, DeKalb 32
Northridge 33, Wawasee 12
Angola 27, Culver Military Academy 7

Sectional 19 Second Round
NorthWood 52, East Noble 35
Angola 34, Northridge 0
Sectional 19 Championship
Angola 27, NorthWood 26

Sectional 20 First Round
Fort Wayne Wayne 50, Fort Wayne South 12
New Haven 24, Columbia City 14
Leo 35, Jay County 21
Fort Wayne Dwenger 42, Logansport 14
Sectional 20 Second Round
Fort Wayne Wayne 53, New Haven 14
Fort Wayne Dwenger 42, Leo 9
Sectional 20 Championship
Fort Wayne Dwenger 14, Fort Wayne Wayne 13

Sectional 21 First Round
Marion 49, Pendleton Heights 35
Delta 28, Lebanon 14
Yorktown 53, Frankfort 7
Mississinewa 35, Western 9
Sectional 21 Second Round
Marion 37, Delta 0
Mississinewa 24, Yorktown 14
Sectional 21 Championship
Marion 26, Mississinewa 9

Sectional 22 First Round
Mount Vernon (Fortville) 56, Shelbyville 0
Greenwood 35, New Castle 34, 2 OT
Mooresville 49, Beech Grove 21
Richmond 31, Connersville 7
Sectional 22 Second Round
Greenwood 14, Mount Vernon (Fortville) 7
Mooresville 48, Richmond 21
Sectional 22 Championship
Mooresville 49, Greenwood 14

Sectional 23 First Round
East Central 41, Franklin County 6
South Dearborn 48, Jennings County 16
Edgewood 28, Madison 19
Silver Creek 55, Scottsburg 21
Sectional 23 Second Round
East Central 9, South Dearborn 7
Edgewood 23, Silver Creek 15
Sectional 23 Championship
East Central 57, Edgewood 22

Sectional 24 First Round
Boonville 42, Evansville Bosse 35
Jasper 34, Evansville Harrison 12
Northview 55, Owen Valley 0
Evansville Central 30, Evansville Reitz 14
Sectional 24 Second Round
Boonville 17, Jasper 6
Evansville Central 35, Northview 21
Sectional 24 Championship
Evansville Central 49, Boonville 20

Regional Championships
Mishawaka 28, Lowell 14
Fort Wayne Dwenger 40, Angola 7
Marion 19, Mooresville 13
Evansville Central 28, East Central 24

Semi-State Championships
Fort Wayne Dwenger 24, Mishawaka 6
Evansville Central 30, Marion 14

State Championship
Fort Wayne Dwenger 16, Ev. Central 10, 4 OT

Class 3A
Sectional 25 First Round
Hanover Central 34, Wheeler 14
Andrean 49, Benton Central 0
Twin Lakes 49, Hammond Clark 8
West Lafayette 43, Calumet 12
Sectional 25 Second Round
Andrean 44, Hanover Central 12
West Lafayette 74, Twin Lakes 0
Sectional 25 Championship
West Lafayette 51, Andrean 24

Sectional 26 First Round
Brebeuf Jesuit 50, Southmont 14
Guerin Catholic 49, Crawfordsville 19
North Montgomery 54, Hamilton Heights 20
Blackford 51, Northwestern 0
Sectional 26 Second Round
Brebeuf Jesuit 20, Guerin Catholic 10
Blackford 38, North Montgomery 0
Sectional 26 Championship
Brebeuf Jesuit 42, Blackford 13

Sectional 27 First Round
Tippecanoe Valley 34, Peru 7
Maconaquah 48, John Glenn 13
Knox 21, Jimtown 14
Mishawaka Marian 42, Fairfield 7
Sectional 27 Second Round
Maconaquah 24, Tippecanoe Valley 6
Mishawaka Marian 31, Knox 6
Sectional 27 Championship
Mishawaka Marian 35, Maconaquah 7

Sectional 28 First Round
West Noble 28, Norwell 21
Fort Wayne Luers 63, Heritage 24
Fort Wayne Concordia 28, Lakeland 13
Bellmont 16, Garrett 6
Sectional 28 Second Round
Fort Wayne Luers 45, West Noble 21
Bellmont 28, Fort Wayne Concordia 21
Sectional 28 Championship
Fort Wayne Luers 27, Bellmont 14

Sectional 29 First Round
Indianapolis Chatard 40, Indianapolis Ritter 7
Indian Creek 51, Indpls. Crispus Attucks 12
Sectional 29 Second Round
Indianapolis Chatard 62, Rushville 6
Indian Creek 33, Indianapolis Manual 0
Sectional 29 Championship
Indianapolis Chatard 42, Indian Creek 6

Sectional 30 First Round
Danville 27, Greencastle 7
Tri-West 28, South Vermillion 17
Sullivan 34, West Vigo 12
Monrovia 69, Brown County 6
Sectional 30 Second Round
Tri-West 29, Danville 7
Sullivan 27, Monrovia 7
Sectional 30 Championship
Tri-West 31, Sullivan 27

Sectional 31 First Round
Lawrenceburg 22, North Harrison 14
Batesville 59, Greensburg 19
Brownstown Central 55, Corydon Central 13
Salem 27, Charlestown 20
Sectional 31 Second Round
Batesville 28, Lawrenceburg 22
Brownstown Central 56, Salem 15
Sectional 31 Championship
Brownstown Central 35, Batesville 28

Sectional 32 First Round
Vincennes Lincoln 56, Pike Central 6
Evansville Memorial 52, Princeton 14
Heritage Hills 47, Mount Vernon 0
Gibson Southern 54, Washington 6
Sectional 32 Second Round
Evansville Memorial 52, Vincennes Lincoln 6
Gibson Southern 24, Heritage Hills 14
Sectional 32 Championship
Evansville Memorial 56, Gibson Southern 28

Regional Championships
West Lafayette 24, Brebeuf Jesuit 10
Fort Wayne Luers 42, Mishawaka Marian 6
Indianapolis Chatard 56, Tri-West 14
Evansville Memorial 56, Brownstown 14

Semi-State Championships
West Lafayette 27, Fort Wayner Luers 14
Evansville Memorial 42, Indpls. Chatard 17

State Championship
West Lafayette 47, Evansville Memorial 42

Class 2A
Sectional 33 First Round
Boone Grove 71, Bowman Academy 20
Whiting 34, North Newton 7
Gary Roosevelt 46, River Forest 34
Sectional 33 Second Round
Boone Grove 47, Lake Station 0
Whiting 48, Gary Roosevelt 0
Sectional 33 Championship
Whiting 37, Boone Grove 19

Sectional 34 First Round
Bremen 35, Woodlan 27
Central Noble 30, Wabash 22
Bluffton 35, Manchester 0
Prairie Heights 28, Whitko 22
Sectional 34 Second Round
Bremen 52, Central Noble 19
Bluffton 41, Prairie Heights 8
Sectional 34 Championship
Bremen 42, Bluffton 13

Sectional 35 First Round
Rensselaer Central 21, Delphi 6
Lewis Cass 56, Eastern (Greentown) 0
Eastbrook 49, Oak Hill 14
Rochester 55, Taylor 8
Sectional 35 Second Round
Lewis Cass 14, Rensselaer Central 7
Eastbrook 48, Rochester 20
Sectional 35 Championship
Eastbrook 27, Lewis Cass 25

Sectional 36 First Round
Shenandoah 53, Madison-Grant 12
Alexandria 34, Elwood 6
Northeastern 14, Winchester 8
Lapel 62, Frankton 16
Sectional 36 Second Round
Shenandoah 51, Alexandria 13
Lapel 11, Northeastern 8
Sectional 36 Championship
Lapel 42, Shenandoah 41, OT

Sectional 37 First Round
Heritage Christian 21, Eastern Hancock 0
Indianapolis Scecina 42, Centerville 2
Triton Central 28, Milan 10
Knightstown 40, Union County 0
Sectional 37 Second Round
Indianapolis Scecina 47, Heritage Christian 26
Triton Central 20, Knightstown 0
Sectional 37 Championship
Indianapolis Scecina 34, Triton Central 30

Sectional 38 First Round
Cascade 44, Park Tudor 7
North Putnam 21, Cloverdale 7
Western Boone 49, Indianapolis Washington 0
Tipton 62, Speedway 13
Sectional 38 Second Round
North Putnam 15, Cascade 6

Western Boone 28, Tipton 20
Sectional 38 Championship
Western Boone 49, North Putnam 8

Sectional 39 First Round
Perry Central 27, Eastern (Pekin) 6
Providence 64, Switzerland County 7
Mitchell 46, Clarksville 6
Paoli 37, Crawford County 0
Sectional 39 Second Round
Providence 28, Perry Central 6
Paoli 42, Mitchell 16
Sectional 39 Championship
Paoli 21, Providence 17

Sectional 40 First Round
Linton-Stockton 42, Forest Park 7
Evansville Mater Dei 35, North Posey 7
Southridge 49, South Spencer 7
North Knox 14, Tell City 8, OT
Sectional 40 Second Round
Evansville Mater Dei 40, Linton-Stockton 21
Southridge 40, North Knox 22
Sectional 40 Championship
Southridge 35, Evansville Mater Dei 25

Regional Championships
Bremen 42, Whiting 13
Eastbrook 52, Lapel 21
Western Boone 19, Indianapolis Scecina 7
Southridge 42, Paoli 35

Semi-State Championships
Eastbrook 34, Bremen 33
Western Boone 48, Southridge 7

State Championship
Western Boone 34, Eastbrook 20

Class 1A
Sectional 41 First Round
Triton 34, Culver 12
Winamac 38, Caston 16
North Judson 21, LaVille 6
South Central (Union Mills) 50, West Central 30
Sectional 41 Second Round
Triton 48, Winamac 18
North Judson 42, South Central (U.M.) 25
Sectional 41 Championship
Triton 29, North Judson 17

Sectional 42 First Round
Carroll (Flora) 21, Frontier 14
Pioneer 86, South Newton 0
Tri-County 46, North Miami 27
Lafayette Central Catholic 50, North White 0
Sectional 42 Second Round
Pioneer 74, Carroll (Flora) 0
Lafayette Central Catholic 40, Tri-County 16

Sectional 42 Championship
Pioneer 70, Lafayette Central Catholic 7

Sectional 43 First Round
Southwood 44, Eastside 6
Fremont 25, Southern Wells 14
Adams Central 34, Northfield 23
Churubusco 28, South Adams 21
Sectional 43 Second Round
Southwood 37, Fremont 6
Adams Central 35, Churubusco 10
Sectional 43 Championship
Adams Central 38, Southwood 0

Sectional 44 First Round
Sheridan 35, Tri-Central 14
Monroe Central 34, Clinton Central 13
Clinton Prairie 20, Wes-Del 6
Union City 41, Anderson Prep Academy 16
Sectional 44 Second Round
Monroe Central 8, Sheridan 0
Union City 32, Clinton Prairie 12
Sectional 44 Championship
Monroe Central 29, Union City 0

Sectional 45 First Round
Traders Point Christian 14, Covenant Christ. 7
South Putnam 44, Indianapolis Shortridge 13
Indianapolis Howe 37, Indiana Deaf 6
Sectional 45 Second Round
Traders Point Christian 30, Indpls. Tindley 8
South Putnam 30, Indianapolis Howe 14
Sectional 45 Championship
South Putnam 55, Traders Point Christian 8

Sectional 46 First Round
Edinburgh 24, Cambridge City Lincoln 12
Hagerstown 14, Oldenburg Academy 0
Indianapolis Lutheran 42, South Decatur 12
North Decatur 33, Tri 0
Sectional 46 Second Round
Hagerstown 40, Edinburgh 12
Indianapolis Lutheran 27, North Decatur 12
Sectional 46 Championship
Indianapolis Lutheran 32, Hagerstown 13

Sectional 47 First Round
North Vermillion 44, Riverton Parke 7
Parke Heritage 37, Covington 21
Attica 40, Fountain Central 12
Sectional 47 Second Round
North Vermillion 35, Seeger 14
Attica 20, Parke Heritage 16
Sectional 47 Championship
North Vermillion 22, Attica 6

Sectional 48 First Round
Tecumseh 32, North Daviess 7
Eastern Greene 46, Rock Creek Academy 6

West Washington 27, Springs Valley 20
Sectional 48 Second Round
North Central (Farmersburg) 57, Tecumseh 0
West Washington 20, Eastern Greene 13
Sectional 48 Championship
North Central (Farm.) 14, West Washington 0

Regional Championships
Pioneer 66, Triton 0
Adams Central 38, Monroe Central 12

Indianapolis Lutheran 36, South Putnam 20
North Vermillion 34, North Central (Farm.) 14

Semi-State Championships
Pioneer 38, Adams Central 7
North Vermillion 14, Indianapolis Luthern 7

State Championship
Pioneer 60, North Vermillion 0

Class 6A postseason champions

Class 6A Northern Sectionals

Year	S1	S2	S3	S4
2013	Lake Central	Penn	Carroll (FW)	Carmel
2014	Merrillville	Penn	Carroll (FW)	Carmel
2015	Merrillville	Penn	Homestead	Carmel
2016	Crown Point	Penn	Homestead	Carmel
2017	Crown Point	Penn	Fort Wayne Snider	Carmel
2018	Crown Point	Valparaiso	Fort Wayne Snider	Carmel

Class 6A Southern Sectionals

Year	S5	S6	S7	S8
2013	Pike	Warren Central	Southport	Center Grove
2014	Ben Davis	Warren Central	Southport	Center Grove
2015	Avon	Ind. Cathedral	Warren Central	Center Grove
2016	Ben Davis	Ind. Cathedral	Warren Central	Center Grove
2017	Fishers	Ben Davis	Avon	Center Grove
2018	North Central	Warren Central	Avon	Center Grove

Class 6A Regionals

Year	Champion	Champion	Champion	Champion
2013	Penn	Carmel	Warren Central	Center Grove
2014	Penn	Carmel	Ben Davis	Center Grove
2015	Penn	Carmel	Avon	Center Grove
2016	Penn	Carmel	Ben Davis	Center Grove
2017	Penn	Carmel	Ben Davis	Avon
2018	Valparaiso	Carmel	Warren Central	Center Grove

Class 6A Semi-State

Year	North Champion	South Champion
2013	Carmel	Warren Central
2014	Carmel	Ben Davis
2015	Penn	Center Grove
2016	Carmel	Center Grove
2017	Penn	Ben Davis
2018	Carmel	Warren Central

Class 6A State Champions

Year	School	Coach
2013	Warren Central (11-3)	Jayson West
2014	Ben Davis (12-2)	Mike Kirschner
2015	Center Grove (14-0)	Eric Moore
2016	Carmel (10-4)	John Hebert
2017	Ben Davis (14-0)	Mike Kirschner
2018	Warren Central (14-0)	Jayson West

Class 5A postseason champions
Class 5A Northern Sectionals

Year	S1	S2	S3	S4
1985	Merrillville	Valparaiso	FW Snider	Kokomo
1986	Highland	Valparaiso	FW Snider	Marion
1987	Highland	Valparaiso	Penn	Carmel
1988	Crown Point	Mishawaka	FW North	Marion
1989	Gary Wallace	Valparaiso	Penn	Lafayette Jefferson
1990	Lake Central	Mishawaka	FW North	Marion
1991	Crown Point	Mishawaka	Penn	Lafayette Jefferson
1992	Merrillville	South Bend Riley	FW Snider	Carmel
1993	Lake Central	Portage	Homestead	Huntington North
1994	Lake Central	Portage	FW Snider	Harrison (W.L.)
1995	Portage	Penn	FW Snider	Carmel
1996	Portage	Penn	FW Snider	Carmel
1997	Valparaiso	Penn	FW Snider	Noblesville
1998	Portage	Penn	Homestead	Carmel
1999	Lake Central	Penn	FW Northrop	Carmel
2000	Valparaiso	Penn	FW Snider	Noblesville
2001	Valparaiso	Penn	FW Snider	Carmel
2002	Valparaiso	Penn	FW Snider	Lafayette Jefferson
2003	Portage	Penn	FW Snider	Carmel
2004	Merrillville	Penn	FW Snider	Carmel
2005	Merrillville	Penn	FW Snider	Hamilton SE
2006	Crown Point	LaPorte	Homestead	Carmel
2007	Merrillville	Penn	FW Snider	Carmel
2008	Merrillville	Penn	FW Snider	Carmel
2009	Merrillville	Mishawaka	FW Snider	Carmel
2010	Valparaiso	Mishawaka	FW Snider	Fishers
2011	Crown Point	Penn	FW Snider	Hamilton SE
2012	Merrillville	Carroll (FW)	FW Snider	Fishers
Year	**S9**	**S10**	**S11**	**S12**
2013	Mishawaka	Concord	Westfield	FW Snider
2014	LaPorte	Elkhart Central	Westfield	FW Snider
2015	Mishawaka	FW Snider	Westfield	Kokomo
2016	Mishawaka	FW Snider	Westfield	Kokomo
2017	Michigan City	Concord	Kokomo	Zionsville
2018	Michigan City	Concord	Harrison (W.L.)	New Palestine

Class 5A Southern Sectionals

Year	S5	S6	S7	S8
1985	Carmel	Warren Central	Southport	Bloomington South
1986	Carmel	Warren Central	Perry Meridian	Terre Haute North
1987	Ben Davis	Lawrence Central	Center Grove	Jeffersonville
1988	Ben Davis	Lawrence North	Terre Haute South	Evansville Central
1989	Carmel	Lawrence North	Columbus North	Castle
1990	Ben Davis	Lawrence North	Southport	Evansville Harrison
1991	Ben Davis	Richmond	Bloomington South	Jeffersonville
1992	Ben Davis	Richmond	Bloomington South	Evansville North
1993	North Central	Franklin Central	Bloomington South	Evansville Harrison
1994	Carmel	Warren Central	Martinsville	Castle
1995	Ben Davis	Lawrence Central	Martinsville	Evansville North
1996	Ben Davis	Lawrence Central	Martinsville	Evansville Harrison
1997	Lawrence Central	Ben Davis	Bloomington South	Evansville Harrison
1998	Ind. Arlington	Ben Davis	Bloomington South	Jeffersonville
1999	Ind. Arlington	Ben Davis	Bloomington South	Evansville Reitz
2000	Warren Central	Ben Davis	Center Grove	Castle
2001	Warren Central	Ben Davis	Bloomington South	Evansville Reitz
2002	Warren Central	Ben Davis	Center Grove	New Albany
2003	Warren Central	Ben Davis	Center Grove	Evansville Reitz
2004	Warren Central	Ben Davis	Columbus North	Castle
2005	Warren Central	Decatur Central	Avon	Evansville Reitz
2006	Warren Central	Ben Davis	Columbus North	Evansville Reitz
2007	Hamilton SE	Pike	Columbus North	Jeffersonville
2008	Warren Central	Ben Davis	Center Grove	Castle
2009	Warren Central	Brownsburg	Center Grove	Floyd Central
2010	Lawrence Central	Avon	Bloomington North	Castle
2011	Carmel	Ben Davis	Center Grove	Bedford NL
2012	Lawrence Central	Pike	Center Grove	Castle

Year	S13	S14	S15	S16
2013	Ind. Cathedral	Whiteland	Bloomington North	Terre Haute North
2014	Ind. Cathedral	Whiteland	Bloomington South	Terre Haute South
2015	Zionsville	New Palestine	Bloomington South	Castle
2016	Zionsville	Columbus East	Bloomington South	Castle
2017	Ind. Cathedral	Bloomington South	Columbus East	Terre Haute North
2018	Decatur Central	Bloomington South	Columbus East	Castle

Class 5A Regionals

Year	Champion	Champion	Champion	Champion
1985	Valparaiso	FW Snider	Warren Central	Bloomington South
1986	Valparaiso	FW Snider	Carmel	Perry Meridian
1987	Highland	Carmel	Ben Davis	Center Grove
1988	Crown Point	Marion	Ben Davis	Terre Haute South
1989	Valparaiso	Penn	Carmel	Castle
1990	Lake Central	Marion	Ben Davis	Southport
1991	Mishawaka	Penn	Ben Davis	Bloomington South
1992	Merrillville	FW Snider	Ben Davis	Bloomington South
1993	Lake Central	Homestead	North Central (Ind.)	Bloomington South
1994	Portage	FW Snider	Carmel	Castle
1995	Penn	Carmel	Ben Davis	Evansville North
1996	Penn	Carmel	Ben Davis	Martinsville
1997	Penn	FW Snider	Ben Davis	Bloomington South
1998	Penn	Homestead	Ben Davis	Bloomington South
1999	Penn	FW Northrop	Ben Davis	Bloomington South
2000	Penn	Noblesville	Ben Davis	Center Grove
2001	Valparaiso	FW Snider	Ben Davis	Evansville Reitz
2002	Valparaiso	FW Snider	Ben Davis	Center Grove
2003	Penn	FW Snider	Warren Central	Center Grove
2004	Penn	FW Snider	Warren Central	Columbus North
2005	Merrillville	Hamilton SE	Warren Central	Avon
2006	LaPorte	Carmel	Warren Central	Columbus North
2007	Merrillville	Carmel	Pike	Columbus North
2008	Penn	Carmel	Ben Davis	Center Grove
2009	Merrillville	Carmel	Warren Central	Center Grove
2010	Valparaiso	Fishers	Lawrence Central	Bloomington North
2011	Penn	FW Snider	Carmel	Center Grove
2012	Merrillville	FW Snider	Lawrence Central	Center Grove
2013	Concord	Westfield	Indpls. Cathedral	Terre Haute North
2014	LaPorte	FW Snider	Indpls. Cathedral	Bloomington South
2015	FW Snider	Kokomo	New Palestine	Castle
2016	FW Snider	Westfield	Columbus East	Bloomington South
2017	Michigan City	Kokomo	Indpls. Cathedral	Columbus East
2018	Michigan City	New Palestine	Decatur Central	Columbus East

Class 5A Semi-State

Year	North Champion	South Champion
1985	Valparaiso	Warren Central
1986	Fort Wayne Snider	Carmel
1987	Highland	Ben Davis
1988	Marion	Ben Davis
1989	Penn	Carmel
1990	Marion	Ben Davis
1991	Penn	Ben Davis
1992	Fort Wayne Snider	Ben Davis
1993	Lake Central	Bloomington South
1994	Portage	Castle
1995	Penn	Evansville North
1996	Penn	Ben Davis
1997	Penn	Bloomington South
1998	Homestead	Bloomington South
1999	Penn	Ben Davis
2000	Penn	Center Grove
2001	Valparaiso	Ben Davis
2002	Fort Wayne Snider	Ben Davis
2003	Penn	Warren Central
2004	Fort Wayne Snider	Warren Central
2005	Hamilton Southeastern	Warren Central
2006	Carmel	Warren Central
2007	Carmel	Pike
2008	Carmel	Center Grove
2009	Carmel	Warren Central
2010	Fishers	Lawrence Central
2011	Penn	Carmel
2012	Fort Wayne Snider	Lawrence Central
2013	Westfield	Indianapolis Cathedral
2014	LaPorte	Indianapolis Cathedral
2015	Fort Wayne Snider	New Palestine
2016	Westfield	Columbus East
2017	Kokomo	Columbus East
2018	New Palestine	Decatur Central

Class 5A State Champions

Year	School	Coach
1985	Warren Central (14-0)	Jerry Stauffer
1986	Carmel (14-0)	Jim Belden
1987	Ben Davis (12-2)	Dick Dullaghan
1988	Ben Davis (14-0)	Dick Dullaghan
1989	Carmel (13-1)	Jim Belden
1990	Ben Davis (13-1)	Dick Dullaghan
1991	Ben Davis (14-0)	Dick Dullaghan
1992	Fort Wayne Snider (14-0)	Russ Isaacs
1993	Bloomington South (14-0)	Mo Moriarity
1994	Castle (12-2)	John Lidy
1995	Penn (14-0)	Chris Geesman
1996	Penn (13-1)	Chris Geesman
1997	Penn (14-1)	Chris Geesman
1998	Bloomington South (14-0)	Mo Moriarity
1999	Ben Davis (15-0)	Dick Dullaghan
2000	Penn (14-1)	Chris Geesman
2001	Ben Davis (15-0)	Dick Dullaghan
2002	Ben Davis (12-3)	Dick Dullaghan
2003	Warren Central (13-2)	Kevin Wright
2004	Warren Central (14-1)	Kevin Wright
2005	Warren Central (14-1)	Kevin Wright
2006	Warren Central (15-0)	Steve Tutsie
2007	Carmel (13-2)	Mo Moriarity
2008	Center Grove (14-1)	Eric Moore
2009	Warren Central (13-2)	John Hart
2010	Fishers (14-1)	Rick Wimmer
2011	Carmel (14-1)	Kevin Wright
2012	Lawrence Central (15-0)	Jayson West
2013	Indianapolis Cathedral (10-5)	Rick Streiff
2014	Indianapolis Cathedral (9-5)	Rick Streiff
2015	Fort Wayne Snider (13-1)	Kurt Tippmann
2016	Westfield (12-2)	Jake Gilbert
2017	Columbus East (14-1)	Bob Gaddis
2018	New Palestine (14-0)	Kyle Ralph

Class 4A postseason champions
Class 4A Northern Sectionals

Year	Champion	Champion	Champion	Champion
1983	Hobart	Portage	Penn	Anderson Highland
1984	Hobart	Mich. City Elston	Fort Wayne North	Carmel
Year	**S9**	**S10**	**S11**	**S12**
1985	Munster	Hobart	FW Dwenger	Harding (FW)
1986	Munster	Hobart	DeKalb	Logansport
1987	Munster	Hobart	Goshen	Fort Wayne Wayne
1988	Hammond	Hobart	Goshen	New Haven
1989	Andrean	Hobart	DeKalb	Harrison (WL)
1990	Andrean	Hobart	Fort Wayne South	Harrison (WL)
1991	Andrean	Hobart	New Haven	Fort Wayne Wayne
1992	Lowell	Hobart	DeKalb	Fort Wayne Wayne
1993	Hamm. Gavit	Hobart	Columbia City	Fort Wayne Wayne
1994	Lowell	Hobart	DeKalb	Muncie South
1995	Griffith	Hobart	DeKalb	Fort Wayne Wayne
1996	Munster	Hobart	Goshen	Fort Wayne Wayne
1997	Griffith	Hobart	Elkhart Memorial	FW Dwenger
1998	Griffith	Plymouth	Concord	Carroll (FW)
1999	Lowell	McCutcheon	Goshen	East Noble
2000	Hammond	Plymouth	Goshen	East Noble
2001	Griffith	Plymouth	Carroll (FW)	Delta
2002	Griffith	South Bend Clay	FW Dwenger	Muncie Central
2003	Lowell	East Noble	FW Dwenger	Muncie Central
2004	Lowell	Wawasee	Logansport	Muncie Central
2005	Lowell	Concord	Fort Wayne South	Delta
2006	Lowell	Concord	FW Dwenger	Muncie Central
2007	Griffith	Lowell	FW Dwenger	Jay County
2008	Griffith	Lowell	FW Dwenger	Delta
2009	Hamm. Morton	Lowell	FW Dwenger	Delta
2010	Hamm. Morton	Concord	FW Dwenger	New Haven
2011	Hamm. Morton	SB Washington	NorthWood	Leo
2012	Hamm. Morton	Mishawaka	Concord	FW Dwenger
Year	**S17**	**S18**	**S19**	**S20**
2013	E.C. Central	New Prairie	FW Dwenger	New Haven
2014	Lowell	New Prairie	Northridge	Norwell
2015	Lowell	SB St. Joseph	Plymouth	FW Dwenger
2016	Lowell	Hobart	NorthWood	New Haven
2017	Lowell	New Prairie	Angola	FW Dwenger
2018	Lowell	Mishawaka	Angola	FW Dwenger

Class 4A Southern Sectionals

Year	Champion	Champion	Champion	Champion
1983	N. Central (I.)	Ind. Washington	Bloomington South	Castle
1984	N. Central (I.)	Warren Central	Martinsville	New Albany
Year	S13	S14	S15	S16
1985	Brownsburg	Ind. Chatard	New Albany	Evansville Reitz
1986	I. Washington	Ind. Chatard	East Central	Evansville Harrison
1987	Harrison (WL)	Franklin Central	Franklin Central	Jasper
1988	Logansport	Franklin Central	East Central	Evansville Bosse
1989	Franklin Cen.	East Central	Greenwood	Evansville Reitz
1990	Franklin Cen.	Franklin County	Mooresville	Evansville Bosse
1991	Avon	Mooresville	Greenwood	Seymour
1992	Harrison (WL)	Greenwood	Franklin County	Evansville Reitz
1993	Ind. Cathedral	Ind. Washington	East Central	Vincennes Lincoln
1994	McCutcheon	Ind. Washington	East Central	Evansville North
1995	Avon	Hamilton SE	East Central	Evansville Bosse
1996	Ind. Cathedral	McCutcheon	Franklin County	Vincennes Lincoln
1997	Hamilton SE	Seymour	East Central	Vincennes Lincoln
1998	Hamilton SE	East Central	Avon	Floyd Central
1999	Muncie South	Seymour	Ind. Cathedral	Evansville North
2000	Delta	East Central	Ind. Cathedral	Evansville North
2001	Ind. Cathedral	Seymour	Plainfield	Jasper
2002	Roncalli	East Central	Zionsville	Jasper
2003	Roncalli	Mooresville	Zionsville	Vincennes Lincoln
2004	Roncalli	Mooresville	East Central	Boonville
2005	Roncalli	Greenwood	Columbus East	Jasper
2006	Ind. Cathedral	Whiteland	East Central	Vincennes Lincoln
2007	Westfield	Ind. Cathedral	Columbus East	Evansville Reitz
2008	Zionsville	Ind. Cathedral	Columbus East	Jasper
2009	New Palestine	Ind. Cathedral	Columbus East	Evansville Reitz
2010	Pendleton Hts.	Ind. Cathedral	East Central	Evansville Reitz
2011	Pendleton Hts.	Ind. Cathedral	East Central	Evansville Central
2012	Mt. Vernon (F)	Ind. Cathedral	Columbus East	Evansville Reitz
Year	S21	S22	S23	S24
2013	New Palestine	Ind. Chatard	Columbus East	Jasper
2014	New Palestine	Roncalli	Columbus East	Evansville Reitz
2015	Roncalli	Delta	East Central	Evansville Harrison
2016	Roncalli	Delta	East Central	Evansville Reitz
2017	Mississinewa	Greenwood	East Central	Evansville Central
2018	Marion	Mooresville	East Central	Evansville Central

Class 4A Regionals

Year	Champion	Champion	Champion	Champion
1983	Hobart	Penn	Indpls. Washington	Bloomington South
1984	Hobart	FW North	Warren Central	Martinsville
1985	Hobart	Harding (FW)	Brownsburg	East Central
1986	Munster	DeKalb	Ind. Chatard	Franklin Central
1987	Hobart	FW Wayne	Harrison (WL)	Jasper
1988	Hammond	Goshen	Franklin Central	Greenwood
1989	Hobart	Harrison (WL)	Franklin Central	Mooresville
1990	Hobart	Harrison (WL)	Franklin Central	Greenwood
1991	Hobart	FW Wayne	Avon	Seymour
1992	Lowell	FW Wayne	Harrison (WL)	Evansville Reitz
1993	Hobart	FW Wayne	Indpls. Washington	East Central
1994	Lowell	DeKalb	Indpls. Washington	East Central
1995	Hobart	FW Wayne	Avon	Franklin County
1996	Hobart	Goshen	Indpls. Cathedral	Vincennes Lincoln
1997	Griffith	FW Dwenger	Hamilton SE	Avon
1998	Plymouth	Concord	Indpls. Cathedral	East Central
1999	Lowell	Goshen	Indpls. Cathedral	Seymour
2000	Plymouth	East Noble	Delta	Plainfield
2001	Plymouth	Delta	Indpls. Cathedral	Jasper
2002	SB Clay	FW Dwenger	Roncalli	Jasper
2003	East Noble	FW Dwenger	Roncalli	East Central
2004	Wawasee	Logansport	Roncalli	Columbus East
2005	Lowell	FW South	Roncalli	Jasper
2006	Concord	FW Dwenger	Indpls. Cathedral	Columbus East
2007	Lowell	FW Dwenger	Indpls. Cathedral	Evansville Reitz
2008	Lowell	FW Dwenger	Indpls. Cathedral	Columbus East
2009	Lowell	FW Dwenger	Indpls. Cathedral	Evansville Reitz
2010	Hamm. Morton	FW Dwenger	Indpls. Cathedral	Evansville Reitz
2011	SB Washington	Leo	Indpls. Cathedral	Columbus East
2012	Mishawaka	Concord	Indpls. Cathedral	Columbus East
2013	EC Central	FW Dwenger	New Palestine	Columbus East
2014	New Prairie	Northridge	New Palestine	Columbus East
2015	SB St. Joseph	FW Dwenger	Roncalli	East Central
2016	Lowell	NorthWood	Roncalli	East Central
2017	Lowell	FW Dwenger	Greenwood	East Central
2018	Mishawaka	FW Dwenger	Marion	Evansville Central

Class 4A Semi-State

Year	North Champion	South Champion
1983	Penn	Indianapolis Washington
1984	Hobart	Warren Central
1985	Hobart	Brownsburg
1986	DeKalb	Franklin Central
1987	Hobart	Jasper
1988	Goshen	Franklin Central
1989	Hobart	Franklin Central
1990	Hobart	Franklin Central
1991	Hobart	Seymour
1992	Fort Wayne Wayne	Harrison (West Lafayette)
1993	Hobart	East Central
1994	DeKalb	East Central
1995	Fort Wayne Wayne	Franklin County
1996	Hobart	Indianapolis Cathedral
1997	Griffith	Hamilton Southeastern
1998	Concord	Indianapolis Cathedral
1999	Goshen	Indianapolis Cathedral
2000	East Noble	Plainfield
2001	Delta	Jasper
2002	Fort Wayne Dwenger	Roncalli
2003	East Noble	Roncalli
2004	Wawasee	Roncalli
2005	Lowell	Roncalli
2006	Concord	Indianapolis Cathedral
2007	Lowell	Evansville Reitz
2008	Fort Wayne Dwenger	Indianapolis Cathedral
2009	Lowell	Evansville Reitz
2010	Fort Wayne Dwenger	Indianapolis Cathedral
2011	South Bend Washington	Indianapolis Cathedral
2012	Mishawaka	Indianapolis Cathedral
2013	Fort Wayne Dwenger	Columbus East
2014	New Prairie	New Palestine
2015	Fort Wayne Dwenger	East Central
2016	NorthWood	Roncalli
2017	Lowell	East Central
2018	Fort Wayne Dwenger	Evansville Central

Class 4A State Champions

Year	School	Coach
1983	Penn (14-0)	Chris Geesman
1984	Warren Central (14-0)	Jerry Stauffer
1985	Brownsburg (14-0)	Mike Godan
1986	DeKalb (13-1)	Dale Hummer
1987	Hobart (14-0)	Don Howell
1988	Goshen (14-0)	Randy Robertson
1989	Hobart (13-1)	Don Howell
1990	Franklin Central (14-0)	Chuck Stephens
1991	Hobart (13-1)	Don Howell
1992	Harrison (West Lafayette) (13-1)	A.J. Rickard
1993	Hobart (13-1)	Don Howell
1994	East Central (14-0)	Rod Ballart
1995	Fort Wayne Wayne (12-2)	Mark Newlin
1996	Indianapolis Cathedral (14-0)	Rick Streiff
1997	Griffith (14-1)	Russ Radtke
1998	Indianapolis Cathedral (13-2)	Rick Streiff
1999	Indianapolis Cathedral (13-2)	Rick Streiff
2000	East Noble (14-1)	Tim Able
2001	Jasper (13-1)	Jerry Brewer
2002	Roncalli (10-4)	Bruce Scifres
2003	Roncalli (12-3)	Bruce Scifres
2004	Roncalli (13-2)	Bruce Scifres
2005	Lowell (11-4)	Kirk Kennedy
2006	Indianapolis Cathedral (13-2)	Jim O'Hara
2007	Evansville Reitz (15-0)	John Hart
2008	Indianapolis Cathedral (12-2)	Rick Streiff
2009	Evansville Reitz (15-0)	Tony Lewis
2010	Indianapolis Cathedral (12-3)	Rick Streiff
2011	Indianapolis Cathedral (12-3)	Rick Streiff
2012	Indianapolis Cathedral (10-5)	Rick Streiff
2013	Columbus East (15-0)	Bob Gaddis
2014	New Palestine (15-0)	Kyle Ralph
2015	Fort Wayne Dwenger (14-1)	Ernie Bojrab
2016	Roncalli (15-0)	Bruce Scifres
2017	East Central (12-3)	Justin Roden
2018	Fort Wayne Dwenger (14-1)	Jason Garrett

Class 3A postseason champions
Class 3A Northern Sectionals

Year	Champion			
1975	Valparaiso			

Year	S1		S2	
1976	Merrillville		South Bend St. Joseph	
1977	Portage		South Bend Washington	
1978	Hammond		Fort Wayne Dwenger	
1979	Hobart		Penn	
1980	Hobart		Mishawaka	

Year	S1	S1	S2	S2
1981	Griffith	Hobart	Fort Wayne Snider	Lafayette Jefferson
1982	Highland	Hobart	Fort Wayne Snider	Lafayette Jefferson

Year	Champion	Champion	Champion	Champion
1983	Hammond	SB St. Joseph	FW Dwenger	Mississinewa
1984	Griffith	Concord	FW Dwenger	Kankakee Valley

Year	S17	S18	S19	S20
1985	Kank. Valley	Wawasee	Hamilton SE	Mississinewa
1986	Hamm. Gavit	NorthWood	West Lafayette	Mississinewa
1987	NorthWood	FW Dwenger	West Lafayette	Elwood
1988	NorthWood	FW Dwenger	Tipton	Mississinewa
1989	Hammond Noll	NorthWood	FW Dwenger	Crawfordsville
1990	Griffith	SB St. Joseph	FW Dwenger	Northwestern
1991	Griffith	Central Noble	FW Dwenger	Tipton
1992	Griffith	Central Noble	FW Dwenger	Northwestern
1993	Twin Lakes	NorthWood	FW Dwenger	Tipton
1994	Griffith	SB St. Joseph	Norwell	Tipton
1995	Twin Lakes	SB St. Joseph	Harding (FW)	Hamilton Heights
1996	Andrean	NorthWood	FW Dwenger	Frankfort
1997	Andrean	Lebanon	NorthWood	Harding (FW)
1998	Andrean	Twin Lakes	NorthWood	Harding (FW)
1999	Mish. Marian	Zionsville	NorthWood	Norwell
2000	Culver Military	Zionsville	NorthWood	Rochester
2001	Andrean	Frankfort	NorthWood	New Haven
2002	Andrean	Twin Lakes	SB St. Joseph	FW Concordia
2003	Andrean	Hamilton Heights	NorthWood	Norwell
2004	Andrean	Hamilton Heights	New Prairie	Norwell
2005	Griffith	Hamilton Heights	NorthWood	FW Luers
2006	Griffith	Frankfort	New Prairie	Norwell
2007	Andrean	SB St. Joseph	FW Concordia	Western
2008	Andrean	NorthWood	Bellmont	Yorktown
2009	Andrean	Jimtown	Eastbrook	West Lafayette
2010	Andrean	SB St. Joseph	Leo	West Lafayette
2011	SB St. Joseph	Jimtown	Bellmont	West Lafayette
2012	Mish. Marian	Heritage	Eastbrook	Hamilton Heights

Year	S25	S26	S27	S28
2013	Andrean	Jimtown	FW Concordia	West Lafayette
2014	Andrean	Jimtown	FW Luers	Yorktown
2015	Mish. Marian	Culver Military	Bellmont	West Lafayette
2016	Mish. Marian	Garrett	FW Concordia	West Lafayette
2017	West Lafayette	Brebeuf Jesuit	Mishawaka Marian	FW Luers
2018	West Lafayette	Brebeuf Jesuit	Mishawaka Marian	FW Luers

Class 3A Southern Sectionals

Year	Champion			
1975	Carmel			

Year	S3		S4	
1976	Indianapolis Cathedral		Evansville Reitz	
1977	Ben Davis		Evansville Reitz	
1978	Carmel		Columbus East	
1979	Ind. Chatard		Columbus East	
1980	Carmel		Martinsville	

Year	S3	S3	S4	S4
1981	Carmel	Ind. Marshall	Martinsville	Castle
1982	Carmel	Ind. Chatard	Martinsville	Castle

Year	Champion	Champion	Champion	Champion
1983	McCutcheon	Roncalli	Rushville	Jasper
1984	Brownsburg	Roncalli	Franklin	Boonville

Year	S21	S22	S23	S24
1985	West Vigo	Roncalli	Providence	Ev. Memorial
1986	Zionsville	Ind. Cathedral	Batesville	Princeton
1987	Ind. Cathedral	New Palestine	Zionsville	Ev. Memorial
1988	Roncalli	Lawrenceburg	Zionsville	Ev. Memorial
1989	Roncalli	New Palestine	Greensburg	Charlestown
1990	Ind. Chatard	New Palestine	Edgewood	Tell City
1991	Zionsville	Ind. Cathedral	Lawrenceburg	Ev. Memorial
1992	Owen Valley	Ind. Cathedral	Lawrenceburg	Ev. Memorial
1993	Danville	Roncalli	Charlestown	Ev. Memorial
1994	Danville	Roncalli	Salem	Jasper
1995	Zionsville	Roncalli	Brown County	Jasper
1996	Zionsville	Roncalli	Charlestown	Heritage Hills
1997	Mt. Vernon (FV)	Franklin County	Ind. Chatard	Heritage Hills
1998	Yorktown	Franklin County	Ind. Chatard	Ev. Memorial
1999	Mt. Vernon (FV)	Roncalli	Whiteland	Mount Vernon
2000	Elwood	Roncalli	Whiteland	Heritage Hills
2001	Tipton	Ind. Chatard	Batesville	Heritage Hills
2002	Hamilton Hts.	Ind. Chatard	Batesville	Heritage Hills
2003	Blackford	Ind. Chatard	Batesville	Heritage Hills
2004	New Palestine	Ind. Chatard	Batesville	Heritage Hills
2005	New Palestine	Ind. Chatard	Batesville	Heritage Hills
2006	Mt. Vernon (FV)	Ind. Chatard	Batesville	Ev. Mater Dei
2007	Danville	Ind. Chatard	Heritage Hills	Mount Vernon
2008	N. Montgomery	Ind. Chatard	Heritage Hills	Ev. Memorial
2009	Ind. Chatard	Batesville	Heritage Hills	Ev. Memorial
2010	Ind. Chatard	Hamilton Heights	Indian Creek	Evansville Bosse
2011	Ind. Chatard	Indian Creek	Corydon Central	Ev. Memorial
2012	Ind. Chatard	Greensburg	Charlestown	Gibson Southern

Year	S29	S30	S31	S32
2013	Brebeuf Jesuit	Guerin Catholic	Brownstown	Gibson Southern
2014	Tri-West	Guerin Catholic	Charlestown	Heritage Hills
2015	Ind. Chatard	Batesville	Brownstown	Gibson Southern
2016	Danville	Lawrenceburg	Brownstown	Ev. Memorial
2017	Ind. Chatard	Danville	Lawrenceburg	Ev. Memorial
2018	Ind. Chatard	Tri-West	Brownstown	Ev. Memorial

Class 3A Regionals

Year	Champion		Champion	
1976	Merrillville		Indianapolis Cathedral	
1977	Portage		Evansville Reitz	
1978	Fort Wayne Dwenger		Carmel	
1979	Hobart		Columbus East	
1980	Hobart		Carmel	

Year	Champion	Champion	Champion	Champion
1981	Carmel	FW Snider	Hobart	Castle
1982	Hobart	FW Snider	Carmel	Castle
1983	SB St. Joseph	FW Dwenger	Roncalli	Jasper
1984	Concord	FW Dwenger	Brownsburg	Boonville
1985	Wawasee	Mississinewa	Roncalli	Ev. Memorial
1986	NorthWood	West Lafayette	Indpls. Cathedral	Batesville
1987	FW Dwenger	Elwood	New Palestine	Zionsville
1988	FW Dwenger	Tipton	Roncalli	Ev. Memorial
1989	Hammond Noll	Crawfordsville	Roncalli	Charlestown
1990	SB St. Joseph	FW Dwenger	New Palestine	Tell City
1991	Griffith	FW Dwenger	Indpls. Cathedral	Ev. Memorial
1992	Central Noble	Northwestern	Indpls. Cathedral	Ev. Memorial
1993	NorthWood	FW Dwenger	Roncalli	Ev. Memorial
1994	Griffith	Tipton	Roncalli	Jasper
1995	SB St. Joseph	Harding (FW)	Roncalli	Jasper
1996	NorthWood	FW Dwenger	Zionsville	Heritage Hills
1997	Andrean	Harding (FW)	Franklin County	Indpls. Chatard
1998	Andrean	NorthWood	Franklin County	Indpls. Chatard
1999	Mish. Marian	Norwell	Roncalli	Whiteland
2000	Zionsville	NorthWood	Roncalli	Heritage Hills
2001	Andrean	New Haven	Indpls. Chatard	Heritage Hills
2002	Andrean	FW Concordia	Indpls. Chatard	Heritage Hills
2003	Hamilton Hts.	NorthWood	Indpls. Chatard	Heritage Hills
2004	Andrean	New Prairie	Indpls. Chatard	Heritage Hills
2005	Griffith	NorthWood	Indpls. Chatard	Heritage Hills
2006	Griffith	Norwell	Indpls. Chatard	Ev. Mater Dei
2007	SB St. Joseph	FW Concordia	Indpls. Chatard	Heritage Hills
2008	NorthWood	Bellmont	Indpls. Chatard	Ev. Memorial
2009	Jimtown	West Lafayette	Indpls. Chatard	Ev. Memorial
2010	SB St. Joseph	Leo	Indpls. Chatard	Indian Creek
2011	SB St. Joseph	West Lafayette	Indpls. Chatard	Corydon Central
2012	Mish. Marian	Hamilton Heights	Indpls. Chatard	Gibson Southern
2013	Andrean	West Lafayette	Brebeuf Jesuit	Gibson Southern
2014	Andrean	Fort Wayne Luers	Tri-West	Heritage Hills
2015	Mish. Marian	West Lafayette	Indpls. Chatard	Gibson Southern
2016	Garrett	FW Concordia	Lawrenceburg	Brownstown
2017	Brebeuf Jesuit	Mish. Marian	Danville	Ev. Memorial
2018	West Lafayette	Fort Wayne Luers	Indpls. Chatard	Ev. Memorial

Class 3A Semi-State

Year	North Champion	South Champion
1981	Carmel	Fort Wayne Snider
1982	Hobart	Castle
1983	Fort Wayne Dwenger	Roncalli
1984	Concord	Brownsburg
1985	Wawasee	Roncalli
1986	NorthWood	Indianapolis Cathedral
1987	Elwood	Zionsville
1988	Tipton	Roncalli
1989	Hammond Noll	Roncalli
1990	Fort Wayne Dwenger	New Palestine
1991	Fort Wayne Dwenger	Indianapolis Cathedral
1992	Northwestern	Indianapolis Cathedral
1993	NorthWood	Roncalli
1994	Tipton	Roncalli
1995	South Bend St. Joseph	Jasper
1996	Fort Wayne Dwenger	Zionsville
1997	Andrean	Indianapolis Chatard
1998	NorthWood	Indianapolis Chatard
1999	Norwell	Roncalli
2000	Zionsville	Heritage Hills
2001	Andrean	Indianapolis Chatard
2002	Andrean	Indianapolis Chatard
2003	NorthWood	Indianapolis Chatard
2004	Andrean	Heritage Hills
2005	NorthWood	Indianapolis Chatard
2006	Norwell	Indianapolis Chatard
2007	South Bend St. Joseph	Indianapolis Chatard
2008	Bellmont	Evansville Memorial
2009	West Lafayette	Evansville Memorial
2010	South Bend St. Joseph	Indianapolis Chatard
2011	South Bend St. Joseph	Indianapolis Chatard
2012	Hamilton Heights	Indianapolis Chatard
2013	Andrean	Brebeuf Jesuit
2014	Andrean	Tri-West
2015	West Lafayette	Indianapolis Chatard
2016	Fort Wayne Concordia	Lawrenceburg
2017	Brebeuf Jesuit	Evansville Memorial
2018	West Lafayette	Evansville Memorial

Class 3A State Champions

Year	School	Coach
1973	South Bend Washington (12-0)	Robert Van Camp
1974	Indianapolis Washington (12-0)	Bob Springer
1975	Valparaiso (12-0)	Tom Stokes
1976	Merrillville (11-1)	Ken Haupt
1977	Portage (12-1)	Les Klein
1978	Carmel (13-0)	Dick Dullaghan
1979	Columbus East (13-0)	John Stafford
1980	Carmel (13-0)	Jim Belden
1981	Carmel (14-0)	Jim Belden
1982	Castle (14-0)	John Lidy
1983	Fort Wayne Dwenger (14-0)	Andy Johns
1984	Brownsburg (14-0)	Mike Godan
1985	Roncalli (13-1)	Bill Kuntz
1986	Indianapolis Cathedral (12-2)	Mike McGinley
1987	Zionsville (14-0)	Rick Wimmer
1988	Roncalli (12-2)	Bill Sylvester
1989	Hammond Noll (13-1)	Jerry Vlasic
1990	Fort Wayne Dwenger (14-0)	Andy Johns
1991	Fort Wayne Dwenger (13-1)	Andy Johns
1992	Indianapolis Cathedral (12-2)	Rick Streiff
1993	Roncalli (14-0)	Bruce Scifres
1994	Roncalli (12-2)	Bruce Scifres
1995	South Bend St. Joseph (14-0)	Frank Amato
1996	Zionsville (14-0)	Larry McWhorter
1997	Indianapolis Chatard (14-1)	Craig Barr
1998	Indianapolis Chatard (13-2)	Craig Barr
1999	Roncalli (15-0)	Bruce Scifres
2000	Heritage Hills (15-0)	Bob Clayton
2001	Indianapolis Chatard (11-4)	Tom Dilley
2002	Indianapolis Chatard (15-0)	Tom Dilley
2003	Indianapolis Chatard (14-1)	Vince Lorenzano
2004	Andrean (13-2)	Brett St. Germain
2005	NorthWood (9-6)	Rich Dodson
2006	Indianapolis Chatard (14-1)	Vince Lorenzano
2007	Indianapolis Chatard (11-4)	Vince Lorenzano
2008	Bellmont (14-1)	Toney Bergman
2009	West Lafayette (15-0)	Marshall Overley
2010	Indianapolis Chatard (11-4)	Vince Lorenzano
2011	Indianapolis Chatard (13-2)	Vince Lorenzano
2012	Indianapolis Chatard (13-2)	Vince Lorenzano
2013	Andrean (15-0)	Phil Mason
2014	Tri-West (14-1)	Chris Coll
2015	Indianapolis Chatard (12-3)	Vince Lorenzano
2016	Fort Wayne Concordia (13-2)	Tim Mannigel
2017	Evansville Memorial (14-1)	John Hurley
2018	West Lafayette	Shane Fry

Class 2A postseason champions
Class 2A Northern Sectionals

Year	Champion
1975	Mishawaka Marian

Year	S5		S6	
1976	Mishawaka Marian		McCutcheon	
1977	Plymouth		Delphi	
1978	Goshen		Delta	
1979	Concord		Blackford	
1980	NorthWood		Norwell	

Year	S5	S5	S6	S6
1981	Goshen	New Haven	Delta	Harrison (WL)
1982	Peru	Norwell	McCutcheon	Twin Lakes

Year	Champion	Champion	Champion	Champion
1983	Tipp. Valley	FW Luers	Oak Hill	Crawfordsville
1984	NorthWood	FW Luers	Western	West Lafayette

Year	S25	S26	S27	S28
1985	Rochester	FW Luers	North Miami	Hagerstown
1986	Rensselaer	FW Luers	Whitko	Shenandoah
1987	North Newton	FW Luers	Rochester	Western Boone
1988	River Forest	Woodlan	Manchester	Western Boone
1989	North Judson	FW Luers	Manchester	Western Boone
1990	River Forest	FW Luers	Lewis Cass	West Lafayette
1991	Lake Station	FW Luers	Manchester	Southwood
1992	Rensselaer	FW Luers	Tippecanoe Valley	South Adams
1993	North Newton	West Lafayette	Jimtown	FW Luers
1994	Rochester	Lewis Cass	Bremen	Garrett
1995	Bremen	Jimtown	Leo	Southwood
1996	North Judson	Jimtown	FW Luers	Oak Hill
1997	Bremen	Northwestern	Jimtown	Eastbrook
1998	Lake Station	Rochester	Jimtown	Heritage
1999	North Judson	Eastbrook	Jimtown	FW Luers
2000	North Judson	Winamac	Jimtown	FW Luers
2001	John Glenn	Eastbrook	Jimtown	FW Luers
2002	North Judson	Eastbrook	Central Noble	FW Luers
2003	Rensselaer	Garrett	Harding (FW)	Eastbrook
2004	North Judson	John Glenn	Heritage	Eastbrook
2005	Rensselaer	Jimtown	Lewis Cass	Eastbrook
2006	Rensselaer	Jimtown	Harding (FW)	Madison-Grant
2007	Wheeler	Lewis Cass	FW Luers	Northwestern
2008	Rensselaer	Lewis Cass	Jimtown	Madison-Grant
2009	Rensselaer	Fairfield	FW Luers	Lewis Cass
2010	Rensselaer	Bremen	FW Luers	Tipton
2011	Wheeler	Bremen	FW Luers	Tipton
2012	Andrean	Lewis Cass	FW Luers	Tipton

Year	S33	S34	S35	S36
2013	Rensselaer	Bremen	Tipton	Oak Hill
2014	Rensselaer	Bremen	Lafayette CC	Lapel
2015	Whiting	Bremen	Woodlan	Winchester
2016	Whiting	Winamac	South Adams	Eastbrook
2017	North Newton	Woodlan	Eastbrook	Lapel
2018	Whiting	Bremen	Eastbrook	Lapel

Class 2A Southern Sectionals

Year	Champion
1975	Greenfield-Central

Year	S7		S8	
1976	Roncalli		Jasper	
1977	Mooresville		Jasper	
1978	Brownsburg		Vincennes Lincoln	
1979	Noblesville		Tell City	
1980	Franklin Central		East Central	

Year	S7	S7	S8	S8
1981	Brownsburg	Franklin Central	Tell City	Jasper
1982	Avon	Franklin Central	Providence	Jasper

Year	Champion	Champion	Champion	Champion
1983	Ind. Chatard	Yorktown	Mitchell	Ev. Mater Dei
1984	Ind. Chatard	Hagerstown	Lawrenceburg	Ev. Mater Dei

Year	S29	S30	S31	S32
1985	Tri-West	Indianapolis Ritter	Lawrenceburg	Tell City
1986	Danville	Indianapolis Ritter	Lawrenceburg	Tell City
1987	Ind. Ritter	Triton Central	Tell City	Ev. Mater Dei
1988	Tri-West	Triton Central	Tell City	South Spencer
1989	Tri-West	Lapel	Monrovia	Ev. Mater Dei
1990	Ind. Scecina	Lapel	Greencastle	Ev. Mater Dei
1991	West Lafayette	Ind. Scecina	Greencastle	Tell City
1992	Westfield	Lapel	Cascade	Tell City
1993	Eastbrook	Westfield	Providence	Ev. Mater Dei
1994	Eastbrook	Ind. Scecina	Providence	Ev. Mater Dei
1995	Ind. Chatard	North Montgomery	Brownstown	North Posey
1996	Ind. Chatard	North Montgomery	Brownstown	North Posey
1997	Westfield	Clarksville	Western Boone	Ev. Mater Dei
1998	Speedway	Lawrenceburg	Western Boone	Ev. Mater Dei
1999	Western Boone	Danville	Lawrenceburg	Ev. Mater Dei
2000	Ind. Scecina	Danville	Brownstown	Ev. Mater Dei
2001	Western Boone	Speedway	Brownstown	Ev. Mater Dei
2002	Seeger	Ind. Scecina	Indian Creek	Southridge
2003	Tri-West	Speedway	Brownstown	South Spencer
2004	Tri-West	Speedway	Brownstown	Southridge
2005	Tri-West	Speedway	Lawrenceburg	North Posey
2006	North Putnam	Speedway	Brownstown	Southridge
2007	Heritage Chr.	North Putnam	Providence	Southridge
2008	Heritage Chr.	Speedway	Brownstown	Southridge
2009	Ind. Ritter	Monrovia	Paoli	Ev. Mater Dei
2010	Speedway	North Putnam	Brownstown	Ev. Mater Dei
2011	Guerin Catholic	South Putnam	Triton Central	Ev. Mater Dei
2012	Shenandoah	Ind. Ritter	Lawrenceburg	Ev. Mater Dei

Year	S37	S38	S39	S40
2013	Ind. Ritter	Ind. Scecina	Paoli	Southridge
2014	Monrovia	Shenandoah	Triton Central	Ev. Mater Dei
2015	Ind. Scecina	Indianapolis Howe	Monrovia	Ev. Mater Dei
2016	Ind. Ritter	Milan	Monrovia	Ev. Mater Dei
2017	Ind. Scecina	Western Boone	Providence	Southridge
2018	Ind. Scecina	Western Boone	Paoli	Southridge

Class 2A Regionals

Year	Champion	Champion	Champion	Champion
1976	Mishawaka Marian		Jasper	
1977	Plymouth		Jasper	
1978	Goshen		Brownsburg	
1979	Blackford		Noblesville	
1980	NorthWood		Franklin Central	
Year	**Champion**	**Champion**	**Champion**	**Champion**
1981	Goshen	Delta	Franklin Central	Jasper
1982	Peru	McCutcheon	Franklin Central	Jasper
1983	FW Luers	Crawfordsville	Indpls. Chatard	Ev. Mater Dei
1984	NorthWood	West Lafayette	Indpls. Chatard	Lawrenceburg
1985	FW Luers	Hagerstown	Indianapolis Ritter	Lawrenceburg
1986	FW Luers	Whitko	Danville	Tell City
1987	North Newton	Rochester	Indianapolis Ritter	Tell City
1988	Woodlan	Western Boone	Tri-West	South Spencer
1989	FW Luers	Western Boone	Tri-West	Ev. Mater Dei
1990	River Forest	West Lafayette	Indpls. Scecina	Ev. Mater Dei
1991	FW Luers	Southwood	Indpls. Scecina	Greencastle
1992	FW Luers	South Adams	Westfield	Tell City
1993	West Lafayette	Fort Wayne Luers	Westfield	Providence
1994	Lewis Cass	Bremen	Indpls. Scecina	Ev. Mater Dei
1995	Bremen	Southwood	North Montgomery	North Posey
1996	Jimtown	Fort Wayne Luers	North Montgomery	North Posey
1997	Bremen	Jimtown	Clarksville	Western Boone
1998	Rochester	Jimtown	Speedway	Western Boone
1999	Eastbrook	Fort Wayne Luers	Danville	Ev. Mater Dei
2000	Winamac	Fort Wayne Luers	Danville	Ev. Mater Dei
2001	Eastbrook	Fort Wayne Luers	Speedway	Ev. Mater Dei
2002	North Judson	Fort Wayne Luers	Indpls. Scecina	Southridge
2003	Garrett	Harding (FW)	Tri-West	South Spencer
2004	John Glenn	Eastbrook	Tri-West	Brownstown
2005	Jimtown	Lewis Cass	Speedway	North Posey
2006	Jimtown	Harding (FW)	North Putnam	Southridge
2007	Lewis Cass	Fort Wayne Luers	Heritage Christian	Southridge
2008	Lewis Cass	Jimtown	Heritage Christian	Brownstown
2009	Rensselaer	Fort Wayne Luers	Monrovia	Paoli
2010	Rensselaer	Fort Wayne Luers	North Putnam	Ev. Mater Dei
2011	Bremen	Fort Wayne Luers	Guerin Catholic	Ev. Mater Dei
2012	Andrean	Fort Wayne Luers	Indianapolis Ritter	Ev. Mater Dei
2013	Rensselaer	Tipton	Indianapolis Ritter	Paoli
2014	Rensselaer	Lafayette CC	Monrovia	Ev. Mater Dei
2015	Whiting	Woodlan	Indianapolis Howe	Monrovia
2016	Whiting	Eastbrook	Indianapolis Ritter	Monrovia
2017	Woodlan	Eastbrook	Indpls. Scecina	Southridge
2018	Bremen	Eastbrook	Western Boone	Southridge

Class 2A Semi-State

Year	North Champion	South Champion
1981	Franklin Central	Goshen
1982	McCutcheon	Franklin Central
1983	Fort Wayne Luers	Indianapolis Chatard
1984	West Lafayette	Indianapolis Chatard
1985	Fort Wayne Luers	Lawrenceburg
1986	Whitko	Tell City
1987	Rochester	Indianapolis Ritter
1988	Western Boone	South Spencer
1989	Fort Wayne Luers	Tri-West
1990	River Forest	Indianapolis Scecina
1991	Fort Wayne Luers	Indianapolis Scecina
1992	Fort Wayne Luers	Westfield
1993	West Lafayette	Providence
1994	Bremen	Evansville Mater Dei
1995	Bremen	North Montgomery
1996	Fort Wayne Luers	North Montgomery
1997	Jimtown	Clarksville
1998	Jimtown	Western Boone
1999	Fort Wayne Luers	Danville
2000	Fort Wayne Luers	Evansville Mater Dei
2001	Fort Wayne Luers	Evansville Mater Dei
2002	Fort Wayne Luers	Southridge
2003	Harding (Fort Wayne)	Tri-West
2004	Eastbrook	Tri-West
2005	Jimtown	North Posey
2006	Harding (Fort Wayne)	Southridge
2007	Fort Wayne Luers	Heritage Christian
2008	Lewis Cass	Heritage Christian
2009	Fort Wayne Luers	Monrovia
2010	Fort Wayne Luers	North Putnam
2011	Fort Wayne Luers	Evansville Mater Dei
2012	Fort Wayne Luers	Indianapolis Ritter
2013	Tipton	Indianapolis Ritter
2014	Rensselaer Central	Evansville Mater Dei
2015	Whiting	Monrovia
2016	Eastbrook	Indianapolis Ritter
2017	Woodlan	Southridge
2018	Eastbrook	Western Boone

Class 2A State Champions

Year	School	Coach
1973	Greenfield-Central (12-0)	Clayton Myers
1974	Blackford (12-0)	Eldon Leeth
1975	Mishawaka Marian (11-0)	Mike Hecklinski
1976	Mishawaka Marian (12-0)	Mike Hecklinski
1977	Plymouth (13-0)	Bill Nixon
1978	Goshen (12-1)	Ken Mirer
1979	Blackford (13-0)	Charles Lori
1980	Franklin Central (13-0)	Chuck Stephens
1981	Franklin Central (13-1)	Chuck Stephens
1982	Franklin Central (12-2)	Chuck Stephens
1983	Indianapolis Chatard (14-0)	Chuck Schwanekamp
1984	Indianapolis Chatard (13-1)	Chuck Schwanekamp
1985	Fort Wayne Luers (11-3)	Steve Keefer
1986	Whitko (14-0)	Bryan Sprunger
1987	Rochester (12-2)	Mark Miller
1988	Western Boone (13-1)	Jeff Pearson
1989	Fort Wayne Luers (12-2)	Matt Lindsay
1990	Indianapolis Scecina (9-5)	Ott Hurrle
1991	Indianapolis Scecina (11-3)	Ott Hurrle
1992	Fort Wayne Luers (13-1)	Matt Lindsay
1993	West Lafayette (14-0)	Ernie Beck
1994	Bremen (12-2)	Marty Huber
1995	North Montgomery (13-1)	Charley German
1996	North Montgomery (13-1)	Charley German
1997	Jimtown (15-0)	Bill Sharpe
1998	Jimtown (15-0)	Bill Sharpe
1999	Fort Wayne Luers (13-2)	Matt Lindsay
2000	Evansville Mater Dei (15-0)	Mike Goebel
2001	Fort Wayne Luers (14-0)	Matt Lindsay
2002	Fort Wayne Luers (12-3)	Matt Lindsay
2003	Tri-West (14-1)	Mark Haste
2004	Tri-West (15-0)	Mark Haste
2005	Jimtown (14-1)	Bill Sharpe
2006	Harding (Fort Wayne) (12-3)	Sherwood Haydock
2007	Fort Wayne Luers (11-4)	Matt Lindsay
2008	Heritage Christian (14-1)	Ron Qualls
2009	Fort Wayne Luers (10-5)	Matt Lindsay
2010	Fort Wayne Luers (14-1)	Matt Lindsay
2011	Fort Wayne Luers (13-1)	Matt Lindsay
2012	Fort Wayne Luers (11-4)	Steven Keefer
2013	Indianapolis Ritter (13-2)	Ty Hunt
2014	Rensselaer Central (15-0)	Chris Meeks
2015	Monrovia (14-1)	Kevin Hutchins
2016	Indianapolis Ritter (11-4)	Ty Hunt
2017	Southridge (13-2)	Scott Buening
2018	Western Boone (15-0)	Justin Pelley

Class 1A postseason champions
Class 1A Northern Sectionals

Year	Champion
1975	Wes-Del

Year	S9		S10	
1976	Lafayette Central Catholic		Oak Hill	
1977	Seeger		Tippecanoe Valley	
1978	Fountain Central		Tippecanoe Valley	
1979	North Judson		Tippecanoe Valley	
1980	North Judson		Southwood	

Year	S9	S9	S10	S10
1981	North Judson	John Glenn	Woodlan	Woodlan
1981	LaVille	Carroll (Flora)	Adams Central	Oak Hill

Year	Champion	Champion	Champion	Champion
1983	Bremen	Jimtown	Churubusco	Frontier
1984	North Judson	Mishawaka Marian	Adams Central	Carroll (Flora)

Year	S33	S34	S35	S36
1985	North Judson	Jimtown	Winamac	Adams Central
1986	North Judson	Jimtown	Frontier	Adams Central
1987	Bremen	Jimtown	Frontier	Adams Central
1988	Bremen	Churubusco	Frontier	Bluffton
1989	Bremen	South Adams	Tri-County	Southwood
1990	Jimtown	South Adams	Frontier	Southwood
1991	Bremen	Jimtown	Frontier	Tri-Central
1992	Bremen	Jimtown	South Newton	Sheridan
1993	Whiting	Adams Central	North Miami	North Vermillion
1994	North White	Adams Central	North Miami	Rockville
1995	Tri-County	Adams Central	Carroll (Flora)	Seeger
1996	Whiting	South Adams	Carroll (Flora)	Fountain Central
1997	Whiting	Pioneer	Adams Central	Hagerstown
1998	West Central	North White	Adams Central	Frankton
1999	Culver	Lafayette CC	Adams Central	Hagerstown
2000	Culver	North White	Adams Central	Hagerstown
2001	Culver	Southern Wells	Pioneer	Shenandoah
2002	LaVille	Southwood	Pioneer	Eastern Hancock
2003	LaVille	Adams Central	Seeger	Carroll (Flora)
2004	West Central	Adams Central	Seeger	Sheridan
2005	West Central	Adams Central	Lafayette CC	Sheridan
2006	South Newton	Adams Central	Pioneer	Sheridan
2007	Triton	Churubusco	Tri-County	Sheridan
2008	Triton	Southern Wells	Pioneer	Sheridan
2009	Culver	Lafayette CC	Southern Wells	Knightstown
2010	South Central	Lafayette CC	Churubusco	Hagerstown
2011	South Newton	Lafayette CC	Adams Central	Sheridan
2012	Winamac	Lafayette CC	North Miami	Sheridan

Year	S41	S42	S43	S44
2013	Winamac	Pioneer	South Adams	Tri-Central
2014	Winamac	Pioneer	South Adams	Tri-Central
2015	Pioneer	Lafayette CC	Northfield	Adams Central
2016	Pioneer	Lafayette CC	Southwood	Adams Central
2017	LaVille	Pioneer	Southwood	Monroe Central
2018	Triton	Pioneer	Adams Central	Monroe Central

Class 1A Southern Sectionals

Year	Champion			
1975	Lawrenceburg			

Year	S11		S12	
1976	Sheridan		Lawrenceburg	
1977	Indianapolis Ritter		Paoli	
1978	Hamilton Southeastern		Lawrenceburg	
1979	Hamilton Southeastern		Lawrenceburg	
1980	Sheridan		Lawrenceburg	

Year	S11	S11	S12	S12
1981	Hamilton SE	Sheridan	Lawrenceburg	North Posey
1982	Hagerstown	Frankton	North Decatur	Southridge

Year	Champion	Champion	Champion	Champion
1983	Sheridan	Eastern Hancock	Fountain Central	North Daviess
1984	Sheridan	Eastern Hancock	Tri-West	Linton-Stockton

Year	S37	S38	S39	S40
1985	South Putnam	Sheridan	Eastern Hancock	Clarksville
1986	South Putnam	Westfield	Tri	Linton-Stockton
1987	Sheridan	Eastern Hancock	South Putnam	Tecumseh
1988	Sheridan	Eastern Hancock	South Putnam	Springs Valley
1989	Lafayette CC	South Decatur	South Putnam	Springs Valley
1990	Sheridan	South Decatur	North Putnam	Springs Valley
1991	Tri	Ind. Ritter	South Putnam	Tecumseh
1992	Knightstown	Ind. Ritter	Cloverdale	Springs Valley
1993	Tri-West	Hagerstown	West Washington	North Daviess
1994	Sheridan	Hagerstown	West Washington	Tecumseh
1995	Tri-West	Lapel	Milan	Tecumseh
1996	Tri-West	Hagerstown	Milan	Wood Memorial
1997	Clinton Central	Knightstown	Rockville	Linton-Stockton
1998	Sheridan	North Decatur	Fountain Central	Linton-Stockton
1999	Ind. Ritter	Seeger	Clarksville	Perry Central
2000	Clinton Central	Attica	Milan	Perry Central
2001	Frankton	South Putnam	South Decatur	Perry Central
2002	Clinton Central	South Putnam	Park Tudor	Perry Central
2003	Eastern Hancock	Ind. Ritter	Turkey Run	Tecumseh
2004	Shenandoah	Ind. Ritter	Fountain Central	Linton-Stockton
2005	Knightstown	Park Tudor	Riverton Parke	Perry Central
2006	Eastern Hancock	Ind. Ritter	Fountain Central	Perry Central
2007	Ind. Ritter	Tri	Rockville	Linton-Stockton
2008	Ind. Ritter	Lapel	Rockville	Linton-Stockton
2009	Clinton Central	Ind. Lutheran	Fountain Central	Linton-Stockton
2010	Guerin Catholic	Milan	Fountain Central	Perry Central
2011	Ind. Scecina	North Vermillion	Milan	Linton-Stockton
2012	Ind. Scecina	North Vermillion	West Washington	Linton-Stockton

Year	S45	S46	S47	S48
2013	Eastern Hancock	South Putnam	Fountain Central	Linton-Stockton
2014	Eastern Hancock	Ind. Lutheran	North Vermillion	Linton-Stockton
2015	N. Vermillion	Ind. Lutheran	West Washington	Linton-Stockton
2016	Fountain Cent.	Ind. Lutheran	Eastern Greene	Linton-Stockton
2017	Ind. Arlington	Ind. Lutheran	Fountain Central	Eastern Greene
2018	South Putnam	Ind. Lutheran	North Vermillion	North Central (F.)

Class 1A Regionals

Year	Champion	Champion	Champion	Champion
1976	Lafayette Central Catholic		Lawrenceburg	
1977	Tippecanoe Valley		Indianapolis Ritter	
1978	Fountain Central		Lawrenceburg	
1979	Tippecanoe Valley		Hamilton Southeastern	
1980	North Judson		Sheridan	
Year	**Champion**	**Champion**	**Champion**	**Champion**
1981	Hamilton SE	Woodlan	North Judson	North Posey
1982	LaVille	Oak Hill	Hagerstown	Southridge
1983	Jimtown	Churubusco	Sheridan	Fountain Central
1984	North Judson	Adams Central	Sheridan	Tri-West
1985	Jimtown	Adams Central	South Putnam	Eastern Hancock
1986	North Judson	Adams Central	South Putnam	Linton-Stockton
1987	Jimtown	Frontier	Sheridan	South Putnam
1988	Bremen	Bluffton	Sheridan	Springs Valley
1989	Bremen	Southwood	South Decatur	Springs Valley
1990	Jimtown	Southwood	South Decatur	North Putnam
1991	Jimtown	Frontier	Indianapolis Ritter	Tecumseh
1992	Bremen	Sheridan	Indianapolis Ritter	Springs Valley
1993	Adams Central	North Miami	Tri-West	West Washington
1994	North White	North Miami	Sheridan	West Washington
1995	Tri-County	Carroll (Flora)	Tri-West	Tecumseh
1996	Whiting	Carroll (Flora)	Tri-West	Milan
1997	Pioneer	Adams Central	Knightstown	Linton-Stockton
1998	North White	Adams Central	Sheridan	Linton-Stockton
1999	Lafayette CC	Adams Central	Indianapolis Ritter	Perry Central
2000	North White	Adams Central	Attica	Perry Central
2001	Southern Wells	Pioneer	South Putnam	Perry Central
2002	Southwood	Pioneer	South Putnam	Perry Central
2003	Adams Central	Seeger	Indianapolis Ritter	Tecumseh
2004	West Central	Seeger	Indianapolis Ritter	Linton-Stockton
2005	Adams Central	Sheridan	Knightstown	Perry Central
2006	South Newton	Sheridan	Indianapolis Ritter	Perry Central
2007	Churubusco	Sheridan	Indianapolis Ritter	Rockville
2008	Southern Wells	Sheridan	Indianapolis Ritter	Linton-Stockton
2009	Lafayette CC	Southern Wells	Clinton Central	Fountain Central
2010	Lafayette CC	Churubusco	Guerin Catholic	Fountain Central
2011	Lafayette CC	Sheridan	Indpls. Scecina	Linton-Stockton
2012	Lafayette CC	Sheridan	Indpls. Scecina	Linton-Stockton
2013	Winamac	Tri-Central	Eastern Hancock	Linton-Stockton
2014	Pioneer	South Adams	Indpls. Lutheran	North Vermillion
2015	Lafayette CC	Northfield	North Vermillion	Linton-Stockton
2016	Pioneer	Adams Central	Indpls. Lutheran	Linton-Stockton
2017	Pioneer	Monroe Central	Indpls. Lutheran	Eastern Greene
2018	Pioneer	Adams Central	Indpls. Lutheran	North Vermillion

Class 1A Semi-State

Year	North Champion	South Champion
1981	Woodlan	Hamilton Southeastern
1982	Oak Hill	Southridge
1983	Churubusco	Fountain Central
1984	North Judson	Sheridan
1985	Jimtown	Eastern Hancock
1986	North Judson	South Putnam
1987	Jimtown	Sheridan
1988	Bremen	Sheridan
1989	Bremen	Springs Valley
1990	Southwood	South Decatur
1991	Jimtown	Indianapolis Ritter
1992	Sheridan	Indianapolis Ritter
1993	North Miami	West Washington
1994	North White	Sheridan
1995	Carroll (Flora)	Tri-West
1996	Carroll (Flora)	Tri-West
1997	Pioneer	Knightstown
1998	North White	Sheridan
1999	Lafayette Central Catholic	Perry Central
2000	Adams Central	Attica
2001	Southern Wells	Perry Central
2002	Southwood	South Putnam
2003	Seeger	Indianapolis Ritter
2004	Seeger	Indianapolis Ritter
2005	Sheridan	Knightstown
2006	Sheridan	Indianapolis Ritter
2007	Sheridan	Rockville
2008	Sheridan	Indianapolis Ritter
2009	Lafayette Central Catholic	Fountain Central
2010	Lafayette Central Catholic	Fountain Central
2011	Lafayette Central Catholic	Indianapolis Scecina
2012	Lafayette Central Catholic	Indianapolis Scecina
2013	Tri-Central	Eastern Hancock
2014	Pioneer	North Vermillion
2015	Lafayette Central Catholic	Linton-Stockton
2016	Pioneer	Linton-Stockton
2017	Pioneer	Eastern Greene
2018	Pioneer	North Vermillion

Class 1A State Champions

Year	School	Coach
1973	Mishawaka Marian (10-2)	Mike Hecklinski
1974	Garrett (11-0)	Dave Wiant
1975	Lawrenceburg (11-1)	Dick Meador
1976	Lafayette Central Catholic (11-2)	Paul LaRocca
1977	Indianapolis Ritter (11-1)	Jacob "Duffy" Hagist
1978	Lawrenceburg (13-0)	Dick Meador
1979	Tippecanoe Valley (13-0)	Charles Smith
1980	Sheridan (13-0)	Larry "Bud" Wright
1981	Hamilton Southeastern (14-0)	Dave Enright
1982	Oak Hill (13-1)	Terry Lichtenberg
1983	Fountain Central (13-1)	Rick Malone
1984	Sheridan (14-0)	Larry "Bud" Wright
1985	Eastern Hancock (13-1)	Bob Copeland
1986	South Putnam (11-3)	Mark Wildman
1987	Sheridan (12-2)	Larry "Bud" Wright
1988	Sheridan (14-0)	Larry "Bud" Wright
1989	Bremen (11-3)	John Kucela
1990	South Decatur (13-0)	Ken Wendling
1991	Jimtown (12-1)	Bill Sharpe
1992	Sheridan (10-4)	Larry "Bud" Wright
1993	North Miami (11-3)	Bob Bridge
1994	North White (14-0)	Jim Davis
1995	Carroll (Flora) (13-1)	John Hendryx
1996	Tri-West (14-0)	Mark Haste
1997	Pioneer (15-0)	Mike Johnson
1998	Sheridan (14-1)	Larry "Bud" Wright
1999	Lafayette Central Catholic (14-0)	Scott Muncy
2000	Adams Central (12-3)	Rick Minnich
2001	Southern Wells (14-1)	Mark Lefebvre
2002	Southwood (13-1)	Terry Siddall
2003	Indianapolis Ritter (12-2)	Jim Boswell
2004	Seeger (15-0)	Brian Moore
2005	Sheridan (13-2)	Larry "Bud" Wright
2006	Sheridan (15-0)	Larry "Bud" Wright
2007	Sheridan (15-0)	Larry "Bud" Wright
2008	Indianapolis Ritter (15-0)	Ty Hunt
2009	Lafayette Central Catholic (15-0)	Kevin O'Shea
2010	Lafayette Central Catholic (15-0)	Kevin O'Shea
2011	Lafayette Central Catholic (15-0)	Kevin O'Shea
2012	Lafayette Central Catholic (14-1)	Kevin O'Shea
2013	Tri-Central (14-1)	George Gilbert
2014	North Vermillion (15-0)	Brian Crabtree
2015	Lafayette Central Catholic (15-0)	Kevin O'Shea
2016	Linton-Stockton (15-0)	Brian Oliver
2017	Pioneer (15-0)	Adam Berry
2018	Pioneer (15-0)	Adam Berry

Most times qualifying for playoffs

From 1973 to 1984, the Indiana High School Athletic Association had a qualification process for teams to participate in the postseason. During that 12-year period, here is a list of how many times each playoff participant qualified:

Team	#	Team	#	Team	#
Lawrenceburg	7	Hagerstown	2	Jimtown	1
Carmel	6	Hammond	2	John Glenn	1
Hobart	6	Indianapolis Cathedral	2	Kankakee Valley	1
Jasper	5	Indpls. Washington	2	Lafayette CC	1
Sheridan	5	Lafayette Jefferson	2	LaVille	1
Indianapolis Chatard	4	Mishawaka	2	Linton-Stockton	1
Martinsville	4	North Central (Indpls.)	2	Merrillville	1
Mishawaka Marian	4	NorthWood	2	Michigan City Elston	1
North Judson	4	Norwell	2	Mississinewa	1
Tippecanoe Valley	4	Penn	2	Mitchell	1
Blackford	3	Portage	2	Mooresville	1
Brownsburg	3	Providence	2	New Albany	1
Castle	3	South Bend St. Joseph	2	New Haven	1
Fort Wayne Dwenger	3	SB Washington	2	Noblesville	1
Franklin Central	3	Tell City	2	North Daviess	1
Hamilton Southeastern	3	Woodlan	2	North Decatur	1
McCutcheon	3	Anderson Highland	1	North Knox	1
Oak Hill	3	Avon	1	North Posey	1
Roncalli	3	Ben Davis	1	Paoli	1
Adams Central	2	Bloomington South	1	Peru	1
Boonville	2	Bremen	1	Plymouth	1
Carroll (Flora)	2	Churubusco	1	Rushville	1
Columbus East	2	Crawfordsville	1	Seeger	1
Concord	2	Delphi	1	Southridge	1
Delta	2	East Central	1	Southwood	1
Eastern Hancock	2	Fort Wayne North	1	Tri-West	1
Evansville Mater Dei	2	Franklin	1	Twin Lakes	1
Evansville Reitz	2	Frankton	1	Valparaiso	1
Fort Wayne Luers	2	Frontier	1	Vincennes Lincoln	1
Fort Wayne Snider	2	Garrett	1	Warren Central	1
Fountain Central	2	Harrison (W.L.)	1	Wes-Del	1
Goshen	2	Highland	1	West Lafayette	1
Greenfield-Central	2	Indianapolis Marshall	1	Western	1
Griffith	2	Indianapolis Ritter	1	Yorktown	1

IHSAA Football State Tournament records & championships by school

Here is a list of every football-playing school that has participated in the IHSAA Football State Tournament, along with the total number of tournament games played, their win/loss record and championships won.

(x) indicates a school that has closed, consolidated or no longer participates.

Team	Total	W-L	Championships Sect.	Reg.	Semi.	State
Adams Central	118	83-35	20	12	1	1
Alexandria	47	12-35	0	0	0	0
Anderson						
Anderson	44	9-35	0	0	0	0
x Highland	36	10-26	1	0	0	0
x Madison-Hts.	15	3-12	0	0	0	0
Prep Academy	4	0-4	0	0	0	0
Andrean	114	82-32	17	8	6	2
Angola	54	19-35	2	0	0	0
Attica	67	30-37	1	1	1	0
Avon	86	51-35	9	6	0	0

Team	Total	W-L	Championships Sect.	Reg.	Semi.	State
Batesville	78	43-35	9	1	0	0
Bedford North Lawrence	46	11-35	1	0	0	0
Beech Grove	48	14-34	0	0	0	0
Bellmont	70	36-34	3	1	1	1
Ben Davis	131	105-26	22	17	11	9
Benton Central	46	12-34	0	0	0	0
Blackford	55	16-39	2	1	0	2
Bloomington						
North	53	19-34	2	1	0	0
South	97	63-34	14	10	3	2
Bluffton	56	21-35	1	1	0	0
Boone Grove	15	7-8	0	0	0	0
Boonville	57	21-36	2	1	0	0
Bowman Academy	14	5-9	0	0	0	0
x Brazil	1	0-1	0	0	0	0
Brebeuf Jesuit	64	30-34	3	2	2	0
Bremen	104	69-35	15	8	4	2
x Brookville	5	1-4	0	0	0	0
Brown County	51	17-34	1	0	0	0
Brownsburg	72	36-36	5	3	2	2
Brownstown Central	93	57-36	13	3	0	0

Team	Total	W-L	Championships Sect.	Reg.	Semi.	State
Calumet	44	10-34	0	0	0	0
Cambridge City Lincoln	44	10-34	0	0	0	0
Carmel	159	125-34	30	21	12	8
Carroll (Flora)	76	41-35	5	2	2	1
Carroll (Fort Wayne)	64	30-34	5	0	0	0
Cascade	52	18-34	1	0	0	0
Castle	93	55-38	13	5	2	2
Caston	46	12-34	0	0	0	0
Center Grove	99	67-32	14	13	4	2
Centerville	44	10-34	0	0	0	0
Central Noble	59	23-36	3	1	0	0
Charlestown	66	31-35	5	1	0	0
Chesterton	53	19-34	0	0	0	0
Churubusco	74	39-35	4	3	1	0

The Complete History of the the Indiana High School Football State Tournament

Team	Total	W-L	Championships			
			Sect.	Reg.	Semi.	State
Clarksville	56	21-35	3	1	1	0
Clinton Central	67	33-34	4	1	0	0
Clinton Prairie	57	23-34	0	0	0	0
Cloverdale	49	15-34	1	0	0	0
Columbia City	63	28-35	1	0	0	0
Columbus						
East	106	70-36	13	11	3	3
North	65	31-34	4	3	0	0
Concord	91	53-38	10	5	3	0
Connersville	39	5-34	0	0	0	0
Corydon Central	47	13-34	1	1	0	0
Covenant Christian	5	1-4	0	0	0	0
Covington	42	8-34	0	0	0	0
Crawford County	12	0-12	0	0	0	0
Crawfordsville	55	18-37	2	2	0	0
Crown Point	75	40-35	7	1	0	0
Culver						
Culver High	57	23-34	4	0	0	0
Military Academy	61	27-34	2	0	0	0

Team	Total	W-L	Championships			
			Sect.	Reg.	Semi.	State
Danville	92	57-35	8	4	1	0
Decatur Central	65	31-34	2	1	1	0
DeKalb	66	32-34	5	2	2	1
Delphi	57	22-35	1	0	0	0
Delta	93	55-38	9	3	1	0

Team	Total	W-L	Championships			
			Sect.	Reg.	Semi.	State
East Central	116	83-33	19	8	4	2
East Chicago						
Central	49	17-32	1	1	0	0
x Roosevelt	1	0-1	0	0	0	0
x Washington	1	0-1	0	0	0	0
East Noble	60	27-33	3	2	2	1
Eastbrook	97	63-34	14	6	3	0
Eastern (Greentown)	45	9-36	0	0	0	0
Eastern (Pekin)	16	4-12	0	0	0	0
Eastern Greene	27	11-16	2	1	1	0
Eastern Hancock	82	46-36	10	2	2	1
Eastside	51	17-34	0	0	0	0
Edgewood	70	32-38	1	0	0	0
Edinburgh	41	7-34	0	0	0	0
Elkhart						
Central	52	18-34	1	0	0	0
Memorial	53	19-34	1	0	0	0
Elwood	59	25-34	2	1	1	0
Evansville						
Bosse	67	33-34	4	0	0	0
Central	70	36-34	4	1	1	0
Harrison	70	36-34	6	0	0	0
Mater Dei	131	96-35	20	12	5	1
Memorial	106	74-32	13	9	4	1
North	63	29-34	5	1	1	0
Reitz	104	70-34	16	6	2	2

Team	Total	W-L	Championships			
			Sect.	Reg.	Semi.	State
Fairfield	55	21-34	1	0	0	0
Fishers	33	21-12	3	1	1	1
Floyd Central	64	30-34	2	0	0	0
Forest Park	13	2-11	0	0	0	0
Fort Wayne						
Concordia	72	39-33	4	3	1	1
Dwenger	148	115-33	25	21	10	5
x Elmhurst	26	1-25	0	0	0	0
Luers	156	131-25	24	19	15	11
North	57	22-35	3	1	0	0
Northrop	51	16-35	1	1	0	0
Snider	141	106-35	27	16	7	2
South	64	31-33	2	1	0	0
Wayne	79	46-33	6	5	2	1
Fountain Central	90	52-38	11	4	3	1
Frankfort	55	21-34	3	0	0	0
Franklin	46	10-36	1	0	0	0
Franklin Central	93	59-34	9	7	6	4
Franklin County	70	40-30	5	3	1	0
Frankton	70	35-35	3	0	0	0
Fremont	49	14-35	0	0	0	0
Frontier	72	36-36	6	2	0	0
			Championships			
	Total	W-L	Sect.	Reg.	Semi.	State
Garrett	68	34-34	3	2	0	1
Gary						
x Mann	20	1-19	0	0	0	0
Roosevelt	38	4-34	0	0	0	0
x Wallace	39	10-29	1	0	0	0
West	44	10-34	0	0	0	0
x Wirt	27	3-24	0	0	0	0
Gibson Southern	72	38-34	3	3	0	0
Goshen	78	43-35	7	5	3	2
Greencastle	56	22-34	2	1	0	0
Greenfield-Central	57	21-36	1	0	0	1
Greensburg	63	29-34	2	0	0	0
Greenwood	78	44-34	5	3	0	0
Griffith	111	75-36	15	5	1	1
Guerin Catholic	36	23-13	4	2	0	0
			Championships			
	Total	W-L	Sect.	Reg.	Semi.	State
Hagerstown	87	51-36	10	2	0	0
x Hamilton	1	0-1	0	0	0	0
Hamilton Heights	82	47-35	7	2	1	0
Hamilton Southeastern	89	51-38	10	4	3	1
Hammond						
Hammond High	72	34-38	4	1	0	0
Clark	45	11-34	0	0	0	0
Gavit	52	17-35	2	0	0	0
Morton	69	35-34	4	1	0	0
x Noll	60	26-34	1	1	1	1
Hanover Central	6	2-4	0	0	0	0
x Harding (Fort Wayne)	69	44-25	6	5	2	1
Harrison (West Lafayette)	76	42-34	7	4	1	1
Heritage	62	28-34	3	0	0	0
Heritage Christian	37	21-16	2	2	2	1
Heritage Hills	106	73-33	12	9	2	1

Team	Total	W-L	Championships			
			Sect.	Reg.	Semi.	State
Highland	61	25-36	3	1	1	0
Hobart	131	95-36	20	14	9	4
Homestead	79	44-35	5	2	1	0
x Howe Military	1	0-1	0	0	0	0
Huntington North	48	14-34	1	0	0	0
			Championships			
	Total	W-L	Sect.	Reg.	Semi.	State
Indian Creek	68	33-35	3	1	0	0
Indiana Deaf	34	5-29	0	0	0	0
Indianapolis						
x Arlington	43	13-30	3	0	0	0
x Broad Ripple	43	10-33	0	0	0	0
Cathedral	144	119-25	22	18	13	12
Chatard	152	125-27	27	19	14	13
Crispus Attucks	2	0-2	0	0	0	0
Howe	39	14-25	1	1	0	0
Lutheran	41	28-13	6	4	0	0
Manual	38	7-31	0	0	0	0
x Marshall	9	2-7	1	0	0	0
x Northwest	44	11-33	0	0	0	0
Ritter	117	87-30	16	14	10	4
Scecina	101	69-32	11	7	4	2
Shortridge	8	2-6	0	0	0	0
Tech	42	8-34	0	0	0	0
Tindley	7	1-6	0	0	0	0
Washington	44	20-24	4	3	1	1
			Championships			
	Total	W-L	Sect.	Reg.	Semi.	State
Jasper	112	74-38	13	11	3	1
Jay County	51	17-34	1	0	0	0
Jeffersonville	62	27-35	4	0	0	0
Jennings County	40	6-34	0	0	0	0
Jimtown	135	102-33	22	12	6	4
John Glenn	63	28-35	3	1	0	0
			Championships			
	Total	W-L	Sect.	Reg.	Semi.	State
Kankakee Valley	51	16-35	2	0	0	0
Knightstown	75	40-35	4	2	2	0
Knox	50	16-34	0	0	0	0
Kokomo	60	26-34	4	2	1	0
			Championships			
	Total	W-L	Sect.	Reg.	Semi.	State
Lafayette						
Central Catholic	104	76-28	11	8	6	7
Jefferson	72	33-39	5	0	0	0
Lake Central	70	36-34	5	2	1	0
Lake Station	47	13-34	2	0	0	0
Lakeland	48	12-36	0	0	0	0
Lapel	61	26-35	8	0	0	0
LaPorte	59	25-34	2	2	1	0
LaVille	68	33-35	4	1	0	0
Lawrence						
Central	79	46-33	6	2	2	1
North	58	23-35	3	0	0	0
Lawrenceburg	109	70-39	18	5	2	2
Lebanon	48	14-34	1	0	0	0
Leo	64	29-35	3	2	0	0

Team	Total	W-L	Championships			
			Sect.	Reg.	Semi.	State
Lewis Cass	86	51-35	7	4	1	0
Linton-Stockton	104	69-35	14	10	2	1
Logansport	54	20-34	3	1	0	0
Lowell	100	67-33	15	9	4	1
	Total	W-L	Championships			
			Sect.	Reg.	Semi.	State
Maconaquah	45	11-34	0	0	0	0
Madison	41	7-34	0	0	0	0
Madison-Grant	55	21-34	2	0	0	0
Manchester	56	22-34	3	0	0	0
Marion	66	32-34	4	3	2	0
Martinsville	70	31-39	7	2	0	0
McCutcheon	69	32-37	6	1	1	0
Merrillville	93	57-36	11	6	0	1
Michigan City						
Michigan City	37	13-24	2	2	0	0
x Elston	16	4-12	1	0	0	0
x Rogers	13	3-10	0	0	0	0
Milan	72	37-35	6	1	0	0
Mishawaka						
Mishawaka	97	59-38	11	3	1	0
Marian	80	45-35	9	5	0	3
Mississinewa	67	32-35	5	1	0	0
Mitchell	47	12-35	1	0	0	0
Monroe Central	23	12-11	2	1	0	0
Monrovia	77	43-34	5	4	2	1
Mooresville	70	35-35	6	1	0	0
Mount Vernon	56	22-34	2	0	0	0
Mount Vernon (Fortville)	66	32-34	4	0	0	0
Muncie						
Central	58	24-34	4	0	0	0
x North	6	2-4	0	0	0	0
x South	51	22-29	2	0	0	0
Munster	70	34-36	4	1	0	0
	Total	W-L	Championships			
			Sect.	Reg.	Semi.	State
New Albany	47	12-35	2	0	0	0
New Castle	41	5-36	0	0	0	0
New Haven	76	37-39	7	1	0	0
New Palestine	93	59-34	10	6	4	2
New Prairie	69	35-34	5	2	1	0
Noblesville	62	25-37	3	2	0	0
North Central (Farm.)	50	16-34	1	0	0	0
North Central (Indpls.)	80	40-40	4	1	0	0
North Daviess	60	25-35	2	0	0	0
North Decatur	52	17-35	2	0	0	0
North Harrison	46	12-34	0	0	0	0
North Judson	98	58-40	12	5	2	0
North Knox	47	12-35	0	0	0	0
North Miami	65	32-33	4	2	1	1
North Montgomery	74	42-32	3	2	2	2
North Newton	56	20-36	3	1	0	0
North Posey	75	39-36	4	4	1	0
North Putnam	70	35-35	4	3	1	0
North Vermillion	78	45-33	6	3	2	1
North White	64	31-33	3	3	2	1
Northeastern	50	16-34	0	0	0	0

Team	Total	W-L	Championships			
			Sect.	Reg.	Semi.	State
Northfield	49	14-35	1	1	0	0
Northridge	52	18-34	1	1	0	0
Northview	41	7-34	0	0	0	0
Northwestern	67	33-34	4	1	1	0
NorthWood	131	95-36	18	11	6	1
Norwell	81	45-36	8	2	2	0

Team	Total	W-L	Championships			
			Sect.	Reg.	Semi.	State
Oak Hill	66	28-38	5	1	1	1
Oldenburg Academy	5	1-4	0	0	0	0
Owen Valley	43	9-34	1	0	0	0

Team	Total	W-L	Championships			
			Sect.	Reg.	Semi.	State
Paoli	65	28-37	4	2	0	0
Park Tudor	55	23-32	2	0	0	0
Parke Heritage	2	1-1	0	0	0	0
Pendleton Heights	60	26-34	2	0	0	0
Penn	153	118-35	24	18	12	5
Perry Central	83	49-34	7	6	2	0
Perry Meridian	58	24-34	1	1	0	0
Peru	53	16-37	1	1	0	0
Pike	62	27-35	3	1	1	0
Pike Central	35	1-34	0	0	0	0
Pioneer	97	66-31	11	7	5	2
Plainfield	58	22-36	1	1	1	0
Plymouth	83	48-35	5	4	0	1
Portage	77	40-37	8	2	1	1
Prairie Heights	42	7-35	0	0	0	0
Princeton	49	15-34	1	0	0	0
Providence	86	45-41	6	1	1	0

Team	Total	W-L	Championships			
			Sect.	Reg.	Semi.	State
Rensselaer Central	92	58-34	10	4	1	1
Richmond	62	23-39	2	0	0	0
River Forest	53	19-34	2	1	1	0
Riverton Parke	44	12-32	1	0	0	0
Rochester	76	43-33	5	2	1	1
Rock Creek Academy	1	0-1	0	0	0	0
x Rockville	65	31-34	4	1	1	0
Roncalli	135	106-29	19	15	12	9
Rushville	51	16-35	1	0	0	0

Team	Total	W-L	Championships			
			Sect.	Reg.	Semi.	State
Salem	59	25-34	1	0	0	0
Scottsburg	2	0-2	0	0	0	0
Seeger	67	33-34	6	2	2	1
Seymour	71	34-37	4	2	1	0
Shelbyville	55	20-35	0	0	0	0
Shenandoah	81	47-34	5	0	0	0
Sheridan	128	98-30	19	14	10	9
Silver Creek	13	5-8	0	0	0	0
South Adams	69	35-34	7	2	0	0
South Bend						
Adams	54	20-34	0	0	0	0
Clay	59	25-34	1	1	0	0
x LaSalle	22	5-17	0	0	0	0
Riley	49	15-34	1	0	0	0

School	Total	W-L	Sect.	Reg.	Semi.	State
South Bend						
St. Joseph	104	68-36	10	7	4	1
Washington	63	28-35	2	1	1	1
South Central (U.M.)	54	20-34	1	0	0	0
South Dearborn	46	12-34	0	0	0	0
South Decatur	60	27-33	3	2	1	1
South Newton	61	26-35	3	1	0	0
South Putnam	90	57-33	11	5	2	1
South Spencer	73	38-35	2	2	1	0
South Vermillion	40	6-34	0	0	0	0
Southern Wells	71	38-33	3	3	1	1
Southmont	54	20-34	0	0	0	0
Southport	60	26-34	4	1	0	0
Southridge	91	56-35	9	6	4	1
Southwood	85	51-34	8	5	2	1
Speedway	82	47-35	8	3	0	0
Springs Valley	72	37-35	4	3	1	0
Sullivan	51	17-34	0	0	0	0
Switzerland County	4	0-4	0	0	0	0

School	Total	W-L	Sect.	Reg.	Semi.	State
Taylor	43	9-34	0	0	0	0
Tecumseh	71	35-36	5	3	0	0
Tell City	80	41-39	9	4	1	0
Terre Haute						
North	66	32-34	3	1	0	0
South	50	16-34	2	1	0	0
Tippecanoe Valley	66	28-38	5	2	0	1
Tipton	89	55-34	9	3	3	0
Traders Point Christian	3	2-1	0	0	0	0
Tri	67	32-35	3	0	0	0
Tri-Central	54	21-33	3	1	1	1
Tri-County	55	21-34	3	1	0	0
Trinity Lutheran	2	0-2	0	0	0	0
Triton	56	22-34	3	0	0	0
Triton Central	68	34-34	4	0	0	0
Tri-West	103	70-33	12	9	6	4
x Turkey Run	45	12-33	1	0	0	0
Twin Lakes	73	37-36	5	0	0	0

School	Total	W-L	Sect.	Reg.	Semi.	State
x Union (Dugger)	34	5-29	0	0	0	0
Union City	49	15-34	0	0	0	0
Union County	43	9-34	0	0	0	0

School	Total	W-L	Sect.	Reg.	Semi.	State
Valparaiso	93	58-35	11	7	2	1
Vincennes Lincoln	71	35-36	6	1	0	0

School	Total	W-L	Sect.	Reg.	Semi.	State
Wabash	40	6-34	0	0	0	0
Warren Central	116	90-26	18	9	9	9
Warsaw	47	13-34	0	0	0	0
Washington	48	14-34	0	0	0	0
Wawasee	56	21-35	2	2	2	0
Wes-Del	45	9-36	1	0	0	0
West Central	57	23-34	3	1	0	0
West Lafayette	102	69-33	14	9	5	3
West Noble	45	9-36	0	0	0	0

Team	Total	W-L	Championships			
			Sect.	Reg.	Semi.	State
West Vigo	51	17-34	1	0	0	0
West Washington	70	36-34	4	2	1	0
Western	69	32-37	2	0	0	0
Western Boone	92	60-32	9	5	3	2
Westfield	79	45-34	9	4	3	1
Wheeler	34	15-19	2	0	0	0
Whiteland	65	31-34	5	1	0	0
Whiting	83	48-35	6	3	1	0
Whitko	57	24-33	1	1	1	1
Winamac	73	38-35	6	2	0	0
Winchester	49	15-34	1	0	0	0
Wood Memorial	42	10-32	1	0	0	0
Woodlan	77	40-37	5	4	2	0

	Total	W-L	Championships			
			Sect.	Reg.	Semi.	State
Yorktown	73	38-35	4	0	0	0

	Total	W-L	Championships			
			Sect.	Reg.	Semi.	State
Zionsville	99	67-32	14	3	3	2

Most tournament games played (at least 100)			
No.	School (W-L)	No.	School (W-L)
159	Carmel (125-34)	116	Warren Central (90-26)
156	Fort Wayne Luers (131-25)	114	Andrean (82-32)
153	Penn (118-35)	112	Jasper (74-38)
152	Indianapolis Chatard (125-27)	111	Griffith (75-36)
148	Fort Wayne Dwenger (115-33)	109	Lawrenceburg (70-39)
144	Indianapolis Cathedral (119-25)	106	Columbus East (70-36)
141	Fort Wayne Snider (106-35)		Evansville Memorial (74-32)
135	Jimtown (102-33)		Heritage Hills (73-33)
	Roncalli (106-29)	104	Bremen (69-35)
131	Ben Davis (105-26)		Evansville Reitz (70-34)
	Evansville Mater Dei (96-35)		Lafayette Central Catholic (76-28)
	Hobart (95-36)		Linton-Stockton (69-35)
	NorthWood (95-36)		South Bend St. Joseph (68-36)
128	Sheridan (98-30)	103	Tri-West (70-33)
118	Adams Central (83-35)	102	West Lafayette (69-33)
117	Indianapolis Ritter (87-30)	101	Indianapolis Scecina (69-32)
116	East Central (83-33)	100	Lowell (67-33)

Most tournament wins (at least 100)			
Wins	School (W-L)	Wins	School (W-L)
131	Fort Wayne Luers (131-25)	115	Fort Wayne Dwenger (115-33)
125	Carmel (125-34)	106	Fort Wayne Snider (106-35)
	Indianapolis Chatard (125-27)		Roncalli (106-29)
119	Indianapolis Cathedral (119-25)	105	Ben Davis (105-26)
118	Penn (118-35)	102	Jimtown (102-33)

Best tournament win percentage (.667 or better)			
Pct.	School (W-L)		
.840	Fort Wayne Luers (131-25)	.725	NorthWood (95-36)
.826	Indianapolis Cathedral (119-25)	.719	Andrean (82-32)
.822	Indianapolis Chatard (125-27)	.716	East Central (83-33)
.802	Ben Davis (105-26)	.703	Adams Central (83-35)
.786	Carmel (125-34)	.698	Evansville Memorial (74-32)
.785	Roncalli (106-29)	.689	Heritage Hills (73-33)
.777	Fort Wayne Dwenger (115-33)	.684	Pioneer (67-31)
.776	Warren Central (90-26)	.683	Indianapolis Scecina (69-32)
.771	Penn (118-35)	.683	Indianapolis Lutheran (28-13)
.766	Sheridan (98-30)	.680	Tri-West (70-33)
.756	Jimtown (102-33)	.677	Center Grove (67-32)
.752	Fort Wayne Snider (106-35)	.677	Zionsville (67-32)
.744	Indianapolis Ritter (87-30)	.676	West Lafayette (69-33)
.733	Evansville Mater Dei (96-35)	.676	Griffith (75-36)
.731	Lafayette Central Catholic (76-28)	.673	Evansville Reitz (70-34)
.725	Hobart (95-36)	.670	Lowell (67-33)
		.667	Traders Point Christian (2-1)

Most sectional championships			
No.	School		
30	Carmel		Mishawaka Marian
27	Fort Wayne Snider		Southridge
	Indianapolis Chatard		Tell City
25	Fort Wayne Dwenger		Tipton
24	Fort Wayne Luers		Western Boone
	Penn		Westfield
22	Ben Davis	8	Danville
	Indianapolis Cathedral		Lapel
	Jimtown		Norwell
20	Adams Central		Portage
	Evansville Mater Dei		Southwood
	Hobart		Speedway
19	East Central	7	Crown Point
	Roncalli		Goshen
	Sheridan		Hamilton Heights
18	Lawrenceburg		Harrison (West Lafayette)
	NorthWood		Lewis Cass
	Warren Central		Martinsville
17	Andrean		New Haven
16	Evansville Reitz		Perry Central
	Indianapolis Ritter		South Adams
15	Bremen	6	Evansville Harrison
	Griffith		Fort Wayne Wayne
	Lowell		Frontier
14	Bloomington South		Harding (Fort Wayne)
	Center Grove		Indianapolis Lutheran
	Eastbrook		Lawrence Central
	Linton-Stockton		McCutcheon
	West Lafayette		Milan
	Zionsville		Mooresville
13	Brownstown Central		North Vermillion
	Castle		Providence
	Columbus East		Seeger
	Evansville Memorial		Vincennes Lincoln
	Jasper		Whiting
12	Heritage Hills		Winamac
	North Judson	5	Brownsburg
	Tri-West		Carroll (Flora)
11	Fountain Central		Carroll (Fort Wayne)
	Indianapolis Scecina		Charlestown
	Lafayette Central Catholic		DeKalb
	Merrillville		Evansville North
	Mishawaka		Franklin County
	Pioneer		Greenwood
	South Putnam		Homestead
	Valparaiso		Lafayette Jefferson
10	Concord		Lake Central
	Eastern Hancock		Mississinewa
	Hagerstown		Monrovia
	Hamilton Southeastern		New Prairie
	New Palestine		Oak Hill
	Rensselaer Central		Plymouth
	South Bend St. Joseph		Rochester
9	Avon		Shenandoah
	Batesville		Tecumseh
	Delta		Tippecanoe Valley
	Franklin Central		Twin Lakes
			Whiteland

4	Woodlan Churubusco Clinton Central Columbus North Culver Evansville Bosse Evansville Central Fort Wayne Concordia Guerin Catholic Hammond Hammond Morton Indianapolis Washington Jeffersonville Knightstown Kokomo LaVille Marion Mount Vernon (Fortville) Muncie Central Munster North Central (Indianapolis) North Miami North Posey North Putnam Northwestern Paoli Rockville Seymour Southport Springs Valley Triton Central West Washington Yorktown		South Newton Southern Wells Terre Haute North Tri Tri-Central Tri-County Triton West Central
3	Bellmont Brebeuf Jesuit Central Noble Clarksville East Noble Fishers Fort Wayne North Frankfort Frankton Garrett Gibson Southern Heritage Highland Indian Creek Indianapolis Arlington John Glenn Lawrence North Leo Logansport Manchester Noblesville North Montgomery North Newton North White Pike South Decatur	2	Angola Blackford Bloomington North Boonville Crawfordsville Culver Military Academy Decatur Central Eastern Greene Elwood Floyd Central Fort Wayne South Greencastle Greensburg Hammond Gavit Heritage Christian Kankakee Valley Lake Station LaPorte Madison-Grant Michigan City Monroe Central Mount Vernon Muncie South New Albany North Daviess North Decatur Park Tudor Pendleton Heights Richmond River Forest South Bend Washington South Spencer Terre Haute South Wawasee Western Wheeler
		1	Anderson Highland Attica Bedford North Lawrence Bluffton Brown County Cascade Cloverdale Columbia City Corydon Central Delphi East Chicago Central Edgewood Elkhart Central Elkhart Memorial Fairfield

Fort Wayne Northrop
Franklin
Gary Wallace
Greenfield-Central
Hammond Noll
Huntington North
Indianapolis Howe
Indianapolis Marshall
Jay County
Lebanon
Michigan City Elston
Mitchell
North Central (Farmersburg)
Northfield
Northridge
Owen Valley
Perry Meridian
Peru
Plainfield
Princeton
Riverton Parke
Rushville
Salem
South Bend Clay
South Bend Riley
South Central (Union Mills)
Turkey Run
Wes-Del
West Vigo
Whitko
Winchester
Wood Memorial

Most regional championships

No.	School
21	Carmel
	Fort Wayne Dwenger
19	Fort Wayne Luers
	Indianapolis Chatard
18	Indianapolis Cathedral
	Penn
17	Ben Davis
16	Fort Wayne Snider
15	Roncalli
14	Hobart
	Indianapolis Ritter
	Sheridan
13	Center Grove
12	Adams Central
	Evansville Mater Dei
	Jimtown
11	Columbus East
	Jasper
	NorthWood
10	Bloomington South
	Linton-Stockton
9	Evansville Memorial
	Heritage Hills
	Lowell
	Tri-West
	Warren Central
	West Lafayette
8	Andrean
	Bremen
	East Central
	Lafayette Central Catholic
7	Franklin Central
	Indianapolis Scecina
	Pioneer
	South Bend St. Joseph
	Valparaiso
6	Avon
	Eastbrook
	Evansville Reitz
	Merrillville
	New Palestine
	Perry Central
	Southridge
5	Castle
	Concord
	Fort Wayne Wayne
	Goshen
	Griffith
	Harding (Fort Wayne)
	Lawrenceburg
	Mishawaka Marian
	North Judson
	South Putnam
	Southwood
	Western Boone
4	Danville
	Fountain Central
	Hamilton Southeastern
	Harrison (West Lafayette)
	Indianapolis Lutheran
	Lewis Cass
	Monrovia
	North Posey
	Plymouth
	Rensselaer Central
	Tell City
	Westfield
	Woodlan
3	Brownsburg
	Brownstown Central
	Churubusco
	Columbus North
	Delta
	Fort Wayne Concordia
	Franklin County
	Gibson Southern
	Greenwood
	Indianapolis Washington
	Marion
	Mishawaka
	North Putnam

	North Vermillion	Clarksville
	North White	Clinton Central
	Southern Wells	Corydon Central
	Speedway	Crown Point
	Springs Valley	Decatur Central
	Tecumseh	East Chicago Central
	Tipton	Eastern Greene
	Whiting	Elwood
	Zionsville	Evansville Central
2	Brebeuf Jesuit	Evansville North
	Carroll (Flora)	Fishers
	Crawfordsville	Fort Wayne North
	DeKalb	Fort Wayne Northrop
	East Noble	Fort Wayne South
	Eastern Hancock	Greencastle
	Frontier	Hammond
	Garrett	Hammond Morton
	Guerin Catholic	Hammond Noll
	Hagerstown	Highland
	Hamilton Heights	Indian Creek
	Heritage Christian	Indianapolis Howe
	Homestead	John Glenn
	Knightstown	LaVille
	Kokomo	Logansport
	Lake Central	McCutcheon
	LaPorte	Milan
	Lawrence Central	Mississinewa
	Leo	Monroe Central
	Martinsville	Mooresville
	Michigan City	Munster
	New Prairie	New Haven
	Noblesville	North Central (Indianapolis)
	North Miami	North Newton
	North Montgomery	Northfield
	Norwell	Northridge
	Paoli	Northwestern
	Portage	Oak Hill
	Rochester	Perry Meridian
	Seeger	Peru
	Seymour	Pike
	South Adams	Plainfield
	South Decatur	Providence
	South Spencer	River Forest
	Tippecanoe Valley	Rockville
	Wawasee	South Bend Clay
	West Washington	South Bend Washington
	Winamac	South Newton
1	Attica	Southport
	Batesville	Terre Haute North
	Bellmont	Terre Haute South
	Blackford	Tri-Central
	Bloomington North	Tri-County
	Bluffton	Vincennes Lincoln
	Boonville	West Central
	Central Noble	Whiteland
	Charlestown	Whitko

Most semi-state championships

No.	School
15	Fort Wayne Luers
14	Indianapolis Chatard
13	Indianapolis Cathedral
12	Carmel
	Penn
	Roncalli
11	Ben Davis
10	Fort Wayne Dwenger
	Indianapolis Ritter
	Sheridan
9	Hobart
	Warren Central
7	Fort Wayne Snider
6	Andrean
	Franklin Central
	Jimtown
	Lafayette Central Catholic
	NorthWood
	Tri-West
5	Evansville Mater Dei
	Pioneer
	West Lafayette
4	Bremen
	Center Grove
	East Central
	Evansville Memorial
	Indianapolis Scecina
	Lowell
	New Palestine
	South Bend St. Joseph
	Southridge
3	Bloomington South
	Columbus East
	Concord
	Eastbrook
	Fountain Central
	Goshen
	Hamilton Southeastern
	Jasper
	Tipton
	Western Boone
	Westfield
	Zionsville
2	Brebeuf Jesuit
	Brownsburg
	Carroll (Flora)
	Castle
	DeKalb
	East Noble
	Eastern Hancock
	Evansville Reitz
	Fort Wayne Wayne
	Harding (Fort Wayne)
	Heritage Christian
	Heritage Hills
	Knightstown
	Lawrence Central
	Lawrenceburg
	Linton-Stockton
	Marion
	Monrovia
	North Judson
	North Montgomery
	North Vermillion
	North White
	Norwell
	Perry Central
	Seeger
	South Putnam
	Southwood
	Valparaiso
	Wawasee
	Woodlan
1	Adams Central
	Attica
	Bellmont
	Churubusco
	Clarksville
	Danville
	Decatur Central
	Delta
	Eastern Greene
	Elwood
	Evansville Central
	Evansville North
	Fishers
	Fort Wayne Concordia
	Franklin County
	Griffith
	Hamilton Heights
	Hammond Noll
	Harrison (West Lafayette)
	Highland
	Homestead
	Indianapolis Washington
	Kokomo
	Lake Central
	LaPorte
	Lewis Cass
	McCutcheon
	Mishawaka
	New Prairie
	North Miami
	North Posey
	North Putnam
	Northwestern
	Oak Hill
	Pike
	Plainfield
	Portage
	Providence
	Rensselaer Central
	River Forest
	Rochester
	Rockville

Seymour
South Bend Washington
South Decatur
South Spencer
Southern Wells
Springs Valley

Tell City
Tri-Central
West Washington
Whiting
Whitko

Most IHSAA state championships

No.	School	6A	5A	4A	3A	2A	1A
13	Indianapolis Chatard	0	0	0	11	2	0
12	Indianapolis Cathedral	0	2	8	2	0	0
11	Fort Wayne Luers	0	0	0	0	11	0
9	Ben Davis	2	7	0	0	0	0
	Roncalli	0	0	4	5	0	0
	Sheridan	0	0	0	0	0	9
	Warren Central	2	6	1	0	0	0
8	Carmel	1	4	0	3	0	0
7	Lafayette Central Catholic	0	0	0	0	0	7
5	Fort Wayne Dwenger	0	0	2	3	0	0
	Penn	0	4	1	0	0	0
4	Franklin Central	0	0	1	0	3	0
	Hobart	0	0	4	0	0	0
	Indianapolis Ritter	0	0	0	0	2	2
	Jimtown	0	0	0	0	3	1
	Tri-West	0	0	0	1	2	1
3	Columbus East	0	1	1	1	0	0
	Mishawaka Marian	0	0	0	0	2	1
	Pioneer	0	0	0	0	0	3
	West Lafayette	0	0	0	2	1	0
2	Andrean	0	0	0	2	0	0
	Blackford	0	0	0	0	2	0
	Bloomington South	0	2	0	0	0	0
	Bremen	0	0	0	0	1	1
	Brownsburg	0	0	1	1	0	0
	Castle	0	1	0	1	0	0
	Center Grove	1	1	0	0	0	0
	East Central	0	0	2	0	0	0
	Evansville Reitz	0	0	2	0	0	0
	Fort Wayne Snider	0	2	0	0	0	0
	Goshen	0	0	1	0	1	0
	Indianapolis Scecina	0	0	0	0	2	0
	Lawrenceburg	0	0	0	0	0	2
	New Palestine	0	1	1	0	0	0
	North Montgomery	0	0	0	0	2	0
	Western Boone	0	0	0	0	2	0
	Zionsville	0	0	0	2	0	0
1	Adams Central	0	0	0	0	0	1
	Bellmont	0	0	0	1	0	0
	Carroll (Flora)	0	0	0	0	0	1
	DeKalb	0	0	1	0	0	0
	East Noble	0	0	1	0	0	0
	Eastern Hancock	0	0	0	0	0	1
	Evansville Mater Dei	0	0	0	0	1	0
	Evansville Memorial	0	0	0	1	0	0
	Fishers	0	1	0	0	0	0
	Fort Wayne Concordia	0	0	0	1	0	0
	Fort Wayne Wayne	0	0	1	0	0	0
	Fountain Central	0	0	0	0	0	1
	Garrett	0	0	0	0	0	1

School						
Greenfield-Central	0	0	0	0	1	0
Griffith	0	0	1	0	0	0
Hamilton Southeastern	0	0	0	0	0	1
Hammond Noll	0	0	0	1	0	0
Harding (Fort Wayne)	0	0	0	0	1	0
Harrison (West Lafayette)	0	0	1	0	0	0
Heritage Christian	0	0	0	0	1	0
Heritage Hills	0	0	0	1	0	0
Indianapolis Washington	0	0	0	1	0	0
Jasper	0	0	1	0	0	0
Lawrence Central	0	1	0	0	0	0
Linton-Stockton	0	0	0	0	0	1
Lowell	0	0	1	0	0	0
Merrillville	0	0	0	1	0	0
Monrovia	0	0	0	0	1	0
North Miami	0	0	0	0	0	1
North Vermillion	0	0	0	0	0	1
North White	0	0	0	0	0	1
NorthWood	0	0	0	1	0	0
Oak Hill	0	0	0	0	0	1
Plymouth	0	0	0	0	1	0
Portage	0	0	0	1	0	0
Rensselaer Central	0	0	0	0	1	0
Rochester	0	0	0	0	1	0
Seeger	0	0	0	0	0	1
South Bend St. Joseph	0	0	0	1	0	0
South Bend Washington	0	0	0	1	0	0
South Decatur	0	0	0	0	0	1
South Putnam	0	0	0	0	0	1
Southern Wells	0	0	0	0	0	1
Southridge	0	0	0	0	1	0
Southwood	0	0	0	0	0	1
Tippecanoe Valley	0	0	0	0	0	1
Tri-Central	0	0	0	0	0	1
Valparaiso	0	0	0	1	0	0
Westfield	0	1	0	0	0	0
Whitko	0	0	0	0	1	0

Teams that have won IHSAA state championships in more than one class

Three different classes:
Carmel (6A-5A-3A)
Columbus East (5A-4A-3A)
Indianapolis Cathedral (5A-4A-3A)
Tri-West (3A-2A-1A)
Warren Central (6A-5A-4A)

Two different classes
Ben Davis (6A-5A)
Bremen (2A-1A)
Brownsburg (4A-3A)
Castle (5A-3A)
Center Grove (6A-5A)
Fort Wayne Dwenger (4A-3A)
Franklin Central (4A-2A)
Goshen (4A-2A)
Indianapolis Chatard (3A-2A)
Indianapolis Ritter (2A-1A)
Jimtown (2A-1A)
Mishawaka Marian (2A-1A)
New Palestine (5A-4A)
Penn (5A-4A)
Roncalli (4A-3A)
West Lafayette (3A-2A)

COACHING RECORDS IN THE STATE TOURNAMENT

Most sectional championships (Top 10)
No.	Coach
19	Don Howell
	Russ Radtke
	Larry "Bud" Wright
17	Bill Sharpe
	Rick Streiff
16	Dick Dullaghan
	Matt Lindsay
	Rick Minnich
	Mo Moriarity
14	Jeff Adamson
	Bob Gaddis
	Vince Lorenzano

Most regional championships (Top 10)
No.	Coach
14	Dick Dullaghan
	Don Howell
	Rick Streiff
	Larry "Bud" Wright
13	Matt Lindsay
	Vince Lorenzano
12	Bob Gaddis
	Eric Moore
	Mo Moriarity
11	Bruce Scifres

Most semi-state championships (Top 10)
No.	Coach
12	Matt Lindsay
11	Rick Streiff
10	Vince Lorenzano
	Larry "Bud" Wright
9	Dick Dullaghan
	Don Howell
8	Chris Geesman
	Bruce Scifres
7	Mo Moriarity
6	Bill Sharpe
	Chuck Stephens
	Kevin Wright

Most IHSAA state championships (Top 10)
No.	Coach
10	Rick Streiff
9	Matt Lindsay
	Larry "Bud" Wright
8	Dick Dullaghan
7	Vince Lorenzano
	Bruce Scifres
5	Chris Geesman
	Kevin O'Shea
4	Jim Belden
	Don Howell
	Bill Sharpe
	Chuck Stephens
	Kevin Wright

About the Author

Dan Engler's love for Indiana high school football goes back over a quarter of a century. The 1996 graduate of F.J. Reitz played all four years while also covering the sport for his school's newspaper.

With the help of his brother Joe, who covers soccer while lending his coding skills to make the site work, the two have created the go-to source for football history in the Hoosier state, AlmanacSports.com.

In addition to playing, Engler has also coached, refereed and attended hundreds of games.

Engler and his wife, Melissa, have two sons, Logan and Micah. Engler has visited every state in the country and traveled all over the world but is proud to call Indiana and the West Side of Evansville his home.

Thank you!

Thank you so much for purchasing this book. The author has spent years researching this information and I hope you find it useful.

Comments? Find any mistakes? Please email me at dengler@almanacsports.com.

Other books in this series:

Check out these other books in the Indiana High School Football Almanac series, all available on Amazon!

- Indiana High School Football All-State Player Database
- A History of the Northern Indiana Football Playoff
- The Reitz Football Encyclopedia: 100 Years of Mighty Panther Football
- What a Cluster! The Story of Indiana High School Football's Infamous Cluster System

Follow us online!

- AlmanacSports.com
- facebook.com/almanacsports
- Instagram.com/almanacsports
- twitter.com/almanacsports

Thanks again!

Made in United States
Orlando, FL
07 November 2023

HERO

The Traveler Series Book 7

Tom Abrahams

A PITON PRESS BOOK

HERO

A Traveler Series Story
© 2019 by Tom Abrahams
All Rights Reserved

Cover Design by Hristo Kovatliev
Edited by Felicia A. Sullivan
Proofread by Pauline Nolet
Interior design by Stef McDaid at WriteIntoPrint.com

This book is a work of fiction. People, places, events, and situations are the product of the author's imagination.

Any resemblance to actual persons, living or dead, or historical events is purely coincidental.

No part of this book may be reproduced, stored in a retrieval system, or transmitted by any means without the written permission of the author and publisher.

tomabrahamsbooks.com

FREE PREFERRED READERS CLUB: Sign up
for information on discounts, events, and release dates:

eepurl.com/bWCRQ5